HOLE IN MY HEART

Praise for *Hole in My Heart*

"A profound and deeply moving love story between a mother and the daughter she gave up for adoption. With straightforward and sometimes brilliant prose, Dusky brings to life the struggles of women who wanted a career in an earlier era when abortion was illegal and single motherhood difficult to imagine. Dusky goes well beyond her personal story and forces us to reflect on the most important questions in human life: who we are and who we might become. Meticulously researched, her story shows how she slowly became a major force in the advocacy for open adoption."

—DRUCILLA CORNELL, adoptive mother, professor emeritus in political science, comparative literature and gender studies at Rutgers University, author of *At the Heart of Freedom: Feminism, Sex, & Equality*

"Lorraine Dusky writes with the depth and vulnerability of a mother who has endured great loss, faced her demons, and turned inconsolable grief and heartache into a powerful advocate's voice. A tour de force full of insight and inspiration."

—RICHARD UHRLAUB, adoptee, president of Adoption Search Resource Connection

"A fascinating story of how Dusky turns her grief about losing her daughter to adoption into activism for opening birth records to adult adoptees. Her devastating research shows that the scars she and her daughter received from the adoption industry were not unique."

—MARIANNE NOVY, adoptee, founding co-chair of the Alliance for the Study of Adoption and Culture, professor emeritus of English, University of Pittsburgh, author of *Reading Adoption*

" . . . should be required reading for all parents who are contemplating placing a child or adopting for this precautionary tale offers poignant lessons about the importance of adoption being an option of last resort; about the inadequacy of openness and/or reunion as a salve for lifelong adoption losses; and about the ongoing need for adoption reform and adoptee rights legislation in America. *Hole in My Heart* is an intricately-crafted, tender and painfully honest reminder of the collateral damages suffered by parents and children amidst even the best-intentioned of adoption decisions."

—ELIZABETH JURENOVICH, director of Abrazo Adoption Services, San Antonio

"I felt that I was listening in to Lorraine's experiences across the years somewhere between her heart and her skin. Dusky writes as most people think."

—PAM HASEGAWA, adoptee, former board member, American Adoption Congress

"Dusky disproved the myth of the natural mother in the closet in 1979 with *Birthmark*; now she exposes the hard realities at the core of adoption before—and after—reunion. *Hole in My Heart* will change the way people think about adoption.

—FLORENCE FISHER, founder of ALMA (Adoptees Liberty Movement Association) and author of *The Search for Anna Fisher*

"*Birthmark* changed my life. Dusky's words gave me the courage to search for the mother who lost me to adoption. Now Lorraine has done it again. *Hole in My Heart* is high drama—and a riveting case for adoption reform. Dusky shines a spotlight on the harmful outcome of closed adoption and the lasting impact of secrecy upon relationships."

—JEAN A. S. STRAUSS, adoptee, author of *Birthright* and filmmaker of the documentary *A Simple Piece of Paper*

"Stunning . . . Dusky's writing is passionate and eloquent. Her restraint in telling her tragic, timeless and redemptive story is an extraordinary feat. A tour de force that should be read by everyone."

—KIANA DAVENPORT, author of *The Spy Lover* and *Shark Dialogues*

"Dusky eloquently evokes the painful circumstances and social pressures that led to the loss of her child to adoption, and the multi-layered complexities of reunion and relationship with her daughter . . . a compelling manifesto for why our culture and legal system must re-think and reform adoption down to its roots."

—DAVID SMOLIN, adoptive father, professor of law and director, Center for Children, Law, and Ethics, Cumberland Law School, Samford University

". . . a powerful memoir you won't be able to stop reading till the final page. Her story is modern and retro, tough and tender, romantic and profoundly honest. She illuminates the power of transgenerational longings and enduring genetic attributes, all richly enhanced by historical details about adoption laws and practice. Another masterpiece by a gifted writer."

—DELORES TELLER, natural mother, post-adoption therapist, past president of the American Adoption Congress

"Dusky's courageous, honest book puts a human face on the emotional minefield of adoption while navigating an often-hidden truth—that at the heart of every adoption there are issues of loss, guilt, emptiness, abandonment and an incomplete sense of identity. Much more than a good read, *Hole in My Heart* integrates important research findings that support the universality and truth of Dusky's personal experience."

—DAVID KIRSCHNER, psychoanalyst, author of *Adoption: Uncharted Waters*

"Dusky's compelling memoir is a tough reminder of the shame of being an 'unwed mother' in the sixties, as we both were. With lyrical prose and unwavering commitment, she advocates eloquently for adoption-law reform."

—FAITH IRELAND, natural mother, Washington State Supreme Court Justice (Ret.)

"Dusky writes the truth, but with a gentle poetic quality which makes those truths easy to understand and accept. There is laughter and there are tears, evoking more tears than laughter as adoption is wont to do . . . not only for the adoption community, but for anyone who values family and connections. It is beautiful, powerful, and painful. But most of all it is the truth."

—NANCY VERRIER, adoptive mother, psychologist, author of *The Primal Wound* and *Coming Home to Self*

Also by Lorraine Dusky

Birthmark
Total Vision
The Best Companies for Women
Still Unequal: The Shameful Truth about
Women and Justice in America

HOLE
IN MY
HEART

Love and Loss in the

Fault Lines of Adoption

LORRAINE DUSKY

Grand Canyon Press
Tempe, AZ
www.grandcanyonpress.com

Grand Canyon Press
Tempe, Arizona
www.grandcanyonpress.com

Publisher's Note: Grand Canyon Press is an independent publisher committed to bringing works of high literary merit to a new generation of readers. Some names have been changed. Locales and public names are used when events are part of the public record. There are no composite characters in this book, and events are reported as accurately as possible.

Cover design by Richard Ljoenes Design LLC
Cover photographs from Shutterstock by Maks_Nova and roroto12p
www.richardljoenes.com

Names: Dusky, Lorraine, author.
Title: Hole in my heart : love and loss in the fault lines of adoption / Lorraine Dusky.
Description: Second edition. | Tempe, AZ : Grand Canyon Press, [2022] | Includes bibliographical references and index.

Identifiers: ISBN: 978-1-951479-79-4 (hardcover) | 978-1-951479-80-0 (hardcover: library edition) | 978-1-951479-84-8 (paperback) | 978-1-951479-82-4 (Kindle) | 978-1-951479-83-1(epub)

Subjects: LCSH: Dusky, Lorraine. | Birthmothers—United States—Biography. | Women journalists—United States—Biography. | Adoptees—United States—Biography. | Mother and child—United States—Psychological aspects. | Adoption—Psychological aspects. | Adopted children—Psychology. | Mothers and daughters—United States—Biography. | Adoptees—United States—Identification. | Birthmothers—United States--Identification. | Registers of births, etc.—United States. | Confidential communications—United States. | Open adoption—United States. | Parental grief. | Loss (Psychology)

Classification: LCC: HV874.82.D87 D87 2022 | DDC: 362.734/0973—dc23

Printed in the United States of America

To the memory of my daughter

We all remember things in our own way. This is what I remember, how I remember it. The names of some individuals have been changed.

It is a law of nature that we stand in a kinship network, related by blood to others of our kind; pluck us out of that network and we are like refugees without passports—some friendly nation may take us in, but it is never a completely adequate substitute for home.

—ANTHONY BRANDT

Contents

Preface   xv

Conception

1   Coda   2

2   Backstory   3

3   The Next Story   40

4   Conception   46

5   Rude Reality   58

6   Mystery Woman or Cosmo Girl   72

     White Woman's Disease   81

7   Reentry   85

8   Adrift   96

     Aftershock   103

9   Moving On   109

Search

10   The Personal Becomes Political   119

11   Taking a Stand   131

12   Is Anyone Watching?   149

13   Looking for Cracks in the Wall   157

14   SOS in the Night   171

15   Birthmark   173

16   Meeting Mr. Right   190

17   She Is Found!   200

     Open vs. Closed Adoption   205

Reunion/Reality

18   A Girl Named Jane   215

19   Reunion   224

     Mothers Who Reject Reunion   236

20   Jane Meets the Relatives   240

21   Getting to Know You   246

       The Wily Persistence of DNA   260

22   No-Show Dad   268

23   The Opposite of Happiness   272

       Being Adopted   281

24   Moving On   287

25   Another Birthday   290

26   'Not Now' Becomes Never   297

27   The Heart of the Matter   305

28   The Things People Say   320

       The Injustice of Sealed Birth Records   328

29   What to Wear When You Are a Moving Target   333

30   Here Today, *Pfft* Tomorrow   341

31   End Game   353

32   Peace at Last   367

       Epilepsy, Adoption, Pharmaceuticals, and Suicide   373

Resolution

33   Albany, Redux   381

34   Dream a Little Dream   387

35   Karmic Kickback   390

36   The Missing Granddaughter   399

37   How Dare She?   408

38   Justice Arrives in New York   411

39   House with the Red Door   417

Appendix   421

Additional Reading   423

Resources   424

Acknowledgments   426

About the Author   429

Bibliography   431

Preface

A few words about language.

> They call me "biological mother."
>
> I hate those words. They make me sound like a baby machine, a conduit, without emotions. They tell me to forget and go out and make a new life.
>
> I had a baby and I gave her away. But I am a mother.

Those words are emblazoned on the jacket of my memoir *Birthmark*, the first to break the silence of mothers who gave up a child for adoption. At the time of publication in 1979, the debate over what to call women who relinquished children was just beginning. Before that, we were "natural mothers."

But as adoptions increased in number that term was thought to be offensive to adoptive parents, and "birth mother"—supposedly the writer (and adoptive mother) Pearl S. Buck coined the label—came into wide usage. When Lee Campbell founded Concerned United Birthparents (CUB) in 1976, she embraced the concept, using the conjoined word "birthmother."

Yet not all of us to whom the term applies have been comfortable with this, as it subtly but surely implies that we are there only for the act of giving birth and then gone. However, with time the term has made its way into the American lexicon and has taken on a more neutral and inclusive meaning. It is universally used in internet searches. Still the debate continues, sometimes furiously. Some women prefer "first mother," which some adoptive parents and adoptees find offensive. "Biological mother" sounds clinical and cold, but I have, on occasion, preferred it, for it typically indicates the speaker is not aware that there are more politically correct terms, and indeed, I am my daughter's flesh-and-blood biological mother.

When possible I have avoided the use of any modifier before the word *mother* unless clarity demanded it, or I was quoting someone, and generally use *other* and *natural. Birth mother* remains when in a quotation.

Other changes in adoption language have also occurred, as adoption workers and lawyers attempt to obfuscate the reality of the deep, abiding wound left by the separation of mother and child. Today we are not supposed to "give up" our children, but "make an adoption plan," words that obscure the emotional crisis and imply that the loss is simple, unemotional, clean and done, once a child is handed over. The adoption industry has pushed the idea that some mothers give up their children out of "love" for the child. It is a statement that taken at face value would mean that mothers with fewer resources than others would, out of love, hunt for wealthier parents, say, in the supermarket, and ask them if they would take their children because they could give them a life with more of what money and position can buy.

But we humans are not rigged like that. Women who give birth (in nearly all circumstances) want to love and raise their own children. Every species operates this way, and any other concept is laughable. When one's life situation makes that impossible, adoption is what comes to mind, but as a last resort.

Some mothers will only say they "surrendered" their children, implying they were overcome by forces they could not withstand. Lawyers use the term "relinquished" to mean privately arranged adoptions and "surrendered" for those facilitated by an agency.

I gave up, relinquished, and surrendered, but I no more made a "plan" because I "loved my baby so much" than a person who falls overboard from an ocean liner makes a "plan" to swim to the life preserver thrown to them.

The language issue is so heated that one can find hundreds of scholarly and popular articles on the internet about "positive adoption language" and lists of what is approved and what is considered "negative adoption language." The number of words written about adoption language in general and the moniker of *birth mother* (sometimes written as one word) in particular is a testament to the intensity of feelings on the subject. Some support groups and conferences ban the use of *birth mother*.

The term *real mother*, as in, "Are you ever going to search for your real mother?"—which comes out of the mouths of many not schooled in the correct adoption idiom—drives most adoptive parents around the bend. Yet people, being people, use the term and know what it means, and they also know that the adoptive parents are the ones who do the day-to-day raising of a child. Both women who give up their children and the women who raise them are real mothers. Different, but both real.

Modifiers other than *natural* to my ears shut us up in a delineated time frame: between conception and birth, then ipso facto gone. Why is *natural* better than the other words? Because it refers to nature, and implies an un-bending, unbreakable connection. *Biological* is the more clinical choice and just as accurate.

In many ways, once a child is available for adoption, a part of our role as mother is replaced by another; a connection is partly severed and will never be the same as if it had remained intact. We trust someone else to do the nurturing. But the maternal bond, the biological, hereditary link, remains.

No matter the conflicted feelings I had when I first learned of her exis-tence, I gave birth to my baby, and once she was born, I became her mother, in body and in soul, a fact that a mere signature on a surrender paper, and the adoption that followed, can never undo.

I had a baby and I gave her away.

But I am a mother.

When I began this book more than a decade ago, and published the first edi-tion in 2015, my aim was to illustrate the full story of a single relinquishment and adoption with my own saga, and do so with supporting research to present the gamut of complexities that are unavoidably a part of every adoption. Too often society sees adoption as a simple, singular act. The focus is on the joy of one family getting a newborn. The mother who created that infant—the other side of the story—is conveniently ignored because to be reminded of her is to be confronted with her sadness, possibly her poverty, or other life situations that led her to give up her baby.

We women who have lived with that hole in the heart throughout our lives—and it does permeate our lives—know that relinquishment of a child, and the adoption that follows, is a lifelong series of events, emotional and physical, that we—mother and child—carry with us every day.

I do what I can to change the way people think about adoption, and in so doing, I hope to change adoption as we know it. If along the way I am able to provide solace and support to others like me so they can know they are not alone, and, yes, let adopted people know that we mothers never forget—that some of us spend our lives hoping for reunion and forgiveness—well, that would be a boon.

Today this book is more relevant than it was before because abortion rights in this country have been rolled back, and some states are ushering in draconian laws that take away a woman's right to control her own body and destiny. The midterm elections of 2022 indicate that in the long run such measures will not stand. In a small footnote in the Supreme Court decision in *Dobbs v. Jackson Women's Health Organization*, adoption is offered as an antidote to abortion. No mention is made of the impact of adoption on the adopted. As for the women involved, the clear implication is that one has a baby, gives it up, and returns to society and goes about her business unaffected. And, likewise, the adopted individual suffers not.

Nothing could be further from the truth.

—Lorraine Dusky, Sag Harbor, New York
November 26, 2022

Conception

1   Coda

The mother walks in following a child who runs ahead of her. The child is two, could be three. I'm sitting at Starbucks in the morning reading the *New York Times*, wishing the music was turned down a tad. Sun is streaming through the window behind me. My husband, Tony, is doing the crossword puzzle. Both of us are writers, and it's nice to get out of the house in the morning.

But for the moment—fifteen seconds or so—my attention is diverted to the child, and then to the mother, and back to the child. Unconsciously I look to see if the child resembles his mother.

I want to be able to tell myself he is not the child of someone else.

I want to reassure myself that the woman is his only mother.

I have been doing this ever since my daughter was born.

Probably before. As soon as I knew I was pregnant.

2   Backstory

FEBRUARY 13, 1965—We are making small talk as we walk across the Genesee River on my first day of work city side at the Rochester *Democrat & Chronicle*. I don't know it yet, but I am brushing up against a man with whom I will soon fall truly, deeply, madly in love. Our love will thrust me into a life I never could have imagined, but at this moment I am merely walking across a bridge.

He is somewhat older, already established in the profession that I have dreamed about since I was ten. It's early evening, dusk is hurtling toward dark, but it's not cold for February, it's foggy and damp but not quite raining. A silk scarf is tied at the back of my neck à la a French movie star, and I am wearing a slick, soldier-blue trench coat with a red lining—MADE IN FRANCE !—that cost a week's salary. I am high on life at that moment—hell, I am practically gliding across the bridge in three-inch heels—for I'm the first woman to be hired for the hard news section at the *Democrat & Chronicle* since World War II emptied the newsroom of men.

To get here had taken more than cracking a certain glass ceiling in the office—it also meant breaking through at home, starting at the end of the eighth grade, when I had to convince my father that taking Latin and algebra in the ninth grade—the college prep courses—was crucial to the rest of my life. A parent had to sign off on what I would take that fall. Latin was the only language offered at the local parish school, St. Alphonsus, and the Latin especially hit a nerve with him: *What good is Latin going to do you? You're only*

going to get married and have kids. You're a girl! Who do you think you are? Some
movie star's daughter? We're not that kind of family!

My father's reaction to my plan seemed to come out of nowhere. This
was the daddy who taught me to fall straight back into his arms as he caught
me just before I hit the ground. This was the daddy who, I'd heard innu-
merable times, was so taken with my ability to pronounce big words when
I was a year old that he urged friends and family to try to stump me. This
was the daddy who reveled in my winning the kids' races at family reunions,
the daddy who taught me how to play Scrabble but didn't let me win until
I could win on my own, the daddy I adored—up until these last few weeks.
Now he meant to ruin my life by telling me I can't go to college when my life
depends on my going to college?

Who was this man? Didn't he know me at all? Or that I could do this?

Dad himself had gone from Appalachian coal miner at thirteen to master carpenter—the guy who makes custom cabinets and bookcases—to construction manager in Detroit for a builder who was putting up houses left
and right during the city's auto-industry boom of the fifties. He might have
made a great leap himself on the scaffolding of the American Dream, but
now, he couldn't fathom that the next logical step was college for his children.
College was not part of my older brother's equation—he was off in the navy
by then—but college was definitely in mine.

Though I had not talked about the career I imagined for myself, for it
would have struck my parents as the daft dream of a silly girl, my life's plan
had been real to me since the fourth grade, when what I was meant to be
opened up like the pages of a book. An extremely shy child, I was the quiet
kid in the back of the class who took a fistful of valentines to school in the
second grade and came home teary-eyed with two. After school, I'd hole up
in my room and read novels from the library about the adventures some girls
got into, especially girls fortunate enough to go off to boarding school. Going
away sounded exciting and full of freedom, with possibilities well beyond
Dearborn, Michigan, the tidy, humdrum suburb where we lived. My mother
was worried I didn't play enough with the kids on the block. She was forever

saying, *I don't know what's going to happen to you. You're going to grow up to be a hermit.* I ignored her.

In the fourth grade, a teacher read one of my assignments to the class, a story in which I'd anthropomorphized a banana on its journey from Central America to a pie in my mother's kitchen. When the teacher finished reading—a nun, of course, since this was St. Al's—she told the class that I had written the story, and the kids turned around to look at me, the quiet girl nobody knew in the back of the room.

That was it.

I would be a writer.

That decided, I moved on to, What kind? I soon figured out that writing novels was too precarious a career because you had to have somebody support you until you made it big. We weren't that kind of people. I needed a job. With a salary. Lickety-split, I had the answer: I'd write for newspapers—you got paid to do that. I already had a comic-strip heroine who showed it could be done, Brenda Starr, the glamorous, red-haired reporter—single and childless—who, besides the exploits that took her to exotic places, had a romance with a mystery man who periodically came and went. Her life was fantastic! Brenda Starr came into my life through the Detroit *Free Press*, one of three newspapers we had delivered to the house daily. It was not lost on me that as a reporter I'd have an excuse to talk to people, a way around my innate shyness. And if you think about it, the banana assignment was journalism of a sort: Facts make a story. Newspaper reporter/writer was perfect. Mom and Dad would be amused at my lofty ambition—we weren't that kind of people, after all. So I never told them. Their aspirations for me stopped at secretary.

First, I had to go to college.

The end of the eighth grade was the make-or-break point. That was when you signed up for courses—either college prep or vocational courses, which for girls were home economics and typing. Typing was okay because reporters—and college students—needed to know how. I had to return a form, signed by a parent, stating the courses I would take in the fall.

A kind of war broke out at home. It was as if I'd said I was going to walk over Niagara Falls on a tightrope. I had a few weeks before the form had to be turned in. Mom supported the college plan—I don't think I said I wanted to be a reporter, that would have been too absurd—but we knew Dad had to agree. I never heard them argue about it. But through a closed door, I did hear Dad argue at length with a friend of the family, a teacher named George who had been a neighborhood kid and who was like an older brother to me. Now he taught high school, but way back when I was in the second grade, he'd been in college and had read a paragraph I'd written for a school assignment, and after that, he'd never doubted that I should be university bound. My dad must have missed that. Mom had not, and she let me know she was quietly on my side in this pitched battle.

The college-or-not quarrel simmered below boiling for weeks, infusing our nightly family dinners and straining the easy banter Dad and I had many mornings at the kitchen table. He had made it plain, and my mother seemed to agree, that surely I was headed for motherhood. And that would be the end of any career. Now I turned my attention to my gender. Why was I born female? What a huge stink bomb being a girl was if you wanted to have a different life than Mom's! It had never occurred to me that I would grow up to have her life. Oh, I played with dolls and paper cutouts you dressed up in different outfits, but when she said, as mothers are wont to do, *Someday, when you have a child, you'll understand*, and I thought, *We'll see about that.*

How could I be a writer—especially a "writer with a career"—and have kids who needed feeding, burping, changing, cookie baking? In short, everything that went into being a mom.

When Mom told me where babies come from—mommies' tummies— I don't recall my reaction to that biological fact, but I do remember telling her, quietly, deliberately, and repeatedly, that I would die if I ever had a baby. I must have been five, maybe six, but I was old enough to know that to make my point I had to go for the jugular: *I would die if I had a baby.* I couldn't just say, *I don't want to have a baby, I don't want to be a mommy,* now could I? Where would I have ever gotten that idea? Did I think she would agree? Not likely. So, I made a pronouncement that didn't involve me changing my mind. It stated that an outside force would overcome the circumstance of childbirth or, if it did not, I would die. She said women didn't die anymore when they had babies, it was plenty safe, and surely I'd change my mind one day. I kept repeating, *I will die.* After we went a few rounds like this, I was aware that I'd never win her over to my point of view, and so I simply stopped responding. She stopped talking.

I never brought this up again.

I did have a real-life role model, Dad's older sister from New York City, Aunt Jean. She didn't have children. She had a boyfriend who called her long distance when she visited every summer. Jean had blond hair like mine, she introduced me to frogs' legs in a restaurant when I was five, and when I was twelve, she left *Bonjour Tristesse* in my bedroom (which we shared when she visited). Of course, I read it. Mom found out, and, as the main character has a rather libertine attitude toward sex, the book's discovery led to a certain amount of commotion in our house. When I went out with Mom and Aunt Jean, strangers assumed Jean was my mother—not Mom. Relatives said we sounded uncannily alike on the phone. When Jean was not visiting us, she worked as a waitress near city hall in Manhattan, and she knew all the big shots who worked there. She made Manhattan as enticing as Shangri-La. It didn't matter that she had not gone to college. However, I was of a different generation and I would definitely need to.

While I was putting forth my plans for college, what did not cross my mind was that I was the same age as my dad when he had to quit school and go down into a dank, dream-killing coal mine in southwestern Pennsylvania. He'd never gone beyond the eighth grade. He never spoke of the smothering layer of coal dust that would have coated him from head to toe every evening as he emerged from the pit. What I knew about the coal mines was tied up in the romance of the folk songs—some about the mines, some old English/ Scottish ballads—that he'd sung to me when he'd put me to bed as a little girl, snug in my cozy bed with a blue leather-tufted headboard.

The morning the form was due—it was the size of a note card—I placed it and a pen in front of Dad at the kitchen table. I was ready to run out the door as soon as I got his signature. He was drinking his coffee, reading the

Free Press. That morning, sun streaming in through the kitchen windows, I stood there, resolute, refusing to budge, my determination as sharp as the pleats in my navy-blue uniform. He looked it over briefly and signed, saying, "Now this doesn't mean anything."

He was conceding this battle with a dare.

Oh yes, it does, Daddy, you wait and see. I heard what he said, I would never forget what he said, but it only made me more determined to prove him wrong.

Throughout high school, neither I nor my parents ever spoke about my college plans. In the meantime, I seized every opportunity to lay the building blocks of a journalism career. By the end of my freshman year in high school, I had a weekly column in our local newspaper, the *Dearborn Guide*, about the goings-on at high school. At the end of my junior year, I signed up for a two-week journalism seminar for high school students at the University of Detroit. I can't remember how I got there every day, but certainly Mom made it happen. Senior year, I was editor-in-chief of my high school newspaper.

Boyfriends were not a distraction because I didn't have any. Not in high school, not with my nose. I sustained a crush on one guy who kissed me more than once at more than one party in the seventh grade, and—while my girlfriends had real boyfriends—I swooned over him until the tenth grade, when he acquired a real girlfriend. I managed to go to the junior prom with the class president because we were friends, not of the flirty sort. I was a safe date. Lusty fumbling was not on the agenda. He was headed to the seminary after graduation. To the senior prom I took the twenty-something nephew of a family friend. The nephew, recently arrived from Germany, barely spoke any English. He was on the hunt for a wife, and I might do.

Back to my nose. Understand, this was not simply a somewhat prominent proboscis. My nose was thin and pointy, long, with ski-jump—a remarkable Roman nose, but remarkable is not a plus for noses. Consider the hag. Consider Cyrano. Consider the sixth-grade boy who called me Big Nose when we were chasing each other around after school. In my senior yearbook photograph, some kind photographer's assistant had shortened and straightened my nose. I always turned my head if I caught someone staring at my profile. New acquaintances did stare at it—instead of into my eyes—when we first met. I acted as if I didn't notice, or I moved my head so they would stop staring an inch below my eyes, and I simply endured. When the subject of a nose job came up at home, and it did, Mom worried the surgery would cause some other problem—I had the runny nose that came with fall allergies. Surgery could make that worse. Anyway, where would we get the money? College was going to be enough of a financial hurdle.

When I applied to Wayne State University in downtown Detroit—I'd live at home so room and board wouldn't be an issue—my mother and I did not mention it to my father. The day I skipped school for the admissions interview, she drove me downtown, and we didn't tell him. When the acceptance letter came, I shared it only with my mother. When I was growing up, she had occasionally voiced concern that I was "too smart" to have an easy time finding a mate, and throughout high school, she'd supported my college bid. She had not finished high school herself, but for me, she harbored an in-

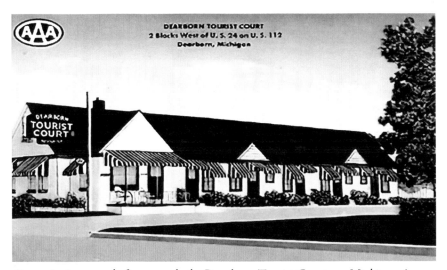

Figure 1. A postcard of our motel, the Dearborn Tourist Court, on Michigan Avenue near Telegraph Road in Dearborn. The motel has since been torn down and a beverage store stands in its place.

ner ambition and kept her eye on the long game. College-graduate Lorraine leads to college-graduate partner, right?

Dad and I never spoke of the fact that, come fall, I was college bound. He must have known because my mother wrote the check for tuition.

So, one morning in September, I put on the new clothes I'd bought for school and waited for the carpool I'd arranged with other students from Dearborn. Before coming home that first day, I joined the staff of the *Daily Collegian*. Feeling shy and overwhelmed, I had walked into the *Collegian's* office—it was bustling with energy and kids exuding confidence—and to my surprise, the news editor, a slight and quiet guy, immediately handed me a press release to rewrite. I sat down at the big table where four typewriters were bolted down next to outside phone lines, read the release, made a phone call, and got a fresh quote. When I turned in my copy—I already knew newspaper lingo—I anxiously waited for him to read it, in case he had questions, which is the way it goes.

"What's your background?" he said as he looked up.

The next morning my story was on the front page with my byline. The story had not seemed important, so I was surprised. My carpool friends were impressed.

By this time, my parents had moved us from the east side of Dearborn to the west side, where they'd purchased a small motel—the kind of place that proudly displayed its AAA rating, with red-and-white-striped awnings, family and pet friendly, a nondescript place drivers passed on the highway without noticing until they were desperate for a room for the night. Dad quit his management job in construction.

That motel nearly killed him. Or maybe it was his decades-long habit of smoking Lucky Strikes. Whatever the cause, making the mortgage during the off-season was a problem, and Dad went back to work as a finish carpenter. In January, at the end of my first semester, he had a massive heart attack. He was in the hospital for two weeks. I took a leave from the *Collegian* and kept my head down and my grades up. Once at home Dad became dead set on me quitting school, getting a job, and helping with the mortgage.

After all that commotion getting to college, I was supposed to quit now? One semester under my belt, established at the *Collegian*, the second semester already paid, and—this is a very big *and*—I already had a boyfriend in college, and now Dad wanted me to drop out and get some lousy job? Doing exactly what? My terrible typing precluded my becoming anyone's secretary. Would I be a waitress all my life? Is that how my life would end?

Any truce was off. My mother quietly supported me. I didn't quit college, but now Dad and I barely spoke beyond a quick "Please pass the salt" at the infrequent meals we had together. My parents must have argued over my not quitting school, but I never heard them. I went back to the *Collegian* and finished the semester. It would take decades before I would understand how much I had let him down.

After the heart attack it was a given that I would pay all my college expenses—tuition, books, lunches, clothes, and transportation to and from school. I still took the carpool in the morning, but the *Collegian*'s late afternoon hours didn't jibe with the return trip to Dearborn. I had a bus ride that could last up to two hours. Tuition was nothing like it is today; mine was less than a grand a year (in today's dollars, that's roughly $8,600), and I was able to cover all the fees and living expenses as long as I lived at home.

And I had a summer job.

That *boyfriend* mentioned above was much more than a casual crush. Maybe our relationship wasn't tied up with whether or not I stayed in school or dropped out, but at the moment, my determination to finish college made it almost impossible to spend time together. I'd met him the previous Thanksgiving Day at my cousin's big Polish wedding, the kind with an oom-pah-pah polka band and a bar where guys congregated and drank vodka shots all night until old grievances erupted and a fist fight broke out in the side alley. The wedding was in Jackson, my mother's small hometown, seventy miles from Dearborn.

Tom and I were attracted to each other the second he walked up to me, sitting alone at the edge of the dance floor in cranberry velvet with satin pumps dyed to match, and thinking, *This is going to be a long night*. Dinner was over, but hours stretched ahead. Though I was the maid-of-honor, I didn't know most of the guests, even though many of them were my mother's extended kin.

"You're not from around here," announced this young man suddenly standing in front of me. I hadn't noticed him until that moment.

Since I looked upon Jackson with barely concealed disdain, his opening paved the way for me to act distant and cool. I was from the "big city." But, damn, he was tall, trim, and attractive in his olive-green corduroy suit with vest, a button-down Oxford shirt, and striped blue-and-green tie. Yes, I remember those details as if it were yesterday. He had a killer smile and glasses thick enough to ensure he was brainy. He was appealing, all right, but I was icily reserved as we worked out his connection to the festivities. He hadn't actually been invited. Home for Thanksgiving from school, he'd dropped in to hang out with his best friend, whose family was close to the bride's family—did I know them? No. I did not. And, he added, he lived practically around the corner, as if to say, of course it was fine that he was there.

"Oh, I get it," I finally said. "You're almost a wedding crasher." Within minutes I learned we were both college freshmen. He went to John Carroll University in Cleveland, which sounded extravagant and enticing—he went away to school—even though I had never heard of John Carroll. We were chatting along breezily when I asked him if he wanted to sit down. He did.

I told him I was going to be a newspaper reporter. He said he was planning to major in English and be a college professor and write novels—did I know the writer Frank Yerby? Actually, no. All of this was more than intriguing; it was absolutely alluring. As for the newspaper business, he countered that an uncle of his covered state government for a string of Michigan newspapers, another data bit that was delicious, though I didn't let on. Soon we were both quoting the lyrics to Harry Belafonte's "Jamaica Farewell," and that mysteriously led to Milton and Shelley, both of us finding good use for what we had memorized at our respective Catholic high schools. He recited "Ozymandias" without a blip, and—believe it or not—we then went on to discuss the metaphor therein. Okay, not obscure, to be sure, but hey! We were eighteen, and this chance meeting was turning into a dream date. If I had filled out a questionnaire for a "desirable mate" and he had popped up, both my mother and I would have swiped right. He seemed to have ignored my nose. So did I. Supposedly it was less noticeable because my hair was done up in a French twist, adding volume to the back of my head to counteract what was going on in the front. Maybe it did.

Much too soon I was called away for the maid-of-honor chore of passing out wedding cake from a big, silver tray to a couple of hundred guests on both floors of the hall. Forty-five minutes later, I found him with his best friend, and we three hung together for a while. Eventually, the best friend melted away. Tom met my father, he met my mother, and we danced to a slow tune. He wrote my address on a wedding napkin. By midnight, we had kissed under the bright lights on the dance floor.

None of this went unnoticed. The next morning my mother warned me that she'd heard from the mother of the bride—her sister, my Aunt Clara— that Tom Sawicki had lots of girls chasing him, and I ought not to get my hopes up. How did Aunt Clara happen to know this? Aunt Clara's best friend was, indeed, the mother of Tom's best friend. Clearly, they had already chatted. My mother said he had to write first.

Tom's letter arrived Tuesday. So smitten were we that a few letters later, we made plans for me to spend the week between Christmas and New Year's in Jackson. We'd be going there on Christmas Day, as usual, I'd stay at Aunt Clara's, and my parents would pick me up on New Year's Day. He wrote that we would go tobogganing and I ought to bring slacks that "weren't too slack." Though we were both under legal age for drinking, he asked if he should get some alcohol for me for New Year's Eve. As I already knew from the wedding, he didn't drink at all, having observed an uncle who habitually over-imbibed. I wrote, Don't bother.

Overnight, Jackson had taken on an appealing glow. For the first time, I had the prospect of a boyfriend. Or maybe I already had one.

Christmas evening after dinner, he showed up at Aunt Clara's, and now he had to pass close inspection by not only my parents, but everyone else who happened to be there, and the living room seemed to be packed with relatives, the way it might have been in a Jane Austen novel. There was not much to do on Christmas night in Jackson, Michigan, except drive around, talk—we spent a lot of time talking—and park, right? In the letters that had flown back and forth for a month, our relationship had blossomed.

I assumed I'd see him several times that week leading up to New Year's Eve, but no. His mother, he said, in a hurried phone call, was making it terribly difficult for him to get away. In retrospect, I can imagine that his parents were concerned. *You met her one night and now she's spending a week in Jackson?*

One afternoon he phoned and said he was taking his four-year-old brother to the movies, and could I be ready in ten minutes? Tom had a maroon Karmann Ghia, and his smiling kid brother, thrilled to be a part of a grown-up adventure, managed to fit in the small space behind the two seats. Going into the theater, Tom made some remark about how we were like parents taking our child to the movies. I gave him a look that said, *Hold on! We're not there yet!* Tom settled his brother two rows in front of us, and we continued getting to know one another as some unremembered movie played on.

New Year's Eve arrived and by the time Tom came to pick me up, looking swell in that same corduroy suit, my aunt and uncle were already gone for the evening. He was early. I let him in and ran back upstairs to finish getting ready. At the bottom of the stairs, he sounded like a whimpering puppy when he asked if he could come up. His suggestion seemed pretty racy, but I let him anyway, and now my last-minute fussing took a suggestive turn—after all, we were in a bedroom! I probably extended the time by putting on more eye makeup than usual—might as well have the smoky eyes I'd seen in magazines. If not now, when? We would just be hanging out with his best friend and his girlfriend at her house, but dressed up we were going to be. At some point our eyes caught each other in a gaze of no more than ten seconds, but that wordless exchange telegraphed some primeval code, as if one day getting ready to go somewhere together would be our normal. I felt myself flushing, looked away, and distracted myself by slipping the chain of my grandmother's gold watch around my neck. As we were leaving, he helped me with my jacket, a mouton chubby, and gave my arms a squeeze. When I got to his car, he opened the door for me, the way young men did back then when they were courting.

When he brought me back to my aunt's house, sitting in the Ghia with the clunky gearshift between us, in the midst of kissing, he said, "I've never told anyone this before . . . I love you."

"I've never told anyone this before either . . . I love you," I said back. Immediately. Even while startled that our declarations tumbled out so soon.

Bursting with the intense high of first love that can never quite be repeated, I returned to Dearborn the next day.

A week later, my father had that near-fatal heart attack.

In March, Tom came to Detroit for a dance at Wayne. He'd spend the night—actually, two—in one of our motel rooms. I picked him up downtown in the family's Plymouth, and we stopped to park before we got home, for there was really no place for us to have privacy in our small apartment, other than my bedroom, and that wasn't going to fly that night. But soon after we parked, he said, "I have to make something of my life because I want to marry you."

I pulled back to look him in the eye and replied, "Yes, but I am keeping my name because I am going to have a career," the words tumbling out in one breath so he understood this was nonnegotiable. In the early sixties, it was necessary to get that out in the open straightaway.

Despite the heat of our passion, it was of paramount importance that I not get pregnant. A girl could get pregnant amazingly easily, I understood, given the famous "iffiness" of the birth control of the day. I don't think I even knew what a condom was. There were no pills, no foams, no intrauterine devices. With the admonitions of the Catholic Church dancing in my head, it was more than a good idea not to go all the way; it was a given. Abortion was not an option, and getting pregnant now would be a catastrophe of seismic magnitude.

So after the dance at Wayne State, while my parents were asleep below and I was in my bedroom with neither foot on the floor, I told Tom that I only wanted to go all the way with one man in my life, and that would be him—after we married. He did not push his luck. Besides, there is a lot of leeway between a kiss and all the way. Even for a Catholic girl. Who had decided this was no business of any priest. As long as we did not do the deed.

When I told my mother about this fortunate turn of events that included the magic word "marriage," she stopped saying, as she had all through high school when I talked of a Career with a capital C, *I don't know what is going to happen to you, Lorraine.* Meaning: Women do not have careers like that. What about the normal thing—marriage, children?

Now I was supposedly going to have the normal thing, but what I did not think about was having babies. My version of our life included complementary careers in some city that was not Jackson or Detroit—the Motor City had never felt like my city—but my plans didn't go beyond that. Tom and I would figure out the "beyond that" tomorrow.

Back in our separate towns, getting together required planning, fortitude, and frequently concealing his whereabouts from his parents. They were against our liaison. Tom said he didn't know why. I assumed it was because they thought we were too young to get as serious as we obviously were. My mother wondered if it might be because they knew she had been divorced, and maybe divorce ran in the family. I couldn't quite dismiss her musing because in that era, a divorced woman was considered a loose woman—and besides, according to Catholic doctrine remarriage meant my mother was living in a constant state of mortal sin. Back then, divorce was serious business.

Tom wrote that he was coming to Dearborn for a weekend with his buddy Pierre. Could I get him a date? Then they didn't come. I don't remember if I canceled, or he did. Dad's recovery and the continuing issue of the motel's finances left no space to foster this romance. My spirits rose and fell with Tom's letters, or lack of them. His classes were not going well; he liked his roommate; there was a dance in a few weeks, could I come for the weekend?

No, I couldn't come for the weekend. How could I afford it?

Not with the issue of me dropping out of school permeating our apartment like stale smoke.

I didn't even ask.

SUMMER 1961—That summer did not start out well. I was abruptly fired from the coffee shop where I'd been assured, weeks earlier, that I could work full-time, as I had the summer before. In a tone as cut-and-dried as macaroni in a box, the manager explained she was giving my shift—the only extra summer shift—to her daughter, as if I should have expected this all along. I was devastated, but there was nothing I could do. I must have gone in and out of twenty places looking for a job, and finally landed at a busy diner that was hard for me to get to. One evening after about a week, the owner drove me home—to the motel, that is—and he wanted more than a simple thank-you. I mumbled a few words that amounted to no and jumped out of the car without being assaulted. Desperate to stay employed, I did not tell my mother, and went back to work the next day. The owner fired me after the lunch shift.

I helped my mother clean rooms at the motel in the morning and, making a pact with myself to read a novel a day, I sequestered myself in my bedroom in the afternoon. Since there was still time to sign up for courses at the local community college, I did. Though my dad said nothing, I knew that I had further exasperated him.

Hallelujah, another job materialized. As a bonus, it was within walking distance from the motel, one of those beef houses that are cafeteria style with table-side help. I had classes from nine to eleven, Monday through Friday, in east Dearborn—a twenty-minute drive—then I'd race home to change from coed to cafeteria server, get to work before noon, back home by three, study, back to work at five, home around ten. Exhausted. But the bosses were fine and the money decent. I didn't take off a single shift that summer, seven days a week; I had to make enough money for school that fall. Loans didn't seem possible then, and certainly not without my father's support—and signature.

Now that Tom and I were little more than an hour apart and he had his Ghia, I'd hoped we'd see more of each other, but my crammed schedule meant I only saw him when he showed up unannounced and infrequently during the hours I had off between lunch and dinner. Life was a grainy black-and-white photograph enlivened by Tom's sporadic letters. Our apartment at the motel was small, with a single bathroom, and putting Tom up on the couch didn't seem remotely feasible—nor did giving him a motel unit in high season. I didn't even ask. When he asked his parents if he could transfer to Wayne State that fall, his father responded by announcing he wasn't going to let his son go to "some school" because he had "some broad" there. I went from girlfriend to *broad* in the time it takes to say the word, understanding all the implications of the word. His father had reduced me to a passing fancy that he could dismiss at will.

Yet our social situations were not dissimilar. His parents had a corner grocery store; mine owned that motel. Metaphorically, we both lived above the store, even if our apartment was on the ground floor, except for the small bedroom Dad built for me under the roof. We were both in college, we were both Polish Catholics, all of which should have given me suitable credentials, as the Poles back then were tribal, and the familial pressure to marry one of your own kind was robust. Never mind. His parents were adamant in their opposition, ignoring the fact that Number One Son was a testosterone-fueled, good-looking lad in need of a steady girlfriend. Girls liked him, that was true, but he was not, in today's parlance, a player. He wanted a girlfriend, not a raft of them. For a magical while there, he wanted me.

That fall Tom wound up at Jackson Community College. But I did not see him any more than when he was at John Carroll in Cleveland. Aware of his parents' attitude toward me, I was leery of writing since my letters had to go to his home. The frequency of his letters dwindled, but when he wrote, he always signed off with, "I love you, Tom." I held on to that, but fretted, uncertainty nibbling at desire. This was someone who wanted to marry me? Yes, I thought, but you can't make someone write you more or love you more or be constant when they aren't. I knew that love has to come freely, openly, for if one has to cajole or compete for affection, how deep is the love, how lasting could it be? Had that yellow light of caution grown out of an ingrained awareness of my physiognomy? Girls elected to homecoming courts—as one of my best friends was—might have a sense of assurance about their powers of enticement, but not me.

With Dad and me still in our wary truce, I went back to Wayne and the *Collegian* that fall. Now with more duties at the paper, I got home even later, well after dinner. We almost never had meals together, and never had a real conversation even when we exchanged the news of the day.

I did not dare invite Tom to visit. The seventy miles between Dearborn and Jackson was now a long, winding road full of detours and dangerous curves. Everything would be fine, I told myself, if only we lived in the same town—at least part of the year. If only we went to the same school. If only we lived in the same city in the summer. If only I didn't have to work every available hour. If only I had a home where Tom could spend the night. If only his parents didn't object.

Understand, this was well before the era of constant communication: before email, cell phones, instant messaging, texting, Twitter, Instagram, and whatever the next new thing is. This was when lovers depended on letters in longhand delivered by the US Post Office to keep their passion intact. This was when long-distance phone calls—and Dearborn to Jackson was long distance—were listed separately on one's phone bill, time and charges noted, meaning parents knew if you called someone in a distant city. So you didn't do it. Oh, you could stand at a pay phone with a stack of quarters, when quarters were like dollars, and hope your beloved was home. But he didn't call, and I couldn't call him at home—it wasn't done and would have only fanned his parents' hostility. I felt they were opposed not only to the idea of me, but to me in particular. Their disapproval was a little brown bird outside the window chirping a warning: Danger Ahead. My mother was the only cheerleader for this romance, but what could she do?

At Wayne, I became co-feature editor of the *Daily Collegian*, sharing the title and an on-campus office with another woman, Gael McCarthy. I put up a framed print of one of Buffet's sad clowns and immediately felt at home in that cramped, dark, windowless office. With a desk and phone and a door I could lock, such a retreat was a luxury, especially for a student who did not live on campus. Gael and I both wondered why each of us weren't named sole feature editor, but our initial chill quickly dissolved into a fast friendship.

That fall I also walked into the *Dearborn Guide*—where I'd written my high school column—and left with a part-time gig writing features. By January I was also covering the Dearborn school board and occasionally ended up with the lead story on the front page. I was nineteen. My mother was proud of me, but now and then she still said, *I don't know what's going to happen to you.* My dad revealed nothing. Now I was home even less than I had been before.

While Tom had been drifting away, someone else sidled up. I put him off for months, but he was relentlessly attentive, he was nearby, and he would never hurt me. I mean, he *could* never hurt me because I didn't love him. I saw Tom on Christmas Day, and instead of spending the week between Christmas and New Year's in Jackson, the way I had done the year before, I worked at the *Guide* all week. Letters, even though signed "I love you," were infrequent. No words had been spoken about breaking up, but there hardly seemed a need to declare the relationship over. I had accepted, with lots of tears in my room at night, that we were hardly a couple by then.

On Easter that year, in Jackson as usual, instead of falling deliriously into Tom's arms when he picked me up after the dinners we'd had with our respective families, I told him that someone in Dearborn was pursuing me, that I was fed up feeling like he, Tom, had me on a string, that he almost never wrote, that I hadn't seen him for months . . . and that I was breaking up with him. How I wanted him to object, to promise he would write more, to tell me that he would get to Dearborn frequently! But he seemed more stunned than sorry, and while I wanted to take my words back—*Please say something Tom, talk me out of this*—I didn't hit that mental delete key. Oddly enough, I didn't think about, or ask him, if he was dating anyone in Jackson.

But of course, he was.

I dated the guy back home. Within six months, I broke up with him.

I know I hurt him badly. I didn't mean to, but that is what happened. I couldn't manufacture love.

However, I couldn't call Tom up and say, Hey! What's up? Can we talk? Besides, *some broad* ricocheted in my mind. How could a broad like me call him at home and risk his father or his mother answering? How could I leave my name? If I did, would they tell him I'd called? Writing him at home didn't seem like an option either because I'd be *that broad* chasing him.

Over the next year my mother reported there were occasional hang-ups on Saturday nights—she suspected it was Tom—but I was always at the movies with a girlfriend. I so wanted Mom to be right. But if it was him, why didn't he leave his name? I would have braved his parents' disdain and phoned. Yet without the caller's name, I was stymied. What if it wasn't him?

A girl has to have some pride.

By then my parents had sold the motel, and we were living in the bottom floor of a modest two-story house. My room was a narrow nook alongside the living room, big enough for a twin bed and a desk barely wider than a typewriter. A walk-in closet underneath the stairway held a small bureau. My father had turned his lifelong hobby of coin collecting into a business. Village Coins was never a big moneymaker either, but the business sustained us and he loved it. Relations between us smoothed out, and our conversations evolved into pleasant, grown-up banter. Various pieces of jewelry come to coin dealers, and he gave me a sapphire ring (which I lost at college) and a gold men's pocket watch that I wore on a chain around my neck. But with classes, the *Collegian*, my job at the *Guide*, and a two-to-three-hour chunk of time every day for commuting to and from school, my time at home when I wasn't behind a shut door studying or sleeping was rare. But everything on the career front was clicking into place.

Until Mom realized I had declared journalism my major.

Both parents descended on me one Sunday afternoon, insisting that my major could not, must not, be something as chancy—for a woman especially!—as journalism. Education or nursing it must be! Not only would these professions lead to an actual job, they would allow me to have a schedule compatible with being home with the kids. Their insistent message was that women (like me) did not make lives as writers for newspapers, and even if a few did, it was out of the question that I could ever be one of them. Again: *Who do you think you are? You're not some movie star's daughter. When you have kids . . . .*

What seems like a reasonable goal today was a leap too far for them, both the children of immigrants, children who had lived through the Great Depression. No matter what kind of credentials I was racking up, as they not-so-incorrectly assumed, wealthier wannabes with pedigrees and connections always had a leg up on someone like me. They said I wasn't being realistic, I was only setting myself up for a fall, a nurse or teacher I must be, blah blah blah. I wasn't the only one who had this kind of go-round with her parents. My friend at the *Collegian*, Gael, ran into the same row with her mother; Gael simply said she had switched her major to education. When she had not.

While my parents presented a united front, I suspect my mother had turned on this cold shower because she was the practical one who wanted me to have a nice, safe job. After all, Dad had a younger brother who'd landed in California after fighting in World War II, and Dad had sent him money to go to art school—one of his oil paintings hung in our home. After the initial battle over college, Dad had projected a laissez-faire attitude about the course I'd set. He often said I was like his sister Jean, and Mom wasn't too happy with that comparison. Jean now had a husband, but never had children. By then I knew that she had broken away from that drab mining town of their youth—Jenners, Pennsylvania—by getting on a bus at sixteen and going to New York City. It was clear that my inner Dusky was taking precedence over Mom's side of the family.

' I pointed out rather vociferously that I was already making money in my chosen career—not only did I get a small stipend as an editor of the *Daily Collegian*, but I was also working as a writer for the *Dearborn Guide*! This heated discussion seemed to go on for quite some time, but realistically, it was probably less than an hour. They gave up, and eventually the skirmish wound down. I did not switch majors. The subject was never brought up again.

By then, Tom had transferred to a school in central Michigan. It might as well have been in Patagonia. We had no mutual friends, we would never bump into each other on the street, and we had no easy way to get a message to each other.

Summer came. I worked full-time at the *Guide*, where a mentor—a re-

Figure 2. My father, Harry Dusky, in the 1950s.

covering alcoholic there on the way down from one of Detroit's dailies—
made the promise of working on a big-city paper seem real. By the end of the
summer, I had set aside money for college. Because of a tuition scholarship
my senior year, I had enough to splurge on an overnight Greyhound to New
York City with a friend.

Our rooms for a week at a once-grand hotel in Brooklyn were gratis
in exchange for ads that the *Guide* ran back in Dearborn. We crammed in
every tourist thing you could name, saw four Broadway shows at a steep discount, and visited my Aunt Jean in Queens. On the overnight bus back to
Detroit—with the city behind us basking in the setting sun's golden glow and
silver beams glinting off the skyscrapers' windows—I was consumed with the
thought of making this glittering Gotham my own.

I told no one. Mom would have been horrified. Most likely Dad would not have been surprised.

Just like Jean, I could hear both of them thinking.

Shortly before the end of junior year, a student-faculty committee selected the *Collegian*'s editor-in-chief for the following year. You declared you were in the running, wrote a proposal, and a committee of students—not from the newspaper, but student government—interviewed everyone in the running and elected the editor. It seemed rather arbitrary. The year before, they had overlooked the guy the staff assumed was the obvious choice and selected someone most of us did not even know. We were flabbergasted. Our choice, a terrific writer, the kind of guy who had printer's ink for blood, left the *Collegian* and was hired immediately by one of the dailies downtown.

This year's anointed—a guy, of course, there had never been a female editor-in-chief—had a great backstory to boot. A year earlier, Jim had suffered a debilitating stroke. We heard he might never walk again. Yet he came back to school with a limp and a leg brace, and otherwise he was the same quick and acerbic guy as he'd always been.

We all knew he had the support of the *Collegian*'s adviser for the top job. But Gael convinced me I had a shot; she'd be my managing editor, second in command. Even my mother, now used to the idea that I was staying in journalism, got behind the idea. I plunged ahead. So did another guy.

We three came to school that day in suits. I was both euphoric and anxious as I clacked around campus in spike heels and a smart purple-and-black tweed suit. But hope was dashed when I walked into the interview and knew instantly that any enthusiasm for my bid had been vacuumed up by Jim. I went ahead with my presentation as briskly as I could, yet no one would engage me. Where there should have been questions, there was silence. The single woman on the committee would not even make eye contact. She stared stonily at the floor. Finally, some kind soul—a guy—thought of something to ask.

Your losses teach you how to be strong. How to pick yourself up. How to start over again. How to believe in yourself despite the odds.

I did not quit the paper that fall. Within weeks, Jim's choice for managing editor washed out. When Jim offered the job to me, I said yes and moved into the office we would share. It had windows.

To carve out enough hours during the day for the *Collegian* and my part-time job at the Dearborn weekly, I looked for a night course that would fulfill my requirements, and settled on Greek and Roman drama, eagerly ripping into tales of men and women whose vanity would lead to their downfall.

What I could not foresee was how prescient those ancient stories of hubris would turn out to be.

Sometime that fall, fortune took a flier on Tom and me in the improbable form of his mother. At another wedding in Jackson, one to which we were not invited, Tom's mother turned to my Aunt Clara in the ladies' room and said, "I shouldn't have broken up Tom and Lorraine."

Well.

Weeks later this news flash made its way back to me, and I sent one of those thinking-about-you cards to his home in Jackson, timing it so it would get there a day or two before Thanksgiving Thursday, when I figured Tom would be home. He called Wednesday evening. Indeed, it was he who had made those anonymous hang-ups on Saturday nights. He'd driven to Dearborn and called from a phone booth. In my mind it was always raining.

By Sunday afternoon we were sitting in a Wayne coffee shop and again talking marriage. Crazy, right? It did not seem so then.

I was sure that if we were only in the same city at the same time, everything would be as it should. Soon enough, our plans grew to include where we would live (some big city where I would work on a newspaper and he would teach), how we would decorate our house (modern with Asian accents), what we would drive (sports car, make undetermined). The question of children bounced around in my head—I knew he assumed he would be a dad—but while we mentally furnished our house, we did not speak of children, either by unconscious design on my part or obvious assumption on his. Other than this rather large vacancy in our plans, our future together seemed bright and glorious. His letters came often enough, signed as before with "I love you, Tom."

For a while.

Once again, he pulled a disappearing act.

But that year again I did not have the luxury of spending that week in Jackson over Christmas break. I wrote Tom that I needed to work the entire week at the *Guide* to replenish my dwindling cash reserves. Since I couldn't see my parents giving Tom permission to spend the night on the living room couch, feet away from my bed, I didn't raise the issue with either Tom or them. My parents got dressed up and went to their usual New Year's Eve gathering with friends. I spent the night, that long night, in my bedroom studying. How I wished he'd just turn up! That the doorbell would ring and he'd be standing there and I'd fall into his arms. We would work something out with my parents when they got back. Mom would be relieved to see him there. Dad would have gone along.

Or he could just call. Ring, phone, ring!!!

None of that happened.

When a letter to Tom in early January went unanswered, I did not write again. I was having a hard time accepting that he was disappearing again, but the proof was in his lack of response—no letters. Because it was too embarrassing, I didn't tell anyone, including my mother, how much I was hurting. But she knew. Tom and I had been talking marriage, and now he was gone. Again? The swift communication of today's email and messaging apps might have kept us together—but that is now. This was then. I felt deserted. I knew there was another girl at college, someone from Jackson. He'd even told me about her, but not in a way that made me concerned. I had dated that other guy, too. I was more hurt than angry, but I was busy getting ready for the next chapter of my life and didn't have the luxury of taking to my bed and moping.

At the *Collegian*, Jim and I spent most weekdays together, entertaining each other and the rest of the staff with our sparring. And eventually we shared our Saturday nights.

But it didn't start out so smoothly. One Friday evening sometime that January, Jim phoned and asked me to go to a screening the next night of *Dr. Strangelove, or: How I Learned to Stop Worrying and Love the Bomb*. He had press passes. It seemed unlikely that between the time I'd seen him at the *Collegian* a few hours earlier and the phone call the passes had miraculously come into his possession, so I assumed I was a late fill-in for someone else. I assessed all this as I said yes. I had no plans for Saturday night. But I couldn't help noting to myself that the passes were another perk of being editor-in-chief rather than the managing editor.

The big bonus, other than the top job itself, was the red-and-white Mustang convertible that Jim was driving. The year was 1964, the year the Mustang came out—mid-year. To promote it as a cool car for the young and hip, the Ford Motor Company gave the editor-in-chief of thirty college newspapers around the country one to drive—gratis—for the semester.

Let me point out that on the way to school every morning in the carpool, I passed the world headquarters of the Ford Motor Company on Michigan Avenue in Dearborn, and sometimes I'd look at the Glass House, as it is called, and momentarily reflect that somewhere up there was the guy—of course it was a guy—who came up with the plan that added glitter to the dividends of being born male: guys became editors-in-chief, and editors-in-chief got free cars for a semester.

But you take life as it comes.

And now, instead of staying home on Saturday night and wondering if I might find a way to call Tom at college—I didn't have the number of the phone in the hallway at his dorm—I had plans. With Jim. In the Mustang. I wasn't terribly surprised he'd asked me out, since our bantering at the office often veered into a kind of snappy flirting, and I chose to treat our evening out as a real date. I put on my favorite dress, one that Mom had made: a coral mohair number patterned on Pierre Cardin's A-line style—simple, sleeveless, and quietly sexy.

After the film, Jim and I must have gone out for a meal or a drink. I don't remember. I do remember we kissed goodnight rather enthusiastically. His blue blazer was covered with telltale bits of coral mohair.

Back at the office come Monday, we acted as if nothing had changed. We did our jobs, we kidded around, we put out the next day's paper.

While the chemistry was nothing like it was with Tom, I assumed we'd go out again. By then, it was February. No word from Tom. Valentine's Day came and went. Jim and I were together several hours a day, three times a week. Because we both had jobs one full day a week at our local suburban newspapers and didn't come to school that day, each of us had one day out of five when we were solely in charge at the *Collegian*. Jim was surprised and chagrined—but he didn't admit it until later—when I turned out the first twelve-page edition of the *Collegian*. He learned about it the next morning when he picked up a paper on the way to class.

One night after everyone else had gone, he pulled me to him and we kissed. Jim lived miles to the east; I lived west. It didn't occur to me that dating someone from the office came with complications, but maybe that had floated through Jim's mind. If so, then he shouldn't have initiated kissing at the office after hours.

Jim and I kissed again at the office.

And still he didn't ask me out.

And still I didn't hear from Tom.

I didn't tell Jim about the relationship I had with someone in another city who had stopped writing to me.

Jim and I kissed again at the office.

Still he didn't ask me out.

Was I confused? Yes. And no. He liked me, but not enough to go public. I felt tawdry and terrible. *Next time, I will stop it*, I thought. *I'm not pretty enough for him to want to show me off. It's the nose.*

When it was still cold outside, someone gave a *Collegian* party at their house; someone else from the paper asked me to go as their date, a sweet guy who would later come out as gay. Like back in high school, I was the safe date who wouldn't expect more. I knew Jim was going. I had another good dress in my closet—this one mostly black—and off I went, determined to act as if I didn't care about you-know-who.

Jim's date was someone who hung around the paper and had written a few stories. She was pretty enough, and she had no off-putting feature. Jim asked me to dance, the Beatles' "I Want to Hold Your Hand" came on, and like a dog who wants a treat, he stared into my eyes while singing along with the words. Now that was confusing. We each left with our respective dates.

But after that night, Jim and I were a couple for the rest of the semester. Everyone knew. The other woman quit the paper. Dating Jim was diverting and heady and fun—he was good-looking and hunky, bright and ambitious, and he had ample choices for the role of girlfriend, which did add to the buzz. It was like getting the ring on *The Bachelor*, but for an engagement that would only last until the end of the semester. We were not in love, neither one of us. We were young and having a fling.

Tom?

There had been no tearful goodbye, no letter calling our affair kaput, no night when I wept for what might have been. We had faded in increments, like a well that slowly, but finally, dries up. You put the bucket down the well, and one day there's no water at all. I focused on the next chapter of my life, and now, it would be alone.

The *Collegian*'s faculty adviser, a crusty Irish newspaperman named Frank Gill, called me into his office one afternoon and said I ought to pack up and Go East or Go West—but get thee to a coast! You'll find better pickings there than in the stodgy center of the country. Fusty women's departments were likely to be all the Midwest would be serving up for some years to come, and someone like me would be cracking her head on multiple glass ceilings. But I didn't have the money to strike out for the coasts; I simply had to find a job. New York City would have to wait.

The best offer I got—the only one that made any sense—was, alas, in a women's department of the *Saginaw News*. One of my assignments would be to write up engagements and weddings, a task that requires no more skill than knowing that verbs follow subjects in sentence structure and how to spell peau de soie. At least the *News* was a daily, ninety miles north of Dearborn. Jim and I made no plans for the future.

Dad came to the graduation ceremony but never made much of it—nor that I was one of a handful of seniors inducted into Wayne State University's honor society. There are a few snapshots from the day, but none of those proud-parent-with-graduate photos everyone else seems to have. My dad seemed particularly low-key that day. Perhaps our battle had been too protracted for my father to let on that, so far, I was succeeding. Was he proud, or bitter? He gave no indication.

What I did not consider during those years was how my not helping out financially at a time of need affected him—while I single-mindedly pursued my dream instead—and how that might have left a lingering burn. What I did not realize then was that my father found himself the chief provider for a household of seven at roughly the same age as I had been when refusing to help with the family finances. Two months after he turned eighteen, his father died, and as the oldest son, my father became the breadwinner for his family, with his mother and five younger children at home. By then he had risen to gang boss in the local mine, just as his father had been—as high as you could go as a miner who works in the pits.

Sometime in the next decade, he moved the family from Appalachia to the booming Motor City. Jean was already in New York by then, the other sisters drifted to other states, his brothers were caught up in World War II. I knew the vague outlines of my father's journey but had not been aware of how our ages converged at the time of family need—eighteen—when he asked me to help our family in distress. Certainly, the responsibilities that had been thrust on him shaped what he expected of me, but none of this percolated into my eighteen-year-old consciousness. I believed that if I dropped out of school, I would never make my way back—I wasn't some movie star's daughter. Would my quitting school have saved the motel? Maybe as a stopgap. Most likely my parents would have sold it anyway. Its mom-and-pop style was already going out of fashion. But no matter. What I know now is that I surely let him down. However, what I absorbed in every cell of my being was that if I stayed in school, I had to prove my worth. I had to demonstrate that the effort, and the cost, had not been in vain, that I must make them—him—proud. *Daddy, I'll show you I can do it.*

After I was offered the job in Saginaw—a month or two before graduation—my mother reacted as if I'd gotten a job in a whorehouse in Hades. She went berserk: *Nice girls don't leave home. None of your cousins have!* became her mantra. With a you-are-killing-me look, she never broke character. Now Dad did something surprising. He said he'd help me move. He'd drive me up to

Figure 3. At the Saginaw News. The watch and chain once belonged to my maternal grandmother.

Saginaw with my stuff. We'd find a place for me to live. Thank you, I said, thank you ever so much.

Dad must have spoken to my mother, for soon after that, Mom woke up with a totally different mindset. Together we went through the house. She pulled out all the sheets and towels and pots and pans that I might need. I still have a few of those things—an aluminum pizza pan, a Pyrex measuring cup with most of the red ink worn off, a cast-iron frying pan. I packed it all up, along with the three or four outfits she'd sewn for me—one a copy of a Chanel suit.

She and I drove to Saginaw, and within a day we'd found a small-but-adequate furnished apartment on the second floor of a home. It was within walking distance of the paper, as I did not yet have a car. The owner and her two young daughters lived downstairs. An older woman lived across the hall. The rule was this: No men overnight. No exceptions.

It did not seem like a problem.

JULY 3, 1964—I am being pursued, presumably because I was initially stand-offish, by the good-looking scion of a wealthy Michigan family who is obviously destined for greater things than the police beat of the *Saginaw News*. He has a law degree from the University of Michigan, a socialite mother, a publisher father on a sister newspaper—but three desks away from me is where he is for the time being. Someday he will marry someone named Pru who went to a Seven Sisters college or its near cousin. This I know instinctively, but being the object of his attention for the moment is insanely flattering. It is a given that he is lobbing pretty women like tennis balls from one of those thingamabobs that automatically shoots them into the air, one after another.

It is Friday night, we have had drinks, he has taken me grocery shopping and made me dinner at his fabulous single-guy studio on the top floor of a still-grand house on Saginaw's Mansion Row. I am a virgin, I say, disentangling myself from this guy who is so smooth his cologne should be called Savoir Faire. He is astounded—how could this be in this day? It's 1964! The promise I'd made to Tom bounces around in my head. I'm not going to give that up for a quick flash in the sheets, despite his insistence, despite how Victorian I suddenly feel.

With my virginity still intact, Dashing Scion drives me home around ten p.m. in his hardtop, maroon Karmann Ghia. What do you know. Tom, grinning as if he hadn't been MIA for five months, is there on the street, leaning against his own hardtop, maroon Karmann Ghia. I am not sure what I am thinking or feeling, I am not sure of anything, but I am not incredibly surprised. I say goodnight to Dashing Scion, who comments favorably on my surprise suitor's choice of wheels. It is unbearably hot and humid, so damp the sky is wringing out its hair as a fine drizzle mists the air. It's been like this for days. When will the weather break?

Tom follows me up the steps while I try to assess how I feel. Numb is the answer. Groceries deposited in the kitchen, I can't decide where we should sit. Where have you been? I ask. I want to smack him and kiss him at the same time.

I've been really depressed, he says. I didn't have enough credits to graduate. My mother isn't speaking to me. I've got a room and a crummy summer job in Flint. I wrote once, he says, but it was just a list of how bad things are. I didn't send it.

Hmm. Let's go out, I say. This place is stifling.

We go to a drive-in—Tom still doesn't drink, so a bar is out of the question. Not having heard from him for months, I am doing a slow burn inside. I don't have a hold on my emotions. Do I want to fall into his arms? No. *Yes.* Do I want him to go? No. An hour passes. Another. We talk and talk, and I still want to fall into his arms and smack him. This is someone who made me feel strong, confident, secure, attractive—when we were together. I never suspected my looks were the reason for Tom's silence. He was brainy, no matter what his grades were, and we fit each other. But. Will he stay? Can I trust him?

"Let's get married now," he says.

Huh? After all those months of me wondering what in the hell happened to you? After you doing this twice? I did NoDoz nights; you did College Lite—now you didn't even graduate. Am I a tad irritated? Confused? Did you think I'd always be there, waiting on ice without so much as a word from you? I thought I'd never hear from you again.

I don't even ask if he has been seeing someone else—what difference would it make? How can we make plans? He still had to graduate. Getting a degree—the first in my family to do so—had been all-important to me, had been so hard to do over my father's objections, it was difficult to accept Tom squandering his opportunity. His mother had gone to college; maybe it didn't seem so critical to him.

"I don't know anymore," comes out of my mouth. But we keep on talking. I don't want him to go.

It's two a.m., and we're now back in my apartment, it's creeping toward three, we are trying to be quiet, talking barely above a whisper. *I am not supposed to have gentlemen overnight* runs through my head as I think of the woman who lives across the hall, the owner of the house downstairs, the private entrance that's not that private. I'll never be able to get him out of here in the morning without everybody knowing, it's too late to ask for an exception, even the cat across the hall is sleeping. I feel for Tom, who looks desolate and tired. I want to explore more about what I—we—are going to do, but I can't get thrown out of this place. I don't have a car, and I can walk to work from here. I need this apartment.

"You need to come back tomorrow," I say. "We'll have the whole day. It's the Fourth of July."

"Can I spend the night?" The question compresses the reality that Flint is forty miles away, it's two-thirty already, we are both tired. A reasonable request.

I explain the rule. He asks again, I do not relent, though I do not really want to send him away. *You know he loves you, and you love him still, right?* Really, do I? *Why didn't he write all semester?* I'm always having these conversations with myself.

"Promise me you will come back tomorrow," I say, standing across from him in the tiny sitting room with a dark, fuzzy maroon couch and matching overstuffed armchair. Where could he sleep anyway? Should I break the rule, run down in the morning, and tell the landlady it was too late for him to drive home? What will happen then? I just moved in. I barely know her.

He nods.

"Say, I promise," I insist.

"I promise," he says.

This should be sealed with a kiss flits across my consciousness. *Say that, Tom, and I'll meet you in the middle.* Should I say it? I have been awfully distant. Should I take the two steps toward him, and hold out my arms, saying, Let's seal that with a kiss?

But pride gets in the way, and I do not, and he does not, and down the front steps he goes into the unforgiving swelter of the night.

JULY 4, 1964—Another scorcher, blistering hot and humid all over again. That teasing shower the night before has not broken the heat wave. I wake when the sun comes up, and it comes up before six. The ceiling above my bed has no writing revealing the future. I shut my eyes, hoping for a few more moments of oblivion to stop the constant questions, but I might as well have hoped to stop time. I was either going to marry him, or not, and I'd know the answer before the day was done. If you really want to marry someone, you know without questioning it. It's not like picking something from column A and column B at Won Ton Charlie's Take-Out. It's either yes or no. The months when I hadn't heard from him had taken their toll.

I shower, slip into navy shorts and a hot-pink tube top, and make my coffee strong so it will stand up to ice. I curse the milk gone sour. I cannot leave to buy fresh milk, and besides, would any store be open? It's a holiday.

We need some time. I need to be sure he will be constant.

I write out *Mrs. Thomas Sawicki* on a scrap of paper and stare at it. Even if I don't really change my name legally . . . Mrs. Thomas Sawicki.

His wife. I like the sound of that. Meet Tom's wife, Lorraine Dusky. I like the sound of that better.

Okay, he hasn't finished college yet, like he should have.

But he's no dummy. We'll figure this out.

Nine-fifteen. He will be here any minute. The apartment is already oppressive, it barely cooled off at night, there is no breeze, I have no fan. When he gets here, I will give him a big hug when I open the door. I'll know. When we got back together before, I wanted to be with him forever as much as I did before, no question about that. He is smart and kind and supportive, and he will be a good mate, a husband, a partner for life. But why hadn't he graduated? He is the one, right? Life will be settled. We will figure this out.

It will be better to be with him than not. I really don't do so well alone.

I am leaning to yes.

Yes! Hurry up and get here.

Ten. The heat is crawling up my mind. It was late when he left, he needed rest, maybe he overslept.

But remember the time he woke you up after only three hours of sleep? He'll be here any minute. Is that a car on the road I hear? Yes . . .

The car goes on by.

Eleven.

I can hardly believe this is happening. Exactly how far is Flint?

He will not do this now. He will be here.

Noon.

I cannot see the street from my rear apartment so I cannot look for cars. I cannot go out because I must wait. Besides, Miss, where would you go? I cannot call him because I do not have a phone yet. Nor does he. Even if I find a phone downtown—who do I call? He's not at home, his mother is not speaking to him, and I'm some broad—or maybe not anymore—and what if he comes while I'm gone? After last night, he'll assume the worst. If I had a car, I would have gotten his address last night and driven up to Flint myself.

I make myself read. Something.

One.

Is it possible he's not coming? If someone wants to marry you, he shows up, right?

I have to wait.

Tick-tock two o'clock.

Three.

I sit in the backyard. No one is having a barbecue on the block, there is no calling over the fences to neighbors, no sound of bottles being opened or kids playing with sparklers. The lady downstairs and her girls have been gone for hours, off to some family picnic, I imagine, and the woman across the hall was picked up by someone a while ago. The silence is deafening, the heat is oppressive, the apartment is suffocating, my heart is already lamenting. How did something once so fine get lost?

I can do nothing but wait. I have nowhere to go. I have no friends in town. I have no car, I can't take off just to be away from this place where he is not coming, I have nowhere to go.

Four.

He has not come. He is not coming. Why didn't I say, Let's seal this with a kiss? That would have made all the difference. He would be here if I had done that. I was so . . . cool. So this is how it ends. He is not coming.

Five. Six. Seven. Eight.

Finally, night comes, bearing a shroud.

That Monday morning I could have called his uncle, the one who ran the Lansing bureau for the same chain of newspapers I now worked for, and said I'm worried about Tom, he was supposed to show up on Saturday, is he all right, how can I reach him? But that oozed desperation. He'd wonder how he'd gotten involved in his nephew's love life, he'd probably think I was pregnant, maybe he even knew about *some broad* that Tom had been infatuated with a while back.

I do not make the call.

By that Monday, my virginity, such as it still remains, seems as outdated as a lorgnette, pretty to look at but impractical to use. Dashing Scion continues to pursue me with the kind of charming intensity that such men possess when their goal is a reluctant cherry. I am a modern woman, am I not? I am hip, right? It is 1964! Even though all I know about birth control could fit in a thimble, I am hardly the good Catholic who once believed in mortal sin or someone who would reveal this transgression in a confessional.

Yet. The piercing remembrance of my pledge to Tom—that I would only sleep with one man in my life, my husband who would be him—is there in the bed with me and this ardent Lothario a few weeks later. He might have lust in his heart; I have only despair. Sex is awful in all the ways that sex for the sake of simply doing it is awful.

Soon enough, I buy a car. A Karmann Ghia, the same kind both Dashing Scion and Tom own. The Ghia has a Volkswagen engine in a sleek, sexy body, and it is the cool car of the era unless you can afford a real sports car—or want a Mustang. I did not.

My Ghia is a creamy pale yellow, and a convertible. I also move into the building where Dashing Scion lives, a big, old mansion—Saginaw once boasted lumber barons—that had been carved up into several quirky and inviting apartments. There are no rules about who can spend the night. Either one of these later realities—car or accommodating lodging—occurring mere months earlier, likely would have altered the course of my life.

That January, a call comes out of the blue—an offer of a flight to Rochester, New York, for a tryout on the morning paper there, for a job city-side, not in the stultifying ghetto of a women's department. The guy who had lost out on the editor-in-chief job at Wayne the year before me had offered up my name when a friend of his—Ron Martin, the assistant city editor on the *Democrat & Chronicle*—said they were looking for a feature writer, and did he know anybody? I leap at the opportunity, fly there in the middle of a snowstorm in January for a tryout, and when the job offer comes I do not hesitate, even when the editor/publisher of the *Saginaw News* makes a counteroffer, saying they will revamp the women's department—they want to modernize it—call it Lifestyle or some such thing, and put me in charge. The women's editor, who is on the way to retirement anyway, will be eased out sooner rather than later.

But I will be Nellie Bly, Ida B. Wells, Brenda Starr! Not some lifestyle editor in a middling town in central Michigan, which now feels like a place that might as well be named Podunk. *Get thee to a coast* bounces around in my head, and Rochester is at least in the right direction and in the same state as the golden mecca of New York City. Besides, and this is a very big besides, Mom told me that Tom had married—at the end of the year to a girl he'd met at Jackson Junior College and who had followed him to his new school.

So.

Goodbye Tom. Goodbye Midwest.

I am not thinking of any of this as I walk over the Genesee River and headlong into the life I've dreamed of since the fourth grade. I have broken out of the sideshow of a women's department where recipes rule and important stories never run. The *Democrat & Chronicle* in Rochester is a bigger newspaper in a bigger city. I am in Metro, the lone woman there. *I'm on my way, Daddy, you wait and see.*

I do not acknowledge it—I barely know it—but my heart is plenty sore. First love cuts deep, leaves a lasting scar, and the memory is always suffused with nostalgia. Tom did love me, I tell myself, but not enough, a voice would whisper back. I'd learned that while absence might make the heart grow fonder, proximity leads to marriage. Without being aware of it, I am ripe for the attentions of someone who is substantial, fervent, and present. *Present* is very important.

Tom might not have been on my mind that afternoon as I walked over the Genesee River in the oncoming dark, but the gods were playing chess with us, and we were the pawns.

Fate was not yet done with Tom Sawicki and me.

3   The Next Story

Today, Rochester might be a struggling upstate city, but back then, Rochester was someplace. Bausch & Lomb and Kodak and Xerox (which hadn't yet become a verb) were all headquartered there, giving the place a raw, vibrant energy. Kodak controlled most of the US photography market, and manufacturing jobs had not yet gone overseas. Rochester natives knew that the Mafia was around, providing services. The University of Rochester, the Eastman School of Music, and Rochester Institute of Technology (which had a hip art department) added intellectual and creative flair. A new downtown mall—they were novelties then—had a posh restaurant with a cocktail lounge on top where the city's power elite ordered Tanqueray gin martinis, seduced their secretaries (which is what they were called then), and acted like big shots.

The *Democrat & Chronicle* is a morning paper, deadlines are in the evening and the Metro staff works afternoons, three to eleven p.m. It's my first day on the job, and I've been hired to write features. Though the city room has been emptying for the dinner break, I have no idea where the guys are going or what to do for sustenance. I certainly haven't brought a snack. In the meantime, I'm sitting there trying to look busy. No one's asked me to join them. I am not only the new face, I am The Girl.

The city editor who hired me, Dick Dougherty, comes to my rescue, suggesting he take me to the Towpath—where everybody has been going—and introduce me around. Dick is done for the day and normally would be heading home. The front page and the local section are mostly made up for the night—as well as the morning edition. The night editor will shepherd the stories coming in onto the pages. Dick is thoughtful, silver-haired, tall, thin, distinguished and handsome enough to be a model for expensive men's suits. As we head out, Dick turns to the guy at the big desk next to a window who sits across the aisle from me and asks if he wants to join us. His name is Patrick Brasley.

We are headed to the Towpath that evening, a gritty joint that serves as an unofficial outpost of the *D&C*. The tavern sits directly across the bridge from where the *D&C* and Rochester's afternoon daily, the *Times-Union*, are housed. The papers occupy a huge classic revival structure that looks like a newspaper headquarters straight out of an old movie, tough and imposing. Surely something important goes on there—and I'm about to be part of it!

As we three make our way across the long span of the bridge, Dick comes upon his conveniently parked car and decides to go home. You'll take her over to the 'Path? he says as a half statement of fact as he hands over the job of introductions to Brasley. Dick nods goodbye as he folds himself into his silver Volkswagen bug. Patrick later would tell me his immediate reaction was, *Damn, we're going to spend an hour saying where did you go to school, what did you major in, et cetera. How did I get stuck with her?*

I know as much, instantly intuiting that this other guy with whom I have not shared ten words is not elated at suddenly being my tour guide. A woman knows when she cannot count on her looks to carry the day, and I understood that I never could. Fresh in my mind were the barely heard words of that single man in possession of a good fortune—Dashing Scion, that is— who had said of me only months earlier—when I came breezing through the revolving door of the *Saginaw News*—"You would be perfect if . . ." *You didn't have that nose*, I mentally filled in as I pretended not to hear. The incident is so imprinted on my brain I can tell you today exactly what I was wearing, down to my black patent-leather heels.

Crossing the bridge that evening with this guy, there's nothing to do except keep walking and talking and depend on the kindness of someone who is nearly a stranger. Patrick later insists that I kept brushing up against him. I might have, as with Dick gone, I am now walking in high heels on the outside of the sidewalk over a bridge with traffic, and I have a sense that the busy street is perilously close.

At the Towpath, the other reporters have already filled up a large table, and there's no room to squeeze in. Patrick makes quick introductions, and we end up at a table for two some distance away from the group, certainly not what he or I had in mind, the awkwardness of my being thrust upon him increasing by the moment. Yet he is polite.

The linguine's good here, he says. Fine, I'll try it, I say. Somehow the conversation flows easily like the house red we're drinking. My college and career up until then are dispensed within ten minutes, then his (he grew up in Rochester, went to the University of Rochester, English major), and before you know it we are churning rapidly through recent movies, the imagery in Polansky's *Knife in the Water* (I found out later he was winging this one), Hemingway's books, which I was not winging as I'd read a couple, including *For Whom the Bell Tolls*, which naturally leads us to John Donne, and soon enough I'm rattling off Donne's "No Man Is an Island," suddenly appreciating that Sister Jane Edward had made us memorize those lines, and that somehow leads to Patrick quoting Andrew Marvell, which is kind of cheeky when you realize this is the guy who had a coy mistress.

The waitress asks if it's one check or two.

"Two," we fairly shout in unison. This is not a date, this is not what it looks like, we both are in a rush to tell her. I'm the new kid on the block, I say.

Uh-huh, she says, dubiously.

She reads the cues right. It is the beginning.

The next evening around seven, Patrick appears in front of my desk. He is already in his trench coat, his Irish wool cap in hand. "Going to dinner?" I notice how blue his eyes are, how inviting his smile.

"Yes!" An ice maiden I'll never be.

If Patrick hadn't asked me to join him, I probably would not have taken a dinner break that night, or the next, or the one after that, just stayed at my desk and read newspapers or otherwise kept busy, the new girl without friends. The guys on the city staff are not overtly hostile, not a single one; they simply take a wait-and-see attitude. I am an object of curiosity, someone to observe but not ask, "Hey, Dusky, want to join us at the 'Path?" Anyway, what's the protocol? I am young and female and an outsider. Almost everyone is older and married and grew up around here. There's a woman covering the arts, and another, religion, but by the time I take a dinner break somewhere between six and seven, they are gone for the day. The women in the women's department? By the time I come to work at three p.m., they are wrapping up. As for the young, pretty redhead giving me the flinty eye? Is she thinking, Why is *she* working Metro and not me?

While the guys are seemingly neutral, waiting for me to prove myself, I obviously get the dander up of an old-timer at the paper who writes a twice-weekly column about this and that. He has an office on another floor, and I haven't met him. I'd seen an older guy in the newsroom one night but hadn't paid any attention to him. But he obviously had seen The Girl. The only one there late at night, acting like she belonged. One morning I open the paper to find that he's written a column about how women are flooding the newsroom. Why, he could barely get a drink at the water fountain without lining up behind them! When did this happen? How did this happen? Oh, the pity of it all!

I am livid and whip off a stinging retort noting his reeking sexism. Because I am in a hurry to drop my memo in the interoffice mail, I correct my typos in pen. A day or two later I am sitting at my desk when the Old Geezer makes the rounds of the newsroom. I see Patrick—only a few feet away—talk to the Old Geezer. He is brandishing a piece of paper. Patrick appears to be brushing him off. "What was that about?" I ask later. Geezer, Patrick says, was showing my note to anyone he saw as a compatriot, that is, any white male. As I'm the only woman in the city room, Geezer surely has seen me sitting at my desk directly across the aisle from Patrick. I am embarrassed only because of the note's typos; I'd been too angry to retype it.

While I'm making my own way at the paper—reporting is entrepreneurial and not dependent on merely being assigned a story—Dick and the assistant city editor, Ron Martin, both my champions, are off two of the five days I work. As I have no contacts calling up with feature ideas and I haven't been assigned a beat that would give me license to prowl for stories, I am largely dependent on the desk for assignments. When Dick and Ron aren't there, an older and cranky chauvinist on the paper's exit ramp is in charge.

Oh, he might throw me a few press releases to rewrite or an unimportant obit, but he did give me one good assignment. *Go see what the commotion is all about over this group called the Rolling Stones, Dusky. They're at the War Memorial.*

Mick Jagger was gracious and soft-spoken during the fifteen minutes we talked before he went onstage, and I did a fluff interview. A phalanx of cops, still reeling over race riots in the city the year before, stood arm-in-arm in front of the stage, giving off a tough military vibe. The kids were noisy and screamed a lot, threw stuffed animals at the stage, and when Jagger removed his sports coat and held it over his shoulder with his finger, the noise level rose to what the chief of police found unacceptable. He took to the stage and shut down the show during the seventh song. Mayhem ensued as the kids, now angry at the police, rushed the stage and began throwing used flash bulbs and unidentified flying objects. One girl was injured in the angry rush. My initial story, written for a first-edition deadline, landed on the front page of the city section without a byline, which was at the discretion of the night editor. I put the blame for the melee squarely on the police chief.

After I left the paper around midnight, a police spokesperson must have insisted to the night editor that the kids breached the phalanx of the cops before the show was cut short, and that's why they shut it down. That is not what I witnessed, and that is not what I wrote, but that's what ended up not only on the front page but also on the state Associated Press wire. I was the only reporter there that night, with a photographer from the *D&C*. I'm telling the story here in some detail because the concert made a kind of weird footnote in Stones lore, and it's the second version—this one slanted to make the cops look blameless—that you can find online.[1] I didn't see the revised story until the following afternoon when I went to the office, too late to change anything, and I

_____

[1] "Long-haired Rolling Stones Cut Short by City Police," *Democrat & Chronicle* (Rochester, NY), Nov. 2, 1965, A-1, https://web.archive.org/web/20220920171525/http://therollingstonesbrianjonesyears.blogspot.com/2013/09/the-rolling-stones-rochester-democrat.html.

knew running a correction of this magnitude was never going to happen. The cops had their story, I had mine, and who was I to call them liars? Sure, I could grumble to Patrick about the rewrite—much good it would do me—but I was too green and new at the paper to raise a commotion.

As I soon learn, Patrick is the consummate newspaper man—with a nose for a good story, an innate love of the business, writing talent, and the indispensable cigarette and cup of coffee from a machine that dispenses murky black dreck for a dime. His beat is city and state politics. He has his own Saturday political column, accompanied by a small engraved image of his face. Not only is he a good reporter and writer, but he can also turn out a memorable phrase on deadline, all of which makes him a big deal on the paper. With his reddish, sandy hair, weathered skin, and broad nose, Patrick looks as Irish as anyone named Paddy. A few inches beyond six feet, he has the wiry, rangy body of someone who might be a tennis pro on his way to the country club, which is how he always dresses—navy blazer and tie, gray flannels, often in need of a pressing. He is irrepressibly appealing to have as a friend. He's way more than an ordinary newsman. He is Someone. I swear I do not presume a flirtation or presume anything—but then, what am I doing? I am fitting in. I had male friends on the other papers. Was this any different? No line has been crossed. I am playing with fire, but I am too young, too inexperienced, too lonely to know it.

As I am swimming solo in a sea of men, Patrick's friendship is a lifeline. So when he asks me to join him at the Towpath—we sometimes sit with the other guys there, sometimes not—those three nights of the week when our schedules coincide, why say no?

No one is waiting for me back home.

I am not aware, not really, that I am falling for this man. He's married. He's taken. We are just buddies, right?

How foolish that sounds now.

4   Conception

A month after our fateful walk on the bridge, Patrick and I kiss. Kiss! It is on the eve of the Ides of March, a bad omen we make light of. No strings, we hurriedly agree the next day. I don't want you to get the wrong idea, he says. I'm married. I've got a family.

I understand, I say. I don't expect anything. How in charge I sound. I am not the guardian of his fidelity—that is up to him—and I am not cheating on anyone. I don't feel like a seductress, nor do I feel like the one being seduced. All is light and breezy, I tell myself.

His wife dislikes—make that hates—his job: the long hours, the not-enough pay, the whole dirty business of working on a newspaper. He might be a hotshot in the city room and a man respected about town, but at home he is a husband and father who ought to have a better job. One could smell trouble right there, because for those of us who love the work—the story, the buzz of a deadline, the satisfaction of front-page bylines—no better job can be imagined. What I admire, she berates. He does not complain, but his unhappiness comes out in chance comments.

Though he sits directly across the aisle from me—a few feet from my desk (no one has a cubicle)—we are cool comrades. For a while there, it would have been possible for me to walk away from what is drawing me in more deeply week after week, month after month, but nothing and no one stems the flow. Though we do not talk of love, I am too young and too reckless to see where my heart is racing full speed ahead, or to have any sense of dangerous roadblocks fortune has set out on the way. Without being aware, I am falling madly in love with this man, although I have not yet admitted this to myself. I am making no plans, nor am I thinking about tomorrow. I am on a toboggan without brakes.

Instead of talking to each other in the city room, we type each other notes and leave them in our mailboxes. To arrange where and when we will meet for our dinner break—and avoid walking out together and set tongues wagging—we call each other on the interoffice phone. When I hang up, he stays on the line and talks to the dial tone for another minute so no one will notice that we both hang up at the same time. As the weeks—and then months—drift by after that first kiss, we take to having dinner at another joint—Bryan's—where the other reporters seldom come. For an entire hour we are likely to be alone in a red-leather booth. Yet Bryan's is not so out of the way that if we run into other reporters, we can't carry off the fiction that we just happen to have chosen Bryan's instead of the Towpath. Come on, join us? They usually do, and that's fine too. Dinner is often a bacon-lettuce-and-tomato sandwich and a drink—his a martini, mine a glass of wine.

He reads my stories and offers a compliment or critique. He suggests I read the *New York Times* to stay informed. We note a graceful turn of phrase here, a detail to savor there. Patrick is my friend, my mentor, my lover.

Almost.

We do not jump into bed that first night we kiss, or the night after that. Oh, no. My Catholic guilt might have been left back in Michigan, but his is running up and down his Irish-Catholic psyche. He's never had an affair before. I'm in love with someone who clearly cares for me back, who treats me well, who is where he says he is going to be when he says he is going to be there, who calls when he can't be there, who even calls from his home late at night, and who says he loves me. His body is lean and tall, and it feels perfect as it curls around mine. I try on his fedora. It practically falls down over my eyes. He says he has a big head and has to buy large hats. I say he must have a big brain. Aren't there studies that show that? His body isn't as taut and smooth as Tom's, but it'll do. The years—he's fourteen years older than me—don't seem *fourteen* when we're together. I don't feel naive and inexperienced; I feel like his equal, only younger. He smokes all the time, and I was smoking too, French cigarettes that came in a box and made me cough. I didn't inhale but still got the effect I wanted—one part smoke, one part attitude.

He has a martini, or two, after work, but isn't that what newspaper people do? They drink. They smoke. They are smart and interesting. Their jobs are more than jobs: They are a lifestyle, a meaningful career, a calling to a higher purpose. To tell the truth. To be a watchdog. To record the history of the moment. To tell the world's stories. I am in love with it all: our shared dedication to the work, the seamless compatibility, my head on his shoulder, the endless stream of our conversation that roamed from the civil rights movement in the South to local politics in Rochester—his beat—to our personal histories, to whether or not E. E. Cummings was a poet whose popularity would last. He wasn't so sure. I demurred. In the stolen moments we find to be together, he introduces me to Billie Holiday and I introduce him to Joan Baez. He is pleased to find that I have my own short stack of Dinah Washington albums. He tells me that the *VSOP* on a bottle of cognac means it is the good stuff: Very Superior Old Pale, something I might want to know when doing a cross-word puzzle one day. He might be married, I couldn't make out the future, but he is constant. He is what Tom had not been.

But while I might not have any qualms about our deepening bond as we lie on the backless couch in my living room, the all-systems-go switch in his brain turns off. Back then, there are no little blue Viagra pills to get us over the hump.

For me, this was a plus of sorts. I did not have to do something smart about birth control. I didn't have to think about it, and naturally I was not prepared. All things considered, his impotence—that went on for weeks—was a kind of a gift. This I did not share with Patrick.

But all good things come to an end.

It happens in Manhattan. He is to cover a big Republican dinner there in June. He asks me to come along. He'll arrange everything so we can be together without hiding for a couple of days; he'll do an extra interview with someone so we can have more than a single night in Manhattan. I ask for the time off.

Everything is planned so no one would connect the two of us. I will take an early flight down, by myself, and meet him later in the day at a hotel on the east side of Manhattan, far from the west-side hotel where the event is taking place and everyone else will be staying.

Except that my flight is packed with what appears to be the entire upstate Republican Party contingent, as well as other editors and reporters. Hello, everyone, what a surprise! Everyone going to the dinner is on that flight—on a suddenly very small plane—except Patrick, who is taking a later flight. Charming and chatty, the Republican county chair sits next to me. Why am I going to New York midweek? Seeing friends. Do I know Pat Brasley, the paper's political reporter? Of course. Where am I staying? With those friends. Could he buy me a drink in the next few days? I'll be busy. Do I want to ride into town in their limo? No, a friend is meeting me in Manhattan. I'll take a cab. Since nobody with a shred of street smarts would turn down a limo ride into midtown, that probably was a tip-off I was meeting the one person who should have been on that plane but wasn't. All I had to do was get off in midtown and say thank you.

It being a Wednesday, and early enough to take in a Broadway matinee, I take myself to see *Any Wednesday*, that biting romantic comedy about a young single woman and her married lover. Why not? It's my story now. It was amusing, the humor close enough to singe.

That's what you went to see? Patrick asks, momentarily taken aback, when we meet later. I nod and smile knowingly in return. I can control this, I tell myself. I won't get hurt, right?

We dine at a fancy restaurant called La Caravelle, feeding trough of the haut monde and anyone with an expense account. I order vichyssoise for a starter, how delicious; we drink stingers after dinner, how sophisticated; we hop a cab downtown for jazz at the Village Vanguard, how hip; and on the second day in the late afternoon, we become lovers in the sense that the world understands.

It is too late to not be in love. The words have been said. And said again. It's a story as old as time, as common as roses in rhyme.

But of course, I am keenly aware of his young children, three—he spoke of them the day after our first kiss, how "this couldn't mean anything"—but we have both given in to the heady intensity of our romance. He gives me gold earrings and Billie Holiday albums; I buy him silk ties. Occasionally, we meet at a restaurant that has a single rose on each table and big menus on thick, cream paper. Saturday afternoons we might listen to Herbie Hancock—the pianist that night at the Vanguard—on my stereo. Although guilt had once set out its snare, Patrick had beaten it back, and I rejected being the schoolmarm of his marriage.

If Tom was raw and unfinished, Patrick is the opposite: he is already a star in the firmament that matters most to me. And married lovers are so caring, so constant, so unlike careless young men who do not yet see how easily love can get lost.

A Chinese woman at the newspaper is known to read palms. What do you see in mine? I ask one day. She must have told me more than this, but this is all I recall, as she curled my palm into a fist: *You will have one child, but there is something wrong, like it's adopted.*

How very odd. Why would I adopt? I put it out of my mind.

By mid-summer I am trying desperately to live out the fiction that I do have a separate life, one that is not totally bound up with Patrick. But play the field? Not an option. There is no one to play with. I did have a few dates with one of the two single guys on the paper, but he got nasty after a few drinks, and besides, I'd learned it was his leaden copy I'd rewritten when I came for my tryout. I'd be with him and find myself humming Dylan's "It Ain't Me, Babe." The other unmarried guy? He's engaged to someone out of town, soon to be imported.

Even though I still have to work around the old-school sexist running the desk nearly half of my work week, I'm getting more stories in the paper, features that start on the front page of the Metro section—or the real front page, A1. Will I stay in Rochester forever? I have no idea. Will I go to a bigger city? Time to think about that later. And Patrick? What about Patrick? He is still not saying anything about tomorrow. Our relationship is a poignant cocktail of ecstasy and misery.

Patrick's tenth wedding anniversary marches in like an icy, stinging wind in July. To stave off the long night cursing fate and eating too much popcorn while he and The Wife are out having a swell dinner, I ask the guys—and the religion and arts writers, both women—if they would like to come by after work for a drink. That night being a Saturday, most would be leaving work around eight or nine, maybe even earlier. We'd all become friendly enough. I didn't consider inviting the crew from the women's department—I barely knew them, and my gut told me they all were still irritated I had swooped in from elsewhere and taken a plum job none of them had been considered for.

I wrap thin slices of salami around cream cheese, put out a crock of cheddar spread and crackers, set out some booze and ice, and slip into what was then called a hostess gown. My apartment, with an entrance foyer, two good-sized rooms, and a sliver of a kitchen, wraps around the corner of the top floor of a three-story apartment building. It's got good light and no rules about who can stay the night. The previous tenant, an artist, left behind some serviceable furniture, and thrift stores supplied the rest. It's a given the guys are curious about me and where I live. The religion editor stops by briefly, so it isn't just me and the guys—but still, the whole event is an exercise in desperate madness. I am trying to prove to myself that I am an independent person, not someone caught up in a tawdry triangle.

Around eleven, Patrick calls, saying, The Wife and I just had a big argument, I took her home and left, are people still there, I want to come up.

I get rid of the few laggards as soon as I can. I light candles, turn off the lights, and put on Dinah Washington. I sit and wait as her bluesy, soulful voice reminds me of the perilous journey I am on. Patrick shows up before midnight. He's clearly had one too many. Who was there and how was it, he wants to know, and soon enough we are making love on the slim and lumpy couch. Sometime that night, in a voice fogged by booze and cigarettes, Patrick says, I cannot go on leading this double life, we will be together, just give me time, I promise. You are my woman. We're rare, do you know how rare this is, what we have? We are two of the lucky ones, to be in love this much. You are my woman, he repeats, and I cling to that.

By the time he leaves, it's getting light. I stay up a while longer, picking up, emptying ashtrays, wondering if what he says will come to pass. A voice inside me is taking a wait-and-see attitude.

Patrick's three children, two boys and a girl, are all under ten. He and I were both raised Catholic—but those Catholic rules were shedding like a molting skin. My own mother had been divorced. The day Mom told me, I was seven, about to make my First Communion, and I asked why she never took Communion. When she explained why, we both wept—the rules I had learned in school meant that unless she had time to renounce my father to a priest as she lay dying, she would go straight to hell! This meant my older brother had a different father, news to me. She was so ashamed of this that none of our neighbors in Dearborn knew—for her marriage had been in Jackson, where her ex lived. I was to tell no one. No one.

So I know how Patrick's Irish-Catholic family would react. For added zest—when none was needed—his mother is the secretary to the bishop of Rochester. Could she ever admit that a son of hers is divorcing? To the bishop? To the rest of the very Catholic kin? To her friends in the parish? She would mentally take to her bed with smelling salts and rosary beads once she felt the ill wind of d-i-v-o-r-c-e. Tears and entreaties would be followed by novenas, and special masses would be ordered up. His brother would talk to him and set him straight. I would forever be the harlot, the home wrecker.

That is July.

By December, I am pregnant. Very pregnant, to be sure. Four months pregnant.

Why was I so careless? I can think of answers, I can fill pages with answers. Nineteen sixty-five was a time when girls (like me) decidedly did not keep condoms on the nightstand. When guys (like Patrick) who said they did not like to use condoms got away with it. When women felt they had to lie and say they were married, or about to be, even when they went to the doctor to ask for a prescription for birth control. Why didn't I take the Pill? The Pill was already around; it had been approved by the Food and Drug Administration (FDA) in 1960.

It might have been approved by the FDA, but information about the Pill that reached women of that era was scant. There was no internet on which to look up information about the Pill. If there had been pieces in *Cosmopolitan* about the Pill, I missed them. My mother assumed—and prayed, I am sure— that I would stay virginal, and the words "birth control" or "the Pill" never passed her lips. If my college friends slept with their boyfriends, I did not know. We did not talk about sex. No one I knew admitted to me that she was in a relationship that included going all the way. Only in June of that year—1965—had the Supreme Court decided in *Griswold v. Connecticut* that all married persons had the legal right to use birth control![2]

So call up a doctor and brazenly ask for a prescription for the Pill? Or a diaphragm? It sounded so racy and sinful and demanded a boldness beyond me. Was it even legal? Who knew? Respectable young women who were not married but who were having sex at least had fiancés and fixed wedding dates. They simply did not waltz in and ask for the Pill. Maybe they did elsewhere, maybe they did that in big cities, maybe they did not have the cultural admonitions to be chaste before marriage resounding like chapel bells inside their heads. I might think I had left the Church because I questioned the existence of God, but I hadn't gotten away that easily. The idea that if-I'm-having-sex-I-should-be-married lingered in me. Maybe it was the fear of pregnancy as

---

[2] The Pill was not universally available to unmarried women in all states until 1972. Not until 1965 did the U.S. Supreme Court rule in *Griswold v. Connecticut* that it was unconstitutional for the government to prohibit married couples from using birth control. Activist Bill Baird was arrested in 1967 for distributing a contraceptive foam and a condom to a student during a lecture on birth control and abortion at Boston University. Baird's appeal of his conviction led to the U.S. Supreme Court case, *Eisenstadt v. Baird* (1972), that finally made it legal in all states to allow unmarried couples to have and use birth control and thereby legalized it for all Americans. While these rulings were catching up to the fact that unmarried couples were having sex and not hiding it, they do indicate the puritanical ethos of that era. How different it was back then is hard to convey to young women today.

much as the mortal sin aspect of it—Go straight hell, no stopping in purgatory until redemption!—that the Church imprinted in me, but there it was.

As for those chic outfits I wore that my mother made for me from Vogue patterns? A thin veneer, hiding a greenhorn aching for love and for what had slipped away.

My daughter is conceived on a Saturday afternoon in August—I know enough about the rhythm method touted by the Catholic Church (three weeks, Go; ten days, No) to know it is a time not likely to be safe. I warn Patrick. *Not this afternoon. I could get pregnant.*

He says he will pull out.

I am dubious. He is persistent.

After the grief over guilt and impotence, I am chary of upsetting our delicate balance. I notice the beads of sweat on his brow, how blue are his eyes, and hear him say, We are rare, I love you, You are my woman. We will be together.

When my period is late, I go to a doctor I find in the phone book. I lie and say I am engaged to a law student. I take a pregnancy test. When the results come back negative, Patrick and I celebrate with champagne. I get a prescription for the Pill. I take it faithfully. My stomach is often a tad queasy, but I ignore it. I'm on the Pill. Morning sickness is not on my radar.

When my next couple of periods are light to nonexistent—and that had often been the case—I phone the doctor and ask if I should come in again. No need, he says. The test was negative and you're on the Pill. I believe him because I do not have the courage to doubt him. I believe him because my life up till then was predicated on the idea that I would not get pregnant like any silly girl. I believe him because after years of dreaming, praying, working to get the kind of job that I had, opposing my father, then opposing my mother, for all those years, I am not ready to face that it could all disappear because of one act of intemperance when I yielded instead of coming to a full stop. If there had been a blinking neon sign outside my window announcing

YOU ARE PREGNANT! I would have assumed it was not meant for me. I was on the Pill.

Reality does not set in until late December. I manage to hide my thickening waistline from my family at Christmas, and even from myself. I'm on the Pill, right? I can't be pregnant. But once back in Rochester, I can no longer avoid my rounding belly, even if I haven't gained a pound. The day after I get back from Detroit, I am in the doctor's office the next morning.

"You are almost five months pregnant," the doctor says icily, as he fingers me inside, as I lie splayed open on the examining table, a chicken ready for the carving. "The test is not accurate in the very early stages of pregnancy."

Crash, boom, the world will end at five p.m.

"I cannot have this baby."

He walks over to the sink and washes his hands, Pontius Pilate in a white coat. He knows I am desperate, but abortion is illegal, and I am too frightened to ask him if he knows "anyone who can help me" with all the implications that has. A furtive hysteria surrounded the mere mention of abortion, at least in my world.

Yet the circumstances should have snapped his code of ethics to attention. Regardless of his personal feelings, this man of the Hippocratic oath—First, Do No Harm—should have recognized that after I've ingested birth control pills with god knows how many hormones for more than three months—including that perilous first trimester—the fetus is almost certainly at risk.

The world had been through the ravages of thalidomide, a drug originally intended as a sedative but soon used for a wide range of other conditions, including colds, flu, nausea, and morning sickness in pregnant women. Though thalidomide was never approved by the FDA, thousands of women took it and gave birth to babies born with serious birth defects—or who were stillborn. Thalidomide had only been taken off the market a few years earlier, in 1961. Who knew what effect the rich soup of hormones in the Pill would have on a fetus? Probably not a good one. My baby should not be a test case. Termination—yes, abortion—surely should have been an option.

But the doctor says nothing, does nothing. He offers no advice and does not suggest I make another appointment—even though I am pregnant and he is an OB/GYN. When I had asked if I should come in again because something wasn't right earlier in the pregnancy, he had said, No need to. He clearly wants me out of his office, out of his life. He does not want the problem my baby and I have suddenly become. Those birth control pills? He never mentions them. His message: Leave. I can't help you.

I do not yell or scream at him, for a part of me is not surprised. I should have known. I have ignored the mornings when I felt like throwing up. Having had irregular periods for much of my life, I ignored my lack of real periods. "Spotting" does not count. Have I noticed my waist thicken? Too slight to acknowledge. Until just recently. Every way I possibly could, up until that moment, sitting on the examining table, I have been whispering to myself: You cannot be pregnant. You must not be pregnant. Not after all that it has taken to get here. Not after fighting against what my parents insisted— that I am destined only for motherhood, that my life will be constrained by my sex. Not after finally breaking out of a women's department and landing on a daily newspaper in a substantial city. In New York.

But now, crash, boom, everything has changed. I am indeed pregnant. Resignation clamps down on my shoulders like a yoke. I cannot even scream. I do not cry. My mind is reeling. While abortions happened in 1966, they happened in New York City, they happened if you knew somebody who knew the right person, they happened for serious medical reasons in cities other than the Rochester I knew. Years later I would learn that with the agreement of two MDs, I could have received a therapeutic abortion for "medical reasons," probably in a New York City hospital—probably even at this late stage, given that I had taken birth control pills for so long, and through almost the entire first trimester. However, if the reason for the abortion was that I was a threat to my own person, or "psychologically unsound"—and that was the reason for 80 percent of the therapeutic abortions then—I needed two shrinks to sign off on this. In other words, to get a legal abortion I had to be suicidal or nuts, and for good measure, probably both. And sometimes the conclusion was that the psychosis would go away once the pregnancy was over and the baby born so the abortion was not needed after all. Half of the hospitals in the country required the approval of a medical board—and that board could include the caveat that, since I was crazy, it might be best for me to be sterilized at the same time to prevent further pregnancies.[3] Usually that meant a hysterectomy. First, do no harm? When it came to women and pregnancy, misogyny prevailed.

I could hear a voice ringing in my head: I told you so. You're a girl. *Who do you think you are? Some movie star's daughter?*

Now look what I have done.

I burn with shame. I would be a family disgrace, I would be a laughing-stock, I would be the object of both pity and scorn, no matter what else I ever accomplished in my life. I could hear my mother's recrimination and tears; I could see the keen resignation and disappointment on my father's face.

I could not imagine facing them.

---

[3] Rickie Solinger, *Wake Up Little Susie: Single Pregnancy and Race before Roe v. Wade*, (New York: Routledge, 1992), 4. Solinger quotes a professor of obstetrics in a large university hospital who says they haven't done a therapeutic abortion in ten years because "we don't recognize psychiatric indications." Some hospitals had panels of doctors vote on whether a woman could have a therapeutic abortion for psychiatric reasons. She adds that the "committee may have, in fact, agreed with the outside specialists that the abortion petitioner was psychotic, but the panel often claimed the problem was temporary, with sanity recoverable upon delivery."

5   Rude Reality

But the day is not done with me yet. Fate has one more cruel joke up its ragged sleeve. As soon as I get back to my apartment from the doctor's appointment, I call Patrick. His day starts earlier than mine, and he'll be at the office. *Please pick up*, Patrick. I don't mince words. He doesn't doubt me.

We'll figure this out, he says. How? I wonder. Will we marry, will he actually leave his wife and kids? We'll talk at dinner, he says. You're coming in, right? I change and go to work. My shift starts at three.

We stare at each other when I walk in, desperation seeping out of every pore. He barely nods—we didn't want anyone to notice—and I sit down, say hi to the guy sitting next to me. We're friendly, but not friends.

My small desk is at the end of a row, each desk pushed up against the other. By chance—my desk had been empty when I took the job—I sit in the front row at the end of the aisle, facing the city desk. Patrick, at his larger, important desk against the wall, is a few feet from me. We do not speak.

General controlled commotion is underway: People coming and going, talking on the phone or to each other, smoking, typing their stories, drinking coffee while reading some other newspaper from around the state. A light haze of afternoon light already slanting toward sunset and a filter of smoke soften the edges. I am less than two years out of college, I am the only woman in the room, I am a figure in this tableau of a daily newspaper going about its business, and I am exactly where I have wanted to be since I was eleven years old.

And I'm pregnant.

I could not allow myself to stare into space, so I am working hard at looking busy. Maybe I'll get some simple assignment, an easy obit or a rewrite will do, anything to take up the hours—three, maybe four—until Patrick and I can have dinner. Somewhere private. It must be private tonight.

My mind is a sinkhole of despair when Dick walks over and gives me the kind of assignment you can wait years for. A career changer.

In 1966 the country is in the throes of the Vietnam war, and the First Cavalry, based at Fort Benning, Georgia, is losing a lot of men, one of them a young man from Rochester. I am to go down to Fort Benning for a few days and do a mood piece—many of the widows continue to live there, including the widow of a local boy. "You know what to do, Dusky," Dick says, signaling his confidence in me. This kind of story is what I do best. A mood piece. With a widow of Vietnam. I know it's a big deal, an assignment that half of the guys in the room would have eagerly grabbed for themselves. My reputation is riding on this. Any late kvetching over my hire will be stilled.

At dinner with Patrick, elation over the assignment is smothered by the larger issue: pregnancy. He says that while I am at Fort Benning, he will find a doctor for an abortion. Don't worry, he says, I'll take care of this. But he doesn't sound that confident. He says he knows someone to ask about a doctor—surely there is someone in Rochester who does abortions—but it does mean that he has to lay himself open to whomever he asks. We are still keeping our affair under wraps, but he has become less cautious in the last few months. We know word has gotten out. At the office Christmas party—he brought his wife, and I went alone—one of the other wives told him, "Don't screw up your marriage."

What we do not talk about at dinner is the other solution. That he could leave his wife and family. That it has been six months since he said we would be together, that I was his woman. I don't bring it up. I sense that he is not ready.

Within a couple of days, I'm on the plane to Georgia. The widow has a good story to tell. Her husband wrote on the bathroom mirror with her lipstick that he loved her before he left. She hasn't washed it off. On the third day, the chief photographer flies down.

When I return to Rochester, Patrick tells me that he's borrowing a grand from someone who has a secretary from Puerto Rico, and she says that while abortions are still illegal there, they are easy to come by—Why, you can ask any cab driver and he will give you the name of an obliging doctor.

You're kidding, I say. For a story, I could do it. For real, no way.

Yet that is the scenario that unfolds.

Instead of waiting until I get back to my apartment that day—it will be after eleven, too late to call—I phone the secretary from a pay phone in the building's lobby. Too risky to make the call from my office phone. Too many people around, anyone might hear, the operator could listen in. The secretary is encouraging and supportive, she gives me names and numbers of people who will help me when I get to San Juan—a hotel desk clerk, a restaurant manager, her sister. I tell Dick I have to make an emergency trip home. My father is deathly ill and I need a few days off.

Once I am in San Juan, however, the only person who can be found is the woman's sister, who does have the name of a real doctor I could call. She actually offers to take my baby, but that sounds unreal. How could this work out? Where would I have the baby? How would I support it? No, this cannot be.

It takes a day to get an appointment. An airmail letter from Patrick informs me that my story from Fort Benning will be splashed all over the front page on Sunday, that Dick told him I'd written a hell of a story. I should be celebrating, thinking of sending the clip home to my parents, but instead I am sitting on a beach fending off some American guy who is trying to pick me up. And I am hysterically worried I am too pregnant.

I am. Too pregnant.

That is ten dollars, the doctor says evenly. He dismisses my protestations with a wave of his hand. "Ten dollars," he says.

I am the most desperate person on earth. How can I have this baby? My parents must never know. I would rather die.

It is gray and cold when I land in Rochester. I return to the office with hearty congratulations all around for my big story. I am actually doing what I set out to do.

But I am female.

Now I am a pregnant woman.

Within the week, I announce to Dick that my father is dying of some disease I do not mention, and that I must quit to go home and help my mother take care of him. All I know is that I must be out of there before my burgeoning belly shows. Even married women quit jobs before they show; for an unmarried woman—unthinkable.

Dick is stunned and suggests a leave of absence. That didn't even cross my mind—how could I go back? Surely everyone would suspect I'd left because I'd been so incredibly stupid and gotten pregnant.

Would I let him know when I could come back?

Yeah, sure.

I grimly pack up my desk. I get a whiff of everyone's wonder as I leave, positive they suspect the real reason. Why would I quit after the triumph of the big story from Fort Benning? Call my parents and ask for their help? Not in a million years. Face my father? Not ever. I hear *You're only going to get married and have kids* clanging in my head as insistently as if a Salvation Army bell ringer were standing on every street corner. Now I am going to have a kid without the married part. Now every argument, every job, every late night, every step I took to get here is being squandered. My life is over. Will I ever come back from this? I cannot go home. I wish I could just disappear.

Why was I born female?

I would stay in my apartment, and when my own slender savings ran out, Patrick would take care of the bills, pay the rent, make my car payments, and give me money for groceries.

At night, trying to sleep, I go over various ways I might kill myself. In a bathtub with a razor blade. Running in front of a truck, right outside my apartment. Getting my hands on enough sleeping pills. Jumping off the top of the downtown mall. Turning on the gas oven. Suicide seems like a reasonable option.

I try none of them.

That is January.

The times kept a-changin' with the music, but no cultural shift happens all at once. While the sexual strictures were loosening, and hip young women like myself were supposed to be sophisticated about sex—not only having sex but wildly enjoying it—the heartbreaking irony was that becoming pregnant without someone to marry you revealed a society still stuck in the sexual shaming of earlier decades. Good girls still didn't do it. Smart girls didn't get caught. Some found ways to get an abortion. The lucky ones got married. It's estimated that more than a quarter of all children born to women between the ages of fifteen and twenty-nine in the decade between 1960 and 1970 were conceived before marriage.[4] That's a lot of people having sex outside of marriage, but it was, at least in my world, all sub rosa.

The stories of women who got pregnant when they weren't supposed to are as varied as the culture itself. This one was a debutante, with her engagement already announced to an appropriate young man in the pages of the *New York Times*. This one thought that her college boyfriend would marry her. This one had sex in the backseat of her boyfriend's parents' Buick—once. This one had sex the night of her prom when she'd had too much to drink. This one had sex with a lot of different guys because it was what the cool girls did at her high school. This one or that one was raped by her boyfriend or a friend of her father's or a stranger who jumped out of the bushes. This one had sex with someone when he temporarily broke up with his girlfriend. I had an affair with a married man I met at work, a man who promised that we would be together one day. Later.

After.

In 1970, four years after I hid in shame and fear of discovery, New York made abortion legal. Three years after that, in 1973, the Supreme Court's *Roe v. Wade* decision made abortion legal in all fifty states.

By February, "it" shifts to "the baby." And the baby is always "he." No matter

---

[4] Marcia A. Ellison, "Authoritative Knowledge and Single Women's Unintentional Pregnancies, Abortions, Adoption and Single Motherhood: Social Stigma and Structural Violence," *Medical Anthropology Quarterly* 17, no. 3 (2003): 326.

that I had wanted to abort—that was about a blob. Birth gives forth a baby, a living, screaming baby. I love this baby now. I want my baby to be healthy and strong and brave, and I wish for him all good things in life. I take the prescribed prenatal vitamins, I make sure that I have enough calcium in my diet, but I do not walk proudly with my belly forward when I skulk out to buy groceries or walk in a nearby park.

Please leave your wife now, I beseech Patrick. Now! You say you are going to, you've been saying that since July. When is the time going to be right? If you do this now, we can keep the baby. Tell The Wife about the baby. That will make all the difference.

He cannot do that.

We have to get through this first, he says, meaning: We (you) have to give him up.

He tells me the name of the adoption agency in the phone book. He says there is no other choice.

No no no, I can't, I insist, now blubbering uncontrollably.

He hates scenes like this.

You have to.

You will have one child, but there is something wrong. Like it's adopted.

No matter that once I had thought I would never want, could never have, a baby to raise, now I am twenty-three years old and I desperately want this baby, our baby, my baby. The abstract is far different from the real baby gently kicking in my belly, and all I can think is that I want this baby, I am supposed to have and to hold this baby, to love and to cherish all the days of my life. I talk to my baby and say, I am sorry, I am ever so sorry it is like this.

But Patrick has to step up.

That he did not meant that no matter how horrible the idea seemed, no matter that my being was recoiling at the idea, adoption is what someone like me did. We gave up our babies. They would have a better life than we could possibly give them, as advice columnists regularly touted in daily newspapers. A decade earlier, a writer in *Reader's Digest* wrote that an "unwed mother should in fairness to her child give him up for adoption, for otherwise, the child's life will inevitably be damaged by social cruelty."[5] The message still held in 1966: A child needed two parents. If the child had two parents, she or he would not be a bastard; the child would not be the subject of scorn and derision. As Patrick and I also would be if I kept the baby. Adoption for babies born "out of wedlock" by women or teenagers who "got in trouble," the parlance of that era, seemed writ in stone. I did not have the strength to resist or to chart a different course.

My world—the newsroom of stale cigarette butts and late deadlines— was far removed from Woodstock's muddy fields with their pungent aroma of weed and nearly naked flower children. All that would come later. In my world, in the mid-sixties of the Midwest, pantyhose might be on the way in, but Playtex rubber girdles—like the one I had been wearing—were still around, and roles for women were just as constricting. International air travel was opening up, but women didn't fly the plane. They served up "coffee, tea or me," a catch phrase that became a naughty anthem of the generation that came a few years later when the Pill was taken by legions of young women. All that would be later. I would be trapped between those two worlds and, in the process, lose my baby.

Remembering my life then, I can still conjure up Patrick's back retreating down the stairs where they made a half turn. He is wearing his navy blazer. He turns to nod, and I nod back before he continues going away from me. Despite what he says—that we will be together eventually, that we will get through this—I sense that giving up my baby will be the worst thing I ever do in my life.

I will probably never murder anybody or rob a bank or embezzle funds. Instead, I will have a baby and give him up. I know he will miss me and I know he will always wonder why, and I know there is no going back to life as it was before. Yet I cannot protest because that is the way it is.

---

[5] Frederick Brownell, "Why You Can't Adopt a Baby," *Reader's Digest,* Nov. 1955, 57, quoted in Linda Tollett Austin, *Babies for Sale: The Tennessee Children's Home Adoption Scandal* (Westport, CT: Praeger, 1993), 121.

I am a shaft of wheat in a field blown down by the wind. I bow to the inevitable.

"But we'll be able to—find each other when he's eighteen, right—or twenty-one?" I say matter-of-factly—it's half a statement, said in defiance, half a question, because I really don't know the answer. I am talking to the social worker at Northaven Terrace, the inoffensively named adoption agency in Rochester. Her first name is Helen, but to me she is Mrs. Mura. She is in her thirties and could be my older sister. She is my confessor, my therapist, my compassionate conduit to adoption.

Other than Patrick, Mrs. Mura is my primary outside contact for those last months of my pregnancy and the only person I can talk to at length about my predicament. I do have a girlfriend on the afternoon newspaper in Rochester—like me, Christy is the lone woman covering hard news there—and out of proximity and shared need we'd become friends. We are both young, ambitious, and from elsewhere, but she's busy with her own career. I've told her what's happening, but she and I rarely talk.

So, Mrs. Mura. She is nonjudgmental, even sympathetic, as my woes flow out like molten lava. I hadn't known what to expect when we met because I was, after all, owning up to an affair with a married man—an older married man in my office. Why hadn't I insisted that we not go all the way that afternoon—when I correctly calculated the timing was bad? With so much at stake, what kind of an idiot gets into this predicament? I not only feel sorry for myself, I feel like an idiot. I am radioactive with shame. I cannot imagine giving away my baby. I cannot see how I can keep my baby.

I have been sailing along under the silver lining that someday my baby will be able to know who I am, and I will be able to know him. We would meet. I didn't get beyond that. But surely, we would meet one day. That he would have the right to find out who his parents were. Where he came from. That he could make a choice, to meet or not, and of course, in my mind, he—the baby was always a "he"—will want to meet. What Mrs. Mura says next never crossed my mind.

"Lorraine, I thought you knew," she says, speaking barely above a whisper. "Once you sign the papers the adoption is final."

How would I know that? That adoption is worse than I could ever imagine? When I do not respond, she releases a second arrow. That when he's adopted, a new birth certificate will be issued with only the adoptive parents listed. The other is sealed. For all time.

My baby, no matter how old he is, from birth to adoption to the end of eternity, will never be able to know who I am, period, and of course it's a given that I'll never be able to find out what happens to him either.

Ever.

How can they take the right to know who you are from anyone? Erasing a person's history is inhumane. I push back against Mrs. Mura's words, insisting that there must be some way around the law, that there must be exceptions for mothers who want to know their children one day. Surely this cannot be the only option—what monster would make that kind of law? I try to turn my astonishment into a declarative sentence, not a question.

Why doesn't she say something? Something's wrong.

My heart is already on overdrive as understanding comes into focus. I am covered with a hot flash of stickiness, the kind that comes with panic attacks.

She offers me a glass of water and pushes a box of tissues across her desk. She's trying to be gentle, I can tell that, but how can she not see, herself, that this is wrong? I think she does! She's not saying how this is the best for everybody. She's just talking about the new birth certificate, records sealed, it's the law, blah blah blah.

I turn to the windows. They are high up, and all I can see is the sky—the better for privacy, I am suddenly aware. A patch of clear bright blue fills the window. How can today be sunny?

True, I don't want this baby announced in the newspaper under Births, and I have been desperate to keep my pregnancy secret, to not embarrass Patrick and myself—the pathetic pregnant numbskull—but I can hardly believe I am never—we are never—going to be able to meet. I am looking through a chain-link fence as a child goes from baby to toddler to adolescent to teen to adult, and now the fence is covered with black plastic film that one cannot see through.

But I am not down for the count yet. After all, it is my baby, and I am sure that whoever wants this special baby—the child of two college graduates, employed, healthy, in short, desirable breeding stock—would agree to something other than taking away a person's ability to find out how he or she came to be adopted. At the same time, I'm certain that they would not want to shut me out forever. "What about if we ask the adoptive parents? Or can't we find a couple who would agree—can't we do this another way? Can't we have an arrangement that when he is older, that he can find out who I am, and me about him? There must be some people who—"

She is shaking her head, no. I keep interrupting her, until she finally says, "Lorraine, if you won't agree to this, we can't help you. There is no other way."

We can't help you. There is no other way. The impossibility of arranging an adoption privately is incomprehensible—I'm in a strange city with no connections, and Patrick says this is what I must do. I notice the floor is sickly pale green, the color of vomit, even in the place where the sun hits it.

Who am I to go up against the law? I am a mere cog in the busy machinery of passing children out to people more respectable than me. I am an unfortunate nobody. I am a sinner without rights. Nothing I say will change her mind, change the rules, change anything. Speaking further is futile.

"In time this won't be so intense," Mrs. Mura says. "You will never forget your child, but it will get easier. You will move on. There will be another life." At least she has the good grace not to tell me it is best this way. Or that I must forget him.

When I tell Patrick this utterly horrible news, he does not share my outrage. I am more aware than before that I am having this baby alone. He is not having this baby. I am. He is still insisting yes, one day, later, we will be together, he loves me, he loves me—but is that enough?

Patrick brings me a thin gold band, and I slip it on my ring finger. Now, when I go out on the street, I can pretend I am a married lady. As long as I don't run into anybody from the newspaper.

I have no choice but to stay suspended in that slurry fog of hope and doubt.

That is March.

Erasing a paper trail to the natural mother in adoption is a modern phenomenon. Accounts of earlier adoptions clearly show that when adult adoptees—or their mothers—came back asking for information about each other, the agencies complied. In E. Wayne Carp's *Family Matters*, a thorough history of the adoption-reform movement, I read about a desperate woman who gave up a son around the turn of the century when he was four. In 1929—more than three decades later—she wrote to her local welfare agency asking someone to find him because "her mind turn[ed] constantly to the thought of this son."[6]

The letter was forwarded to the Children's Home Society in Washington, where a caseworker, a Miss T., was assigned to the case. She contacted the adult man's last known address; she called the local credit association; she looked him up in an old city directory. Nothing turned up a lead. Yet somehow this tenacious woman found his ex-business partner, who supplied the man's current address in California. To make sure he was the right man, Miss T. wrote to him before forwarding the information to his mother.

Right up until the middle of the twentieth century, whether or not to reveal the information in agency records to either the adopted person or the mother was at the discretion of the social workers, many of them as sympathetic to those separated by adoption as Miss T. had been.

Yet.

Sometimes a single person can have an outsized effect on a social movement. One such person was a canny social worker with a law degree named Georgia Tann. By the mid-1930s, Tann was in the business of illicitly acquiring babies in her home state of Tennessee and selling them to movie stars such as Joan Crawford, Lana Turner, and the married June Allyson and Dick

[6] E. Wayne Carp, *Family Matters: Secrecy and Disclosure in the History of Adoption* (Cambridge, MA: Harvard University Press, 1998), 78.

Powell, as well as wealthy businessmen and politicians, such as Governor Herbert H. Lehman of New York. Lehman had three adopted children, with at least one acquired from Tann. To hide the sketchy and illegal ways she procured children—often duping hapless women into signing papers they did not understand—she promoted sealing the original birth certificates and having new, amended ones issued. These reissued birth certificates replaced the names of the biological parents with those of the adoptive parents.[7] This suited the "people of the better sort," as Tann called them, who used her services. As Tann was the daughter of an influential judge, her methods were given a generous veneer of rectitude, and for decades her operation was largely ignored by authorities who could have shut her down or had her prosecuted for what amounted to stealing children.

It is not as if Tann tarnished a benevolent arrangement for children who needed to be adopted. The orphanages of the era were harsh, squalid places, and the "orphan trains" that transported children found on the streets, in urban slums, or in overcrowded orphanages to farms in the Midwest were no better a solution. Many of the children were exploited as indentured servants. Getting the children to parents who wanted them and could afford Tann's hefty fees—some paid as much as $10,000, the equivalent of close to $200,000 today[8]—was for many children a better option than the unforgiving chaos of life on the street or in an orphanage. But Tann's methods unfortunately ushered in a system that treated human beings as merchandise, goods that could be produced and exchanged and whose history or heritage would be erased.

As adoption became more prevalent, especially among the moneyed class, so did the idea that children came as blank slates who could be molded into the idealized child and heir. Sealing the original birth certificates from the parties whose names were listed on them supposedly de-bastardized the infant, who would become an integrated member of the new, adoptive family

---

[7] Barbara Bisantz Raymond, *The Baby Thief: The Untold Story of Georgia Tann, The Baby Seller Who Corrupted Adoption* (New York: Caroll & Graf, 2007), 108. A state investigation of adoption fraud in Tann's agency was underway when she died in 1950.
[8] Raymond, 118.

with all the rights of a natural child. In the process, the mother was supposedly saved from humiliation, and could go on with her life as if her pregnancy and the birth had never happened.

There have always been naysayers to this harsh and binding severance of blood ties between mother and child, people who understood that cutting off the past of a person is not humane or reasonable. In 1935 the head of the New York Foundling Hospital wrote to Governor Lehman stating her opposition to such proposed legislation for the following reasons:

(1) It legalizes the falsification of permanent public records.

(2) It nullifies the inalienable right of a person to know the actual facts of his birth.

(3) Any special provision for illegitimate children which will single them out from the group of legitimate children is bound to be a cause of embarrassment to them in later years.

—Sister Dominica Maria, April 25th, 1935[9]

The nun's warnings were ignored. Not only did California slam shut its birth records that year[10]—the first state to do so—adoptive father Governor Lehman signed similar legislation the following year. Through the next several decades, nearly all other states followed suit—save Alaska and Kansas.

In a quirky twist, Alabama kept their records open until a movement was well underway to unseal them everywhere. Alabama sealed their records in 1991, only to unseal them nine years later, and in doing so became the first state to give adoptees their original birth certificates by legislative action.

Despite such efforts to sever a child's origins by decree, the laws could never completely quell the human and innate need for connection to one's natural family or stifle curiosity about one's roots. Before the mid-sixties, adopted individuals, their natural mothers, and even adoptive parents were more likely to get identifying information if they went back to the agency than they are today. As late as 1960, some 40 percent of the states left open

---

[9] A copy of the letter is in my files.

[10] Janine M. Baer, *Growing in the Dark: Adoption Secrecy and Its Consequences* (Bloomington, IN: Xlibris, 2004), 49.

the right of the adoptee to access his or her own birth records at various ages.[11]

While this cultural and legal shift was galloping throughout the land, adoption became increasingly acceptable as a way to have a family, and changing sexual customs made more babies available. By 1966 my baby and I were being scooped up whole into the awful net of laws designed to sever our bond.

We were never supposed to know one another.

---

[11] Elizabeth J. Samuels, "The Idea of Adoption: An Inquiry into the History of Adult Adoptee Access to Birth Records." *Rutgers Law Review* 53 (2001): 367.

6 Mystery Woman or Cosmo Girl

I spend the months of my confinement—and that's what it was, despite being free to come and go—playing house. I read the *New York Times* every morning from cover to cover and learn how to cook from *The Joy of Cooking* and a popular how-to manual, *Sex and the Single Girl*, that has a few recipes for seductive meals with your lover. Patrick works through his dinner break to be able to quit early and is usually at my place around seven. Lamb curry! Canard a l'orange (made with poulet)! Linguine with clam sauce! Welsh rarebit! I shower and dress for my date with my lover in one of the two outfits I have: a plaid wool jumper without a waist (an outfit that did not come from a maternity department) or a big sweater and a pair of black pants (that did).

The kid who didn't want to go outside to play is now a grown-up, content with her books, her music, *Time* and the *New Yorker* weekly in her mailbox, her own writing, and solitary walks in the neighborhood. I don't venture much beyond a nearby grocery store, the pharmacy across the street, a reservoir up the street, and the library a few blocks away that coughs up books I missed in college—ones by Fitzgerald, Steinbeck, more of Hemingway. Patrick's read them all, and we create our own literary salon of two. He brings me books from his own collection; one that will turn out to be so very prescient is John O'Hara's *Appointment in Samarra*, with its tale of the inevitable, of fate one cannot outrun.

Since I am not quite cloistered, it is a given that I will run into someone

I am trying to avoid—anyone from the newspaper. And suddenly one day there he is—a D&C reporter with a woman (surely his wife) standing a few feet away from me at the specialty food shop down the road. I drop my basket and dash out, heart racing, unaware if he saw me, assuming he did. At least I got away before he said, Hello! What are you doing here?

My only friend in town, Christy, is sure I will love The Sound of Music, and so I slip into a midweek matinee when I'm not likely to run into anyone I know. Instead, I learn how much I will always hate the movie—all those saccharine singing children, such a happy ending. I have no television, so I can't vegetate. What I do not do is drop into a church, any church, for solace and a conversation with God. I have nothing to say. Does God exist? Maybe. Maybe not. Without vexation I realize I've become a full-blown agnostic.

I allow myself no food cravings—in truth, I have none—and I count the calories of everything I eat. I gain only a few pounds—I will hide this belly from the neighbors under bulky sweaters. I don't even know the neighbors, but I don't want them to see me. Pregnant.

Yet thoughts of the baby-I-will-not-keep fill my days, and I write him a long letter, pages and pages, trying to explain how and why and whatever else I can think of. Patrick thinks he is a boy, and it seems even my unconscious is trying to please Patrick. Surely it's a boy, and no matter what lies ahead, I want him to be healthy and strong. I never forget to take the special vitamins the doctor has prescribed, I switch from wine and martinis to tomato juice, and in time I find books at the library on how to take care of the child inside me—but not what to expect when giving birth. Mrs. Mura and I have not spoken of the physical realities that lie ahead. I have no connection to anyone other than the doctor to talk about what's happening to my body, and she is a reticent Indian woman with whom I do not feel comfortable talking about anything. I am so ashamed of my condition—and know that she must know that I am not married—that I am nearly mute when I see her.

Patrick continues to talk about how we will be together one day. But he can't leave the kids now. He promises that he will. Just not now, the timing is wrong. He's not ready, but he will be. Soon. He says that lots of different ways, and there are days when something in his words lets me have a glimmer of hope that he will find the strength to claim me now, while I am carrying our love child. And then, we can keep our baby.

But another week goes by, and nothing changes except that I learn a new recipe or two and have added a few more rows along the petit-point evening bag I'm stitching. The days drip by.

Maybe Patrick will act, maybe he won't, but for now, he calls two or three times a day from work to say when he'll be there for dinner. By the time he steps through the door, I am all shiny hair and lipstick with the aroma of something good on the stove filling the air.

That is all I can focus on. I cannot see the next chapter, where I will be, how I will be, who I will be.

After.

The muffler on the Ghia blows; a cop stops me; before he can write a ticket for excessive noise, I burst into tears. No ticket ensues. I can see the pity in his eyes as he sends me on my way.

We run out of money. Patrick must find another grand to pay my living expenses—which now include a new muffler. Patrick turns to Dick, and thus he is brought into our closed circle. Dick informs Patrick that despite our in-office subterfuge to shield our affair, everybody knows. Ever the prince, Dick lends Patrick the money and asks if he should come by to cheer the lonely shut-in, and lo! One evening after work he does. We three chat amiably about the news of the day. When I replay this scene in my head, it seems nearly unimaginable—my old boss, Patrick, and me having drinks (me, fruit juice) as if this were just a normal after-work get-together, with nobody noting, Oh my god, you're pregnant! Years later, my mind lingers over Dick's simple act of kindness.

But while I am well informed in current events, such a naïf am I about the process of birth that when my water breaks I don't even realize what is happening. I did know this occurred, but I expected a huge deluge, not simply the feeling that I couldn't hold my bladder. I'm talking to my landlord, a dentist whose office is on the ground floor. I'm wearing an oversized sweat-shirt—I'm pretty sure you can't see my belly—and I have no idea whether he notices the small puddle below me. Retreating back to my apartment, I assume a leaky bladder is a final indignity to be endured for the last weeks. My due date is three weeks away.

When searing pain wakes me at three a.m. I do not even realize I am going into labor—and besides, I don't know what to do. I can't call Patrick at home, I won't wake up Christy, I won't call Mrs. Mura—even though she's given me her home phone number—it's the middle of the night, and what's the problem, this can't be the baby. Right? I take two aspirin. And in an hour, two more.

At six a.m. I do reach the doctor, who tells me to take two aspirin—it's too early for the baby. But I've already gobbled four and don't think I should take more. Sometime after nine I call again—I make no mention of "water breaking," but hearing my insistence, she says I should come to the hospital. I have no plan for how to get there—I am in too much pain to drive myself—cabs are rare, and I cannot call Patrick.

Christy is finally enlisted. She is at the office, but she feigns an interview and picks me up by ten-thirty. She holds my elbow as we go down three flights of stairs. We are in her car. Driving fast. Forsythia in bloom along the roadside mocks me with its cheerful yellow flash, row after row—who knew Rochester had so much forsythia? Hospital, emergency entrance, wheelchair, doctor saying, You are having a baby.

Baby and me, we are alone in a room somewhere, or was it a hallway? There is no Mrs. Mura, no Patrick, and Christy has gone back to work.

The pain is a hot rocket on its determined course, splitting me apart. Another woman is screaming nearby, but I hold back. Screaming is for women who can keep their babies.

Until I can't stand it anymore. The godless woman had been shaken in the night by floating terrors . . . *Woman, be sure your heart is brave—you can take much.*

Which Greek wrote that? Aeschylus. He got it right. My brain isn't totally fried. Cassandra replies. *Only unhappy people ever hear such praise. When will this end, this murderous pain?*

A nurse—she is kind, she is not clucking in condemnation—checks on me periodically and brings me ice. She gives me her hand and my grip is hard, my nails bite into her skin. Does she know I am one of "those women," those stupid young women who got caught? Who furthermore is on a runaway train that leads to giving her baby away?

Only Patrick can stop it.

Nurse says that when this is over and I have my baby, I will forget the pain. She does not know.

I stare into her unknowing eyes. There is nothing to say.

The clock in the OR reads one-thirty as a black mask comes down over my face and I greedily gulp away the misery. If women knew, would they still have babies? Of course they would. Most women get to keep their babies. They forget about the pain. They say it is worth it.

All I would remember is the pain.

I am in a haze when I awake. Mrs. Mura is there, telling me she weighs under five pounds. She asks if I want her baptized.

A girl?

Babies under five pounds are always at risk, Mrs. Mura continues.

Dammit, you can't die now!

I sit up in the bed and wail. Great hulking waves of grief pour out of me, loud, messy, uncontrollable. I am a wild animal who has lost her baby. I have a right to be out of my mind for the moment. Tomorrow I will have to pretend I am normal. Giving her up is what is crazy. Let me be, let me grieve as I have never grieved before, as I will never grieve again. I sit up and slam myself down on the bed. I am sobbing, making noise in the recovery room, disturbing the peace.

I have just had my baby. I have just lost my baby.

The priest who has been hovering at the end of the bed leaves. He will baptize her and name her Mary, and save her from, god forbid, that ineffable place that used to be called limbo, where unbaptized souls went, some forgotten pope's wacky idea of a joke. I might question the reality of God as I once knew Him, but maybe my baby isn't an agnostic.

My howling will not stop. Nurses come in, they rush out and return with a hypodermic. They do not want a deranged, wailing woman, senseless with grief, disrupting traffic like an overturned semi on the expressway. There are rules. All quiet in the recovery room. Decorum must be maintained.

No! I don't want a damn tranquilizer! She is gone, and the only time we will ever have together is over. My hands make my way down to my belly, and I feel my soft, flaccid flesh, empty now, a used-up pea pod that has delivered its fruit. I sit up and throw myself back down on the bed. I don't want a shot, get away, don't you understand, let me have my moment, let me howl now to purge this grief!

That is not to be. The nurses return with a man, they hold me down, in goes the needle and I am gone.

I wake in a beige room. They have burned the fury out of me. I am surrounded by a scrim of fog that mutes but does not hide the beige void of tomorrow and tomorrow and tomorrow when I will not know her. Now I can only submit.

There are flowers on the table. The card says they are from Mrs. Mura. So I have flowers like everyone else on the ward. All acts of compassion are greedily accepted.

There is someone in the other bed. She is so young, a teenager. Is she like me? Is she not keeping her baby, too?

Bearing a white box with a dozen long-stemmed red roses, Patrick arrives in the late afternoon. *Oh, how pretty, thank you,* I say.

I don't need roses, I think. I need you to act. There is still time, Patrick. It is not too late.

How did you find out? is what I say.

Mrs. Mura called me at work, he says. It was the first time they had spoken. Oh.

He says that she asked me if he was going to come and see you tonight. Of course, he was coming tonight.

He says he told Dick, who sends his best wishes.

For a speedy recovery? But there is no coming back from not keeping her.

"I love you, Lorraine." He squeezes my hand, hovers over me, and says once again, "We will be together." He doesn't say "later," but I know that is what he means. That it will be just the two of us, and we will leave our child behind.

He stays for over an hour and then he is gone. Not back to our funny apartment with the burlap I'd put on the walls and the tea cart I had refinished and the small round table where we ate, but to his home in the suburbs, a place I recall as a big white house with a yard out back where his other kids could play. I used to drive by occasionally. Once I saw his daughter outside. I stepped on the gas and sped away.

"I'll be back tomorrow," he says. "We will be together when this is over," he repeats. I think he believes it, and that if he says it often enough, it will come to pass. It would have to do.

But hope is a sparrow that has flown far away. I do not think about tomorrow. I think about getting through the day, the night ahead of me, my baby down the hall.

I stay four nights, five days in the hospital, the norm for that era. While I could walk down to the nursery to see her, I make the choice not to because I can barely hold myself together. To actually see my baby would be unbearable, the seams of my sanity would rip apart. I walk the other way. I avoid the other women in the ward, the married women, happy with their babies, feeding their babies, cuddling their babies.

As suspected, my roommate is unmarried. She is fifteen. She and her high school sweetheart ran away to get married, but one set of parents called the police, who found them in Maryland. Women converge over her bed, women in an ageless diorama. Her mother and an aunt want her to keep the baby. The boy's parents do not. Then they do. She is undecided. The boyfriend, a pimply kid called up to too soon to the major leagues, arrives one afternoon. He is bereft—dazed—but he has a son, and they are clearly a couple. They are too young to have a son. Yet they are old enough to have a son. Together they walk down to the nursery to see him. She is quiet when she returns, alone, sympathetic to my inability to walk that way. She understands my predicament as well as any woman.

God help me, I cannot see how her keeping her son could possibly have a good outcome, so imbued am I in the culture of the day, so much do I not want to be the only villain in the room who gives up her baby. The smart thing for her to do is to finish school, to let her son be adopted. I keep my feelings to myself.

Patrick comes every afternoon. "He loves you," my roommate says. I am grateful for small favors, that someone notices, for believing in his love is all I have to cling to. I am not making it up that he loves me. But he and I do not even discuss whether she will be adopted or not. It is all decided.

The sound of the gravel as Patrick and I drive away from the hospital, leaving our baby there, is crisp and loud. Tears rim my eyes. Don't, says Patrick. Please don't cry. He hates displays of emotion.

I do the best I can.

We do not speak on the drive to my apartment. He stays awhile, and then he is gone. It's Saturday, he has to go to work.

The next day is Easter. Easter was a huge holiday when I was growing up, thick as porridge with aunts and uncles and cousins and bread my mother and I made on Holy Saturday and milk-chocolate-and-cornflakes nests filled with jellybeans we'd made the day before. This Easter morning is gorgeous, an azure sky fills the windows. Following the convention of the era, I tell myself it's too soon for me to be out and about. Though my apartment is the same as I'd left it, now it is a tomb with a cheap Van Gogh print and a stained sisal rug, spilled wine from an earlier time. A *Time* magazine sits on a table with its Easter cover for 1966: IS GOD DEAD? in ninety-point red type against a black background. It had been waiting in my mailbox when I returned.

Baby Mary lies alone in an incubator across town.

Patrick is with his family, doing family things. I won't hear from him until tomorrow. Eventually the day will be over, I remind myself. Tomorrow will be the beginning of the rest of my life.

To keep up the fiction that all is well, I phone my parents, and we chat about god-knows-what. My only concern is hiding the truth. I've kept my baby a secret all through the pregnancy and birth, and I imagine I will go on like this forever, picking up, moving on, living an unruffled life, as far as they and the world are concerned. Other women surely have lived a lie, why not me?

Margaret Drabble wrote somewhere that the world is divided into two: those who have children and those who do not. But that's not quite right: my world is divided between those who have lost children to adoption and those who have not.

I will always be a woman who gave up her baby.

A childless mother.

I wait for the sun to go down, for night to come. I hope for a sleep like death, without dreams. When the dreams do come, they are nightmares—I am throwing a baby down a bottomless stairwell, into the dark void, and I know she is at the bottom of the stairs, trying to crawl up, but she can't make it, she is a baby and I can't go down to rescue her. I awake when I scream. If God isn't dead, He's surely gone.

Two weeks later I drive to Northaven Terrace, this time to sign termination of parenthood papers, documents that will verify that I surrender to forces greater than I can overcome. Though Patrick and I had filled out his family's health history, his signature is not needed. I alone sign her away.

My roommate at the hospital? I ask Mrs. Mura. What did she and her boyfriend decide?

They came to sign the papers, she answers, but first they went to see their baby one last time. Then they took him home.

I will always wonder about the young woman and her son, how everything turned out, but no matter what happened—no matter how young they were—that young woman kept her baby, and today I salute her. No matter whether she and the father married or not, their son grew up knowing a mother and a father who looked like him, acted like him, and shared the same strengths, failings, and foibles.

My roommate falls on the other side of the divide now. She and her son are the lucky ones.

White Woman's Disease

While I felt alone in my catastrophe, I actually had a lot of company. We women who got pregnant when we weren't supposed to in the fifties, sixties, and early seventies were trapped in what has become known as the Baby Scoop Era, a period that began after World War II and continued through the seventies[12] until abortion became legal in 1973.

How many women relinquished their babies during this time is impossible to pin down with any accuracy; statistics were gathered voluntarily and haphazardly, even by government agencies. Some states did not report the data at all. Only three states had laws requiring a hospital to notify a state agency of the mother's plan for her child born outside marriage.[13] The official statistics do not take into account that many babies were born to women who relinquished in what is called the "black market." Babies were delivered by doctors who quietly passed them on to willing customers who wished to avoid the entanglement of investigation by social workers. Some of these were legal adoptions, simply handled privately by an attorney. For an unknown number, the birth certificates were written by a doctor as if the adopting woman had given birth, and so an accurate birth certificate was never issued. According to one estimate, the black market accounted for nearly 40 percent of all babies born outside marriage and adopted in the fifties and early sixties.[14] In short, there simply are no early reliable statistics. However, all things considered, it is generally estimated that between 1945 and 1973 more than 3.5 million mostly white babies were relinquished and adopted.[15]

Many adoptions were within the family—by a relative or a stepparent—

---

[12] Karen Wilson-Buterbaugh, *The Baby Scoop Era: Unwed Mothers, Infant Adoption, Forced Surrender* (self-published, 2017). Wilson-Buterbaugh originated the phrase Baby Scoop Era, sometimes shortened to BSE, which has become a popular descriptor for the period that began after World War II and began declining in the seventies.

[13] Solinger, 33.

[14] Solinger, 32.

[15] Ellen Herman, "Adoption Statistics," The Adoption History Project, last updated Feb. 24, 2012, https://web.archive.org/web/20220825202419/https://darkwing.uoregon.edu/~adoption/topics/adoptionstatistics.htm

and the individual, even when grown, may never have been told who their natural mother or father was. Birth certificates were routinely falsified to hide the reality of an illegitimate birth. The truth would sometimes be revealed when the now-grown child needed his birth certificate. Or at a funeral, when family secrets have a tendency to spill out, and relatives who have always known of the adoption casually mention it—and the adoptee hears of it for the first time.

Today, counting all adoptions, domestic and foreign, between five[16] and seven million[17] people living today in the United States are adopted. Yes, the range is wide, but a more exact count is not possible. In my own case, the numbers say that in 1966, my daughter was one of more than 81,000 children adopted by nonrelatives in the United States. By 1970 that number would rise to more than 89,000,[18] after which the number of adoptions began dropping due to an increasingly liberal attitude to pregnancy outside of marriage and single motherhood as well as the availability of abortion, legal in a few states by then. White babies were the overwhelming majority of these adoptions. By and large, Black women kept their babies. Not only was the loss of children reminiscent of the slave era, when families were split at the will of the slave owner, the reluctance of adoption agencies and social workers to facilitate adoptions of Black children by Black families was widespread.[19] Generally the family made a place for mother and child.[20]

Surrendering a child during that era has been dubbed the "white woman's disease," as the number of white unmarried mothers who gave up their children is thought to be around 70 percent—some estimates put it at 80

---

[16] Ellen Herman, *Kinship by Design: A History of Adoption in the Modern United States* (Chicago: University of Chicago Press, 2008), 5

[17] "US Adoption Statistics," Adoption Network, accessed Sept. 20, 2022, https://web.archive.org/web/20220920182934/https://www.adoptionnetwork.com/adoption-statistics

[18] John B. Turner, ed., *Encyclopedia of Social Work*, 1977, 17th ed. (Washington, DC: National Association of Social Workers, 1977), 2:1654, table 35.

[19] Kori A. Graves, "Before It Was 'A Practice of Genocide:' Transracial Adoption and African Americans in the 1950s and 1960s" (presentation at the Alliance for the Study of Adoption and Culture conference, Minneapolis, MN, Oct. 28, 2016).

[20] Solinger, 6.

percent,[21] and some as high as 95 percent.[22] A social worker at an adoption seminar years ago asked me if there were "commonalities" among mothers who relinquished. Unconsciously, one supposes, she was representative of those experts of an earlier era who "pretty unanimously agreed that only the most profoundly disturbed unwed mothers kept their babies, instead of turning them over to a nice, middle-class man and woman who could provide the baby with a proper family."[23] Not familiar with social workers' jargon—and put off by the question in the seventies—I simply answered no, and stared at her blankly. How I wish I'd said, Yes, we were mostly white. We all had sex. We all got caught, with all the implications that has. I felt alone in my tragedy, but I was merely one of the crowd, all of us separately hiding under a shroud of shame.

My mother presumed—or wanted to believe—that good girls like me (ahem) just didn't do it before marriage. The advice good Catholic girls got back then about birth control, other than the notoriously unreliable rhythm method—and then, only for marrieds! —was nil, or nearly so.[24]

Rare was the white parent sympathetic to an unmarried and pregnant daughter. Girls not so lucky as to be able to marry their sweethearts or, less romantically, the father of the child, were sent to live with relatives in another town, shipped off to homes for unwed mothers, and encouraged not to use their real names—even with each other—or they hid at home and bore the ignominy of their parents' scornful why-did-you-do-this-to-us? gaze. Some were committed to mental institutions for the duration of the pregnancy. Neighbors whispered, fathers held their heads down, and you, the sinner, prayed for this purgatory to be over and knew your life was ruined. Some girls had their babies taken from them in the hospital; their parents made the arrangements, and their daughters had no choice but to go along. Teens

---

[21] Gwendolyn Mink and Rickie Solinger, eds., *Welfare: A Documentary History of U.S. Policy and Politics* (New York: New York University Press, 2003), 177.
[22] Ellison: 326.
[23] Solinger, *Wake Up Little Susie*, 6.
[24] Ironically, today the rhythm method is followed by those desiring to get pregnant. Women take their temperatures and chart their periods to figure out the most advantageous days to procreate.

thought too young to marry—no matter how much the couple were in love and well suited for one another—were urged to give up their babies, finish school, and then get married. They could always have another.

Despite the sexual revolution going on in the background, the two-parent family remained the norm. Married motherhood was idealized; fatherhood was a sign of virility and solid citizenship. No consideration at all was given to the proposition that a child might prefer to grow up with people who looked and acted like them. Nurture trumped nature, if nature meant that the child was born to a single mother. I understood that I was supposed to do the right thing, and the right thing was to give up my baby. Society told me so. Patrick insisted. My parents would never know.

Within a decade, effective contraception as well as legal abortions became increasingly available. Sex education in some schools began to include contraception. The negative connotation of "unwed mother" shifted to a more neutral "single mother," and single mothers were considered brave forerunners of a newer, less restrictive culture. In 2019, the last year for which data is available, nearly 40 percent of all babies in the U.S. were born to single mothers.[25] A 2013 report found that close to half of all first children were born before marriage.[26]

But all that would come later, too late for me and my baby.

---

[25] Centers for Disease Control and Prevention, National Center for Health Statistics, National Vital Statistics Reports, vol. 70, No. 2, March 23, 2021, Births: Final Data for 2019. https://web.archive.org/web/20221202013239/https://www.cdc.gov/nchs/data/nvsr/nvsr70/nvsr70-02-tables-508.pdf

[26] "Kay Hymowitz et al., *Knot Yet: The Benefits and Costs of Delayed Marriage in America* (National Marriage Project at the University of Virginia / National Campaign to Prevent Teen and Unplanned Pregnancy / RELATE Institute, 2013). Data compiled from a number of studies and government surveys.

7 Reentry

One foot really does go down in front of another, and you just keep walking. In those first few days I accepted that my options were limited: I could end up in a padded cell and drugged, if not wrapped up tight in a straitjacket, or I could crawl toward sanity, however slowly.

And so, two weeks later, my figure intact and back into my work clothes—you would be amazed how quickly you can return to your old self when you must—I turned to a temp agency while I looked for a newspaper job in another city. Going back to the *Democrat & Chronicle* was not an option. I would get settled elsewhere, Patrick would disentangle himself from his wife and family, and somewhere we would start a life together. Our families would accept us in time, he promised. Please be patient. I will do it. I will come for you.

I nod, but think, We'll see. Tom promised to return the next day, but had not; Patrick, married with children, is much iffier. My track record is not good.

Ironically the first job offered me reminds me how far I have fallen: proofreader for the *D&C*. I'd gone from rising hotshot to drudge fixer of—typos. Instead, I take a receptionist slot at an office-furniture store, its only drawback that it is located perilously close to the newspaper. If I go outside at lunchtime, I might run into someone I know! So I slink in and out of the building in the rear and stay at my desk at lunchtime.

You're hiding something, says the man who hired me. Umm, I say.

I send clips of my stories to more than two dozen papers all over the country. I am still young and green, and now have a worrisome hiccup in my résumé. Some editors write back and suggest I try the women's department or say that my letter already has been passed on there, both responses throwing me into a tailspin of gloom. I'd been able to break out of that ghetto, and now, would I be forced to pay double the cost of being female? No baby and professionally take a step backward? I'd once thought I could outwit my father and biology, but it now appears that they are winning.

Then a miracle happens. The managing editor of the *Toronto Star* calls, compliments my clips, and mentions a job on the city desk. On the drive from Rochester to Toronto, I am giddy with the expectation that this job will at least get my career back on track. Toronto is a big city and a hip town—more sophisticated than Rochester—and only a few hundred miles away. The *Star* is a lively and respected newspaper. Why, Hemingway used to write for it! If I can get this job, my résumé will not look like a list of shattered dreams, and in a year or two, the break in my working life can be glossed over. I can move to Canada. What an adventure! Maybe Patrick will follow. He is encouraged by the prospect.

But not so fast.

The managing editor is agreeable, but sends me on to the city editor, the man who would be my boss, and when I cannot adequately explain the gap in my employment, the interest in his eyes dims as if a shade rolled down and shut out the light. I use the same lame excuse of having to take care of my father, but he isn't buying. If that was why I quit a promising job in Rochester, why should he count on me to stay in Toronto? Or maybe, as I let my imagination read his mind, maybe he thought I was mentally unstable or had some "man" trouble at the last job. Who wants to hire trouble? The job slips away like a fish that manages to lose the hook.

Patrick is waiting at the apartment that evening. He is still saying, I love you, we're rare, we'll be together, I just can't do it yet. I want to believe him, but I understand the rules—of the times, of Holy Matrimony, of his Irish-Catholic family. His brother and mother might talk to me eventually, but I'd always be that other woman who seduced her son and made him stray. His children? I couldn't even think about them. The divorce rate—among Catholics and non-Catholics alike—had not yet seen the uptick that it would in a few short years. New York did not even have no-fault divorce then—it required infidelity and a guilty party. Leaving his marriage would be no simple matter.

As the job hunt continued up and down the East Coast—Boston, Baltimore, Richmond, even San Juan—Patrick ran in place, and I began to accept that "not now" might mean never. When he says I love you, the woman who hears him is no longer the same person she was before. Now I hope but count on nothing. I do not even resent his inaction. I am not going to beg or cajole or do anything melodramatic like phone The Wife. I always figured if one pleaded, if one pushed the guy in a corner, he would never stay, and even if he did, you'd always be worried he wouldn't stay. Tom had not shown up when he said he would; now Patrick was going to have to show up. I would meet him with an open heart and open arms, but first, he had to show up.

His marriage might be breathing on a respirator, but I would leave town as soon as I could.

After a couple of months of getting nowhere on the job front, I ran an ad for myself in a trade publication called *Editor & Publisher*. "Writer-reporter with metro experience looking for similar position," the ad started. At the time, it felt like a last-ditch effort from a desperate reporter. Yet the editor of the *Knickerbocker News* in Albany calls, and two weeks later I string myself together like a puppet and drive east across upstate New York. While Albany is smaller than Rochester, Patrick points out that Albany is the state capitol, so going there won't be a step backward—in fact, it could be a positive change! I note that Albany is closer to New York City. The best part is that there has been no mention of the dreaded words: women's department.

Unbeknownst to me, Dick, who is aware of my job search, calls the editor in Albany the morning of the interview and apparently gives me a ringing endorsement. I sense that I will get an offer as soon as I shake the editor's hand. He does not ask why I hadn't been working since January. The only question is whether I want education or health and science as my beat.

Hallelujah! This is better than general assignment; this is a real beat to cover. Just like a man. Within seconds, I pass on education—which sounds like a woman's beat—and choose health and science.

The job in Albany turns out to be swell. The shift that would occur in the next decade in city rooms all over America, as barriers were broken and women hired, had already occurred at the *Knick*. I am not The Girl or The Woman, I am one of several—others are already covering hard news. Like the old Alka-Seltzer ad, "Oh, oh, what a relief it is." It is a heady time: We women know we are breaking new ground. We are making news ourselves with our front-page stories.

Medicare and Medicaid are in the works; so is an abortion bill in the state legislature; the Albany Medical Center is doing cutting-edge research, and an observatory in town is involved in space exploration. As an added plus, the city editor gives me great out-of-town features. Stories hang like low fruit.

The one downside has nothing to do with the job itself, but with hours. The *Knick* is an afternoon paper, meaning that deadlines are mid-morning, and we work from early morning to mid-afternoon, when the paper comes out. I mentally do not settle down to write until mid-afternoon—a predilection that seems to be hard-wired—as I'd found the afternoon-to-night schedule in Rochester suited me perfectly. The *Knick's* hours meant I was hitting my stride, actually writing, around the official quitting time at four-thirty. I was often at the paper an hour or two longer than nearly everybody. The phones stopped ringing, the place quieted down, there were no distractions. My story would be in the editor's copy box when he got there in the morning. But though I might not leave the office until six or seven, that still left the long night ahead, yawning with crushing loneliness.

Sunlit mornings and early afternoons might have been bearable, but the nights, the dark and solitary nights! When I do fall apart—and I do periodically—it is in my two-room apartment in a new building that has all the charm of a cheap motel furnished with Danish knockoffs. It had been available and affordable when I was looking, and I was a woman in a hurry. A resident in psychiatry at the Albany Medical Center moved in the same day I did, and so we say, Hello, how did you end up here? Rarely are we there at the same time, but it does happen, and one night over wine I tearfully spill out my woes. In the space of a year, I tell him, I have lost my child, my love, my home, my job. He prescribes uppers, a pretty green-and-white capsule called Dexamyl—and makes himself available when I need to talk, even midday one time when I called him from work saying I am suicidal. Can he meet me right away? When he sees a scabby red rash on the back of my knee grow to the diameter of a grapefruit, he says it's likely a reaction to everything that has happened to me in the last year and prescribes a cortisone cream.

Someone at work asks me out on a date. I go, but I am a contrarian mess. He wants a kiss. No, I can't. Kisses now seem to promise sex, or lengthy disquisitions on why not. I am evasive, but he asks me out again anyway. Doesn't he know I am not normal? I am a loose log in a raging river, crashing about in the turbulence.

Then the reminder of her comes in the mail: a bill from Strong Memorial

Figure 4. Covering a canoe trip with Caroline Kennedy and the Robert Kennedy family in upstate New York, circa 1967. From left in foreground, Courtney, Caroline, Lorraine, Kerry (facing away from camera). Guards in background. (Photo by Eddie Adams)

Hospital for more than a thousand dollars, roughly a month's salary. My daughter had been a preemie. Now I have a bill for her care in the incubator. I might not have a baby, but the billing department makes no exceptions. Patrick immediately pays half. I'll pay off the rest. Every now and then he puts a twenty or two in an envelope and sends it to me. It takes months, but finally the bill is paid in full.

Come August I timidly ask the arts editor if I can score a press pass for the New York City Ballet at the Saratoga Performing Arts Center, which opened that summer. You know anything about dance, he says? A little, I say. I took ballet when I was a kid. Great, he says, you're hired. I need someone to write about ballet all month. Yo! I say, You ought to see my turnout! He doesn't know what I'm talking about—you need a dancer's flexibility for a good turnout at the hips, and mine is impressive—but I'd just become the *Knick's* dancer reviewer.

All month, I work a full day at my regular beat, now pushing myself to leave the paper around five because I've got to grab a bite, chill for a bit, and make the forty-minute drive up the Northway to Saratoga Springs to be in my seat before the eight o'clock curtain. Afterward, I race back to Albany and write my review, usually finishing up around midnight, sometimes after. I'm learning how to write about dance by doing it, by reading everything I can about ballet in short order. The beauty of this double load of work is that I am so busy, I don't have time to be depressed. I am so tired that when I do sleep, I immediately fall into a deep stupor. More than once, I fall asleep on the couch, thinking I'd lie there for a few moments. Then I'd wake in the middle of the night, the lights still on, still in my work clothes. I have to be at work at eight-thirty the next morning.

In those first months, Patrick is still writing: "I think about you a lot and even when you're not consciously in my thoughts, you're part of so many things: brandy, Bogart movies, Lady Day, good third grafs, Andrew Marvell, all the Polish movies I've never seen . . . . I love you . . . Pat." I keep them and wonder what they mean. Will he really come for me? He calls most Friday afternoons. June, July, August go by.

I am still wearing the gold band Patrick gave me on my left hand. One of the doctors at the State Health Department comments on it. Knowing I appear not to be married, he says, There's a story there somewhere.

Our eyes meet but I say nothing.

The abortion bill that is wending its long and torturous way through the state legislature provided a reason to plunge deep into the bowels of state government. It was heaven disguised as work—far from any aroma of what was considered a "woman's story." It was one thing to do features and quite another to go after real news and front-page scoops.

I wasn't the only woman following stories that led to the capitol. We initially had to convince the guards there that our press passes were authentic, but in short order they were cheerfully waving us through. We never talked about it, but we all relished being the advance guard of those who would follow. Soon enough I dug into the effort to undo New York's 1871 law banning abortion "unless necessary to save the life of the woman," an ambiguity, I discovered, that did allow a small number of women—mostly women in private hospitals—to get a safe and legal abortion for mental health reasons. *Could one of them have been me?* I mused then, but beat back the thought.

In reading my stories—including a four-part series that began on the front page every day—from the vantage point of today, it is surprising to see how most people in the religious and medical community were pushing for the liberalization in a way that is unheard of today when, for the time being, legal abortion is in jeopardy or outright banned. The New York Archdiocese of the Episcopal Church, the Union for Reform Judaism, the New York Council of Churches, the state arms of the Academy of Medicine, the American Medical Association, and the Obstetrical Society, all made their support known, as did the Republican governor, Nelson Rockefeller. Dr. Robert C. Lamar of the Albany First Presbyterian Church is quoted: "The present law is overbalanced in favor of the value given a fetus as against the physical, psychological and spiritual health of the mother involved."

Virulent Catholic opposition rose up like Lazarus. The apostolic administrator of the Albany diocese, Rev. Edward J. Maginn—the only bishop in the state to speak out against the bill—preached from the pulpit, on television, and in the print media, calling for a letter-writing campaign against the bill. Preach he might—but I wrote that Catholic doctrine did allow abortion to save the life of the mother, something I had learned in tenth grade biology from Sister Ann. With some digging at the state library, I found that the Church's position as to the "beginning of life" had not been handed down unchanged through history. "Until 1869, it was held that life began 40 days after conception for the male, and 80 days for the female," I wrote without comment. This was from St. Thomas Aquinas, and from what I read, it was unclear if the vaunted thirteenth century saint was against abortion at every stage of life, despite what I read today is the Church's position. I noted that the Bible makes no mention of abortion, but it is outlawed in the rules set down by the twelve apostles. But that reminded me that Sister Ann also taught that any man-made rules in the Church—and the apostles were indeed men—can be changed by fiat of the Pope.

However, my real ace in the hole about the wavering of the Catholic position, always presented as inviolate, were the writings of a Belgian Catholic theologian, Canon Henry De Dorlodot. In a French publication (of which I must have found a translation), he observed "that since it is estimated that at least one-third of all fertilized eggs fail to develop and undergo spontaneous abortion, baptismal water would have to penetrate everywhere" to save that life from an eternity in limbo, the place where the unbaptized go after death.[27]

Well.

Including that tidbit may have been what led to a visit a few days later from a spokesman for the Albany diocese who showed up unannounced at the *Knick,* presumably to harangue whichever heathen had written the ar-

---

[27]   Dusky, "The Abortion Issue," *The Knickerbocker News,* Jan. 27, 1967. p. 1A, 5A. The articles ran from Jan. 24-27.

ticles. He had little to say after I calmly told him I was the product of twelve years of Catholic education.

New York did not make abortion legal until 1970, three years later.

One hot September afternoon, a Friday, when I am still at my desk, Patrick calls from a phone booth from somewhere on the highway and says he is on his way. He should be there in about an hour. He told his wife about us the night before and took the day off. "I'm coming to you," he says. "I'm coming." I run home and shower and stick pantyhose in drawers and pick up the mess of magazines and what-not lying around.

From my window I watch as he gets out of his car. He is as trim as ever, in the same seersucker suit that he wore in Manhattan. He came; he showed up; maybe it is not too late. I open the door before he knocks. This is really happening, we will find a way, I say to myself, but I have been disappointed too many times to rejoice. This must play out before I will truly, finally, believe it.

The next day we drive back to Rochester and check into a motel. We have dinner with his (very Catholic) brother, who tells us in no uncertain terms that Patrick is making a mistake: Think of The (not-quite-blameless, to my mind) Wife, The (innocent) Children, The (omnipresent) Church, The (enormous) Scandal. Think of our mother, this will kill her. Me? I say pretty much nothing beyond hello; I might as well be invisible. I am a mere piffle. I can be swatted away with a few strong words. Of course, Brother John does not know about the baby.

This conversation will change if you tell him about the baby, I think. This is up to you, Patrick: Say something. There are times when one should speak up, when what goes unsaid will be more harmful than keeping silent, but I am too young, too ashamed, too governed by Patrick's willful silence to interrupt the flow of What We Are Doing Wrong. I sit there mute, a seemingly callow woman whose main assets, I am sure, appear to be her long blond hair and good legs—you know, the attributes of a wily seductress. I want to slink down below the table into the floor. Once again, I am merely some broad, someone who can be discarded, and the world will go on spinning as before. Patrick drinks too many martinis that night, has bad dreams that wake us at three a.m. This too shall pass, I tell myself.

Come Sunday around noon, Pat and I say goodbye in a diner at the bus station. I leave him there, smoking a cigarette, drinking black coffee, and reading the morning papers, and get a bus back to Albany. I have to work the next day. He is off to a state Republican convention near Buffalo. I'll be back on the weekend, he says. Do you think you could get next Monday off?

I'll try, I say as I get on the bus.

We talk several times during the week. Everything is going fine; a businessman from Canandaigua is the nominee as predicted. Yet I am keenly aware of ramparts still to clear. I do not have our baby, but if I do not lose my love, I will have this one strong thing to cling to.

Look forward. Do not peer into the rearview mirror.

Saturday late afternoon, he calls. He is back in Rochester, at the office. His voice labors under the weary drone of defeat and exhaustion after a week of long hours fueled by caffeine, cigarettes, booze, and the adrenaline rush of deadlines. I know we are lost as soon as he says my name. I've just wrapped up my column for the Sunday paper, he says.

Pause.

I've got a suitcase full of dirty shirts and I have no place to go. My kids are calling me at the office, saying, *Daddy, when are you coming home?*

Pause.

I can't do it.

The sun is not yet down, golden rays leak through my front window, spilling onto the blah beige carpeting, and I'm standing there listening to him say, I can't do it.

My throat is dry, my body awash with the hot flush of a panic attack. I am too beat-up to cajole or beg, and besides, love has to be freely given, you cannot force an unwilling heart. I do not remind him that we are rare or of promises made and promises repeated. I know he has reached a decision. The Wife is taking him back. He has nowhere else to go. I am in Albany and he is three hundred miles away. Would I always be doomed not to have a place where a weary man could spend the night? You know how they say, Déjà vu all over again?

We never make decisions in a vacuum. We may think we come to them independently, but they are the result of a thousand pinpricks to the mind from the world we live in. Patrick and I were no exception. I gave up our child because I could see no other way, and now he sees no other way than to stay in his marriage. We might always be rare, but now we would be like lovers in a sad song, always kept apart by circumstance.

Yet we were not quite done.

8   Adrift

The panic attack is still in full bore as I dial a friend on the newspaper, Judy Bender, another reporter like me. We've only gotten to know each other recently, but I must get out of my apartment, I have to talk to someone, the doctor upstairs is not home—somehow, he's not the right person anyway—and I am about to explode. Judy hears the desperation in my voice. Come right over, she says. On the two-mile drive there, I blast through a stop sign that in a saner moment I knew was there and almost ram into another car. I screech to a stop. We both get out of our cars, the guy yells at me profusely, and I apologize just as profusely—I'm sorry, I'm sorry, I am sorry, a million times sorry. For being me. For my life. For what I have done. When I arrive, Judy pours me a drink and listens. I tell her the whole story, including the baby. She's compassionate and full of sympathy. The next morning we are back in the office at eight-thirty.

Time doesn't fly until you are sixty-something and look back, and you say, Where did all those years go? But when you are young and aching to get on the other side of something, like your twelfth or eighteenth birthday, time never hurries. So it was with me in that first year. Yet the sun goes down every night and comes up in the morning, and eventually lonely nights turn into days a body can stand, which turn into weeks that are blessedly ho-hum, which turn into tolerable months. Some days—even that very fall—the beauty of upstate New York could not be ignored. On Sundays I'd go for a drive and head straight into a Thomas Cole painting, a brilliant stew of gold and red and burnt sienna.

Despite the dung heap of my love life, work remains a constant that is both meaningful and enjoyable. Staying late at the office makes the nights shorter. When Dudley Observatory announces they have an experiment to collect space dust on one of the Gemini missions, I convince the editor of the *Knick* to let me go with the Dudley crowd that November, not only to Houston but also to follow them around for several more days while they do rocket tests at the White Sands missile base in New Mexico. When I report that one of their rocket launches failed, the director of the Dudley team is upset with me. I explain that I may be traveling with them but I am not "one of the team," all the while hoping there are no more snafus on the trip. Then back to Texas to launch a weather balloon from a town called Palestine. In a small plane, one of the team and I follow the balloon until our plane runs out of gas at four a.m. near Birmingham, Alabama, where we set down. I try to sleep the rest of the night on the floor of the ladies' room, and in the morning, I catch a plane back to Albany. My write-ups have made the front page all week. I send tear sheets home to my parents.

Judy is the only person in Albany who knows I've had a baby. My daughter is a secret that I carry around in my pocket. I even lied to the doctor who examined me for the *Knick's* health insurance. When he asked if I'd ever been pregnant, I said, No.

I find a nicer apartment, the first floor of an elegant townhouse on Lancaster Street, a little more than a mile from the newspaper. Freshly painted in a rich cream color, the apartment has an alabaster fireplace, tall windows that let in great light, and a shoebox kitchen. I make bookcases from bricks and lumber and refinish an oak dining table that had been cut down to serve as a coffee table. Life is turning a corner.

Sometime in January, I begin seeing a *New York Times* reporter who is covering the state legislature while it is in session, which is several months each year. We'd met at the Ambassador, the place out-of-town reporters—and there were a lot of them back in the sixties—found their way to nightly. Dark, sleek, and sophisticated, the Ambassador was a short walk from the capitol, and through a small park, or, if you walked the other way, only a few blocks from the *Knick*. Though most of the reporters from the *Knick* didn't frequent the place, Judy and I stopped in a couple times a week, and one of those nights I met Sydney.

Sydney is bright, he's self-assured, and, as the head of the *Times'* Albany bureau, he's a man going places. Pretty soon, we have dinner nearly every night he's in Albany. He's attentive and affectionate, and soon enough I am trying to keep my emotions in check, but that is not working out so well. Though at work I project the image a strong woman going about my job— my female comrades and I at the *Knick* are the first women to report regularly on the doings of the state legislature—where the heart resides, I am a bottomless well of need, and Sydney is filling it up. Nobody is saying the word "love," but my heart is eager. I am woman. I am lonely. I need a partner! I know he is not married, yet after a couple of months, a nagging inner voice notes that Sydney hasn't asked me to come to Manhattan on a weekend. I am reluctant to bring this up. A part of me suspects why, but I don't want to go there.

A thousand-dollar windfall comes my way when a story of mine—observing and writing about still-novel open-heart surgery—wins an award, and that, combined with my corporate health insurance, gives me the means to have my nose bobbed. Doing so had been in the back of my mind since I first heard you could do that, but it was always out of reach. Weeks earlier, one of the NBC reporters covering the legislature had arranged an on-camera interview for me in Manhattan. You'd be great, he kept insisting as he pulled strings that landed me at NBC talking to the head producer for the local evening news. I was aware of only one woman covering hard news for the national networks. Women on the local networks were nearly as rare, and so an interview at all was a desired plum. But me, hired as an on-camera news reporter? With my nose? Unlikely. I unconsciously, but somehow purposely, flubbed the taping, so I could tell myself it wasn't my profile that cost me the job. It wasn't the first time I'd done something like this. I'd tried out for the high school cheerleading team but turned the wrong way in a group cheer to assure I could use that as the reason I wasn't chosen. I knew I didn't fit in with the popular, prettier girls. The hormonal pull of natural selection always bends toward beauty. Life favors the advantaged. Et cetera. Ah, well.

But now I will take the money from the award and get my nose fixed. By mail I consult Detroit's top plastic surgeon and send off the requested photographs. His reply amuses me: You appear to be a good candidate for the requested surgery.

Damn straight! My body seems to have been so primed for the surgery, I don't even get the normal black eyes that most do. With a dab of concealer, I'm good to go within a week.

I get back to Albany on a rainy, chilly Sunday at the end of March, the weekend of the New York State Legislative Correspondents' annual dinner, when a lot of reporters and editors stay in town for the hoopla. I call Sydney at his hotel, raring to show him my new physiognomy. A woman answers his phone—maybe it's someone from the *Times* and they have converged in his room?—and I'm so taken aback by the female voice I simply ask if he's there. He is. In a grim voice, he says, "I can't talk now."

I have been a side dish all along.

When he calls Tuesday evening, he is profuse in his admission, he is ever so sorry he didn't tell me, but he is engaged, has been engaged, to someone in New York City.

Someone who is Jewish, as he is, and I am not. Someone who will take his name, as I would not. Someone who will bear him children, as I would not. He does not say these things, but I understand them.

Would I have spoken up about weekends if . . . if what? If I'd been a different person, a woman with more assurance in her allure, if I'd been someone who grew up with a different nose? Was this happening because it was clear I would have a career? And had no desire to be a traditional homemaker and helpmate? I have no answer. All I knew then is that is that three times in a row I had come up a loser.

Weeks later, I still cannot run into Sydney in the capitol building without my face flushing and my heart racing. When possible, I speed-walk the other way. Yet I can't avoid the legislative building because I'm covering the fight to get an abortion bill passed. What I can do is stay away from the Ambassador.

Eventually I force myself to walk through the door. I slip into a seat at the bar, relieved that at least for the time being, Sydney is nowhere in sight—had he been avoiding the place, too? The Associated Press (AP) bureau chief in Albany, Charlie, sits down next to me for the first time ever, and we chat affably for half an hour. As he leaves, he says, "I never knew you were so charming."

Right.

He means it as a compliment. I hear it as a recognition of how he now sees me: a woman without that nose. While the men I'd cared for have seen past the nose, or had to get past the nose, his off-the-cuff comment signifies how differently people will react to me from now on. No one is going to stare at my now-upturned nose when I meet them. Men are less likely to tell me I have "beautiful eyes," which is a way of saying my nose is not so great.

But now I start eating. Along with millions of Americans, I discover French cheese. Brie, in particular. Great quantities of it, great for nighttime snacking. I barely remember eating dinner—I certainly wasn't cooking for myself, there was no one to have dinner with, night after night—I just remember gorging myself night after night. Cookies. Crackers, Camembert, and, of course, Brie. The runnier the better.

Afterward, I berate myself, and once or twice try to purge with fingers down my throat. Unsuccessful after a couple of tries, I give up. The stuffing continues, like fattening up a goose. I hate myself in the morning and eat again too much in the evening. If I were to draw a cartoon of myself, it would be of a woman walking around with a dark cloud over her head. A woman in trouble—even if she has an unremarkable nose—packing on the pounds, filling the void with food.

Life indeed has gone on, but every so often I still wake with bad dreams. I'm in a department store with my baby, and somehow she gets left on a floor, and then I'm in an elevator trying to get back to her, to rescue her, but the elevator keeps stopping at the wrong floor, or I can't get out of the elevator when it's at the right floor, and the door closes and takes me to another floor, and over and over again . . . until I wake up in a lather.

That old adage that time heals all wounds?

Not this one.

My daughter's birthday comes and goes that year without me noticing. Weeks and days before her birthday, I remember thinking, How am I going to get through the day? The actual day is a week after Sydney went *poof,* and my consciousness obligingly banishes all thoughts of her to help me cope with my more recent loss. A few days later, a bright flash of forsythia jolts me—*Hello, Mommy, I am here, waiting for you. Where are you?* I visualize her as healthy, strong, vital, and blond like me, but now I am taken aback because I so coolly missed her birthday.

It must have been an act of self-preservation, a nod to sanity, for it was necessary to dull the cutting edge of memory if I were ever going to be able to pick up the pieces of a life gone haywire. I made the choice to survive. Now she sits in the corners of my mind where I do not ruminate daily or dally long, just as Mrs. Mura said. The rash behind my knee is receding. When I recognize how truly sick I had been that first year, I know that I am getting well.

But still, she is there. She is always there.

You would be surprised how many little blond girls there are in the world when you are not looking for them. They are everywhere, filling your sightline like a chorus of charming little dolls, reminding, mocking, making you aware of what you are missing, what you have done. You stare at them, check out their clothes, absorb their little-girl movements and words. The girl in the coffee shop with her mother. Another at the supermarket. Creating a scene at the mall. The daughter of new friends: blond, fine-boned, and only a few months older than yours. Are my daughter's parents good to her? How is she? Who does she look like? Is she blond like me? Does she have my flat feet and Patrick's blue eyes?

But it is more than the girls themselves that comes at you in full frontal attack. An invitation to a baby shower. A picture of a baby in a magazine. Forsythia in the window of a flower shop. A vague reference to somebody's child, or children. My mother asking if I'll come back to Michigan for her extended family's annual reunion, a potluck picnic that would be filled with people to whom my daughter is related. I couldn't go, not without her, the missing link in this family. I don't want to joke with relatives who are sure to ask when I am getting married. Or notice that they have stopped asking. Now I am an outsider, much more than because I moved away. I feel disconnected from everyone—except, in some weird way, Patrick.

And he is gone.

I have this secret that makes me—different. Alien.

Deep inside me there is a gnawing sense that I must find my daughter one day, but I'd never heard of anybody—mother or child—who did it. I hadn't even met another woman who'd given up a baby. Yet surely, I am not the only one in this private hell. Where are the other women?

They are hiding in plain sight.

Aftershock

Adoption is trumpeted today as a universally good thing. For infertile couples who wish to have a family, it is a solution. For religious organizations and fellow travelers, agencies that wrap themselves in the mantle of religion, it is a business. For gays and lesbians, it is a way to have a family. For liberals who want to do good and keep the sense of family about them, it is a way to keep population growth down. Celebrities who adopt get on the cover of magazines, increasing their likability and encouraging ever more people to raise other people's children. A liberal think tank issues a white paper encouraging women and teens to surrender their babies in order that they, the mothers, might have a better life. It says nothing about the impact of adoption on the children.[28]

But what is rarely talked about in general conversation about adoption is the long-term mental and physical effect of surrendering a baby to others. Even though some young women today are lulled into believing that their sacrifice of a child is a cause for some pride and self-congratulation—and announce their plans on social media—the world still understands that this is not the normal order of things.

Adoption equals loss, loss of the biological mother and extended family to the child and loss of the child to the mother, whose body and brain are primed to keep, love and protect that child of her flesh. One expects short-term grief in the aftermath of signing away one's rights to a child one has borne, but what of the long-term lasting impact, four, five—twenty—years later?

We are not doing so well. While for years there was little study of the women who relinquished their children for adoption, today that is no longer true. Studies show—all the studies show—that the grief of losing a child to adoption for most women is deep and long-lasting. What is different today is that some evidence suggests that mothers in old, closed adoptions, such as mine was, where there is not only no contact but no information, continue

---

[28] Jessica Arons, *The Adoption Option: Adoption Won't Reduce Abortion but It Will Expand Women's Choices*

to suffer more and longer-lasting grief than those in open adoptions, where there may be not only shared information but also contact, including continuing visits between mother and child.

That is not to say that we are easy to find and turn into research subjects, even though there are millions of us out there. We do go on and have lives and get swallowed up by a code of silence that many of us assume will last forever. But for a great many of us, the toxic aftermath of relinquishing a child lingers on.

A British study of ninety-three mothers who relinquished children to adoption found that while only an insignificant proportion of these women had been diagnosed with a mental health problem previously (3 percent), in the time between parting and contact, 24 percent had a psychiatric diagnosis, mainly for depression.[29] Not surprisingly, mothers who felt compelled to search for their children fared the worst: they were prone to lower self-esteem, anxiety, and worry over the child; they required more doctor visits and attributed their physical and mental problems over the years to adoption. Seeker mothers (women looking for their children) often cited parental pressure as the main reason for the adoption and reported that they had little emotional support during the pregnancy and relinquishment.

An Australian study of over two hundred natural mothers found that nearly 30 percent reported below-average "adjustment" to the situation at the time they were questioned, many up to twenty years later.[30] Half reported an increasing sense of loss over the years. The women had few opportunities to talk about their feelings related to surrender and no social support, exacerbating their depression.

A survey of a dozen studies[31] identified a grief reaction "unique" to the

---

[29] John Triseliotis, Julia Feast, Fiona Kyle, *The Adoption Triangle Revisited: A Study of Adoption, Search and Reunion Experiences* (London: British Association for Adoption and Fostering, 2005), 80–92. The sample is small—composed of thirty-two seekers and sixty-one mothers who were sought, but the study is one of the few—perhaps the only—to include both seeker and sought mothers.

[30] Susan Livingston Smith, *Safeguarding the Rights and Well-Being of Birthparents in the Adoption Process* (Evan B. Donaldson Adoption Institute 2006, revised 2007), 46–49. The Australian study is one of several included in this report.

[31] Holli Ann Askren and Kathaleen C. Bloom, "Postadoptive Reactions of the

natural mother that left her "at risk for long-term physical, psychologic[al] and social repercussions." The authors concluded that the women's reactions were similar to normal grief, with one notable difference: that this particular sorrow "often leads to chronic, unresolved grief. . . . Although interventions have been proposed, little is known about their effectiveness in preventing or alleviating these repercussions."

A 2007 study of relinquishing mothers from both closed and open adoptions found that the women in open adoptions suffered somewhat less in the long term than those in closed adoptions. The study found that even after many years had passed—between twelve and twenty—after relinquishment, nearly three-quarters of the 127 women were still experiencing grief, which ranged from intense to moderate. Overall, researchers found that more openness benefited some birth mothers and that in the early years after relinquishment the women who suffered the most were those whose open adoptions closed. Showing considerable empathy for their subjects, the authors made this observation: "Must the birthmother show no signs of suffering or sadness regarding the placement for her to have resolved her grief, or is this perhaps a misunderstanding of the nature of birthmother grief? Can we truly expect the loss of a child to be 'resolved' in this sense, or will the resolution look different—like birthmothers who are still sad and perhaps remorseful, but who have built a 'safe place' for that grief in their lives?"[32]

While the authors note that openness in adoption is the current practice, they caution that a "rush to openness" may not be beneficial to all women, depending on their life situation, stresses, and coping mechanisms. One mother may feel relieved to hear that her child has had the flu and is now better, while another may find that news overwhelming and the cause for more worry. For some women the birth of later children renewed the feelings of loss, while for others each birth was a milestone in their healing process.

Relinquishing Mother: A Review," *Journal of Obstetric, Gynecologic, & Neonatal Nursing* 28, no. 4 (July 1999): 395–400.

[32] Susan M. Henney, et al. "Evolution and Resolution: Birthmothers' Experience of Grief and Loss at Different Levels of Adoption Openness," *Journal of Social and Personal Relationships* 24 no. 6 (Dec. 2007): 875–889. doi:10.1177/0265407507084188.

The authors urge agencies to consider offering counseling to mothers for the "lifespan of the adoption." Taken to the fullness of meaning, that would extend to the rest of the woman's life.

As for myself, I eventually lost track of my social worker, Mrs. Mura, but decades later I tried to find her. She had died and I grieved her loss. The psychiatric resident I met at my apartment building had been incredibly helpful, but ten years later when I tried therapy—with a woman psychiatrist—she wanted to pathologize me for being a woman who let herself get into the position of having relinquished a child. What I was seeking was a therapist who would help me deal with the hard reality of relinquishment. I quit after a few visits and did not shop around for another.

The impact of great trauma, whether emotional or physical, does not leave the body unscathed; it digs in and stays. So it is with a pregnancy and birth that results without a child, especially when the heart and mind are aching with a million microwarnings to hold that baby safe and protect it like a lioness. To carry on, we childless mothers must bury the damage, but, like silent worms in the night working quietly but persistently, that trauma has its way with us. The amount of the "love hormone," oxytocin, that nature pumped into me at my daughter's birth turned me into a blubbering mess that wanted only to keep my baby close, and when that was not part of my life's equation, the inchoate sense of ever reaching that physical and emotional state again threw me into a mental panic.[33] True, I never saw myself as or hungered to be a mother before I had my baby, but once I had that baby, I wanted to keep and love and cherish her for all the days of my life. It wasn't that I wanted another baby—I wanted her. Besides, how could I give one away and keep another?

I've got lots of company. One study found that close to 40 percent of

---

[33] Marla Paul, "Study Finds Oxytocin Strengthens Memories of Both Bad and Good Events," Northwestern University Feinberg School of Medicine, July 22, 2013, https://web.archive.org/web/20220825202855/https://news.feinberg.northwestern.edu/2013/07/22/oxytocin_stress/ The research found that oxytocin may intensify a social memory as the hormone activates a part of the brain that stimulates that memory. If the experience was negative or stressful, the memory of it may be exaggerated, thus increasing the susceptibility to feeling fearful and anxious during events that are similar going forward. This study was in mice, but as I read it, my mind said, yes.

women who had relinquished children never had another, either because they chose not to or could not.[34] Another study put the number at more than 30 percent, breaking down the percentage between those who chose not to have another child (17 percent) and those who wanted to but were unable to (14 percent).[35] These studies were done before open adoption was common, and so it is unknown whether these numbers will remain steady.

A study of more than three hundred natural mothers, most of them members of Concerned United Birthparents, found that they perceived that surrendering a child had a profound negative effect on their later lives, particularly regarding marriage, fertility and parenting.[36] Critics might argue that members of any such an organization self-select to be skewed toward pathology; nonetheless, the results mirror the studies done by impartial researchers. The Birthmother Research Project found that on average women who surrender children are more likely to have hysterectomies than women who do not: "The survey results supported other research findings . . .that birthmothers experience difficulties with unresolved grief, traumatic stress symptoms, self-punishment, low self-esteem, arrested emotional development, living at extremes, difficulty forgiving oneself/others, being out of touch with feelings, difficulty giving/receiving love, relationship problems, self-hatred and dysfunctional sexual problems. Unresolved grief, self-punishment, and low self-esteem ranked highest among the difficulties identified as extreme, often, or severe."[37]

Today some come right out and call the effect of adoption on some natural mothers post-traumatic stress disorder (PTSD). The diagnosis includes: involuntary memories or dreams of a traumatic event; avoiding reminders of said

---

[34] Eva Y. Deykin, Lee Campbell, and Patricia Patti, "The Postadoption Experience of Surrendering Parents," *American Journal of Orthopsychiatry* 54, no. 2 (Apr. 1984): 271–80.

[35] Smith, "Safeguarding": 61.

[36] Campbell and Patti, "Postadoption Experience," 274.

[37] Judy A. Kelly, "The Trauma of Relinquishment: The Long-Term Impact of Relinquishment on Birthmothers Who Lost Their Infants to Adoption During the Years 1965-1972," (Master's thesis, Goddard College: 1999). https://web.archive.org/web/20220617184244/http://www.sites.google.com/site/birthmotherresearchproject/.

event, alterations in mood and inability to remember important aspects of the event, behaving in a self-destructive way, self-blaming behavior, and guilt and shame about the event.[38] As I read through the list of symptoms, I remember how I avoid baby showers and can recall immediately the three that I forced myself to attend in the half-century since my daughter was born, and how anxious and uncomfortable I felt just being there; how bad dreams persisted for a long time and recurred years later; how I avoid scenes of births in movies and television; how I never, ever, ask to hold a baby or coo over a friend's pictures of their children or grandchildren; how worthless I felt about myself for such a long time; how for years I felt like such a fake, an impostor pretending to be normal. Yes, I'd say PTSD is a diagnosis that seems about right.

In *The Adoption Triangle*—in 1978, the first book to investigate women who relinquished children—the authors (a psychiatrist and two social workers) found that in numerous letters collected years after surrender, "there was still the intensity of feeling and the need to describe the pain, still carried within. . . . Even if the birth parents had become comfortable with the decision because there were no viable alternatives, they nevertheless felt loss, pain, mourning and a continuing sense of caring for that long-vanished child."[39]

Whenever a fresh flash of forsythia spins into my field of vision, I am reminded of her.

Every. Single. Time.

---

[38] "What Is Posttraumatic Stress Disorder?" American Psychiatric Association. https://web.archive.org/web/20220825203206/https://psychiatry.org/patients-families/ptsd/what-is-ptsd.

[39] Arthur D. Sorosky, Annette Baran and Reuben Pannor, *The Adoption Triangle: Sealed or Opened Records: How They Affect Adoptees, Birth Parents, and Adoptive Parents* (Garden City, 1978), 72.

9 Moving On

The following July my parents come to visit. I had managed to keep the pregnancy and adoption from them, though there had been one close call when they phoned the newspaper in Rochester looking for me. The operator told them I had not been there for months; she transferred the call to the city editor when Mom was insistent. Dick was there that day and was fast thinking enough to tell them I was on a secret assignment and had been for months. Dick called me at home to warn me before they phoned. Because no big exposé ever appeared in print, my mother was suspicious, but I never wavered from my story. She pestered when I visited but eventually gave up. If the move to Albany added to their suspicions, she didn't say. Dad had never really bugged me, and clips from Albany had quieted their curiosity. When they visit nearly a year later, none of this is brought up.

One day, they take down and wash my dusty venetian blinds, swishing them around in the bathtub with soap and water, the way we had done them at the motel, and they are already back up when I come home from work. Knowing Dad would enjoy a day at the track—he used to go to the races in Detroit—I take them up to the grand, historic track in Saratoga Springs. My press pass allows us into the posh turn-of-the-century clubhouse, where we have lunch and watch our horses from the windows, not milling about in the stands with the hoi polloi—but it's rather subdued up there, and so are we, removed from the boisterous earthiness of hanging out with the masses. My parents come up to the *Knick*'s office and meet my boss, the city editor. With Dad out of earshot one afternoon, Mom tells me how proud Dad is of me, how he puts up my stories on a bulletin board at his coin shop and brags about me to everyone—My daughter's covered a space shot, they sent her to Houston, take a look, front page!

Huh, I think. Just, huh. It would mean so much more if he ever said something himself. Coming secondhand, the praise registers like a mental shrug. It doesn't feel particularly swell to have proven his past naysaying wrong, and besides, he's been right, too. I am a woman who had a baby, even if I don't know where she is, even if they don't know I had a baby. I have not outwitted being female. My best-laid plans have turned to ashes. My ambition might have been running in a race against my gender, but fate set out a trap for me that I stumbled headlong into. Sometimes at night I could practically hear a Greek chorus mocking my folly. Hubris might not show up on my official curriculum vitae, but it would be there, writ in invisible ink between the lines. Hold it up to the light, and you'd see it there.

But we do not speak of any of this. A big reality gap yawns between us, and I feel it most keenly with my dad. Maybe because the remembrance of years we had been close, before our falling out, is so deeply embedded, like a thick layer of metamorphic rock resistant to removal. I would always know the words to the folk songs of his youth that he sang to me when he put me to sleep. I would always have his naturally speedy gait when I walked. I would always remember our intense Scrabble games on Mom's bowling nights, and how I ran up the steps to my room when we heard the car in the driveway because I was supposed to be in bed by nine—and it was creeping toward ten. I would always remember how he kidded me that I took up his hobby of collecting coins—Lincoln pennies, in my case—but only between dolls and boys. I would always remember his teaching me how to drive his red Ford pickup with its cranky stick shift when I was sixteen. I would always cherish his offer to drive me to Saginaw to start my new life. He's the one I could have told my secret to without a hue and cry. He would have been understanding, and not full of recrimination and tears, but I couldn't bring myself to tell him because I couldn't ask him not to tell Mom.

On the fourth day, Dad says, *You work all the time. We're leaving.* No words about the fuzzy past have been spoken, but my parents' affectionate visit is a sign that there's a rapprochement between my father and me. Our filial bond has been tested and nearly severed, but finally, time has stitched it back together.

Patrick? He still phones, usually on a Friday afternoon before we both leave the office. Though his calls are devoid of plans for the future and no longer end with protestations of love, I relish these chats. I feel calm hearing his voice. We talk like old friends. He reads the *Knick*—newspaper offices always have papers from around the state, and especially from the state capitol—and praises my stories. He tells me office gossip of people from my former life. He tells me what he has been covering. One Friday he says he has quit the newspaper and taken a job as communications director for Monroe County's Republican committee. Regular hours, better pay, he says.

Wow.

I mentally add: no late meetings to cover, check; no hanging out at the Towpath, check; he will be home for dinner every night, check; The Wife is pleased, check! But Patrick Brasley, a flak for the GOP? Journalism is a calling—his calling—and this is a mere job. He's not even a Republican.

I mute my surprise, though he knows I understand everything unsaid in what he has announced.

The Wife is learning to play chess, he adds.

Can this marriage be saved by chess? I do not say. Way too cheeky.

We are two characters in a tragic love story with roles preordained by circumstance and choice. His choice. No matter what else would happen in our lives, where we would go, how things would turn out, Patrick would always be the father of my child. My only child. Of this, I am sure.

Patrick and I would always be bound by her.

At the end of August, I find myself with a few days off and go to Nantucket. After wandering around by myself for a couple of days, I am in love with the place but as lonely walking aimlessly around as I am in my apartment back in Albany.

Figure 5. In Albany at the Knickerbocker News, recovering from a torn ligament in my knee, which I tore dancing the twist with my future husband at a frat party.

The beaches are inviting—but I am afraid to swim in the ocean alone. The town is charming, but how many pretty blocks of well-kept period houses can I walk down? One afternoon I drop into a bar full of young people, but recoil at the hipness and cheer they radiate. I'm still that shy person. And now I feel fat. Thank god trapeze-style dresses are popular. They hide the nearly twenty pounds I've gained.

Into this quaint setting comes a tall, slim, and appealing young man. I am walking up and down Nantucket's Main Street, looking in windows, just walking, nowhere to go, wondering what to do about dinner. I can't stand eating alone in a good restaurant one more time.

He stops me on the sidewalk. He smiles broadly and says, I said to myself that if you walked by three times, I'd approach you. Would you like to have a cup of coffee. Well, yes, I'd very much like to be rescued from walking aimlessly around.

He is twenty, five years younger than me, still in college. Okay, he's young and inexperienced—and I feel quite the opposite in matters of the heart—but he's nice, we can talk, he makes me comfortable. He's working on Nantucket for the summer. He is going back to his junior year at Bucknell University in a few weeks. The next night he picks me up for dinner. And the next night after that. We make plans to stay in touch after we go back to our off-island lives.

He surprises me by asking me to come to Bucknell for homecoming weekend, and although the idea seems off-the-wall—I am a woman of the world, not a coed—I say, Yes. Why not? I have nothing to lose, and I could see what it might have been like if I'd gone to John Carroll when Tom asked me. I go on a crash water-and-protein diet and shed fifteen pounds. When I get to Bucknell, he doesn't just say I look great, he nonchalantly notes that I've lost weight and that in fact, after he asked me to come, he'd had doubts about having such a, er, chubby date to introduce to his fraternity brothers. Some women might have been put off, but instead, after hearing too many times about "beautiful eyes" as code for ignoring my oversized proboscis, I admire his spontaneous honesty. So would any biologist, which in fact is what he is studying. Body and mind are one package, right, but now the body where my mind resides is not the same as it once was. I had been well schooled in how life was different after my nose job, even if I felt I was the same person.

But I'm not, am I? The world wouldn't see me the same if they knew.

We eat and party at his frat house, I stay at a hotel in town, and a carefree, exuberant weekend unfurls like a beach blanket on warm sand. It is the weekend I'd never had when I was in college myself.

By Christmas my handsome young beau asks me to marry. He is driving my Ghia, and we are going to a restaurant on a sunny day in the countryside around Albany. I look out the window, take a deep breath, and say, Before I say yes, I have to tell you something. I'm not looking at him, I stumble around a bit and finally force the words out without stopping or shedding tears. I add that I know I could never have another child. This is final and nonnegotiable. I make sure he understands.

As he hears the basics of the story, he is calm and does not ask more. He says he does not want children either—he is quite positive about it. Then *yes*, I say. *Yes*. Lickety-split I am diving headlong into a marriage built on a flimsy foundation of utter desperation.

His proper, pillar-of-the-community, Protestant parents protest like holy hell when he announces our intentions, which are to marry at the end of the school year so we can go to Nantucket as a couple for summer. We will work at the Sea Cliff Inn, the big old heap of weathered boards and salty memories where he'd worked the summer before. To make this all possible, I'll quit my job at the newspaper. I know it sounds more than a little daft as I write about it decades later, but it seemed wonderful and madcap and right at the time. He is offering me a taste of a life that eluded me before.

His father eventually offers him a trip to Europe if he drops this absurd idea—but the whole enterprise depends on us getting married. And this time, for the first time, I sense I have the power to make this marriage become my happy landing. His parents' relentless opposition, his father's numerous phone calls to him at school, result in our pushing the marriage forward to his spring break. He tells his father that he is coming to meet my parents that February. That is true, but we now plan to marry then. Our marriage will demonstrate his independence from such a demanding, authoritarian father, a modern-day Montague.

I had told my parents at Christmas that we planned to marry before summer, and they reacted to the new date calmly. Perhaps they suspected something odd about my rush, perhaps they suspected I had some mystery man in those murky months when I was incognito, but whatever they said to themselves, they said nothing to me, and my mother gave off a whiff of relief. Their wandering daughter would be settled. But what would I do after the summer, they wanted to know? Why, I'd get a newspaper job either near Bucknell or—at the *New York Times*! I was already in communication with Charlotte Curtis, the famed women's editor and society chronicler at the paper—yes, it was a women's department, no matter that they called it something else—but it was the *New York Times*! I'd been sending clips to the *Times*' metro editor but getting nowhere. Another *Times*' reporter covering the legislature in Albany who knew Charlotte well—and knew the likelihood of me landing a job outside of women's news was nearly nil—mentioned me to her. Now she'd seen my clippings and hadn't blown me off. Just typing this makes the idea of spending the summer playing hostess in a resort dining room seem off-the-wall, but that was the plan.

I loved my husband-to-be, make no mistake, but there was a manic, desperate quality about all this, especially giving up my job at the *Knick*. Yet going to Nantucket for the summer had an innocent lightness about it, a relief from the years of working to make the writing life I wanted a reality, a vision that began, really began, in the ninth grade when I got on the high school newspaper. Since then, I'd either been working ninety miles an hour toward my goal of having a newspaper career or I'd been binding up my self-inflicted wounds. And now, my young love, naive in some ways, strong in others, accepted me as I was. A summer on Nantucket with him beckoned as a refuge of healing, sunshine, and love. It was irresistible.

Lying through it all—telling the owner of the inn we were married when we were not—did not seem realistic. Not back then, not when unmarried young people like us did not "shack up," as living together was derisively called, at least in my world. Besides, how could I quit my job and go to Nantucket for the summer and not be married? If not for marriage, how could I change my life so drastically?

Indeed.

No, the only way forward was to marry. That would give me respectability. That would prove I was worthy—or at least good enough—to be married. That would be that. I'd be settled. The ring on my finger would be authentic.

Never underestimate the desperate need of a woman who has lost a child to plunge into a hasty marriage. *Damn the torpedoes! Full speed ahead!*

Yes, we must marry.

Then my father dies. Heart attack, like before. A lifetime of smoking unfiltered Lucky Strikes caught up with him. He was fifty-eight years old.

There is a lot I recall about the sadness, the wake and funeral, the family, my younger brother still in high school, worried about what my mother would do now, how fully I would miss my father from that day forward. What had been unsaid between us would always be unsaid, but what I remember most is thinking that he died without knowing about my daughter. I wasn't sure if his not ever having to know made the secret of her existence easier to live with or harder. I throw two pink roses onto the casket as it is lowered—one from me, one for my daughter. Now I wouldn't disappoint him with the news that she was gone, but I wouldn't be able to ever have his solace either. My feelings were a medieval tapestry of a complicated tableau.

Goodbye Daddy, I love you, goodbye.

The wedding goes forward as planned, a small affair in a judge's office, me in a pale pink crepe-and-satin cocktail dress off the rack at Macy's.

It will do.

Search

10 The Personal Becomes Political

JULY 1972—"Adopted Children Who Wonder, 'What Was Mother Like?'" is the headline that rivets my attention when I turn the pages of the *Times* one morning.[40] A woman named Florence Fisher, I read, had an awakening after an accident when the doctor in the emergency room asked for a family medical history and she had no information to give: she was adopted. Assuming she wasn't the only person who experienced this, Florence ran a small ad in the classified section of the *New York Times*. The response was overwhelming—and included, to her surprise, a number of letters from mothers who had relinquished children to adoption. It hadn't even occurred to her that they would be looking too. She ran a second ad, this one directed at mothers. The Adoptees' Liberty Movement Association (ALMA) was born. There were already more than a thousand members.

I knew it!

Adopted people do want to know who their natural parents are! It's not only mothers like me who want information—it's our children, too! Mothers like myself are also in ALMA—I am not the only sad sack out there! Maybe my daughter wants to know me. ALMA's aim, I read with growing elation,

---

[40] Enid Nemy, "Adopted Children Who Wonder, 'What Was Mother Like?'" *New York Times*, July 25, 1972, Family Food Fashions Furnishings, 22, https://web.archive.org/web/20220825203529/https://www.nytimes.com/1972/07/25/archives/adopted-children-who-wonder-what-was-mother-like.html.

is not only to provide support and assistance in searching but to "abolish the existing practice of sealed records." Hallelujah!

After the excitement of reading the story falls away, a kind of serenity comes over me. Adoption curiosity, the need to know one's family, one's blood kin, works both ways. I always wanted to believe it, but I kept my feelings in check, only pouring some of them out in an essay I wrote over the winter: "That will always be the hardest part: never knowing what you are or who you are or what you have become. Every time that I read or hear about an adopted child your age, will I wonder if it is you? And later will I look at engagement pictures in the newspaper and wonder if one of them is you? The guilt I still carry with me today, because she is not with me, weighs me down, doing somersaults in my head every time I talk to a child her age."[41]

The piece is on the stands that July day. It was written with buckets of tears and high hopes, but mainstream women's magazines had rejected it. *Too outré* was the coded message in the politely written rejections. Eventually, a smart new publication called *New Woman* bought it. Since I wasn't ready to put my name on the piece, the editor gave it the innocuous byline of "Phyllis Bernard" and a ridiculous headline: "Things Your Husband/Lover Never Told You about Sex." It is my first piece about giving up my baby, and I'm pretty sure my husband hopes it will be my last. As the cliché goes, once I got it off my chest, I'd be done. But when something is in the air, it manifests itself in multiple places.

One day some obscure book is a crossword clue in the *Times*, the next evening it's a *Jeopardy* clue, and a day later someone says they are reading it and asking if I have. I read and reread the *Times* piece that morning, sitting in a half-empty apartment on a royal-blue velvet couch left by the previous tenant. I'm in Manhattan, in one of those spacious treasures on the west side you'd keep forever. But it's a week after I called it quits on my marriage, and my husband is about to move out. In another week, I'll sell the couch, he'll take the bed, and I will sleep on the floor until I find a new place, one that I can afford. Alone.

Why did my marriage fall apart?

------

[41] Lorraine Dusky [Phyllis Bernard, pseud.] "Things Your Husband/Lover Never Told You about Sex," *New Woman,* June–July, 1972, 24, 26, 28.

I knew soon enough that it would not last. We spent a few days on Martha's Vineyard before we got to Nantucket that summer, and one night a premonition of some tomorrow when we would not be together flitted through my consciousness like the flyby of a hummingbird. Maybe it was something he said or didn't say. Yet I had set my course, and now was not the time to alter the destination. I put the thought away somewhere, like a box in the back of the top shelf in a closet you rarely open.

Nantucket turned out to be grand, just as I'd imagined, and the job offer at the *Times* came through. Indeed, and alas, it was in the women's department—Family Food Fashion Furnishings, the same section that the ALMA story had run in. But this was the *New York Times*, women in hard news on the third floor amounted to two, as I recall, and so I leaped at the offer, squelching any misgivings. Besides, the parameters of what was "women's news" were being interpreted rather broadly. Even so, during the course of several interviews before I was hired, I mentally flinched when the metropolitan editor said in passing, Oh yes, I remember your clips, but I guess it's too late since you're going to work for Charlotte.

My husband and I found a newly renovated but affordable railroad apartment in a part of Manhattan then called Hell's Kitchen, and he went back to Bucknell that fall. I burned up the roads between us on numerous weekends, driving the two hundred miles each way too many times. One Sunday night returning to New York, much too tired to be making this trip and weaving through hairpin turns, I spun out on a mountain road. If someone had been coming the other way, I could have died. If I'd gone over the cliff, I could have died. My life might have seemed as if it was getting back on track, but it was still as out of control as the terrifying moment of my near-fatal accident.

And what a misfit in Charlotte's crew I turned out to be. The copy desk there wanted one of their own to have my slot as a writer, and they were miserable to me and merciless with my copy. Charlotte expected me to jump in and interview third-rate royalty who happened to be in town, or to call socialites for tidbits—so not in my comfort zone—and I couldn't fully appreciate how cool it was that a coworker's kid in private school had playdates with Lennie Bernstein's kids. I never had to write about food or furnishings, but I did have to dream up something clever about how colorful pantyhose had become. I left the *Knick* for this? I didn't last long.

I didn't try the other newspapers in New York City. After the *Times* all else seemed like a comedown. I turned down a job at *TIME* magazine in the women's ghetto of Research, which meant you did a lot of grunt work for a writer—a man, of course—but never got to write yourself or, god forbid, write anything that led to a byline, the signifier that you actually could write as well as any man. But I did need a job, and right away. With a husband in college—I was now paying all the bills—I didn't have time to sit back and lick my wounds.

A woman who sat near me at the paper covered "beauty"—yes, that was a beat—and said she knew of an opening in public relations for Clairol. Though it was something I never would have considered before, public relations sounded like a place to hit a reset button. A place to rest and not think about my career. A place to leave the job when I left the office. The job was to be the assistant of the well-established woman who did media publicity. It paid well, but being an assistant after years of being the master of my own time was like forcing me into a hair shirt that was always going to itch. But soon enough, there I was. I bought clothes of the ladies-who-lunch sort, because now I was expected to lunch with beauty editors. It felt like I had landed on another planet, but soon I learned to read a French menu and never order stuffed artichoke. It took too much time to eat.

This was all happening while young men were still dying in Vietnam. After several nail-biting months, my husband, with his straight-arrow background and Eagle Scout badge, was granted conscientious-objector status and, after graduation, assigned to work in a Manhattan hospital. He grew his hair long and wore bell-bottoms to work while I wore my uptight outfits and took the crosstown bus to Clairol's Park Avenue corporate office. I began writing on weekends. In time, I sold a piece to a magazine, which led to another, and after nearly two years, I had a small collection of bylined pieces, enough, I reckoned, to allow me to chuck PR and turn to freelancing full-time, a precarious occupation that grants freedom, infuses glamour, and eliminates steady income. Risky business, all right.

In the middle of all this, Patrick phoned. He was divorced, working for

Newsday on Long Island, and living in an apartment near the newspaper. Was I surprised? Yes. And no.

We had lunch. I did not tell my husband.

Patrick and I had another lunch.

A spark had been ignited, maybe it had never gone out, and soon enough we flew into our familiar camaraderie and chattered as if we'd never been apart. *Why didn't you leave your marriage when we could have kept her?* sped in and out of my mind like a Formula One race car making lap after lap. But I'd lived through the answer of children and church, and what was the point of speaking of the road not taken? Our daughter was gone. I couldn't be mad at him.

Another lunch. At least four or five over as many months. This one at a cozy French bistro called Chez Napoleon. Before the crème caramel, he asked me to come live with him on whatever terms I wanted. What he was proposing now was what I had once wanted more than anything.

I said I'd think about it.

It was too late. Leaving my husband now, and for Patrick, felt so wrong, so cruel and inexcusable.

Or perhaps my refusing Patrick then was an act of self-preservation, unconscious though it was. Living with him would be a near-constant reminder of what we had not done, the courage we lacked, the child we had lost. One little-known finding is that women who stay in relationships with the father of the relinquished child are at "greater risk for prolonged grieving."[42]

A week later, I said no.

My husband and I stayed together for a couple more years. The marriage was never really bad. We had our usual run of disagreements and arguments and make-up sex, but as time passed, I knew he was wrong for me, and I think by then the marriage was wrong for him too. He had taken to saying

---

[42] Smith, *Safeguarding*, 51. One experienced confidential intermediary, someone who locates and contacts either first parents or adoptees, told me that in her experience the probability of reunion goes down when the biological parents are together. I hazard a guess that the parents' collective guilt over not being able to keep a child when clearly they were a couple is the root cause of this reaction. Both may feel such deep regret and guilt that they are unable to confront their feelings, meet the lost child, and thus have to explain why they were not kept.

"When you leave me . . . " as if he hoped I would, as if he'd found tea leaves in the bottom of a cup or had crawled into the recesses of my mind. Though the little dresses from my days in PR were long gone, I still was not hip enough for him. Now he wanted me to throw out my makeup and care less about my career. He wanted to be married to a different person, but he didn't want to be the one who called it quits. The marriage might once have been right for both of us, but four years later, a marriage based on past needs was only being held together by inertia. Though I could not foresee what my life would become, I knew I had to be free and unhindered by considerations about how what I would write, and say, would affect a partner, no matter who that person might be. My husband's parents, who went to the country club on Saturday evening and to church on Sunday morning, would have bellowed loudly if the story of the baby came out. They knew nothing of her. They'd already had to deal with his secret marriage to an older woman. At the time I had no inkling that my focus would turn so quickly to the birth and adoption of my daughter, or that adoption reform would ultimately consume my life. Only later could I fully grasp that it had been absolutely critical that I be solo during this transformation.

Before the sun went down that evening in July when I first learned of what's called the adoption reform movement, I dashed off a note to an editor at *Cosmopolitan* and proposed a piece on adoption slanted to their audience. I did not mention my connection—Hey! I'm just on top of what's current.

Shame still stuck to me like tar in 1972. You might wear love beads and flowers in your hair, but admit that you had a baby and gave it up for adoption? Wow, man, that's a bummer. My secret must be stuffed down, way down. Six years after my daughter's birth, I'd only told one other person besides my husband, but one afternoon my secret popped out unexpectedly.

A woman I did not know well and I were out to lunch at a funky, festive joint called Bill's Gay Nineties. We sat together in a booth, ordered Bloody Marys and were talking about our lives up to then. Quite unexpectedly, it felt safe to let my secret escape. "Me too," is what she said.

I wasn't alone. I wasn't the only person with this flaming scar on my breast. I wasn't the only woman walking around pretending to be normal.

When she got pregnant, she had dropped out of a Seven Sisters college, moved away, had the baby alone, and finished school elsewhere. Like me, she had found a way back to life after.

Clearly I could tell a friend, but the world? Never. It was too much. Going public in print would change everything. I'd always be the object of either pity or scorn, tarred with scandal, a woman who did *that thing*, an outlier from the rest of humanity. First and foremost, I'd always be a woman who gave away a child. No, I did not imagine that I would ever go public. Not ever. Not in a million years. My mother did not know, and I thought I might never tell her. It would make her so sad.

Soon enough after my husband moves out, so do I—can't afford the rent myself—and within weeks, I am situated in a sixth-floor walk-up in a tenement on First Avenue, sharing my apartment with omnipresent cockroaches and odd or elderly neighbors—but I am free.

By then Patrick is married—to someone from Rochester, someone he met after I left Rochester—and he has another child. A daughter. Of course it would be a daughter. Just like Tom has a daughter. Just like Patrick and I have a daughter. Instead of a daughter, I have an assignment from *Cosmopolitan* to write an as-told-to piece from the viewpoint of an adopted woman who searched and reunited with her natural mother.

I call Florence Fisher, the star of the *Times'* piece. She and I meet one blistering-hot September afternoon at her apartment in upper Manhattan. There are touches of turquoise everywhere. I play it cool—just the journalist, that's me—until halfway through the visit. I'm one of the mothers, I say, stifling back what feels like a deluge about to break through the levee. She says she suspected as much almost as soon as she opened the door. With flaming red hair, plain speech, and a welcoming manner, Florence makes me iced tea and pats my knee. Later I would see the fire in her, but that day she is soft-spoken and kind.

Carrying a secret around is hard work, and now I am finally letting down my guard—with her, at least. She is from the other side of the equation, but she understands my torment, for it is the opposite of hers, and as bottomless. She is the first adopted person I have ever talked to, or at least the first one I know is adopted. Maybe my daughter will be like Florence. Maybe she wants to know me as much as I do her. But *maybe*, where my daughter is concerned, is a bitter brew of hope and fear. I am terrified that she will reject me.

Florence suggests I write about a woman who found out she was adopted from a cousin, while her parents denied it for years. The woman agrees—as long as she is anonymous. The story is accepted within days after I turn it in. Now the long wait till publication.

I write to Northaven Terrace, giving them my new address, in case my daughter's parents ask for it, in case something has gone wrong, in case she needs me now. "To Whom It May Concern: It will be eight years this April since my daughter was born. Can you tell me if she is even alive?" it begins, desperation leaking out of line after line.[43]

An answer comes within days, just before Christmas, from a concerned and kind director of social services. She says she is glad I felt free to write. "I am happy to be able to tell you that your little girl was adopted by a family who have been most delighted with her." She adds that the couple had talked extensively about their feelings toward their children's natural parents, and that they would surely "convey the idea that the child was surrendered because her mother loved her." She ends by saying she knew that while she could not relieve my heartache, she hopes "these few words will give you some measure of comfort."

At least the response is sympathetic. There is that. Yet "most delighted" sticks in my craw. What does that actually mean?

At the time, in almost every state the original birth records of adoptees were sealed. Unless there was some fluke in the system, so was my daughter's. In its place, a new one had been issued, a piece of paper stating that her adoptive parents had given birth to her on the same date and at the same place as I had. It was most likely stamped *amended*, but that merely indicated much of the document was falsified. A lie. A big, fat lie. The court records of the

---

[43] December 12, 1973. Copies or originals of the correspondence are in the author's possession.

adoption itself were also sealed. Adoption agencies by law were not to divulge any information without a court order.

These children were acquiring new identities, ones that would supposedly suffice all of their lives as well as protect the sanctity of the new family and bolster the idea that getting a baby this way was nearly the same as having one the old-fashioned way. Legal scholar Elizabeth Samuels writes, "Over time . . . legal rules established a nearly universal regime of secrecy . . . [that] itself inevitably influenced social attitudes and understandings. Actions once thought natural, such as attempts by adoptees to learn information about their birth families, came to be socially disfavored and considered abnormal. Such attempts acquired negative social meanings: they were the psychologically unhealthful product of unsuccessful adoptions that had failed to create perfect substitutes for natural families created by childbirth, and they indicated adoptees' rejection of and ingratitude toward adoptive parents. Eventually, lifelong secrecy would be viewed as an essential feature of adoptions in which birth and adoptive parents did not know one another." [44]

Cosmopolitan runs the piece the following June—with a line on the cover embellishing the story's importance: "I Found My Mother." I note that no admonishing adjective is added to diminish the word *mother*.

The woman the story is about states that after she confronted her parents about being adopted, they kept up the falsehood that she was their biological child.[45] She caught her adoptive mother in several lies—where and when she was born kept changing—and not until she was twenty-one did her mother admit the truth. In her quest to find her natural mother, the woman became a nurse and got a job at the hospital where she was born. "I would look at the babies headed for the foundling home and feel an acute kinship: We're in this together, and it's not as easy as everyone thinks, growing up and never knowing the truth about yourself. . . " When the hospital yielded no information, she moved on to the Catholic home from which she had been adopted. But the

---

[44] Samuels, "Idea of Adoption," 2–3.
[45] Lorraine Dusky, "I Found My Mother," *Cosmopolitan*, June 1974, 62–69, 134–42.

records were stored on microfilm stashed in the basement. A friendly nun who might have helped didn't have the keys to the filing cabinets.

Eventually the woman became engaged to a man whose brother was a priest, and he—at last—was able to spring her records from the Mother Superior at the adoption agency. Once the woman had her mother's name, finding her turned out to be remarkably easy—she still lived at the same address. Her mother's first words to her daughter were, "I always thought you'd find me." But not everything went smoothly: "My natural mother and I got off to not too good a start when she asked, with what I considered rather too much casualness, how life had gone for me. 'Just fine!' I said sarcastically, and wanted to add, 'What do you really care?'"

Her anger dissipated in time. "My resentment dissolved, however, when she told me how painful it had been for her to live through my birthdays, and how she never stopped wondering about me. Eventually, we got down to the most basic matter: 'Why? Why did you give me away?' She said she'd always been sorry, but that she also knew I'd probably never be able to understand. I guess I never will fully grasp her reasons, but when I left two days later, I felt I'd found a friend."

When she told her adoptive parents she had found her natural mother, only her father would talk to her, meeting her for occasional lunches. But she and her mother eventually reconciled, and she was able to have a relationship with both mothers, one on each coast: "I'm no longer troubled by unanswered questions, I'm a whole person with my own past; this new tranquility makes all the difference for the future."

The story runs with the addresses of ALMA in New York City and Orphan Voyage, an adoptee organization in Colorado.[46] Both are inundated with hundreds of letters from adoptees and natural mothers. I know my daughter is too young to be reading *Cosmopolitan*—but would she be like this woman in ten years? Does her adoptive mother read *Cosmo*? Maybe when she is at a salon sitting under the dryer?

---

[46] Orphan Voyage was the name Jean Paton, an early pioneer of adoption reform, used for her work, which was a one-woman operation but influential in the early days of the adoption reform movement.

At ALMA's monthly meetings I find immense relief simply being with other women who are searching for their children and adoptees looking for their mothers. In the world outside those walls, we must hide our anguish and grieve in silence without sympathy from society or our families, but here we are able to speak freely about what is tearing us apart. We've had it drummed into us that adoption is a good thing, that we are supposed to make new lives and put this all behind us. But the secrecy is suffocating. No one at ALMA brushes me off by suggesting therapy or gets that look in their eyes that conveys that I need to "put this behind me and move on." We all understand that with a living, breathing person out there in the vast unknown, moving on is next to impossible without deadening a part of your soul.

So, month after month, on Saturday mornings, I show up wherever the gatherings are held—in church halls, in meeting rooms somewhere. After the open meetings, search sessions are held for adoptees over eighteen and mothers with children over eighteen. Florence is aware that what she is doing is going up against the entrenched establishment of closed adoption, a revered institution with law on its side. Maybe what she's doing is illegal. To stem some of the criticism, women with underage children like me are kept out of the search sessions. But still I hear whispers: Some women get lucky when they write the state asking for a copy of the child's new amended birth certificate by simply using their name at the time of the birth. Thus encouraged, I write to the state health department in Albany, use my husband's name, and request a birth record of "Unknown Dusky or Brasley," but inexplicably write down the wrong birth date—April 3 instead of April 5—on the application, and enclose a two-dollar fee for a certified copy. A few weeks later, a notice from the Bureau of Vital Records arrives, stating that a "diligent search" was made between the years of 1965 and 1967 for a birth certificate with those names and none was found; I will be mailed a fifty-cent refund at a later date. The next time I see my doctor, I ask him if he would get my records from the hospital. He knows my story. He does not ask why. The records reveal only that she weighed four pounds, four ounces at birth and was jaundiced. All this I already know, but I now have a document to prove she was born.

When Florence takes ALMA nonprofit, I am part of the inner circle and one of the original board members. Our first official meeting is held at the west-side apartment of Betty Jean Lifton, an adoptee and therapist who is in the middle of writing a memoir about searching for, and finding, her mother.[47] B. J., as she is called, is the cool intellectual, but Florence is the engine behind the movement. Short in stature, long on passion, she is quick to laugh and just as quick to push back against critics. We are all are sure we have the wind of justice at our backs. We will succeed one day. Failure is not an option.

To stay afloat and sane, I've been writing for other magazines on a variety of subjects as eclectic as the publications—fasting for health at a spa in Mexico for *Town & Country*, a profile of a hot-air balloonist for the men's magazine *True*, the novel sperm banks that had just sprung up for *Cosmo*, and travel pieces for the *New York Times*. For a story on women skydivers, I end up in Hungary at an international skydiving competition. Unfortunately, the women's sports magazine that gave me the assignment folds before my story runs, and there goes my paycheck. I borrow money from my mother to pay the rent. She worries about me.

I have begun writing more of my own story, and I tell a few more that I am writing a memoir about giving up my daughter for adoption. Ironically, it is easier to tell a man, for he does not pepper me with intimate questions. Going public on this limited level prods me to keep going. If I say I am doing it, I'd actually have to do it. Yet I start and stop and sputter. I write a lengthy prose poem about the experience and never-ending sense of loss and send it off to a publication using a fanciful pseudonym—a play on my name I'm embarrassed to admit I concocted—Alsace Dawn—Alsace for Lorraine and Dawn for Dusky.

The rejection comes back with this written on it: This has the sound of "what might have been."

So? You want an upbeat ending?

I keep on writing.

A sonar beep keeps coming in from somewhere unknown. The message: I need you.

---

[47] Betty Jean Lifton, *Twice Born: Memoirs of an Adopted Daughter* (St. Martin's Press, 1998).

11   Taking a Stand

FEBRUARY 1974—I'm in an airless, overheated courtroom in the Bronx, and I will soon testify—as a natural mother—that we do want to know our children. An accountant named Ann Scharp is trying to get the records that were sealed thirty-seven years earlier when she was adopted. Her identity is likely to be sealed in papers at Spence-Chapin Adoption Services. She's there to show that she has "good cause" to get her records from Spence-Chapin. If any adoptee has taken the trouble to go to court to learn their identity, doesn't that demonstrate prima facie that she ought to be able to find out who she is? But never mind—we know that whether or not her "cause" will be deemed good enough depends solely on one person, this man in a black robe sitting up high in the judge's seat.

Several witnesses will be called. There's Florence Fisher, who testifies not only about the twenty years she spent looking for her mother and father but also about the flood of letters from adopted people she received after she put her first ad in the paper. Now ALMA, the organization she started, has chapters in several cities around the country. Of course Florence would be here. For now, she is the voice and rock of our movement.

Robert Jay Lifton, psychiatrist and author married to Betty Jean, is our outside ace in the hole. As he is a heavyweight in the wider intellectual world on the psychological effects of war and violence, he'll be harder to rebuff than the people personally connected—that's me and Florence. We also have a children's psychologist who will testify for Ann Scharp. Our attorney is a strong, indomitable woman who survived Auschwitz as a child, Gertrude

Mainzer. Spence-Chapin has two lawyers, their own counsel, and a supporting player representing the City of New York. Why has the mayor sent someone? But what we are espousing is revolutionary. Adoption is revered, an institution that should not be threatened or even questioned—and searching certainly is somehow illegal. Spence-Chapin probably asked for the show of officialdom's support against us upstarts.

I'm in some kind of a middle ground, one part expert—as the author now of several magazine pieces on sealed records—one part natural mother myself. I'm wearing the only dress I own, a Betsey Johnson black-and-floral-print number that's far from a miniskirt. Whether or not I'll use my real name is up in the air—Gertrude has told me that I don't have to—but if I don't, what impact will my words have? I'll only represent women in the closet. I am coming to terms with using my name. I'm afraid, but I realize anonymity is gutless. Okay, I can do this. Somebody has to stand up.

Yet.

Telling your story about the daughter that was but isn't is always—always—an internal firecracker. It gets easier with time, but it's never easy. The sympathetic nervous system takes over, the adrenaline pumps, the heartbeat increases. Every time I talk about the loss of my child, I am reminded that no matter how, no matter why, I was a consenting participant in my daughter's relinquishment. I'm hot with anxiety as the words tumble out.

This is different. This is public. This is court. I scan the room to see if any members of the press are there. They don't seem to be. Still, they could be, and if they are, I would be identified.

The trial begins.

The psychological experts testify. The psychologist who examined Ann Scharp testifies that her Rorschach test reveals a lack of trust, isolation and constriction of affection.

Oh, my god, will my daughter be like that, too? Did I do that to her?

And when she draws a tree, the psychologist says, she forgets to put in roots.

She broke off an engagement to a man when she found out he, too, was adopted. He could be her brother. Sounds ludicrous, but it's happened.

I keep eyeing Ann Scharp, who sits there impassively, stiffly, throughout the proceedings. I'd want to hug my daughter when we met, and she would probably stand there like a stone. What is my daughter like? Who would she be, right at this moment?

Soon enough, I'm on the stand. After Gertrude recites my credentials as a journalist, she gets to what makes my testimony relevant. When she asks if I have any other special qualifications for this subject, I say loudly and clearly, It's because I am One of Them—a natural mother. I'm obviously nervous, or maybe the judge is surprised, but he stops and offers me a glass of water and asks if I need a moment to compose myself. I'm fine, I say. This is not going to get easier if I take a moment. I am here to counteract the perception that we natural mothers make new lives without looking back. I'm here to announce that we are desperate to know what happened to our children, desperate to meet them one day. I'm here to say that we do not forget.

This is it. My coming out publicly.

If before I was a ho-hum witness, now attention is focused—so this is what "they" look like. I have suddenly morphed from an anonymous woman in a dress into a many-headed hydra, an unpredictable object of wonder.

The stout, red-faced attorney for Spence-Chapin is openly hostile. How scientific is my research?[48] What are my credentials that allow me to speak for other natural mothers? (I have interviewed many, met them at ALMA meetings.) Am I married? (And this is germane how?) Do I have other children? (And this is germane how? But I am not allowed to ask questions.) He is trying to turn me into a lone voice without a chorus. But his belligerence only serves to peel back my anger, and by the time he asks, "Don't you believe that there are other natural mothers—the ones who do not come forward—who would rather forget what happened, forget that part of their lives?" I find my voice and now boom out my response:

"You don't have someone in your body for nine months and forget."

He sits down. No more questions.

Several months later, the judge rules that while Ann Scharp could examine

---

[48] Direct quotes here are from a transcript of the trial in author's possession.

her birth certificate (which apparently did not have the name of her mother on it), she is denied access to her file at Spence-Chapin. He adds, however, that her file contains no information that would identify her natural parents.

So then why not let her have it?

Precedent.

WINTER 1975—I fly to Michigan to tell my mother. Now back in Dearborn, she has an apartment in a senior-citizen complex. If I am going to be public, she has to know before she reads about me somewhere or sees me on television. I tell my mother at lunch, over gin and tonics, and I see her wince when she understands what I am revealing. Her response is pure gold: Oh honey, how was your labor?

In the time it took for a heart to beat, she flies to what she instinctively knows—that labor must have been hell, that I had been almost certainly alone. It was okay, I say. I do not tell her about the hysteric who was held down and shot up with a tranquilizer.

I tell her about testifying, that I will almost certainly do it again, that the press wasn't there but they are likely to be eventually, and furthermore, I am going to write about this—under my real name. She doesn't blink. I explain the law, sealed records, my hope to be reunited with my daughter—her granddaughter—one day.

"If I were adopted, I'd want to know," she says straightaway. "Everybody must want to know where they came from—don't you think? I can't imagine not knowing or wanting to know." No matter how much she and I had once fought when I was younger—and we had, furiously, frequently—no matter how I felt I could not bear the shame of telling her of the pregnancy at the time, how much I felt I had let her down, no matter what had gone on before, she makes me proud to be her daughter: "You are doing the right thing, honey," she adds, tears glistening behind her bifocals. I mention that there will be a lot of chatter when this comes out because her neighbors include parents of people I went to school with. She brushes that aside.

Telling my brothers is nothing after this. They are surprised but subdued and accepting. You do what you have to do. We'll stand by you.

I write an Op-Ed for the *Times*,[49] which, with a haunting illustration by the prominent Jean-Claude Suares, takes up nearly two-thirds of the page:

"Research to date indicates that most natural mothers do not wish to remain anonymous to their children, and have a compelling desire to know who they are. I'm one of the statistics: I am a natural mother. . . . An ongoing California study of more than a thousand adopted persons and natural parents includes data on close to a hundred reunions without a disaster among them. Even if the adopted individuals were disappointed, they reported that reality was infinitely better than endless fantasy."

This is the first time that I'm aware of anyone coming out as a relinquishing mother publicly in print. Not behind a veil on television, not hiding behind "anonymous." To make an impact, to chip away at the concrete wall of lifelong anonymity and sealed records, to make it possible to find my own daughter, to atone for giving her up—and yes, atone is the right word—to encourage other women to come out of the closet, to let them see they were not alone, one had to stand up and be counted. People would see me in a different light, people would talk about me behind my back, and depending on their mindset, they would censure or empathize, see me as trashy or brave. All this I knew.

Yet someone who had done the deed no one wanted to talk about had to swing the first hammer at the wall of accepted adoption practice and law, an enormous concrete hunk of bad social engineering, emotional and legal, that was held up by legions of adoptive parents and adoption-agency workers. They had bought into the idea that it was permissible, even preferable, to act as if the children they adopted had magically arrived by stork without papers of transport or origin, for who knew what sordid tale the truth might reveal.

The day the piece appears in the *Times*, I am aware that now I am fair game for nasty potshots. But the world goes about its business without notice. Nothing happens. Absolutely nothing. No one phones. I walk out on the street and no one points. The sun still sets that night. And I'm going to

[49] Lorraine Dusky, "Yearning," Op-Ed, *New York Times,* March 1, 1975.

be all right. Coming out is easier than expected, undoubtedly easier because I do not have a husband, or his family, to quibble with or embarrass. I don't know what people say behind my back, but I feel a strong wind behind me.

But word does get around through friends and acquaintances, and people—mostly adopted people—blow in and stop for tea or something stronger in my funky First Avenue flat. The front door doesn't lock, but the buzzer and the walkie-talkie system work. One evening a woman I barely know comes by because she needs to talk to someone—she is reeling with the news of having learned only days before that she is adopted. In the heat of an argument with her husband, she'd said something about "my mother," and he shouted back, She's not even your real mother! You're adopted! The marriage was over, she says, but what about her parents, people who had lied to her for most—all—of her life? *They told him, but didn't tell me? What do I do now? I haven't spoken to them since.*

Revelations like this always brought up my own fears—what about my daughter's parents? Have they told her? Does she know she's adopted? That there is me? Because I know nothing, each story haunts me, every hard-luck story could be mine.

A year later, 1976, the New York state legislature, amazingly enough, is considering a bill that will allow people born and adopted in New York to obtain their original, unamended birth certificates. We are quietly thrilled. The time has come.

Maybe.

Florence is planning a lawsuit to have the amended birth certificates be declared unconstitutional, but holds back now. If New York's law falls, could the rest of the country be far behind? Florence and I troop up to Albany with a handful of others—adoptees (including B. J.), adoptive parents, a phalanx of psychologists and social workers, attorneys, adoption-agency heads, and another natural mother who turns out also to be an adoptee, a double whammy that is confoundingly common but new to me that day. I could barely fathom the double layers of pain.

"If I had known that someday I could meet my daughter it would have been so much easier to sign those papers,"[50] I say, speaking into a microphone in a cavernous and largely empty chamber, looking up at the men sitting high above me—maybe they aren't so far above me, but that's how I remember it—the men who could change the rules looking down on us. "My social worker and I went over this point again and again and again. Never, never, could I see her, not ever. Time heals all wounds, she would say. It does not heal this one."

I am asked about the women who do not want to know the children they gave up for adoption—do I agree that they have the right to not have their identities revealed?

"No, I don't." You have a child, you owe them an identity, you owe them at least this—their place in the chain of life.

But Senator Joseph Pisani, co-chair, needs more convincing. "Suppose she said, 'I don't want anyone to know anything about me. This is a final act on my part and one of the considerations of surrender of this child is that I retain anonymity for the rest of my life. I want to get it behind me.' Let's assume she has that attitude. Right, wrong, or indifferent. Should she be entitled to have it as a matter of right, or should she, somewhere down the line, suffer the trauma of a confrontation?"

Trauma of confrontation—from her own child? How about surfeit of joy instead? I mentally respond. But this is not a time to be flip.

"A, I don't believe a confrontation would be traumatic. And B, no, I don't believe she has the right to that privacy. I think that woman's right is infringing upon the rights of adoptees."

Somewhere in the room, a man lets out a loud, disgusted sigh. I turn to look at him. He is the attorney representing the Louise Wise Services, a major adoption agency in New York City that largely served Jewish clients. His name is Shad Polier. The enemy. Tall, distinguished, a graybeard. The old order.

---

[50] All quotes are directly from the Joint Public Hearing, "New York State Senate/ Assembly: Sealed Adoption Records and Identity," Apr. 28, 1976, Albany, NY, https://web.archive.org/web/20081109045659/http://bastards.org/activism/local/ ny/hearings.html.

I refer to an earlier speaker, a representative of the New York Foundling Home, who spoke of the adoptees who come back looking for names and answers. She said her agency had found about half of the hundred or so natural mothers whom adoptees had asked them to look for in the last few years. No one on the panel had asked her how many of the mothers refused to meet their children. I had sought her out during a break before I spoke. "I asked her how many women did not want to meet their children—the ones they contacted." I speak loudly into the microphone. "It turns out there were none. She said that there was one that was reluctant at first, and then changed her mind."

Then the other side is up. Polier goes on in a windy, sonorous voice. He is here today, he says, to speak for the poor, downtrodden "girls" the agency had helped by placing their children. He rattles on about how the poor women/girls who give up their children go into hiding, how they never want be reminded of this trauma. I am the outlier, the unusual exception. His soliloquy is peppered with words such as "disaster," "havoc," "pathology," "harmful." It is infuriating to listen to him. He knows nothing. Who is he protecting?

The next day my picture is on the front page of the *Knickerbocker News*. I had gone from covering the news in Albany to being the news. I had revealed something I once had been so freaked out by that I even had lied to doctors when they asked if I'd ever been pregnant. Oh no, not me!

That session, the legislature in Albany offered a prospective bill—the original birth records would be open only for adoptions that occurred after the bill became law. It excluded anyone adopted from 1935 on until the new law went into effect—and they reached the age of eighteen. It would affect neither my daughter nor thousands of others born in the decades between. Florence was livid. "The only adoptees affected positively by this bill are those who have just been conceived!!!"[51] she opined in irrefutable logic. The others would be forgotten. She had too many plaintive letters from people in their seventies and eighties to acquiesce to this injustice. For anyone already alive, the proposed law would simply recodify the discrimination of the law already in place.

---

[51] Carp, *Family Matters*, 178–81.

Three months later, riding uptown on a New York City bus jammed with sweaty bodies stuffed like olives in a jar—there is no air conditioning—I am reading the *Times* and come upon Shad Polier's obituary.[52] With some amazement I read that Polier had been one of the lead lawyers involved in the defense of the Scottsboro Boys, but I am not surprised that he had drafted the first law in New York terminating parental rights in 1961. The obit includes nothing about his grinding opposition to giving adopted people their rights. I want to point out the good news to the person sitting next to me. I want to say, Look, the enemy is dying off, they will all be dead, and we will win this yet. Do you know what great news this is, that Shad Polier can no longer testify against us?

What was not in the obit is that Shad Polier had been married to the daughter of Louise Wise, whose namesake agency he represented. The Wise name is mentioned several times in the obit, but only Polier's connection to Rabbi Stephen Wise, his father-in-law. The article omits any mention of Louise, his mother-in-law, a woman who founded her eponymous adoption agency. Decades later, some of the awful, barbaric experiments the agency conducted on the babies waiting to be adopted, and the follow-up studies on identical twins and triplets who were separated and adopted into different homes, would come to light. Some of the twins and triplets would find one another, and these reunions make juicy tabloid fodder. Polier must have known about all this; as the agency lawyer married to the owner's daughter, he was protecting his own dirty interests. Louise Wise's shameful and damaged reputation would ultimately force the agency to close.

But none of that was brought to light that day in Albany, only that he represented the agency, and thus was their legal expert.[53]

---

[52] "Shad Polier, Lawyer, Dead; Active in Civil Rights Cases," *New York Times*, July 1, 1976, 32.

[53] Louise Wise Services went out of business in 2010 after a couple of well-publicized lawsuits. In one, a couple was told that they were adopting the son of a bright, accomplished college student who helped support her mother and whose fiancé had unexpectedly died, and she got pregnant soon after during a rebound affair. In fact, the mother was a lobotomized schizophrenic, and the father was also a mental patient; the couple conceived when both were institutionalized. The adoptee was schizophrenic himself, and at his insistence, his parents sued Louise Wise Services. He died at twen-

Florence wastes no time. She was already taking the fight to the courts, hoping that one good decision would open the records for adoptees everywhere. We assume that we will have to go all the way to the Supreme Court to get these laws repealed. Using ALMA members as the basis for a class action suit, she files a federal lawsuit against New York's sealed-adoption-records law.[54] The suit claims that the right to know one's origins is found in the First, Thirteenth, and Fourteenth Amendments. In brief, adopted people are denied the right to useful information and ideas (First Amendment); adopted people bear a badge of slavery, just as children of enslaved people were sold before they were able to know their parents and were forever denied the right to know their parents (Thirteenth); adopted people are made a "suspect class" by being deprived of information that the rest of us have; and their right to privacy is infringed by not allowing them knowledge of their origins (Fourteenth).

We lose. We lose in the district court for the Southern District. We lose on appeal. The reasons given? Unsealing the records would not only disrupt the adoptive family, it would have a negative effect on adoptions to come— that is, natural mothers, fearful of one day being found, would not give up their babies. Despite how skewed this argument is or how presumptive and paternalistic, despite its callous disregard for the emotional cost of bearing a child that will be relinquished, or even how dated the argument sounds, such was the logic of a Judge James L. Oakes who wrote the opinion. Behind it I hear the drumbeat against abortion: If women couldn't be assured of anonymity, there wouldn't be the babies to keep the adoption system churning.

---

ty-nine of undetermined causes. A 2018 film, *Three Identical Strangers*, exposed how the Louise Wise agency had separated identical twins and triplets, without revealing this separation to either the natural mother or the adoptive parents, for the purpose of a psychological nature/nurture study. The children purposely were placed in homes of differing social and economic class. The study was kept hidden at the time of this hearing. Polier was obviously desperate to keep this study "hidden" from the public for its noxious odor of Nazi-era experiments. *Identical Strangers*, a memoir by Elyse Schein and Paula Bernstein, tells the story of identical twins separated by Louise Wise, who also later found each other.

[54] ALMA Society, Inc. v. Mellon, 601 F.2d 1225 (2nd Cir., 1979), cert. denied, 444 US 995, 1979.

Abortions would stem the supply of infants available to be adopted. Today we know that whether birth certificates are sealed or not has no effect on the rate of adoptions—or abortions. And people have always understood that carrying a child to term to be raised by others is a road to be avoided.

We appeal to the Supreme Court, but it refuses to take the case.

The all-male Supreme Court.

I know who I am: I am the daughter of second-generation immigrants from Poland with some German and a smidgen of Russian/Finnish ancestry, as DNA testing revealed. I have pictures of my grandparents that I treasure. I look for my features in one grandmother's face in particular, for it is what I learn about her, Bronisława Maleszinska Drozdowska, that is so recognizable, so serenely satisfying: she was known for her letters to the local newspaper. *So that's where I got that!* is a familiar notion to the unadopted, instantly acknowledging our familial connections via DNA. I've been writing editorials, opinion pieces, and letters to the editor since I was editor of my high school newspaper.

My mother, who remembered her well, said she was somewhat of a *paniusia*. The literal translation is dame, the wife of a knight, but the word has come to mean a lady who carries herself as if she had rights to property, connections, fine clothes. Aha! I recognize that in me, too. Dad said that she had been educated by a governess and came to America by herself, which translates to plucky and fearless to my young ears. Was she fleeing a broken engagement? Seeking adventure? What made her come, by herself? Dad added that he knew her parents had written—probably before she married and had children—pleading that she return home to Poland. My grandfather, Tomas Drozdowski, had once been in the Russian army and a guard at the palace in St. Petersburg for the last czar. My mind immediately conjured up some spanking-clean, colorful uniforms with gold-braided epaulets and dome hats with feathers that "palace guards" most certainly wore; the truth could have been something else.

"Dirt poor" is the phrase that describes my grandparents' lives in the

Figure 6. My paternal grandmother, Bronisława Maleszinska Drozdowska, paniusia, letter writer, and bootlegger.

coal-mining country of southwestern Pennsylvania. But there were touches of relief, for in my father's bedtime stories I learned that music and news came into the house after a sibling won a radio in a contest. That my father used the dime his mother gave him for lunch money and instead went to the "motion pictures" show—that had a live organist! That he spied an Indian Head penny under the floorboards in his bedroom (shared with two or three brothers), fished it out, and thus began his hobby of coin collecting. That he made skis out of wood—gently curving them after soaking the boards—and learned how to speed down the gentle hills near home. That not only did he square dance, but he was the caller!

That after the eighth grade, he joined his father in the mines.

He didn't tell me much about mining; I focused on his quitting school for a full-time job when he was thirteen. I couldn't imagine it.

For extra cash, Grandma made bootleg whiskey in her copper washtub

Figure 7. My paternal grandparents, Tomas and Bronisława Drozdowski, with my aunt Genevieve, whom I knew as Aunt Jean.

during Prohibition, selling a quart-sized Mason jar of the white lightning for fifty cents. Gutsy! I love this woman! Once, the police shut down her home still, but it was Grandpa who spent the night in jail. The way my dad told it, while his life seemed, yes, poor and foreign, it was far from grim. It was chockablock with adventure and derring-do, and a million years ago and as many miles away from our lives at that moment. The utter dreariness of going down in the pits at thirteen—well, I couldn't even fathom that.

The letter writing, the white lightning, the *paniusia* bravura—in those qualities I recognize myself. My dad might have been onto something, for Mom told me when it came to filling out my birth certificate, he automatically gave me the English version of my grandmother's name as my middle

Figure 8. My pioneering role model, Aunt Jean, sixteen in 1926. I've worn bangs most of my life and had not noticed the similarity until finding this photograph.

name—Blanche—even though a middle name for me had not been broached before. The connection I feel to this woman, this grandmother who died before I was born, is an essential part of my being. It makes me grounded, solid—connected to my heritage. So, Grandma Drozdowska (the feminine ending for a traditional Polish name) was something of a rabble-rouser herself in whatever finery she could afford.

Then there's Aunt Jean, the eldest daughter, looking fierce and strong in a flapper dress and pearls, in a photograph taken when she was sixteen. Yes, I think, so that's where I got that, whatever *that* is.

My other grandmother—my mother's mother, Agnes Augustine—was around when I was young. I have a vague memory of her having an extended visit at our house when I was a toddler. She was not living with her husband, my grandfather, and little was ever said about him. He lived in a small apartment at the rear of an uncle's grocery store, and we rarely visited. When we did it was a brief, pro forma pass-through, icy and stilted. I had no idea why.

We saw my grandmother often. She remarried when I was old enough to understand that she was putting herself outside the official rules of Catholicism. She died not that many years later, and all the sisters wept. When my grandfather died a year later, I was thirteen and old enough to notice how my mother and her older sister were merely grim, not sad, as if good riddance was their send-off. Only their younger sister was bereft.

Decades would pass before my mother told me that he sexually abused her older sister and started in on her once but didn't go all the way. After that one time, she said, he left her alone, and she felt that her older sister, now deceased, bore the brunt of his abuse—until Grandma found out and must have stopped it—and divorced him. Suddenly the family dynamic made sense—my grandmother's divorce, the two older sisters' antipathy toward him, and the younger sister's completely different attitude toward him. She must have not known about the abuse. Now Agnes Augustine was not simply the quiet and sickly woman I remembered. She was a brave woman who defied convention to protect her daughters at a time when divorce among Polish Catholics was exceedingly rare and always scandalous. Now I could be pleased, not simply neutral, that she eventually she found happiness when she remarried. No wonder my mother adored her.

In America we have the delusion that this intimate information—this essential, fundamental stuff of identity—can be shunted aside willy-nilly simply because the adoption system prizes anonymity, and that it's all right to grow up in a vacuum. But this attitude inflicts a murky cloud of genetic bewilderment over the natural curiosity adoptees have about their origins. Where do I belong? Who are my people? What are my ancestral stories? Why was I given up?

Good or bad, rich or poor, celebrated or commonplace, family histories are the connective tissue of future generations. Adoptive parents typically don't acknowledge this void in their adopted child. They want to believe love is enough and covers all else. Many discourage their adopted children, no

Figure 9. My maternal grandmother, Agnes Augustine (Wrozek) Grezesikowski. Not only did her divorce cause a scandal, so did her remarriage.

matter what age, from searching for their original parents, and convey this in word or silence about all matters relating to the particular adoption, as if the adopted person's genetic heritage were not a fact of life. Consequently, many adoptees search in secret, or wait until their adoptive parents die. "Reunion with a grave" is a phrase all too familiar to many adoptees.

We all need to know where we come from. Those who do not are at a clear disadvantage in the world, left with an inexplicable hole in their identity that nothing other than the full and unvarnished truth of their distinct, particular heritage can fill. Knowing that my grandfather was an abuser answered the question I had about the stern demeanor of the two sisters—my mother and an aunt—at his burial, while their younger sister wept. Now I know why we hardly ever visited him, and when we did it was short and stilted, endured, not enjoyed, by my mother. Now I appreciate the strong woman I remembered my Aunt Josephine to be. It made me see my grandmother Agnes in a whole new light, and I felt proud to be her granddaughter. I understood my mother's devotion, where before I'd felt nothing particular about her. Good and bad, this rich history is mine, it is a part of who I am. It gives me

Figure 10. My parents, Victoria (née Wrozek) and Harry Dusky.

roots. It makes me whole. It makes me connected. I don't think any more or less of that grandfather after knowing the truth; I had no reason to like him before because I barely knew him. Some might say, Wouldn't it be better not to know the bad stuff? But if I did not know, I wouldn't have the newfound admiration for these strong women in my background. I prefer not to be ignorant of any of it. Truth is a satisfying reality.

Cicero's famous quote sums it up this way: To be ignorant of what occurred before you were born is to remain always a child.

12 Is Anyone Watching?

Between writing about the aftermath of a school bus colliding with a train for *Good Housekeeping* and a profile of the poet Nikki Giovanni for a long-gone magazine called *Ingénue*, I keep squeezing in adoption among my proposals—and fielding the turndowns. Several women's magazine editors tell me the story is "not appropriate" or "not of interest" to their readers. Despite the naysayers, I hit the jackpot at *Parents* with a piece an editor gave this headline: "The Adopted Child Has a Right to Know EVERYTHING."[55] Whoa! I would not have had the chutzpah to suggest a head that bold.

Freelance writing has its perks, but a living wage is not one of them. After writing a couple of froufrou pieces—and one long, serious one that would later be a finalist for a National Magazine Award—for *Town & Country* (*T&C*), the social chronicle of the rich and richer, I jump at the chance to become a senior editor there. I am so not of *T&C* vintage, but neither is the already-celebrated editor-in-chief, Frank Zachary, a steelworker's son who never went to college.

I know nothing of this the day of the interview. At that time, I am still living in the same rent-controlled tenement I'd moved to when my marriage ended. My bathtub is in a nook in the kitchen; the street entrance still doesn't

---

[55] Lorraine Dusky, "The Adopted Child Has a Right to Know EVERYTHING," *Parents,* October 1975, 40–43. The use of the word "child" when referring to adult adoptees sticks in the craw of those working for reform, as they are adults asking for their original birth records and do not want to be thought of as children. While adult adoptees rightfully object to being called "adopted children," whether we are young or old, we all remain someone's child.

150 LORRAINE DUSKY

have a working lock, and my single "closet" is an armoire my husband left behind when we split. I had given away all the ladies-who-lunch clothes.

The morning of my interview I stop in at a small boutique near my apartment and lock onto a stunning dress. You dress for the job you want, not the one you have, I tell myself, but still—this beauty costs a hundred bucks—way above my pay grade! My rent is $130 a month! After stalling for a ridiculous length of time in front of a mirror, I pull out my American Express card and march off to the interview in my splendid new outfit feeling like—dare I say it—if not some movie star's daughter, close enough. The incongruity of where I came from and where I am going doesn't faze me. I know I can do the job—I just have to get hired first.

When Frank asks why I think I could do the job, I coolly point out that as managing editor of a college daily, I came up with story ideas, assigned writers, and edited copy—skills that suit this job. And I'm in.

Now I have my own office and an assistant, and, of course, a work wardrobe must follow—a few suits, a pricey camel blazer, a dress or two. Pants are still unusual in this office. My mother loves that someone else answers my phone when she calls. Me, I'm happy to have a regular paycheck and health insurance. Six months later, when Frank asks me to put together a special section on the broad subject of children, I include a piece on the sealed-records issue in adoption in the proposed lineup and offer to write it myself. Wealthy people adopt a lot. Why not? I have no intention of including my association—the Op-Ed in the *Times* a year earlier did not raise a fuss. No one at the magazine appeared to have seen it—but wouldn't you know, the minute I sit down to write, this is what comes out of my typewriter: "Ten years ago I had a child whom I gave up for adoption."[56]

When the article is published, the words surprise and ripple through *T&C* and land me on the *Today* show. Interviewer Jane Pauley does not treat me like a pariah. Quite the opposite. She responds as if the sorrow of not knowing my daughter is understandable. I can do this, I tell myself. Outside, a light rain is falling—no more than a sprinkle—but enough for me to open

---

[56] Lorraine Dusky, "A Natural Mother Speaks Out on Adoptees' Right to Know," *Town & Country*, Oct. 1976.

my umbrella as I walk up Fifth Avenue to *Town & Country* in patent-leather pumps. I am aware that outwardly I am some version of who I wanted to be since the fourth grade. I have a decent job in publishing in Manhattan—though I cringe at the frivolous image *T&C* conjures up. I am an adjunct professor teaching magazine journalism at City College of New York. I've traded my tenement walk-up for a large apartment with a roommate in a doorman building. I am in a relationship, but it's one of those iffy kinds that certain men specialized in post-Pill. Always going round and round in a cul-de-sac, making stops now and then, but never arriving anywhere.

Did my daughter's parents have the show on in some bedroom somewhere as they got up, listening while they dressed for work? Or maybe the TV was on in the kitchen and my daughter saw it. She would be ten. Did they leave it on, did they turn it off, did they pay attention, does she look like me?

Who else might have been watching? Patrick? Odds are against it. He's working afternoons and evenings, probably not up yet. What about his wife? Does she even know about our daughter? People I went to school with?

Tom? He'd be shocked, all right, but be sad, not condemning, I decide. His mother? She'd think, I knew it all along. That girl wasn't right for my son! If anyone in Jackson saw me, it will make the beauty-shop gossip mill. Do you know what happened to Vicky's daughter? Yet if Tom and I had married? *What might have been* is a refrain no one wants to have running through their head, but that overcast, moody day, walking up Fifth Avenue, everybody in a rush to get somewhere, I can't shake thoughts of him, or how suddenly alone I feel.

I had seen Tom once after we were both married. Two years after my father died, my mother packed up and moved back to Jackson, her hometown. A cousin in Jackson phoned me, insisting I'd be the ideal commentator for the local March of Dimes fashion show there—since I worked on the *New York Times*, certainly I must write about fashion!? would know something about fashion? could make friendly patter about fashion? The charity would pick up the airfare—but you'll want to stay with your mom, right? Last year, she said, a television personality cost a grand plus expenses—I'd save them quite a bit—how about it? With my husband's college expenses eating up my income, a chance to visit my mother without cost—this was an offer I could not refuse.

Tom is working at the Jackson *Citizen-Patriot*, Mom said the day I arrived. After thinking about it for ten minutes, I called; he answered, and a few hours later we were sitting across from each other in a booth at a café. You look good, we said in unison. We did not make smart remarks or opine on world events, and after twenty minutes of chatter, he pulled out a picture from his wallet. His daughter.

Oh.

Do I tell him? No, I can't. I dialed myself down to numb. She's so cute. She looks like you! How old is she? I had to ask.

Only a few months older than my daughter is what I heard.

He proposed lunch. Tomorrow. There was so much more to say.

Yes. I leave in three days.

He chose the dining room at the big old hotel downtown. It was full of businessmen in suits, smoking cigarettes, slapping backs, doing deals. Tom himself was an up-and-coming young man in a suit, working in advertising at the *Citizen-Patriot*. I wore the expensive-but-blah faux-hippie dress I'd bought for my gig as a fashion commentator.

Will he see anybody he knows, I wondered, and how would he introduce me if he did? As the woman from New York who is the commentator for the March of Dimes fashion show? And we are having lunch because? An old friend? Will this get back to his wife? Does he want it to? Will she be at the fashion show? Or his mother? I couldn't help a little internal gloating. This *broad* had already been interviewed for the *Citizen-Patriot*—his parents couldn't miss that.

I ordered wine and noticed he still wasn't drinking when he asks for a Pepsi. We ran over our lives since I'd sent him away at a quarter to three in the morning. We did not talk about our marriages or spouses, except to explain who they were, but I already knew he'd married the hometown girl. I mentioned that I'd had a nose job. He nodded, right. You know it never bothered me, he said. I said, I know.

Why didn't you show up that day? I finally asked. I did not need to add, I waited all day.

He hesitated, he looked away, seconds passed. By the time his eyes got back to mine, they were glassy. I don't know, he said. I don't know.

Silence.

What to say?

It seemed like we might both be overcome with emotion, going down a rabbit hole that we were not ready to fall in. What could I say now? That I was leaning to yes all day? That was too much, that opened too many doors, and I was leaving the day after tomorrow.

A part of me considered telling him everything. A bittersweet remembrance of what was, and an acute awareness of what had not been, caromed around the room. My eyes were glassy too. Nobody smiled. I wanted to say, We wouldn't be living in Jackson, but we should be married. But that was too bold, too sad, too much. We moved to safer ground, talking about what, I do not know, except that the words between us went on as if they had never stopped.

We might not have wanted lunch to end, but the clock hands kept moving around the dial. When he drove me back to my mother's place, the winter sun was already low, the shadows long. We sat and talked, holding back the inevitable. Just as I was about to open the door, he touched my hand and said wistfully, I'll hear from you again. As on that New Year's Eve so long ago, our eyes locked in some ancient and silent language of lovers. What a mistake we'd made back then, we wordlessly agreed. I nodded, slid out of the car, and turned back to watch as he drove away.

Did Tom watch morning television when he was putting on his pants? Could he have caught me on his way out the door? A few weeks earlier Mom had told me that Tom's marriage was not going well. He and his wife might be splitting up. He'd moved to Indiana. The wife and daughter didn't go. Mom is suggesting that I reach out to him. Is he married still—or isn't he? I need hard facts. I have had it with married men and men whose families find some flaw in me. I swat aside the thought of tracking him down and tell her so.

Besides, the phone works two ways, doesn't it? But would he even know that I'm divorced?

A relationship with a brainy, passionate attorney had ended more than a year ago. We'd lived together for months in my sixth-floor walk-up, the words of love had been spoken repeatedly, I thought our connection was much more than for the time being. But we ran into our own Berlin Wall over his family's conniption because I wasn't Jewish. This involved lengthy phone calls from his sister, a visit from his father from Altoona, and a disquieting lunch with the three of us at the Waldorf-Astoria when his father told us point-blank that we had to break up. It was either me or his family, period.

Yet we lingered on for months, even after he moved out. One night, after dinner at his place, after we'd done the dishes, we came to a dead halt when he said about my memoir-in-progress, You'll never do it. He billed by the hour—Can't you just sit down and write the damn book? Without harsh words or a melodramatic goodbye, I simply took whatever stuff I had there and walked out, never to return.

A year after that, Judy, a friend I'd made while at the *Times*, showed Sydney—back from a stint in Southeast Asia with a Pulitzer Prize—pictures from her summer in Sag Harbor. She'd had me out several times over the summer as her guest, and she had a shot of me at the beach. Ever the match-maker, she purposely included that photo. He asked if that was me, and she made a point of telling him I was again single. As was he also. That evening, he called. I said, I have a terrible cold. He could not be dissuaded. He brought over chicken soup from a deli. We stayed together through the changing seasons until it snowed again. It was good, and then it was stale. On New Year's Eve, we ended up together because there was no one else. After we'd made love, I asked myself what I was doing there. He was his same irascible self, and when he went to brush his teeth, I got up, dressed, and zipped up my high-heel suede boots. He was surprised but didn't try to stop me. I walked out onto Riverside Drive at three a.m. and caught a cab to my own apartment. My relationships were sand sifting through my fingers.

A few weeks after the *Today* show appearance, I am in court again, this time in Superior Court in Atlantic City for four women who were adopted in New Jersey. They are asking for their original birth certificates. Today is nothing like the first time. Today, I am breezing in to push my agenda. The time between the last court appearance and this one has stiffened my back-bone. In a tailored black suit, I look like a lawyer myself. Opposing counsel does not intimidate me. My testimony is sharp, my tone determined. World, hear me roar! "I desperately want those records open so that when my daughter is eighteen, she can find me." This time, the story is covered by the *Times*[57] and ABC-TV in New York. Good thing Mom knows.

In the ladies' room during a break, I come across one of the adopt-ed women bringing the suit. She is standing over a sink weeping profusely. When I try to console her, she says between sobs, "What you said—about never forgetting—it's true—I gave up a child, too."

Sometimes you can't think of the right thing to say. The shock on my face would have to do. Being adopted is terrible enough. Who would go out and willingly add more angst and misery to her life by giving up a child? Or inflict the same on another? What could be worse? This woman wants her original birth record so she can find her mother, but what about her baby? The woman keeps weeping. What do I say? What is there to say? The layers of her sorrow are backed up like planes at LAX—if one leaves, a new one is ready for takeoff.

That double whammy—adoptee/natural mother—is not all that un-usual. Attend an adoption reform conference, and you so often run into the women who did this that your heart spins, your mind has a hard time getting around the thought. Adoption begets more adoption. The one hard statistic I could find indicates that adoptees are seven times more likely than the general population to relinquish a child themselves.[58] Seven times.

---

[57] Donald Janson, "Adopted Children Seeking Changes in Law on Finding Natural Parents," *New York Times*, Oct. 27, 1976, 88.

[58] Nelwyn B. Moore and J. Kenneth Davidson, "A Profile of Adoption Placers: Perceptions of Pregnant Teens during the Decision-Making Process," *Adoption Quarterly*, 2002, 6, no. 2, (2002): 29–41. The sampling was small (178) and in the Southwest, where religious attitudes may have skewed the statistic some-what due to prohibitions against abortion. But clearly something besides chance is at work here. The late Annette Baran, a champion of openness in adoption and one of the authors of *The Adoption Triangle*, confirmed this when we spoke.

Jean Strauss writes in *Birthright* about discovering that her biological mother was also an adoptee. Strauss later found her grandmother, reunit-

I give the woman a hug and wipe away the mascara that's running down her cheeks. We must fold up our sorrow like a pocket square and carry on.

---

ed the two of them, and made a film about connecting of the three of them.

In *Being Adopted: The Lifelong Search for Self,* David Brodzinsky, Marshall Schechter, and Robin Marantz Henig write of a complicated sexual expression for adopted teenagers: "Adopted teenagers who were born to teenage mothers may feel the cycle repeating itself in their own sexual behavior. Adoptive mothers who agonized over their own infertility may feel jealous and resentful of their daughter's developing fecundity. . . . Some [adopted teenagers] deliberately become pregnant to undo what they feel to be their birth mother's mistakes. And some go in the opposite direction, shying away even from healthy sexual experimentation because they are so aware of where that landed their birth mothers," 110–11.

13 Looking for Cracks
in the Wall

1977–1978—To look at me, you wouldn't think anything is wrong. I've got a good job, I'm wearing a suit, I'm on morning television without blubbering. Gone is the sixth-floor walk-up apartment. A friend and I have moved into a two-bedroom, two-bath apartment in a building with an elevator. I freelance a few pieces for the *Times'* travel section, one about being a quality-control inspector for the Intercontinental hotels. This involved checking out anonymously the service and swellness of their five-star lodgings in London and Vienna. A cushy job indeed, as Intercon picked up the bills while I jetted to Europe during the week between Christmas and New Year's. In between noticing if the doorman's shoes were polished to a sheen and if the laundry was returned the same day by four p.m. as promised, I found time to do some sightseeing and meet up with friends of friends. The piece ran over most of the first page of the *Times'* travel section with a seven-panel cartoon AGENT DUSKY OF QUALITY CONTROL. Call me Brenda Starr for a day!

Life is on an upswing, right? But the legions of little girls continue to parade by—on the streets, in the stores, at the park—each year a year older. They don't notice me; I cannot help but see them, marching in the streets, walking by my window, piercing my complacency with their existence, each one a stand-in for my missing daughter. I can't shake the sense that she is calling me, the SOS a faint beep in the night, incessant, demanding. So begins my campaign to find out what I can, however I can.

I write to the New York Health Department in Monroe County, where she was born, once again using the name that would have been on her original birth certificate, Dusky, hoping that some careless clerk by mistake might send the amended—adopted—birth certificate.

Weeks pass.

With some anxiety (you are not supposed to do this!) but fierce determination (so what?), I write again to Northaven Terrace. This time, a long, handwritten letter on two sheets of typewriter paper. I write that I don't want to upset her life or her parents' lives, and would never do anything to hurt them, but that "the desire to know about her [my daughter] is so compelling it rules a great portion of my life. . . . If only I could know who she is my life would be so at peace." Hoping not to sound unhinged, I note that I am a freelance writer as well as a senior editor at *Town & Country*, implying, Respectable! See, I have moved on with my life!

I go on: "I am writing to say that if she is questioning about me, please let her parents know that I am willing—more than that, desire it—that she know" who I am, "just as I believe the same question troubles my daughter."[59] I include a photograph of myself, hoping the letter and the picture will end up in a file they might give her one day.[60]

Then I wait. For a response from the state, the agency, and the judge who is ruling on the case of four adoptees seeking their original birth certificates. Three months go by. The judge's verdict arrives first.

Superior Court Judge Philip A. Gruccio of New Jersey writes that while adoptees have a deep-seated need to learn their origins and should have easier access to their records, he stops short of allowing that they have a constitutional right to their original records.[61] Each will have to go to court individually to prove need. While those four women did not gain access to their

---

[59] The letter, dated January 26, 1977, would one day be sent by the agency to my daughter and is now in my files, with the other correspondence from the agency.

[60] My correspondence with the agency eventually found its way back to me.

[61] Donald Janson, "Jersey Eases Access to Adoption Records," *New York Times*, New Jersey, Feb. 5, 1977, A-1.

original birth records, the wording of the decision makes it seem as if the door to the truth of one's identity is at least ajar. It is something. A partial victory.

A few weeks later, a letter arrives from Monroe County Family Court. Maybe this is it! Maybe I have circumvented the system. I wait until I am inside my apartment before I open the letter, my heart is pounding, I feel flush. Maybe this is her amended birth certificate! With her new parents' names!

No such luck. The reply states that all adoption records are sealed (but I made no mention of adoption in my letter) and can only be opened by an order of a judge. Then it goes on to state that there is "no adoption record of a child bearing the name of Dusky." Now I wonder if I was so crazed with worry that the "Dusky" birth would somehow make its way into the *Democrat & Chronicle* that someone wrote in Droz—the first part of my dad's original name—on my daughter's birth certificate. Now I am worried that my daughter's birth certificate is defiled by my own doing.

But if that were the case, why did this letter mention adoption at all? I had purposefully left out that detail when I wrote. This means that my name and the birth date led them to the amended birth certificate.

I ask an acquaintance, a social worker, if she would write and ask for my daughter's amended birth certificate—the one with her adoptive parents' names—and make up some reason why it is necessary. I am pretty sure she could get it. She shakes her head no. I slink out the door.

One Saturday afternoon the phone rings. A woman is calling from who-knows-where and wants to know my daughter's exact birthday because she can't get it out of her mind that I might be her daughter's mother. She saw me on TV, tracked me down because she thinks her daughter resembles me. The year is right. Could it be? Will she hang up and fade away if she is my daughter's other mother? But the birthdays do not align. And *poof*—the woman is gone. The secrecy that was supposed to protect adoptive families is causing people—in this case, an adoptive mother—to search for answers by shooting arrows at any moving target.

Finally, a response from Northaven Terrace arrives, written by the same woman who wrote to me years earlier, a fact she notes. They have had no further "direct contact" (does that leave open the possibility of indirect contact?)

since she was legally adopted, and that "we have to assume that she is at least as well loved now as she was when the adoption was legalized." She states that they will keep my letter and picture in her record and give it to her should she ever return to search for me.

In the midst of all this angst, my roommate, Barbara, shows me a photograph of a girl who looks to be about ten—my daughter's age—in *People* magazine. The story is about the writers Joan Didion and John Gregory Dunne, at home in Topanga Canyon. With their daughter.

What do you think? Barbara wants to know. I look at the photo again. My lord, she looks like my cousins, the ones I remember from family reunions. And, yikes, she doesn't so much resemble me as a child, she somehow looks like what I might have looked like as a child. But the resemblance is uncanny. Blond, stringy hair, her nose is not a little delicate flower but like mine at that age. Could it be?

"She's adopted," Barbara says. "And she's ten." Barbara flips through more pages and points to more pictures, especially one of the girl washing a car with her father. I inspect the photo—does she have long arms like me? Looks like she might in that photo. I'm trying not to gallop to where Barbara has already gone, but she's enthusiastic about the resemblance. Stay calm. This is bizarre. The chances of this are infinitesimal. But it's not me who sees it, it's someone else; therefore, I am not the crazy one.

Now I think her eyes look like Patrick's.

Her name is Quintana. I had been to Quintana Roo on the Yucatan Peninsula a few years earlier and felt a profound connection to the place, to its stories of virgins sacrificed to the ancient pagan gods, to the deep black cenotes—ink blots embedded in the landscape—to the exotic and mysterious history of the Mayans who once thrived there. One afternoon I climbed the side of the crumbling temple at Tulum—you could do that then—and sat by myself for what I remember as a long time, staring into the aqua ocean, thinking about my daughter, and, yes, communicating with her.

And now this girl is named Quintana. Does this have some sort of synchronistic convergence? Is my daughter reaching out to me from the astral universe?

I need more convincing.

When I show my art-director friend at *Town & Country* the photos and simply say, She's adopted, my friend gets goose pimples. Florence is absolutely positive she is my daughter. When her husband sees the photos and Florence asks whose daughter she might be, he says, "Jesus Christ, Lorraine's." Looking for more stories about Didion, I find that one of them is written by a friend who also writes for *T&C*. When I ask if he has a clue when their daughter's birthday is—and I tell him why I am asking—he doesn't completely discount the story. But I'd better change the subject lest he think I'm completely off my rocker.

A friend of a friend of theirs comes up with the information that he thinks the girl is "from New York somewhere." In another magazine, Quintana turns eleven around the same time my daughter would be.

If she is alive.

Another friend, an editor who actually knows them, tells me I should write them and find out one way or another.

I hesitate. I know the letter will sound ludicrous.

I phone Patrick and tell him about the woman who called and who thought I was her child's other mother and about the Quintana connection, but I sense doubt in his voice. The friend I'd confided in years ago—and learned she, too, relinquished a child—has the guts to tell me that I am mistaken. That this is simply too improbable. That I need to stop this. Part of me says, I know, but another part of me needs proof. I'm not the one who started this!

The editor who knows them gives me their New York address.

In the June issue of *Esquire*, Dunne publishes a piece titled "Quintana." He says they first saw their daughter at a St. John's Hospital, that this was done through a private adoption through the gynecologist who delivered the baby in California. Nothing adds up.

She is not my daughter.

But I will write anyway, even acknowledging his details about Quintana's adoption that do not jibe with mine.

Weeks pass. My birthday comes and goes. I receive a few cards from family and friends.

A few days later, there is a letter from John Gregory Dunne. Sent from Santa Monica.

His words are kind and calm. He writes they would never think of me as a "crazy lady"—I must have put that in my letter to them—and they will show my letter to Quintana. He says Quintana knows her mother's name and that she is from a western state, which I already knew from the *Esquire* piece.

Then all this was a wild and fanciful fugue.

Desperate people do desperate things.

I am not the only woman consumed with a missing child. In Boston, Lee Campbell, who relinquished a son and who has been on television wearing a veil to obscure her identity, founds a national organization called CUB. She uses the conjoined words *birthparent, birthmother, birthfather.* I join, but find I have trouble calling myself a "birthmother." It reminds me of "midwife," someone only there for the birth. I know she has chosen the name to placate adoptive parents—society!—who are not happy that we are coming out of the dark, being bold enough to speak up.

New Woman runs a shortened version of the *T&C* piece.[62] A slew of letters come in response, so many that three months later the magazine runs several of them as a separate piece.[63] The headline is "Love Is Thicker Than Blood," so I brace myself for brickbats from adoptive parents. But the first letter is quite the opposite. An adoptee from Winnipeg notes that at thirty-five, after her mother died, her father "consented" to give her the name of her "mother" and the adoption-consent decree. "There are moments now when I wonder if all this is really happening after all the years of wondering, looking,

---

[62] Lorraine Dusky, "Somewhere Out There Is a Daughter of Mine," *New Woman,* Mar.–Apr. 1977, 34–37, 52–55.
[63] "Love Is Thicker Than Blood," *New Woman,* July–Aug. 1977), 61–62, 64, 66.

anguish and a general floating feeling. All I know is that I am finally going to find out who I am—such a simple thing, yet such an unreality for so long a time."

That is followed by an adoptee from New York City who writes that at twenty-three she has never had one whit of curiosity about her origins and if the woman who gave birth to her ever contacted her, she would refuse to meet her. "That part of my past has no bearing whatsoever on the person I am. My identity has been determined by many things, not the least of which is the support, love, and shared life experiences of a whole wonderful family." She ends with, "Blood may be thicker than water, but love is thicker than both of them."

Ah ha! Whence the headline. But time passes, people change, needs change, desire is fluid.

Someone from Tucson writes, "What is this giving a gift of life, then asking its return?" The writer goes on to state that the consent of foster parents should also be sought before information is released, noting that "foster parents have given their love, and their care, and years of their lives, which the natural parents did not give."

Gift of love? I never thought of relinquishing my daughter as a "gift." It was an act of desperation, of survival, anything but a gift.

An adoptee from Brookline, Massachusetts, wants to be left alone. She suggests that maybe the whole issue could be solved if mothers considering giving up their children for adoption be told the decision is "irrevocable." That adoptive parents should be "sensitive to the special questions and needs their adopted child might have." She recommends that adoptees be told about their adoption in a "healthy, productive way." If this were the case, "there would be fewer mothers regretting their decisions to give up their children, and fewer maladjusted adoptees."

Well, it's not that simple. I know adoption is legally and even emotionally irrevocable.

But.

A twenty-five-year-old registered nurse from Indianapolis happily notes that three years ago she found not only her parents but five natural brothers and one sister! Everything has gone well, even between the two families, she says, adding this twist: "One of my natural brothers and one of my adopted sisters will be married this summer."

Sweet! Now her adopted sister will be her sister-in-law.

Someone from Santa Ana, California, writes that when she was married to her first husband, she was not emotionally equipped to care for a child, and so they gave up a daughter who was three months old, telling everyone she died. The writer says she has never regretted doing so. She is now remarried to a man who knows the truth about her daughter's "death," and she has children (who presumably do not know). She prays "that no one will ever be forced by law to meet someone she does not care to see ever again."

It's going to sting when a searching adoptee reads this—and for that woman, telling the truth after this whopper will be a high mountain to climb.

That letter is followed by someone in Chicago who gave up a child seven months earlier and, while she feels deep down "it was the best thing that I could have done . . . it's the only thing I ever think about." She wants the law to change so that she may "see my daughter whom I love very much."

A woman from Saginaw, Michigan, shares her mindset: "You have given me hope that someday my grown-up young man will find me. Better still, if we can change these stupid laws, I will go and find him."

Well, this is good. But adoptees are going to face both kinds of mothers.

A woman in Milwaukee found peace in meeting her son's adoptive parents at the time of adoption, and now, at twenty-five, she is happily looking to be married this fall.

No matter how much resistance there is now, open adoptions are coming. It would have made it so much easier for me if I could have met her parents. And know who they are.

I would know how she is. And if she is alive.

Adoptive parents from Lancaster, California, write that adoptees have a right to know their natural parents and that they will do everything in their power to find their daughter's parents when she is grown.

There are adoptive parents who get it!

Someone from Redbank, New Jersey, "wants to be protected" from a stranger that could "come knocking at my door someday."

What if she looks just like you? You still going to slam the door on her?

A woman from Fort Lauderdale says that she was pressured to sign the adoption papers two days after her son was born, nine years ago, and her social worker never advised her that she could have put him in foster care while she got her life back together. Lawyers she consulted said it would take ten thousand dollars to even start a case, and she would probably lose. She has written to the agency so that if something ever happened to the adoptive parents, she would be contacted and get him back. "The day that my son comes knocking on my door will be the happiest day of my life, and I'll even let my two daughters know who he is."

A woman from Farmington, Missouri, writes, "When I released Todd for adoption [six years earlier], my mother, the social worker, the paternal grandparents all told me to never mention the 'whole episode.' It was over and I had my entire life ahead of me. They don't understand why I still talk about it—why I have to talk about it. He is my son. It did happen. And it is a part of my life."

So many were told the same thing. One of my friends was told by a priest she had to think of her daughter as dead. Idiot priest. And cruel.

Someone—address unknown—counters that emotion. She writes that her husband deserted her when she was seven months pregnant. Ever since she relinquished her second child, she has been busy supporting herself and an older child. Reminders she does not want: "Don't go around stirring up old memories, Ms. Dusky. Some of us just don't need to remember."

The feature ends with a letter from a woman in Sunnyvale, California who has a "son out there." "Times have really changed in the fourteen years since I gave up my son. I would bring him home today if I were given the opportunity."

Whew. Nineteen letters in all, not a single one is signed. All say, "Name Withheld by Request." Talking about the tragedy with which each adoption begins is still so controversial, no matter where you stand on the issue of open records.

I'd heard these points of view before, but reading them all at once is an emotional gut punch that heightens my agita. How does my daughter feel? Her adoptive parents? Would they welcome me or call the cops? The anonymity of the letter writers also bolsters my sense that coming out publicly had been not only the right thing to do but necessary.

My roommate, Barbara, is dating Lee Salk, a celebrity shrink in Manhattan and brother of Jonas. Ironically, Lee Salk invented the heartbeat device installed in incubators to comfort preemies, and when I hear that I immediately wonder, Did my baby have one? When did he invent that machine? At some point this Dr. Salk says to Barbara, "You don't want to end up like Lorraine."

Am I that pathetic? What he makes me clearly aware of is how the world sees a woman like me: You don't want to end up like Lorraine. Yet there I am, on national television, indeed proclaiming how I have ended up. I am someone I was not supposed to be.

Soon enough, I read in some women's magazine about an adopted girl who ended up being shuttled from boarding school to away camp because the first adoptive mother died, the father remarried, and the new wife didn't want the girl around. So the kid spent a week at home between the end of the school term and before camp began. Nice, huh? It happens. Elsewhere I read about a girl who had been adopted but then ended up back in an institution—where her natural mother was able to track her down. Now we're getting somewhere. This woman found her daughter. But what if that's where mine is—in an institution? What if they sent her back? What if her adoptive mother died?

Until I knew, I wouldn't know. Until I knew, every hard-luck adoptee story could be my daughter's.

What I admit to no one is that I have a second, private purpose in writing the memoir I have begun calling *Birthmark*. I am not just writing a book. I am writing a personals ad:

> Looking for daughter, born April 5, 1966, at Strong Memorial Hospital in Rochester, New York.

Maybe her parents would read it. Maybe they will come to the inevitable conclusion that their daughter is also my daughter. Maybe they will call. Maybe I will meet her. Maybe.

When an editor offers me a contract for a book based on a lengthy piece about eyesight and perception I'd written for *T&C*, I quit my job there. The topic is far removed from adoption—how what you see affects how you think—but it is a way into book publishing. This first, *Birthmark* next. When my friend Judy, the *New York Times* writer, asks if I will move into her apartment for the summer and care for her two parrots while she is recuperating from chemotherapy in the Hamptons, I jump at the chance to be fully alone, to be able to type—clack, clack, clack—late into the night, to answer to no one but myself. It will be my private retreat from what feels like an over-scheduled life in Manhattan.

There's no answering machine, and I ask Barbara not to answer my phone, I move two dozen blocks into my friend's apartment, I put aside the book—for which I have an actual contract—and get to work on *Birthmark*. I write and weep, edit and cut and paste, blow my nose, and get back to work. The parrots and I get along well enough, but they miss their mistress. One bites my finger, cutting it deeply when I am feeding him a blueberry. Not only am I bleeding on the page, now I am literally bleeding. It seems apt. No more blueberries for the green parrot, however. Everything has its limits.

In three months, I have a first draft.

The memoir has taken precedence over everything, including my dating life. The book is my guiding force, my path, my Tao. I have found my life's purpose, and I cannot let anything, or anyone, stop me. The world has to know what happens to the women who give up their babies. That we do not forget. Adopted people have the right to know their true identities, or at least what it says on their original birth certificate. The rules must change. Lawmakers must stop using us women—the mothers of these children—as the reason to keep the adopted people in the dark about their origins. Before all else, I must finish this book.

I know I need to be free to write, unfettered by friends, relationships, a ringing phone. Yet a woman is lonely. A woman has a mother who worries about her daughter. From a distance my mother follows what I tell her of my romances, and she frets. Tom is definitely divorcing, she says. He's living in Ohio now. Is he divorced yet? I ask. She's not sure. She gets the scoop from her sister, my Aunt Clara, who is still the best friend of Tom's friend's mother—who, by the way, was supposed to marry one of my uncles but did not. Another time, Mom tells me about her first love, someone named Richard, which is odd, given that Richard is my older brother's name. She tells me how they drifted apart, and then how he tried to stop her first marriage. Are missed connections everywhere? My mother's and father's marriage was not one of harsh words and loud arguments, but neither was it the kind people write love songs about. I wonder if the world is full of people married to the wrong people.

I will call Tom when I hear that he is actually divorced, I tell Mom. I have had it with not-quite-divorced men, a statement she does not dispute. Besides, years have passed, I'm on the East Coast, and he's in the Midwest. No internet yet, no Facebook, no way to make a casual foray into his life via a coy email. I do not try to track down his phone number or pin down where he's working so I can call him there. Mom would have to ask her sister Clara, who would ask her friend who has a connection to Tom through her son, who would probably have his number, but who would tell his wife—all before I could dial up Tom. Everyone would know my business. Yet if I were to pick up the phone and it was Tom—well, that would be something else. Telephones work both ways, do they not? He'd just have to phone my mother. Okay, that could be awkward too. But my mother would be thrilled.

In the fall my lease with my roommate is up, and we plan to move on, separately. I take a sublet outside the city in Westchester County. My apartment is a few blocks from a train station that connects to Manhattan.

Now I must put aside *Birthmark* to furiously finish the book on eyesight for which I do have a contract. I've blown the deadline and gotten an extension, and I've no time for life-altering, time-absorbing events like tracking down Tom. Yet reaching him is always in the back of my mind. When I'm finished with this book, when I hear that you, Tom, are divorced, I will call. What had he said when we'd had that lunch—I'll hear from you again? Surely that was an invitation to call him. Okay, Tom, I'll make the call. Give me a minute—I mean, a month or three.

I move back to Manhattan—the 'burbs are not for me!—in another sublet, this one comfortable, roomy, furnished, on the tidy east side. By myself.

On deadline, one can work like a crazed person, and I do, through the fall, through Christmas and New Year's, even when I go to Detroit to be with Mom for the holidays. In January, I turn in the manuscript for the book that will become *Total Vision*, and finally I have a chance to take a breath.

I am talking to my mother. It is Saturday. We always talk on the weekend, when the rates are lower.

"Tom Sawicki died," she says. Suddenly. In Ohio. Or was it Indiana? She wasn't sure. Aortic aneurysm. A bubble in the bloodstream, and *boom* he is gone. Last fall—October, she adds.

Last fall?

I knew if I told you then you wouldn't be able to finish the book, she says.

She is talking but I am not really listening, instead trying to remember something he'd said once about his heart, that it was unlikely he would ever be drafted, that he had an irregular heartbeat. What had he said, exactly? It hadn't seemed important at the time, I didn't question it then, I'd forgotten all about it. What the hell was it? Now I'll never know.

It is bitter cold, but I wrap myself up in layers and long johns under my sweats and go for a hard run. I jog down East Seventy-Ninth Street to the East River, downtown to somewhere in the sixties before I turn around and go uptown to Carl Schurz Park at Eighty-Sixth Street and then back to the apartment. The wind off the river stings my face while thoughts of the step not taken, the kiss not given, the call not made reverberate: a cocktail of sorrow, wistfulness, and melancholy. I always time myself on my runs. That day, I forget. *I'll hear from you again.* He said it like that. A statement.

Now it is too late. It is always going to be too late.

A few nights later, I feel Tom there, right there, in my living room. He's come to say goodbye. The times Tom didn't show up recede from my mind. I'll hear from you again, he said. Why did I wait? Why didn't I call? my brain, unbidden, keeps repeating as I light up a joint. What difference could it have made? taunts me back. I don't know, I say, pouring myself a glass of red wine. But. God, you are full of buts. Aren't you being melodramatic? I ask. Probably, I answer, taking another drag. Yet. The call not made would never be made. Why hadn't I called?

I'm sad and I need to say goodbye.

I turn off the lights and open the blinds. City light spills in to illuminate the room. I stare out at the rooftops below me, the angles and lit windows and the traffic below. Manhattan is going about its business. I have another glass of wine, I put on an old Dinah Washington album of mournful love songs, the album I bought that year you and I, Tom, were apart in college. Her heartbreaking voice takes me back to then. "What a Difference a Day Makes" plays on the stereo while I dance around the room in the quasi-dark with his ghost. I don't see anything, no images in the shadows, no funny noises or cabinets opening and shutting on their own, yet that one night I sense Tom there, swirling around the room with me, lingering tenderly before he truly leaves.

I know it sounds dopey. Yet that is what I did.

14   SOS in the Night

Now a new personal nightmare surfaces. In the late seventies, news about a powerful synthetic hormone that doctors prescribed to women who had miscarried, thinking that it would prevent miscarriages, seems to pop up everywhere. The news is stunning: the drug is linked to vaginal cancer in the women's daughters and urinary and genital abnormalities in the sons.[64] The New York State is setting up a registry for the those who took it and their children, as well as screening centers. Women had been taking diethylstilbestrol (DES) for three decades, from 1938 to 1971, but only now was the awful reality coming out.

Oh, my god. I have a fresh set of nightmares. What about birth control pills? What might I have done to my daughter? I already know the dosage of hormones I must have taken in those years was much higher than what was being prescribed a decade later. I had taken them for nearly four months! In the worst of all times, the early stages of my pregnancy! My baby had a couple of weeks without them, I calculated, until my too-early pregnancy test came back negative. And I took them religiously. What had I done? I am frantic. I read everything I can find on DES, looking for some mention of taking birth control pills while pregnant.

I find nothing.

---

[64] Ari L. Goldman, "State Seeks Children with Links to DES," *New York Times*, May 10, 1979, C-7. Goldman describes the effort to find the 100,000 women in New York state who took the drug. Many if not most of their female children would eventually be unable to have children because they repeatedly miscarried.

What do I do that would give me license to call up the experts? I pretend to have an assignment to do a story about the powerful side effects of DES—and hormones. The few magazines I query aren't interested because without more news beyond the initial announcement of problems, the story doesn't have a hook. So I go ahead on my own. I phone up specialists, and while asking about DES, I throw in a question about taking birth control pills while pregnant. No one has heard of such a thing, but everyone I call—at the American Cancer Society, Sloan-Kettering, the Cleveland Clinic—agrees anyone so exposed (that's my daughter you're talking about!) needs to be "followed closely." Checked for any signs of cancer? They do not know, but "get the individual checked, early and often" is the resounding crescendo.

In August, I write to Northaven Terrace with a sense of urgency. Certainly, they will want to contact my daughter's parents immediately. "It is with dismay that I write you this time as new evidence which has just come to my attention indicates that my daughter falls into a high-risk cancer group. Is there any way my daughter can be informed?" I refer them to the third chapter of *Women and the Crisis in Sex Hormones.*[65] I ask for a quick response. "Years must not go by before she is made aware of the danger," I write.

By October, there is still no answer. I write again: "Could you at least acknowledge my letter and tell me if there is anything in my file about the birth control pills, or the name of the doctor who prescribed them for me? I am anxiously awaiting to hear from you."

Still no answer by November. I write once more: "A few minutes ago on the *Today* show, there was a report about a center for children who have cancer. I know the odds of my daughter being the blond little girl who was interviewed are statistically impossible, by anyone's calculation, but I couldn't help wondering about my daughter and if she is all right. More importantly, I couldn't help wondering why you haven't answered my letters. It has been more than two months since I wrote to you."

---

[65] Barbara Seaman, *Women and the Crisis in Sex Hormones* (New York: Rawson Associates, 1977).

15 Birthmark

SPRING 1978—The guy is red in the face and so angry he is practically spitting at me as he talks, his voice getting loud enough to attract attention from nearby tables. He's just learned that I am one of them—a mother who gave away a child—and furthermore, that is the subject of my memoir we are there to discuss. I'm at the Algonquin, once a famous literary watering hole, with the angry man and his boss, Don Fine, an editor who runs his own publishing house. Until this guy Arnold started yelling at me, I was intoxicated with a cocktail of my own elation. Don Fine might have been my publisher!

The veins in Arnold's forehead are bulging as his tirade continues: I am one of those women? What gives me the right to write about this! Who in the hell do I think I am! What gives me the right to even imagine that I might someday know my daughter! The very idea sickens him! Who do I think I am?!

Fine is stunned. I run off to the ladies' room. Jesus, what is going to happen when my memoir is published? How many angry people like that are there? What if my daughter is one of them, what if she hates me as much as Arnold hates his mother? I wait in the ladies' room for at least a quarter of an hour, waiting for Arnold to leave.

Arnold is gone when I return. Fine apologizes, saying that although he's known Arnold for years, he had no idea he grew up without a mother and in an orphanage, and of course he could never consider my book now. We say goodbye in the street. Fine goes one way, and even though my apartment is in the same direction, I purposely walk the other to get away as fast as I can.

Arnold can't be the only one with abandonment issues spelled A-N-G-E-R.

It takes a dozen more rejections before *Birthmark* finds an enthusiastic home with a small publishing house, M. Evans, where the decision to buy it is made by an editor-in-chief whose choices are not subject to the predilections of a committee that would surely have people on it with objections. Adoption, in middle- and upper-class America, is as invasive as kudzu in the South. When one adopts, others of their acquaintance are sure to follow. Mothers who supplied the children were unpleasant reminders of the child's unsavory roots. We women were not only repugnant: the whole story was considered trashy by the classy women who worked in publishing then. They had degrees from good schools and pedigrees from country-club families where this did not happen, or if it did, it was quickly and quietly taken care of (abortion, marriage, a home for this unfortunate lot) and then swept under the rug, never to be mentioned again. Only someone like *her*—working class—would go public! NOCD. Meaning: Not Our Class, Dear, murmured these editors to each other. My agent tried to keep this from me, but it leaked out anyway in her offhand comments.

I do hear that the author James Michener, who set his novels in places all over the world, reacted quite vocally when asked to give *Birthmark* a blurb—something along the lines of *Not on your $#!&ing life!* Michener, I learn, did not know his parents or exactly where he was born. Another Arnold, I presume.

At the end of November, while the process of publishing—editing, cutting, negotiating cuts back into the manuscript, rewriting, settling on flap copy, getting blurbs—goes on, I finally get a response from the adoption agency in Rochester. The letter is from a new director, one who apologizes for the delay. She has only recently taken over. The previous director had retired and her correspondence had gone untended. The letter is friendly, warm, empathetic. "Be assured that we do take seriously the information you present in your letters to us. In fact, we are receiving quite a few communications of the same sort from biological mothers who have taken DES, birth control pills, or other medications during their pregnancy, medications which it is now found pose some health risk to the children."

So, I am not the only distraught mother writing to an adoption agency.

She goes on to say that they will inform the adopting parents and advise them to seek medical advice. Then these kind words: "I hope this will enable you to relax a bit and trust, now that you have done this important service to your daughter."

I tear up. At least this woman, a stranger far away, a stranger whose business it is to facilitate adoptions, recognizes what I am going through. My daughter's parents will know I have not forgotten her. And maybe one day she will, too.

I hang onto slender threads. Hope is all I have.

The following summer, instead of being a weekend guest in the Hamptons, I take a share in a house in Sag Harbor with my friend Judy Klemesrud. She's a rather big deal at the *New York Times*, and thus in the literary Hamptons. Judy's apartment is where I'd written a first draft of *Birthmark* two summers earlier, and her cancer has been stayed for another year. She and I met when I was a sad misfit in what's now called the Style section of the *Times*, which is to say, the penalty box of a women's department. However, Judy thrived there, covering the birth of the women's movement. Her sassy profiles of sports icons and celebrities often appeared elsewhere in the paper. Midwesterners both, we share a certain outsider vibe, a fondness for country music and horses. Manhattan still has a stable, and she and I often ride in Central Park on Sunday mornings.

Before the summer begins, I blow ten thousand dollars, a third of my advance from *Birthmark*, for the car of my youthful dreams—hey, I'm from the Motor City, remember? It's not a Detroit product, however, but a cream-colored convertible 1953 MG-TCD in mint condition, suitable for Isadora Duncan, not someone who wrote *that book*. Who had, furthermore, *done that*. For reasons unknown, I name the MG Esmerelda. To my astonishment, Esmerelda attracts men like a magnet—at gas stations, stop signs, parking lots.

A penitent, I do not resemble. Mary Magdalene, with downcast demeanor and drab garb, should have been my model. Instead, I have Esmerelda.

Mistake. Big mistake.

Judy is invited to nearly everything literary going on in the Hamptons, and then some. She wants me as her sidekick, like Robin to Batman. *Total Vision* has already come out; *Birthmark* is coming that fall. I quickly learn that publishing a book bestows cachet simply because one's words wouldn't be wrapped around tomorrow's fish. I'm taken more seriously than if she'd introduced me as a frivolous *T&C* editor, but controversy is, well, controversy, and it can blow up in your face anytime. Especially when you are driving Esmerelda.

At some party, a guy I'd danced with all evening at a disco—but then turned down for an actual date later—comes right out and says to me that the only reason I wrote "that book" was for the money. Look at the car you bought! he says. You don't care about the kid. I recoil and walk away, but I can't leave because I've come with Judy and won't force my tsuris on her.

Another evening, another backyard, cocktails flowing freely, the sun going down, a woman I do not know hands me a folded piece of paper. She takes a few steps, turns back, and glares defiantly with dark eyes. I open the note to read, "Never forget for a single minute / You grew not under my heart / But in it." Exactly what does she mean? Is she an adoptive mother? Adopted? Someone who was adopted but feels the same as the angry guy in the bar? All I know for sure is that she wishes I would blow away.

If I move quickly, maybe I can avoid the hatchet I feel aimed at my back.

In June I finally hear from the agency director again. She writes that my daughter's family has moved from the Rochester area, and it has taken a while to find them. Naturally, she can't tell me where they are. However, my daughter's doctor has been made aware of "her prenatal conditions," and at present "she has shown no symptoms indicating any such problems as you are concerned about."

So, *she doesn't have cancer*, I translate.

Then this: "She is doing well and is happy in her family."

She is alive. She is well. This is hard information. She is not dead. She is alive. *Birthmark* is coming out in a few months. Maybe it will find its way to her parents.

My correspondent says that they are keeping all my letters in a file that will be given to her should she contact them and ask for information. "I hope this sets your mind at rest. Best wishes to you."

I try to imagine this woman, writing these letters, looking for the right tone, straddling the legal issues, trying to be comforting but not stepping over the line. People dealing with the bureaucracy of an adoption agency often focus their anger at the agency and the people involved, but I never could. We were all players in a grand drama, and each of us knew our lines. Mrs. Helen Mura had never told me that I would forget my daughter. She said it would get easier with time, and that was true. I did stop emotionally wailing on the floor. She also said that I would never forget my daughter. Mrs. Mura did not sugar-coat the truth. She understood my reality and, in doing so, made it easier to bear as time went on.

But how can this woman possibly know that my daughter is "doing well and is happy in her family"?

No, my mind is not at rest; it is roiling in a tumultuous sea. Something is wrong. Something must be.

A few weeks before the book comes out in the fall of 1979, I write a "My Turn"[66] essay for *Newsweek* stating my hope "that she has a mother and a father who love her and give her all the things that daughters need." Nevertheless, further fury ensues. Friends say that when my book came up at a dinner party, the actor/director Ben Gazzara pounded the table in rage. "He actually pounded the table?" I ask dubiously. Surely, they exaggerate. The book isn't even out.

Yes, pounded the table, my friends agree. I am a harridan with a vile request—that I might know my daughter one day—and that was reason

[66] Lorraine Dusky, "Who Is My Daughter," *Newsweek*, October 15, 1979, 27.

enough to explode in anger. What right does that woman think she has? The very idea of one of those women interfering! Unheard of! Who gave her the right!?!

Newsweek publishes a few letters in response: One is from an adoptee who states, "Only other adoptees can understand the rage I feel when told I cannot obtain the truth of my origins." Another adoptee writes he doesn't want to hurt his adoptive parents and doesn't like that people are working to undo the sealed-records statutes and "drag some stranger into their family circle." An adoptive father hopes for a "computer-matching service." Another father is annoyed that so much has been written about the right of the "natural mother and adopted child" and hopes that "a Supreme Court decision would treat adoptive parents better than the media have so far."[67]

In other words, keep the records shut, Supreme Court! Did he ever understand that he was stripping from his own child—and all other adoptees—rights that the rest of us take for granted? That he was asking the Supreme Court to validate a kind of identity theft, that is, taking away for all time one's true ancestry, history, background?

Another night, another party, this one in Connecticut. I am planning to spend the night. The host is a good friend, but around midnight someone I've never met before mentions that the host's girlfriend is going around the room excoriating me for having written *that book*. Whether it was too much booze or buried resentment, I cannot wake up there in the morning. I expected this, I really did, I remind myself—but anticipation is one thing, and feeling the full force of wrath in real life is another.

Curve balls come most unexpectedly. The night before I am to be on *Good Morning America*, I am in my room in a hotel on Central Park South, since I am now living in Sag Harbor. Around eight-thirty that night, the show's producer calls to ask, quite casually, You wouldn't mind going on tomorrow with someone with a different point of view, would you? We think

---

[67] Letters, "Adoption Law," *Newsweek*, Nov. 5, 1979.

it will make for a better segment. You don't mind, do you? His name? Oh, Bill Pierce.

The enemy! Pierce is the ringleader of the opposition to openness in adoption—he even has formed his own lobbying organization, the National Council for Adoption (NCFA), after, I was told, he was not promoted to head the Child Welfare League of America. NCFA is an umbrella association of adoption agencies, and they are all fiercely opposed to the adoptee-search movement. A substantial proportion of the member agencies are under the auspices of this or that Christian church—Protestant, Catholic, evangelical, or the Church of Jesus Christ of Latter-day Saints (LDS).[68] Florence Fisher has taken on Pierce on television before. I have seen the fireworks. Would I object to being interviewed with Bill Pierce? Well, yes, I would. I'm not turning this interview into a nasty debate over open records.

My background in PR kicks in, and I instantly realize that *Good Morning America* does not have a hook to be chatting with Pierce without me—why discuss natural mothers emerging from the closet unless one is sitting there? And the producer is springing this on me at eight-thirty the night before? That's because she correctly assumes that if she had run this by my publicist, she would have said no. Since Pierce works out of Washington, this has been prearranged; he is already in town somewhere. This is an ambush. Screw this.

"I don't think so," I say as evenly as possible, cloaking my annoyance.

"Are you sure?" the producer counters. "We think it will be more interesting—you know, to have the other point of view." But the other point of view owns the day. Birth records are sealed in nearly every state of the union. There is more back and forth until I finally say, "You could have me on another day."

---

[68] At the time, the LDS Church was adamantly opposed to unsealing birth certificates of adopted people, despite the fact that the church maintains the best and largest repository of genealogical records in America, thus making tracing people possible. The LDS Church has long stressed adoption in all cases of unmarried parents, a position that has not changed today, but in 2014, NCFA quietly dropped its policy of opposing legislation unsealing birth records. At this writing, Utah has laws that foster unscrupulous adoption agencies. These agencies arrange questionable adoptions over the objections of the fathers who wish to raise their own children. This has led to several lawsuits.

I wonder if I have overplayed my hand.

The producer caves. I'll do the segment alone.

The interview is neutral, but as I walk off the set, a woman pulls me aside, off camera. "You never forget, do you?" I instantly recognize she is one of us. "I have a twelve-year-old son—I wonder if he'll ever want to find me. I'm married now—I even have another child—but I never stop wondering what happened to him." I recognize in her voice the same shaky ground of guilt and sorrow on which all natural mothers live.

I can't think of anything to say. "Do you think those records will ever be open?" she asks.

"They have to be."

"I can't do what you're doing—be so public. But don't give up."

I clasp her hand and she squeezes mine back. We are like lepers who find one another in the dark.

In Detroit a few days later, a dozen long-stemmed red roses are handed to me as I leave the set. The card says they are from the young man I casually met weeks earlier—who happened to be adopted. I am amazed that he remembered my name, the name of the book, tracked down my publisher, got my media schedule, and found the TV station where I would be that morning. I realize he wants to be sending those roses to his natural mother, not to me, and I know that he understands exactly how controversial what I am doing is. Let the naysayers be damned—I must do this—for him and all the others like him.

Some interviewers are understanding, even sympathetic. Others are not. In Windsor, Canada, across the river from Detroit, a thirty-something, attractive woman practically scalds my skin with her rage and resentment while the camera rolls. My mother is present and she is unbowed. Even though she has to face the gossips of her generation in the senior-citizen complex where she lives, she is my stalwart supporter.

"When people discover what Lorraine Dusky is about, they're likely to cut and run, because Lorraine Dusky is One of Those—a woman who had an illegitimate child, gave her away and now wants to find her"—is the lead in New York City's *Daily News*. "I botched up my life . . . " runs a headline in the *Houston Post.* "Always looking for daughter" is the headline in the *Milwaukee Journal.*[69]

Meanwhile, the reviews of *Birthmark* are up and down—some newspapers had adoptive parents review it; none approved. Many reviewers think I carry on too much about having lost a child to adoption—I'd made that bed, so what did I expect? An anonymous reviewer in *Kirkus Reviews* finds me "hysterical" with a "guilty search that may or may not find sympathizers with the *True Confessions'* crowd." An adoptive mother of four in Dallas at the *News* urges me to come to "better terms" with my life and, instead of working with ALMA, join "birthparent support groups that deliberately do not assist women searching for their children." (Hmm, these would be support groups run by adoption agencies, and I'm not aware that any such "support groups" exist anywhere.) A writer in Vancouver, British Columbia, is irritated that I do not "consider the adoptive parents, how they might feel." Whether unspoken or not, that is the common question that hangs in the air, fueled by popular advice writers like Ann Landers, who has been unwaveringly against searching—no matter who does it. A reviewer for the *Herald-Post* in El Paso says I offered "no solid reasons for revising the laws on adoption." An adoptee in the *Los Angeles Times* is plenty annoyed with me (and probably her own unknown natural mother)—but she does want to know more about the movement to unseal the records. She also asks what my brothers thought about me writing such a scandalous book. Having read the book, she knows that my father's dead, but how do my

[69] Constance Rosenblum, "Searching for a Second Chance," *Daily News* (New York City), no. 15, 1979, 70; Elizabeth Bennett, "I Botched Up My Life...," *Houston Post*, Oct. 21, 1979, 7BB; Lois Blinkhorn, "Always Looking for a Daughter," *Milwaukee Journal*, Oct. 7, 1979; Cynthia Lee, "Unwed Mother: 'Where Is My Child?'" *Detroit News*, 1F; "Birthmark," Kirkus Service, July 1, 1979; Judy Alter, "A Mother's Search for the Child She Gave Up," *Dallas News;* Helen Bateson, "Changing Her Mind Not Enough," *The Province* (Vancouver, BC, Canada), Lifestyles, 1; Elise Voight, "Birthmark," *El Paso Herald-Post*, Dec. 1, 1979; Marilyn Murray Willison, "Emotional Issue of Adoption," *Los Angeles Times*, Oct. 25, 1979, pt. 4, 5; Deborah Lawrence, "*Birthmark's* Important," *San Antonio Light*, Sept. 30, 1979; "Birthmark," *Gazette Times*, (Ferndale, MI), Oct. 25, 1979; "Message to My Daughter," excerpt from *Birthmark, San Antonio Light*, Sunday Woman, Jan. 20, 1980; and numerous other newspapers throughout the country.

brothers feel? Would a male author be questioned about his sisters' feelings in a memoir that doesn't really have anything to do with them? Obviously not.

While these brickbats are bracing to read, they encapsulate the public perception of adoption and those pesky natural mothers who ought to disappear and shut up. I soon realize that *Birthmark* is not being taken seriously as a piece of writing by most reviewers. They do not see me as a writer who happened to write about her experience but as a woman scribbling in her journal to exorcise her demons. Nearly all of the write-ups are not about the book, per se, or the writing; they are about the issue and the woman who dares to attach her name to it.

But there is good news, too. *Library Journal* calls *Birthmark* a "deeply moving account of the biological mother's need for information about the adoptee . . . highly recommended" for public and most academic libraries, adding it was—oh, this is boasting!—"a spectacular addition to feminist literature," words that are balm to my beaten-up ego. *Publishers Weekly* calls the book "powerful. . . . This poignant, candid record should amount to a convincing argument to change laws that prevent adoptees and natural parents from knowledge of each other's lives."[70]

Meanwhile back on the media trail, at a radio station in Texas, an interviewer comes out to greet me in a full-face papier-mâché mask. His point? He intends to stay anonymous to that woman who gave him up for adoption. Clearly, I am disturbing some primordial, buried rage. I brace myself to expect the worst, yet once we are on the air live, he is not vicious at all; he is genuinely curious about what I have to say. Not so with other popular talk-show interviewers, Larry King and Sally Jesse Raphael. Neither will book me, their reps tell the book's publicist—King and Raphael are adoptive parents. What more needs to be said?

But letters like this one—after *Birthmark* is excerpted in *Family Circle*[71]—buoy my spirits:

---

[70] Sallie F. Lowenthal, "*Birthmark*," *Library Journal*, Sept. 1, 1979; unsigned review, *Publishers Weekly*, Aug. 6, 1979.

[71] Lorraine Dusky. "I Gave Away My Baby," *Family Circle*, Oct. 9, 1979, 40+.

I'm adopted . . . I was born in Saginaw, Michigan in 1965 . . . I
can't really remember a lot just what my parents told me when
I was 10 years old. I was adopted at 8 months . . . when I was
12 or 13 I snuck in my parents' room I really don't know what
I was looking for but I found a letter from the adoption agency
telling about my parents and all. And the lady in the picture fits
the description also the man she was going with fits my fathers
description . . . . I really do want to find this lady's address. Is it
possible to get her address for me? I am 14, and I really would
like to know who my real mom is and I think this is my real
Mom.

She's from Saginaw—how odd that this girl would write me—the excerpt
didn't mention my brief stay in Saginaw.

On a national TV talk show I am pitted against a fuming adoptive father, also an attorney, like many other men I will debate over the years to
come. They make such articulate attack dogs. The way they talk about their
children is particularly troubling, for they make them sound like invest-
ments—lots of money does change hands in most infant adoption—and no
one is going to upset that deal. I wonder what these men say, in word or by
inference, to their children about their other mothers. It can't be pretty.

I am still fair game off camera. One attorney/writer at a party in
Manhattan—not a father—corners me in a tiny kitchen. "I know people who
would like to kill you," he says. Since he's not a mob lawyer but a writer with
a law degree, I am only momentarily taken aback. But yet—kill me?

I find myself backing into the refrigerator. Who hates me that much?

He's talking about adoptive parents he knows, not about someone who's
put a hit out on me—though metaphorically it seems to have crossed some
minds, including this guy's, who obviously agrees with his friends who think
Birthmark is an unforgivable crime against humanity—or at least his adoptive-
parent friends. I would like to tell him that the girlfriend of mine he's pursuing
is also a mother like me, but she's not ready to reveal that part of herself.

A fall dinner party in the Hamptons brings a surprise attack from an elder
statesman on the *Times*, known for his incisive obituaries of the famous as well

as his numerous flirtations at the office. I'd turned down lunch with him myself when I was at *T&C*, an invitation by phone after a brief hello at a cocktail party. Now it is three or four years later, and he is sitting next to me when he suddenly begins berating me for writing "that book." No one had brought it up until he did. What gives me the right, who did I think I was, yadda, yadda, yadda, his anger rising with each syllable. If he could stomp me into silence, he would. All other conversation stops, five pairs of eyes turn to us, and on he goes and goes, exuding privilege and outrage until his wife finally speaks up.

"What were we doing all last summer in Wales, looking for the graves of your ancestors?! If you did that, can't you understand this? What is the matter with you?"

After her upbraiding, no one speaks for a long twenty seconds. The host—the *Times'* celebrated food writer, Craig Claiborne—finally pierces the charged atmosphere, changes the subject, and asks if anyone would like more chili. Dinner is interminable; the man and I say nothing else to each other all evening. I am relieved when they leave.

The angry man? Or Ben Gazzara, months earlier? Eventually I come to believe that all the fuming, agitated men I encounter who have no obvious connection to adoption almost certainly have children of their own out there that their wives and other children do not know about. Why else be so angry and take my book so personally? Someone had to father all those relinquished children.

The depth of the fury I encountered was testament to the certainty and strength of the genetic bond. My detractors would not have been so profoundly enraged if they did not instinctively grasp its power. Natural mothers coming out of the closet evoked all kinds of fears—of losing one's child to someone else, to a bond of blood and genes, to eyes and noses that look alike, to similar smiles and idiosyncratic tics, despite everything they had done for their children, every poopy backside wiped, every tearful nightmare calmed, every orthodontics bill paid. No matter that without us their children would not even be in their lives. These people did not want to acknowledge that the original mothers—those who actually had given birth to the children, supplied them, as it were—even existed. Had ever existed. They could not acknowledge that despite the break in the bond, blood had its own inimitable claim and connection. You could denigrate it, you could downplay it, you could even swear at me for breaking the bond of silence, but that longing was still in there, relentless as the pull of the tide, as inevitable as tomorrow. You could not make it go away.

But knowing my cause was just did give me grit. I might not have been able to keep my daughter, but speaking up and saying that we mothers did not forget was a way of making some good out of losing her. Look, I would have done anything to not be that person who wrote that book—to not have lost a child to adoption—but that is who I am, and I cannot play my life backward. I am in this fight to give adopted people the right to their original identities, to give the mothers who want reunion a fair chance at having one, to restore whatever psychic health we natural mothers can salvage from knowing what happened to the children. Without that, there is no real peace, the questions will not quit. While people say we need to "put this behind us" and "get on" with our lives, we walk around in the perpetual aftershock of trauma. Some women stuff down the sorrow better than others, stuff it down so much they cannot, will not, meet their children years later, or even acknowledge their existence.

I am getting on with my life in the only way I know how.

I am not wailing on the floor.

I must have written to the agency after *Birthmark* came out because my pen pal at the agency—now called Hillside Children's Center, as her new stationery announces—writes in January 1980, this time to note that she is placing a letter that I wrote to my daughter, unopened, in the file so that it will be available to her should my daughter or her parents communicate with the agency. She also says she has read *Birthmark* and she is "sorry I can't do more for you at this time. Peace, and good luck."

She knows the law is wrong.

Of course, I write back, gushing out to someone who has some connection to my daughter—who now knows where she is—asking for a photograph, more information about her, more information about her family—education level, ages, siblings for my daughter, born or adopted—and could I have a copy of my surrender papers, and which probate court the adoption was finalized in? I write in detail about the birth control pills, sharing that the experts said it was important that my daughter be monitored for problems. I ask the woman if she had relayed the information to my daughter's physician. I write about the problems of being adopted, problems that emerge during adolescence. I mention that adoptees have higher incidence of alcohol and drug problems. I bring her up to date on Patrick's whereabouts, that he and his wife later divorced, and tell her that he is aware of the book. I thank her for putting my Christmas card—signed by both my mother and me—in my daughter's file. I end by asking if she's ever in New York City, would she give me a call, I'd love to meet her. The letter is two-and-a-half single-spaced, typed pages.

She, too, writes back a long letter with some additional information about the parents: college-educated professionals. At the time of my daughter's adoption, they already had a two-and-a-half-year-old son, and the mother stopped work to become a full-time homemaker. She described them as a "warm, loving, mature couple" whose interests focused on home and family-centered sports and activities. When the adoption was legalized, my child was "definitely blond, and her development was fine." Their physician's office had assured them that they were aware of the significance of new medical information. The family did not respond to her letter, and she interpreted this as meaning that they did not wish or need further input from the agency at this time. She reminded me that state law sealed the official court record. She added that if my daughter or her parents did convey an interest in "her biological parentage," they obviously could contact the agency. "All Hillside Children's Center can legally do at this point is wait for an inquiry, either from her parents, or from the girl independently at her age 21." She said that if my daughter came back, they would serve as an intermediary to arrange a meeting between all parties. "All your letters are placed in your file in preparation of that day. You can help by keeping us abreast of your whereabouts."

She became aware of *Birthmark*, she adds, when she found it on prominent display in her neighborhood public library. As soon as she saw the title, she knew it was about adoption. She noted that what I wrote about my love relationship and pregnancy "was so honest it jibed with their case record."

This was something. It was, in fact, quite a bit. But the gushing wound inside me still told me my daughter needed me. She mentioned age twenty-one; I would strike out to find her when she was eighteen. But that would be another four years.

Birthmark came out in 1979. That year, some "twenty-eight states defeated or allowed bills to die in committee that would have provided adult adoptees with some sort of access to information in sealed adoption records."[72] But despite the intense opposition, some heard our plea. What was then the Department of Health, Education, and Welfare (HEW) held hearings around the country before writing a comprehensive Model State Adoption Act that would cover the whole country. Florence, B. J. Lifton, and I—as well as a whole packed auditorium of people—trooped up to Columbia University to testify. As expected, so did adoptive parents, adoption-agency workers, adoption lawyers, representatives of the NCFA, and fellow travelers, most against the changes being proposed. We cheered when we learned that CUB's president, Lee Campbell, was on HEW's advisory committee, but we didn't hold out much hope for anything for natural mothers.

When HEW subsequently released its proposed legislation in 1980, we were stunned. It advocated open records not only for adoptees, but also for mothers: "It is the philosophy of the Model Act that secrecy is not and has never been an essential or substantive aspect of adoption."

There was more:

> There can be no legally protected interest in keeping one's iden-
> tity secret from one's biological offspring; parents and child are
> considered co-owners of the information regarding the event
> of birth. . . . The birth parents' interest in reputation, which

---

[72] Carp, *Family Matters*, 185.

could be significantly altered by the unexpected appearance a child from the past, is not alone deserving of constitutional protection.[73]

Co-owners of the information regarding the birth ... Even now I thrill to these words and remember how astonished we were. This act alone would slice through the Gordian knot of legal secrecy that had eliminated self-knowledge for the adopted in all states but three at the time: Alabama, Alaska, and Kansas. Lee—savvy, tactful, and unwavering—had accomplished more than we felt we could hope for. In this official federal document, she had managed to wipe away the idea that the mother's secrecy was sacrosanct.

Yet we didn't pop the champagne. Now Congress had to act. Florence Fisher and I were invited to testify in DC at a joint Senate-House subcommittee in May 1980, and so off we went. NCFA produced a birth mother who wept so much she could barely speak or get through her prepared statement. While no media were there, she wanted anonymity so badly that she had to be anonymous, as if her name might one day be discovered in the Congressional Record. Had NCFA suggested this? I wondered.

I was up next. She sniffled noisily all through my testimony. When I passed her on the way back to my seat, she was openly blubbering into the arms of her NCFA handlers. She was crying too hard merely to be worried about something in the distant future. She must have only recently relinquished. Or when her old wound had been opened, she discovered a gushing hole.

We got killed in Washington. Not only were any rights to natural mothers eliminated from the bill, so was the provision that would give adoptees the right to their birth records. NCFA had gone into overdrive, soliciting letters through their many member agencies from adoptive parents, and HEW received more than three thousand such comments. They were overwhelmingly against the proposed legislation. Ninety percent of adoptive parents who wrote objected to allowing their children access to the original birth certificates when they became adults.[74] The late Senator John Tower of Texas—

---

[73] *Federal Register* 45, no. 33, (Feb. 15, 1980): 10691, col. 2, CUB archives.
[74] Carp, *Family Matters*, 187.

known as a drunk and a womanizer all over DC according to the *New York Times*, who put his behavior in more polite terms—was the champion of excising the adoptees' and mothers' rights.[75]

Less well known was that he was an adoptive father, just like Joseph Bruno, one of our main opponents in New York. Bruno ran the state Senate for fourteen years with an iron fist. When Bruno left, under investigation for felony, he passed on the baton to another adoptive father, Dean Skelos, who shared Bruno's stance that the records must stay sealed.[76] I found their attitude nearly unfathomable—because they were denying their own children information about themselves—but I chalk it up to a sense of possession, an unshakable fear of the natural mother and father, a feeling that their own status as a parent might be challenged unless natural mothers were obliterated, erased from memory, and placed beyond the reach of the children—no matter what age.

Years later, Skelos was similarly disgraced and charged with soliciting illegal kickbacks related to providing his adopted son Adam with no-show jobs. Skelos and his son were both eventually sentenced, after two trials, to four years in prison for corruption. At the time of the sentencing in 2018, Skelos and Adam were estranged, and he had reconnected with his biological parents.[77]

---

[75] Philip Shenon, "The Smoke Surrounding John Tower," *New York Times*, Feb. 11, 1989.

[76] Bruno was convicted of two counts of mail and wire fraud. He was acquitted of five felonies, and the jury hung on the last count. His convictions were subsequently overturned on appeal, and he was retried for somewhat different charges. A second jury found Bruno, in his eighties, not guilty of all charges. Bruno died in 2020.

[77] Benjamin Weiser and Vivian Wang, "Dean Skelos, Ex-New York Senate Leader, Gets 4 Years and 3 Months in Prison," *New York Times*, Oct. 24, 2018; Nicole Fuller, "Dean Skelos and Son, Adam, Scheduled to Start Federal Prison Sentence Tuesday," *Newsday*, Jan. 6, 2019.

16 Meeting Mr. Right

WINTER 1981—I am in Sag Harbor. There is a small group of freelance writers—all guys save me—who stay in Sag Harbor year round. Most everybody else has jobs where you had to show up, and they decamped back to the city, known to outsiders as Manhattan/Brooklyn/Westchester. I'm writing a diet book for a doctor who can't write, and I am hanging onto the dregs of a relationship with the same starving and stoned writer that I've been with, off and on, for the past three years. His as-yet-unfinished novel might be a success, might be made into a movie, might require his move to Hollywood! Despite this, being in some sort of a relationship with him—with all his maybes and Saturday nights when he absolutely, positively has to be alone to work—has been better than being alone in Manhattan, home of a million lonely hearts, all with careers going somewhere. I seek commitment. He quotes Shakespeare: "Ripeness is all," a.k.a. "timing is everything." Clearly our cycles are not in sync.

I had tried to end it. When he disappeared over the Fourth of July weekend and I later learned that he was with our friends—and someone from his hometown in Virginia. When he was going to move in with me and then, at the last moment, he wasn't. When he cancels our plans because he wants to be alone.

So when the lawyer I once loved calls from San Francisco and says he is moving back east and joining academia, I consider my options and take the red-eye with a suitcase full of hope. We spend a pleasant few days in Big Sur before driving cross-country, listening to fuzzy Dylan tapes, trying to discern the words. We are mostly successful with Dylan, not so with our own love song. My passion has turned to cold ash and cannot be stoked. I get out in Detroit to visit my mother. He and I say goodbye while waiting for the down elevator in her building. The door slides shut, and another chapter closes.

As always, I end up circling back to the cul-de-sac where the man who can't commit offers frequent, but uneven, companionship—not a small thing as I am sliding through my thirties and still single. Plus, and this is a big plus, he is unflaggingly supportive of my writing *Birthmark* and all that I am doing. So. I am stuck. In almost a relationship with him and his pair of adorable golden retrievers.

My girlfriends roll their eyes.

I hang in there.

Yet sometimes help comes from unexpected sources: freezing weather, my woeful lack of knowledge of houses, and Gael, my friend from the *Daily Collegian*. After another summer in Sag Harbor, I have cozily sequestered myself in an ivy-covered-but-uninsulated cottage. The pipes at this quirky, charming abode freeze when I go back home to Michigan for a week at Christmas. Who knew you were supposed to leave the heat at fifty-five degrees so the pipes won't freeze? I do not. Who knew there would be a week when the temperature never gets above the teens interspersed with single-digit nights? I am paying utilities and thus turning down the heat because that seems like a good way to save on the oil bill. Now that I'm going to be away, I turn the heat off. When I return, even the water in the toilet bowl is frozen. Solid. Only a thin stream of icy water grudgingly emits from the kitchen spout.

My landlord, Arthur, is upset but doesn't throw me out into the street; however, the plumber tells me to relocate until March. This place isn't insulated, he points out. Thus I come to rely on the good graces of my friends, and soon enough I am settled in with Gael in Manhattan. Gael is black Irish, with dark glossy hair and a piercing gaze. She is now a senior editor at *Parade,* the Sunday supplement tucked into newspapers across the country. We'd lost touch for more than a decade, but she phoned after she'd seen an advertisement for *Birthmark* in the *New York Times Book Review*. We are both single again—like me, she is divorced—and we resume our friendship as if there hadn't been a long pause. She has a sofa bed in her studio, and she offers shelter until the spring thaw. A bookcase separates our beds, but not the nightly conversations. She goes off to work in the morning, and I set up at her dining table and proceed to write *How to Eat Like a Thin Person*, which naturally leads me to lose five or six pounds without seemingly thinking about it, but of course I am thinking about it all day.

One Sunday, she suggests I come along to a brunch she has been invited to attend. Before we are out the door, she asks if I had washed my hair that morning—yes was the answer—but I know what she is really commenting on is that my limp, dirty-blond hair needs highlighting. For me, highlighting is as necessary as toothpaste, and I am way behind schedule.

What I don't know is that she is intent on introducing me to a "nice guy" who had broken up with his live-in girlfriend only months before—thus the careful inspection of my appearance. When the nice guy and I do not gravitate to each other—he later tells me he thought I came with someone male— Gael pulls me over to introduce us. His name is Tony. We talk nonstop for well over an hour in the kitchen, oblivious to the rest of the Upper West Side Sunday-brunchers. What was your memoir about? Tony wants to know.

My coming out as a mother who relinquished a child is now as much a part of my identity as the color of my eyes—especially to other writers who understand the importance of writing what you know. Do I occasionally fudge the issue when asked? Yes. Do I sometimes say, Oh, magazine pieces, or, I'm working on a diet book? Yes. The truth sometimes brings casual chitchat to a crashing halt. *You gave up a child? Wow.* And one never knows where a fuming enemy might pop up. Or a woman who will pepper me with questions for the next half hour while my heart is sliced open again. But that day I do not hesitate: it's about giving up a baby for adoption.

I wait.

Mr. Right reacts as if I had said I'd written a book on apple pies. What he says he heard was, This is a woman who has had a child! Swell! She probably won't have baby hunger. As the divorced dad of two teenagers, he is heavily into child support and decidedly not into additional paternity. Yet most of the women he'd been meeting have biological clocks loudly going tick-tock.

I am somewhat amazed at how blasé he is with my revelation—not even a raised eyebrow—but, okay, I think, he doesn't think I'm a slut. Cool. He's a writer; he gets it. However, no matter that this is going swimmingly, somewhere at the forty-minute mark I drop the words "my boyfriend" into the conversation. Possibly I sense he's about to ask me out. I explain that the boyfriend is finishing a novel. A little later, before Tony leaves to meet his daughter, he suggests lunch.

Lunch is safe, right? Lunch doesn't mean I'm dumping the alleged boyfriend. Did I say that as well as being able to talk to this guy about anything and everything, he somewhat resembles Sean Connery? Later, Gael is most interested in the fact that we are having lunch. Now she casually lets me know he is a "nice guy." She mentions a previous girlfriend, adding that she was also at the brunch with her new boyfriend.

Four days later in a nearly deserted tavern on Third Avenue, Tony and I share our life stories, no holds barred—this is not a date, right? This is just lunch, right? We're both dressed as if we might be going to the library, not on a prospective hot date. We sit side by side against a wall. Nothing unusual happens. I'm not even thinking we could be on to something good—nor does he seem to be. We chat amiably. He reveals that when his cousin Joan got pregnant when in high school, her parents in upstate New York shipped her off to live with his family in New Jersey. His mother made her stay indoors and whisked her off to the doctor in a big roomy coat so no one would notice she was with child. The father of her child was a shit who got his buddies to say they also had slept with her when they hadn't, and the family doctor arranged for a private adoption in Tony's hometown. Tony was eleven at the time and barely understood what was happening but later became aware that his favorite cousin got a raw deal from start to finish. She never seemed to be content or happy afterward, he says. There's a couple of broken marriages. Tony knows what giving up a child meant to his cousin, and how it changed her. He understands everything without me having to explain.

His own misery of the moment (besides a wretched divorce and a vindictive ex-wife) is a result of him being sued for libel by a psychiatrist under whose sloppy care a child died, an anecdote that Tony included in his book *Reality Police*. Though it was a muckraking book about the mental health system, his delinquent editor omitted giving the book a libel reading, usually automatic for any such book. His editor later said he "didn't want to rein in" his writer. I am astonished that Tony hadn't asked, precisely because the book was highly critical of the mental health system and its culprits. He explains that he's getting a late start on the dashing-but-dicey life of a freelance writer. Before writing the book, he had published only one magazine article in something called *Foundation News*, and he was clueless about libel. To make matters worse, this was when publishers did not routinely include libel insurance in their contracts, and thus Tony is on his own. His negligent editor will get off scot-free—the publisher's lawyers will protect him—but Tony must pay for his own defense. He has hired the best libel lawyer in the state of Kansas, where the suit was brought. He is getting a robust defense, but nevertheless my lunch companion is going to owe a good-sized chunk of change when it's over, no matter the outcome.

We joke that we each need to marry someone with a job that comes with medical insurance with a family plan so that each of us might have coverage.

He tells me he has an essay about his grandmother (yes, his grandma, but it's no saccharine story) in *The Atlantic* that very month. Hmm. Impressive.

I tell Tony that although my relationship with my, ah, boyfriend has been up and down, I'm giving the guy another year. Another year? says the look in his eyes. Another year? I was thirty-eight, and said boyfriend and I were well into our third year.

When I try to split the check for our burgers, Tony insists on paying, and after I have picked up the check for the other guy more times than I like to recall, the gesture is pleasantly refreshing. We leave the restaurant. Two blocks later, I realize I've left my wallet. We walk back, and it's still on the seat, credit cards and cash untouched. We walk over to a doctor's office nearby where I pick up a manuscript I might take on as an editing job. Just before I jump on the crosstown bus to shop for a dress to wear to a wedding,

I impulsively give Tony a quick kiss. On the lips. Why? The heart already knows what the mind does not.

When I try on a clingy, hot-pink dress an hour later, I have a stroke of insight: This is a dress one could go out on a date in. And not have to pick up the check.

Gael, ever perceptive, listens attentively to my recounting of the lunch but says little. That evening "my boyfriend" calls and says that very day he had come into town from faraway Greenwich, Connecticut (a forty-five-minute train ride), to turn in a first draft of his novel—I didn't even know he was turning it in!—but he hadn't called to tell me ahead of time because . . . I fill in the blanks: You know, the editor might have said, Hey, I'm free, let me take you to a three-hour, two-drink, expense-account lunch. He says that he phoned after he dropped off his manuscript, and gee whiz, no one answered. Oh, I say, thinking, I walked out the door ten minutes earlier.

Kismet.

When my ex-roommate Barbara hears of this lunch, she immediately reads Tony's piece in *The Atlantic* and insists that he is the "real writer," implying you-know-who is not. I am beginning to see a theme here. That is the second week of February.

A week later, after the wedding of one of my guy writer-friends in Sag Harbor, boyfriend and I spend the night together at my cozy cabin, now liberated from its winter chill. But the next morning I hear he's leaving that afternoon. He needs to be alone. Again. After he turned his manuscript in on Wednesday, he says, he's been partying with his friends in Connecticut. Now he needs some downtime. Alone.

You got it, I say.

By the end of February, Tony and I (a) are living together in his book-lined apartment in a Westchester suburb where I have taken over the living room while I finish the diet book, (b) have rented a bigger house with insulation around the corner from the house of frozen pipes where we will move in April, and (c) are planning to get married in the fall.

Summer in Sag Harbor comes along with Tony's son, Evan, who moves in with us. Come fall, he'll be off to college. Now begins the shakedown cruise for Tony and me, and there is a lot to shake out. First of all, I go from living alone for years to living with a partner—and his teenage son, who has teenage child-of-divorce angst. Evan watches a lot of television on our only set while eating potato chips on our couch. Second, Tony and I have to figure out who holds the alpha position.

So, in between heady passion, we scream at each other.

I sell the MG, and what once seemed wildly extravagant turns out to be my nest egg. Esmerelda, still spiffy, is now a liability, like a lover who hangs on after the affair is over. British engineering, as anyone will tell you, is designed to line the pockets of patronizing mechanics who deign to work on your car for enormous amounts of money. Six-foot-two Tony could barely sandwich himself into Esmerelda. She sells for the same ten thousand dollars I had paid. When the money—cash—arrives in a shoebox, I throw the neat pile of hundred-dollar bills up in the air and let them float down. Tony can't stop laughing.

Though Tony and I never quite worked out who's really in charge, we marry anyway on a warm, gray-but-not-quite-raining Sunday afternoon in September in one of those summer cottages of thirty rooms with a name rather than numbered address—Kinkora—in Westhampton Beach. We have a three-tiered mocha cake from a French patisserie, a four-piece swing band, and a write-up in the *Times*, and I wear something that resembles a real wedding dress, a creamy-white satin damask-wrap dressing gown from the thirties, the kind that you might see in a Preston Sturgis movie set in a swank Manhattan apartment. It had the original price tag from Filene's Basement, twenty-nine dollars, still attached when I got it from a vintage shop for three times that. A local dressmaker takes it in, and I jazz it up with a burnt-orange silk cummerbund. I tuck the linen hanky with lacy blue edging my mother crocheted for the occasion somewhere on my person.

The band backs Tony when he sings "Sweet Lorraine" in his resonant basso profundo, which means as low as you can go. My mother, relieved that I'm getting married to someone she senses is the right person, dances the afternoon away with the (unmarried) Episcopal minister who did the honors for us that day. A photographer friend takes pictures, a musician friend of

Tony's plays the wedding march on a keyboard, I have tears in my eyes on and off all afternoon—it must be PMS, right?—everyone dances and joins in when we cut the cake and sing "Bye, Bye, Blackbird"—*Pack up all your cares and woe, there you go, singing low* . . . I can barely carry a tune for more than five notes, but this simple melody I can manage. As long as it's not a solo.

Figure 11. Tony and Lorraine's wedding day 1981 (photo by Star Black)

How did two impoverished freelancers pull off such a gala event, as my father called anything other than a potluck? Nearly two years have passed since *Birthmark* was published, and the money from it is mostly gone—except for the cash from the sale of the MG. The estate where we married? Kinkora belonged to the grandparents of Ted Conklin, owner of the sometimes-rowdy-but-always-elegant American Hotel in Sag Harbor where we hang out and generally raise hell, right beside the well-heeled who order five-hundred-dollar bottles of wine from Ted's extensive cellar. Ted caters the whole she-bang, champagne and chicken curry, at a rate reserved for friends and family. He brings a commercial-sized bag of rice and supplies everyone with fistfuls. Under a pounding hail of rice, we slide into his Continental Flying Spur Bentley and are driven away under an allée of pollarded trees. The wedding feels like a victory party after a long slog into Russia as a foot soldier in Napoleon's army.

Our honeymoon is a trek through five countries and ten cities in South and Central America as the unpaid but all-expenses-paid quality-control inspectors for the Intercontinental hotel chain that I'd written about for the *Times*. The job is clear enough—use all of the hotel's services, from late-night room service to spa treatments, but be canny enough to not tip them off that you are checking out everything from the dust on top of the picture frames to how a waiter reacts when you send back a steak that is too rare. All this is meticulously noted in the reports, each as thick as a PhD thesis. To assure we remained undetected—and thus we will receive no special coddling, no free bottles of champagne—the seventy-plus-page reports are locked up in a suitcase when we are out and about. We visit so many hotels in five weeks that we have a small suitcase designated only for them.

Life indeed is picking up. Left to our own finances, we could have afforded a weekend at an airport Hilton.

But you don't go anywhere without baggage, the kind you can't check. I remember the sweet face of a teenager when we were out walking in Buenos Aires, the gorgeous young girls in their barely-there bikinis on a beach in Rio, a spoiled young beauty—who must have been about my daughter's age—arguing with her mother at a shopping mall in Caracas. I put coins in a tin box in an old stone church in Managua and say a prayer for my daughter. What souvenir would I buy her if I could? A hand-woven belt in Maracaibo, a straw purse from a street market in Ocho Rios? I buy these things, not telling anyone, not even Tony, that I wish I could give them to her one day. Look at those yellow flowers there by the massive monument outside of Valencia— they are the same color as forsythia. I do not think of her every minute of every day, don't get me wrong. Yet try as I might, I can't turn off the Muzak in my mind with its continual chorus.

Find her. She needs you.

17 She Is Found!

Years were going by without me finding my daughter. I had no leads yet—
other than they were not in the Rochester area anymore. I had no plan
about what I would do if I did locate her. So I simply collected and mentally
filed away any information that came my way via the ALMA meetings in
Manhattan. Not the official search sessions—I was still barred from them because my daughter was underage—but you hang around and you hear stuff.
About the elusive searcher who for cash could seemingly find anyone. But my
daughter was too young, I told myself. I wouldn't go there. Not yet.

Some adopted people got their original birth certificates (OBCs) by paying a hundred dollars to a certain clerk at the office where the records were
housed. The clerk copied the original and passed it under a stall in the ladies'
room. Elsewhere adoptees simply got lucky by going to where their birth certificate was filed and a sympathetic clerk simply would get the desired document and let the adoptee furtively look at it—read fast and write quickly!
At some agencies social workers were known to bring the adopted person to
their office, take out the relevant file, leave it open on the desk, and then excuse themselves—to the ladies' room, to a forgotten meeting, whatever. The
adoptee would grab the file and take down the name, the last known address,
whatever was there. A nurse once told me she extracted the information for
her adopted husband from a state agency by befriending someone there and
repeatedly asking for his mother's name and last known address, assuring her
that she and her husband only had the best intentions. He met his natural
mother a few months before she died.

Natural mothers had less success, but still, some did. Some women had found underage children, but I hadn't asked how. One woman, a natural mother named Sandy Musser, had figured out how to do a search, and after finding and reuniting with her daughter, she started a search service. It was successful enough to attract attention. A New Jersey couple pretending to be biological parents looking for their child set her up, and Musser ended up in federal prison.[78] Not only did I not want to be arrested, I had convinced myself that having published a controversial memoir, I must be above reproach. Plus, the slings and arrows of publishing *Birthmark*—of being *that* woman who had the gall to speak out—have beaten me up a bit.

True, after the publication and publicity of *Birthmark*, I received hundreds of letters from adoptees, natural mothers and a few fathers. The letters were full of grief and longing. They were from teenagers, prisoners, and ordinary citizens in their sixties and seventies. I had stationery printed up with my name and address and answered every single one. Even the guy who proposed marriage and sent photos.

I got a phone call from someone who knew somebody who knew me. The caller wanted to know how he could find the airline stewardess he'd impregnated twenty years ago. He did not remember her name. He was pretty sure she had not gotten an abortion. Now, he said, he was wealthy and could help out financially—send his child to school!—if he could find him. Or her. I could offer only empathy.

A few adoptive parents wrote. Their letters were unsigned and angry.

But what did not come was the one letter I was hoping for: a missive from her parents. Or her. I put aside thoughts of looking for her. I would bide my time. I would write about something else.

However.

About two weeks before the wedding, Tony and I are having dinner in Sag Harbor with one of my guy writer-friends. McCabe is a smooth Brit and a man-about-Manhattan magazine editor, and as we are leaving his house the subject of my daughter comes up, who knows how, and McCabe wants to

[78] Musser tells her remarkable story in a memoir, *To Prison with Love: The True Story of an Indecent Indictment and America's Adoption Travesty* (Awareness Press, 2014).

know what is so sacrosanct about waiting until my daughter turns eighteen. You're not going to snatch her, are you? Anyway, at fifteen, she's too old for that. If she's not going to come live with you—then what's the problem? he asks. I stumble around looking for words, but I have no answer. "Dusky, this is killing you, not knowing where she is," he says bluntly, not knowing the rules. "Why are you hesitating?"

Tony looks at me, and I see he is wondering the same thing. If these two perfectly sane guys are saying it is permissible to find her—not in three years, but now—then why not? If it sounds as if I am asking for permission, I am. I need someone—an outsider—to tell me that I am not demented, that my insatiable longing to know her could be understood as reasonable by rational people, people uninvolved in adoption themselves. They act as if my eternal yearning to know my daughter is natural, even normal.

Mere curiosity is much too weak a word for this need to know what happened to one's progeny. English lacks an adequate word. Calling it curiosity diminishes the bottomless thirst for knowing where one's child is, how she is, or if she is even alive. The quest is primal, the need is boundless—unless, like some adoptees, you have had the desire to know beaten out of you by guilt, by society, by the seemingly impossible barriers erected by law and cultural norms. Adoptees are supposed to be grateful and mindful of their parents' tender feelings about how they came into the adoptive family. Often adoptees are schooled into silence by adoptive parents. The adopted must never mention their native curiosity about roots, while "it"—the fact of having been adopted—sits in the center of their relationship like crabgrass that's never quite been killed. Natural mothers are supposed to slink away, never to return, never to be curious, and if they are, too bad. You-made-your-bed-and-now-you-must-lie-in-it permeates the thinking of those who would relegate us to the unspeakable shadows. I'd met women who had been searching for years and found no clues, not even a trail to follow. My greatest fear was that I would be one of them. Despair was always one mental micron away.

Was I afraid? Naturally. Some part of me hesitated to break the rules. Afraid of failing. Of having to explain why. Of possible rejection. Just afraid. But that night, everything changed.

We are standing in McCabe's dining room with oak wainscoting halfway up the walls, the lighting is low, the night is late, we have our coats on, we are about to walk out the door, and Tony and McCabe wait for me to respond. They understand what I can barely acknowledge: How desperately I need to know, how *not* knowing rules my life. Until I have answers, I am stuck in a mire of remorse and recrimination. Time might pass, circumstances might change, but I could not forgive myself. I cannot move forward into my next act.

Until I find her.

"You're right," I finally say, somewhat startled as I find my voice. *I can do this, I can do this* keeps me awake that night.

The next morning, I call someone, who calls someone who knows how to reach someone who is known as The Searcher. It appears that he or she— gender unknown—can find anybody in a matter of days, sometimes hours— mothers for adoptees, adoptees for mothers, people in any state. Is he in the CIA or FBI, someone able to access information that nearly no one else can? Maybe she is a judge or a social worker. Maybe he only has a good cover story: "This is Judge So-and-So from fill-in-the-blank, and I need this information because of a medical fill-in-the-blank reason." Maybe she is a private detective who found a good source of revenue, but how does she do it? Does he have contacts in every state, well-placed clerks he pays off to check the files, fax him the relevant pages? Maybe she believes the records shouldn't be sealed. Maybe he only does it for the money. None of this matters. What matters is that The Searcher succeeds.[79]

The fee to me in 1981 is equivalent to four months of our winter rental

---

[79] Today, though there are search angels (often found through social media) who work simply for expenses, a small private industry has grown up to connect the missing links. The vast increase of people listed in DNA databases has widely increased the avenues of search and connection. Search, however, became so lucrative that when open-records bills came before some legislatures, representatives from search-for-fee operators would lobby against them unless they had a birth-mother veto. If the records were to be opened, oops, there goes their client base. Fortunately, that seems to have ended as more states open—at least partially—original birth records to adoptees. At present, searching appears to be both easier—because of the internet and DNA connections—and harder, because more clerks and social work-

in Sag Harbor. I don't need to pay anything until she is found. I will use money from the sale of the MG. Since *Birthmark* did not smoke her out, maybe the money from it will.

Six weeks later when we return from South America, among the piles of mail waiting for us, among the bills and catalogs and magazines and announcements of gallery openings, is a letter from the woman I'd told I wanted to find my daughter. She has set the search in motion. The letter says my daughter has been located. After a quick bath of adrenaline-induced hot flash, a calmness enters me as I read the letter twice, three times, to make sure it really says what I think it does.

She is found.

I am Lazarus, rising from the dead. Soon I will know where she is. For the moment, that is all that matters.

Now all these years of wonder are sloughing off like an old skin. Is this really happening? Will I be able to know her? Can I explain why I had relinquished her? Will she forgive me?

My sleep is uneasy that night. I have dreams, faces appear and disappear into the ether, numbers melt off the phone as I try to call her, I cannot see the numbers clearly, I hold a phone, but I don't know what the right numbers are, and I wake up, sweaty and agitated. What will her parents say when I call? Will they slam down the phone?

The following Sunday, Tony and I drive to New Jersey with a thick wad of hundred-dollar bills. I hand it to a woman who is part of the pipeline to reach the nameless, shadowy searcher. The cash will be sent in a greeting card, and only after it arrives will I get my daughter's name and address, and maybe some additional information. Twelve hundred dollars in cash through the mail? I say in disbelief. Yes. That is how it is done. It is all so clandestine, so hush-hush, a mother-and-child-reunion railroad.

Now I wait.

---

ers are savvy about their state's closed-records law. And not all DNA searches result in a connection.

Open vs. Closed Adoption

When I relinquished Jane in 1966, all I really wanted—or thought I could ask for—was to be able to know her one day. Even that bare concession to the mother-and-child bond would have made leaving her easier, for it would have held out hope for a future reunion or relationship, and perhaps—*perhaps* is the operative word here—made the years when I did not know where she was or who she was much less traumatic.

Aware of the huge gap between legal, accepted adoption anonymity and the ache in my psyche—and that of the other mothers I met through ALMA—when I pondered what I would say to a woman considering adoption for her child, this is what I wrote in *Birthmark* more than four decades ago:

> I would tell her that if it had to be that way . . . if she couldn't support herself and the child financially and emotionally, if she couldn't go the road alone, in other words, if the child had to be adopted, I would tell her to insist on meeting those parents. She is giving them her child, and she has every right in the world to meet the people . . . . She can demand this no matter what the laws on the books say, no matter what she has been led to believe by people who have never given away a child. There is wisdom the heart knows beyond reason, where logic follows if we let it. And if the experts at the agency say you can't do it that way, I would say, I will find parents to adopt my child another way. I know it can be done.[80]

I would give the same advice today.

What was revolutionary then is commonplace today, for 95 percent of all agency adoptions of infants in the United States today have some degree of openness, supposedly eliminating the wall of anonymity between mother and child. But the words *some degree* are critical. A reliable study from the Donaldson Adoption Institute found that only 55 percent of the roughly 14,000 to 18,000

[80] Lorraine Dusky, *Birthmark* (New York: M. Evans, 1979), 100.

infant adoptions each year were fully open, with the parties agreeing to ongoing contact that includes the child.[81] The rest are semi-open, a classification that means there is some communication between the natural mother and the adoptive parents, but exactly how much is often poorly defined.

Fully open adoption does not come without risks. Meeting the prospective adoptive parents, getting to know them and thinking of them as friends, inviting them into the delivery room, having them cut the umbilical cord—with all the symbolism that implies—makes it more difficult for a mother to change her mind about the adoption and keep her baby. Despite whatever second thoughts she is having, she feels pressured not to let down the nice people who have made their desires for a baby—her baby—so crushingly obvious. Thus, some advocates for mothers understandably are opposed to meeting the parents in person at all.

Therein lies the paradox of semi-open adoption, a fuzzy category that covers 40 percent of infant adoption at this writing.[82] One study found that while mothers with open adoptions experience greater grief resolution in the long run, those who interact with their babies and help choose the adoptive parents actually report more sadness and regret initially, that is, the first few months after birth.[83] Because they continue to cuddle and hold their babies when the love hormone oxytocin is coursing through their bloodstream, the sense of loss may be heightened. I honestly cannot imagine what that must feel like to hold and let go, to walk away without your infant. Yet I do see posts in social media from young women who are at peace with their decision, at least in the early stages, and have good relationships with the adoptive parents, assuming they are living up to whatever arrangements were agreed upon.

Yet not all such arrangements stand the test of time. Women who enter into adoptions believing they will be open, or as open as promised, may later discover that the contact they counted on was merely a mirage hidden in the

---

[81] Deborah H. Siegel and Susan Livingston Smith, *Openness in Adoption: From Secrecy and Stigma to Knowledge and Connections* (New York: Donaldson Adoption Institute, 2012), 7, www.web.archive.org/web/20211201162951/https://njarch.org/wpress/wp-content/uploads/2015/11/2012_03_OpennessInAdoption.pdf.
[82] Smith, *Safeguarding*, 49.
[83] Smith, 49.

fine print of legalese. These women are understandably distraught.[84] Their grief spills out in numerous posts on Facebook and comments on blogs. One woman showed me the latest photograph she had received of her child—it was of the back of his head. Technically, it fulfilled the agreement she had made with the adoptive parents for photographs.

One mother wrote on my blog, *First Mother Forum*, about her devastating experience with verbal assurances not written into the contract.

> I voiced my reluctance about going through with the adoption—if they were unwilling to agree to regular correspondence and pictures of my child until age 18. [The agency agreement stipulated up to age six.] At that point, of course, he would be old enough to make his own decisions. The agency did require that the couple agree to a single visitation when my child was one and held out the promise that there might be more. Yet I was still apprehensive. My hesitation must have been obvious, and so, during our last meeting—shortly before I gave birth to my son—both the man and the woman looked me straight in the eye and promised that they would honor our spoken agreement for an open adoption. I believe they would have said anything to get my child.
>
> Everything ended when he was seven. The adoptive parents moved and left no forwarding contact information. The correspondence and pictures no longer came. I had no way to reach them. I was devastated. A lawyer I contacted after a few years told me that because I did not have a signed legal agreement specifying certain conditions, there was nothing that I could do. The people who adopted my son—supposedly good Christians—were people I trusted, yet they deceived me and destroyed my relationship with my son. To anyone who says that getting a child under these false pretenses is not coercion, you are wrong. I would never have agreed to let my son be adopted if I knew the couple would not honor their promise.[85]

---

[84] Smith, 50.

[85] Quoted in Lorraine Dusky, "An Un-Open Adoption: Adoptive Parents Lie and

Not all open-adoption promises are broken, and if the original agreement is adhered to, natural mothers fare significantly better than those in closed adoptions.[86] Four years after relinquishing their children, women who chose the adoptive parents and who were not coerced by parental pressure report less sorrow and worry and more relief and peace than those who did not have this opportunity. More than half of the respondents had received follow-up pictures and letters. But within four years of the adoption, a mere 12 percent said they had phoned or visited since the child had been placed with a new family.

As open adoption continues to evolve, mothers relinquishing their children need to be aware of the exigencies and loopholes to avoid. Agencies offer what they call "open" adoptions, but the particulars of many of these agreements obfuscate how little control the mother has after she signs the paper. What "communication" means varies dramatically from an annual update to more frequent letters and photographs, and whether the arrangement continues after a certain period is at the discretion of either party. Communication between the natural mother and adoptive parents often is not direct but only through the agency or attorney. Individuals may not actually know each other by name or be given phone numbers or addresses. Even when the names and addresses are well known by both parties, that doesn't mean the arrangement works out as agreed. Verbal promises have no legal standing. A friend who is a magazine editor tells me that someone on her staff refused to do television appearances because the "birth mother [of his adopted child] might recognize" him, the adoptive father. What did that mean? I wondered: Had his child's natural mother picked him and his wife from a photograph? Had there been the promise of contact that he now avoided? Why did he feel the need to hide?

Legally, mothers' rights appear to be improving—but luck is still involved. While numerous states—as of this writing, one site puts the num-

Break a Mother's Heart," *[Birth Mother] First Mother Forum*, March 28, 2009. https://web.archive.org/web/20221205210934/https://www.firstmotherforum.com/2009/03/un-open-adoption-adoptive-parents-lie.html.
[86] Pearila Brickner Namerow, Debra Kalmuss, and Linda Cushman, "The Consequences of Placing versus Parenting Among Unmarried Women," *Marriage & Family Review* 25, no. 3–4 (1997), 175–97.

ber at twenty-nine[87]—give mothers in open-adoption contracts the right to enforce them, the women rarely pursue such cases, typically because they lack the financial wherewithal to do so. Even when they do seek redress, the natural mothers rarely win. Agencies have no prerogative to force the adoptive parents to comply. Some legal websites clearly state that a mother's rights after adoption are chancy, noting that the strength of any relationship with the child depends on a strong bond with the adoptive parents and, even so, "rights are often sparse when adopting a child out to another family."[88]

In some cases, courts have turned down even considering a natural mother's claim because the state has no laws governing open adoption and thus the agency has no standing to offer such a contract! Some agreements include the all-encompassing provision that if the natural mother tries to set aside the adoption for any reason, all visits will stop. Thus, she has a built-in incentive not to upset the adoptive applecart. Given all this, a woman considering an open adoption ought to hire her own attorney to negotiate the provisions of the agreement beforehand. But she is often without funds to do that, and besides, unless it is a private adoption directly with an attorney, the natural mother most likely has placed herself in the hands and supervision of a solicitous social worker, whom she feels has her best interests at heart.

When one of the contestants on *Sixteen and Pregnant*, a discontinued reality TV show, complained to her social worker that she did not know how to reach the parents on her own, the social worker responded by saying something to the effect of, Well, if you wanted a fully open adoption, you should have said so. It was clear that the young—and now anguished—teen mother had not been aware that she had a choice and could have asked for direct contact. If you are made to think that a semi-open adoption sounds as good as you can get, and you are not aware you can ask for more, why would you?

One major problem is that the adoption agency serves as the hub for post-

---

[87] Virginia Spence, "Are Open-Adoption Agreements Legally Enforceable?" The Gladney Center for Adoption, April 19, 2019, https://web.archive.org/web/20220825210205/https://adoption.org/open-adoption-agreements-legally-enforceable-2.

[88] "Birth Family's Legal Rights after Adoption," HG.org Legal Resources, accessed Jan. 2021, https://web.archive.org/web/20220825210831/https://www.hg.org/birth-familys-legal-rights-after-adoption.html.

adoption contact. First and foremost, adoption agencies are businesses. Like any business, they are subject to market whims and the needs and desires of the individuals who run them. Agencies can close. There is no central repository to handle the agency's records and archive them properly, and only luck determines whether anyone will pick up the files. By the time Adoption Services Associates (ASA) in San Antonio shut down in 2012, it had handled some 5,000 adoptions. Many of the women who had surrendered babies had been promised regular updates and photographs until the child was five, as well as the possibility of a reunion at eighteen. Another Texas agency, Abrazo Adoption Services, stepped in to help the frantic women who relinquished through ASA.

But Abrazo was only able to locate the adoptive families of about a dozen of the children, and only half of them were receptive to continuing contact with their child's natural mother. That would be six. Several thousand mothers who thought they had an open-adoption arrangement were out of luck. When Abrazo's director, Elizabeth Jurenovich, suggested to some of the adoptive parents that an actual reunion take place—an ideal that the natural mothers had clung to—the reaction surprised her. "ASA only made us send her a letter and picture once a year for five years afterward, that should be enough!" one adoptive father shouted on the phone. "We didn't want to adopt her and her family, just the baby!" Conversely, a handful of adoptive families did want to keep up contact with the natural mother—but only if Abrazo would act as the go-between. Like most agencies today, Abrazo only handles fully open adoptions. Some agencies will do closed adoptions, but only at the insistence of the mother.

Closing an open adoption is not always the adoptive parents' doing. Some natural mothers do not keep up contact. It may be too hard to visit and not be overcome by grief and guilt; the adoptive family might live in a faraway state; some women are simply less bothered by their children being raised by others and drift away.

Adolescence is precisely the time more contact, not less, is likely to be beneficial to the adoptee. Natural mothers may be led to believe that the openness is merely for their benefit and are unaware how crucial it is for the child. In fact, an adopted adolescent's preoccupation with adoption itself—that is, thinking about one's natural parents, who they might be—is not related to whether the adoption is open or closed or whether the biological parents are known or not.[89]

How do the children fare? Until the 1990s, few adoptions were open. Definitive, long-range research comparing the adoptees from closed versus open adoption has yet to emerge. A few random comments found on the internet suggest that open-adoption arrangements are not necessarily easy for the child. But then, neither is adoption, any sort of adoption. Yet without question open adoption encourages communication with the natural mother, and this communication is likely to give adoptees a better understanding of their backgrounds and complex identities and eliminate "fantasy" parents. Instead, the fantasies are replaced with actual people with whom an adoptee might have a relationship.

The best solution—if a mother cannot raise her child—is for the child to be absorbed into the larger biological, natural family of aunts and uncles and cousins and grow up always knowing who the natural mother is and the circumstances that led to being raised by others in the family. This does not have to mean an adoption. An arrangement called kinship fostering is gaining traction in some places. This keeps the child with a relative—a grandmother, an aunt or uncle, or an older sibling—who receives financial aid and may also assume legal guardianship if the parent in charge is unable to assume that responsibility. Whether in or out of the kinship family, such arrangements do not involve issuing an amended birth certificate and negating the child's origins.

That is not to say that in some cases, adoption outside the family is not a life-affirming choice for the adopted. Adoption can be and may be necessary. Amended birth certificates are not. Open adoption is a step forward, but it is not a panacea for the myriad issues that stem from relinquishing a child to someone with whom they do not have an inalienable genetic connection.

[89] Julie K. Kohler, Harold D. Grotevant, and Ruth G. McRoy, "Adopted Adolescents' Preoccupation with Adoption: The Impact on Adoptive Family Relationships," *Journal of Marriage and Family* 64, no. 1 (Feb. 2002): 93–104.

Reunion/Reality

18 A Girl Named Jane

The call comes the Saturday after Thanksgiving. I take it on the upstairs wall phone, tomato-red in color, and I am standing in the knotty-pine landing, in the half light of early evening, having to say, Hang on, let me get a pen and paper. Writing against the wall, balancing the receiver in the crook of my neck, I methodically write down her name, phone number, and address. She has at least two brothers, one of them probably adopted, says my new friend, the woman I gave the money to, another mother like me, all part of this underground mother-and-child railroad. They belong to such-and-such parish, she adds as an aside. An odd piece of information, but comforting, nonetheless. When I relinquished her, I asked for a Catholic family.

Jane, her name is Jane. Jane. Jane Doe. Not a name I would have chosen, but it's fine. Any name will do. It is her name.

Her father's name is Gary, her mother's, Ann. Their last name is Rhymer. A name. A phone number. An address. In Madison, Wisconsin. Never been to Wisconsin. How did she end up in Wisconsin? People move, don't they? Sure, they do, that's how. Rhymer. Jane Ann Rhymer.

"They are listed in the telephone directory," the voice is calmly saying as if she is giving the weather, "because you will probably want to call information."

Yes, of course, I want to verify that these people actually exist, that this data is real, that she has a home, that she has normal parents who are listed in the telephone directory. I say her last name over and over. It feels strange to my tongue. It is German? English? Dutch? Not Polish. Not Irish. So unlike the Brasley it might have been. Or the Dusky it could have been. Do I like it? Does

215

it matter? No. Nothing matters but that I have a name, address, and phone number. I have her. Well, not quite. There will be hot coals to walk over.

I hang up and let out a scream. I am quickly surrounded by Tony and his children, Evan and Kate, who are there for Thanksgiving, and I'm babbling out the news. Evan is repeating "Jane Rhymer" with a snooty British accent. Now her name sounds cool—it sounds as if it might belong to a real person. Kate hugs me long and hard, and my eyes get misty. I feel as if I had been holding my breath for as long as one possibly could, and then longer still, and now someone has said, You can breathe now. I can exhale, I have permission to exhale and breathe in fresh air.

Sometime later, calmer, I call information solely to hear a woman respond with their number when I say their name. The feeling is magical, unreal. If this information is true, no one can ever take me from her again. Yes, she could walk away, but that will be her choice. That is so very different from the abyss of the unknown.

She—I couldn't call her Jane yet, Jane was too *other*—could tell me to get out of her life, that she didn't want to know me—you didn't want me then and I don't want you now—but at least that would be real, a confrontation between two living, breathing people. Over the next few days, my last thoughts at night and my first thoughts at dawn are these: I have her name. I have her name. She's only fifteen, how is this going to play out? Now I must do the rest, make the connection. Call her. What do I say? What will her parents say? Do? Will they let me see her? Is she all right? Will they call the cops on me? I have her name. I know where she is.

Patrick and I once said what a great, smart kid we'd have, unaware how we were complimenting ourselves. I surmise that if her family is a good one, she is doing fine, and that is what I hope for—that her family loves her and she is flourishing. But now I do not focus on what or who she might be. I want to know who she is.

By Wednesday evening, I am ready—no point in dragging out what I had been waiting fifteen years for. I have a martini with dinner, the meal is over, the dishes done. The phone in the kitchen sits there, mocking me. I kick Tony out. I sit down by the phone. Put it in front of me.

I pause.

Life-altering phone calls are hard. No matter what, one hesitates. One is reluctant. One is afraid. After the phone call, nothing will be the same.

The advice from others who had contacted children under eighteen is to pretend to be doing a survey and try to elicit whether the teenager even knows he or she is adopted. What you didn't want to do was break the news to your child over the phone—Hey, daughter, you're adopted! Oh, you didn't know? After you established what she knew, you were on your own.

My plan is to try the survey, then talk to her parents and tell them right off who I am. And hope for the best. I have a few notes written out on a yellow legal pad. I would say I was from *Seventeen* magazine, just doing a little survey here. Is Jane Rhymer home? I'd ask about clothes, boys, attitudes about drugs, and if she thought adopted people ought to be able to find their natural parents—and keep on going, as if that wasn't the whole point. If she knew she was adopted, she might mention this to the survey taker, right? *Now is the time for all good men to come to the aid of their country*—sentences and stray fragments fill my head as I hesitate—*how now brown cow.* Dial, Lorraine. Just do it. I notice my cuticles are scruffy, the floor needs mopping, the grain of the oak table where I sit makes interesting patterns, tiny rivulets going up and around, everything is in high definition. I'll pass out if I don't dial soon.

She answers on the second ring, and right off I know it's her. She sounds like me. Everything is fading out of focus, but I manage to start my spiel. However, after a few questions, without saying anything, she hands the phone to her mother. I keep talking, continuing my magazine-survey spiel, but her mother interrupts, "Oh, that doesn't apply here—my daughter is LD."

"LD?" Those are my initials. What is she talking about?

"Learning-Disabled."

My daughter is learning-disabled?

I stammer a response and hang up. I do not want to argue with the friendly but firm voice. But learning-disabled?

I call Tony and look at him wide-eyed and fearful—I wasn't counting on this. But there is no turning back. Within fifteen minutes I've written out a different script. Tony can stay. I dial again. After you've fallen off a horse, you have to get back on. Otherwise, the fear sets in, right? Then it gets too scary and much harder to ever get back on. Or it becomes A Thing. How could I sleep if I did not carry this to the end?

Jane Rhymer answers again. This time I am all business. "May I speak to your mother, please?"

She comes on the line. Go.

"My name is Lorraine Dusky, and I have something personal to discuss with you concerning your daughter, Jane. Is this a good time?" Exhale, inhale, stay calm. This may be the most important conversation I ever have in my life. Do not fuck this up.

"Yes, this is fine," she says.

"I—I had a daughter fifteen years ago on April fifth in Rochester, New York, and—I think—I think that daughter is Jane." I feel myself flushing. Back to you, Jane's mother.

There is a long pause. Please say something, say anything.

"What is your name? Where are you calling from?" she sounds unruffled, almost mechanical.

Is she going to call the police, like I'd heard some families do? What now? I answer this woman's questions, name, address, phone number, beating back tears, heart going kaboom, kaboom.

Then it is apparent I am losing the battle with tears. Now I can hear her voice break too. We are both crying. Then she says the words I will never forget—hell, I can hardly write them now without getting goose bumps—"I'm glad you called. I was afraid that you would hang up and we wouldn't know how to find you." If I hung up, there was no way for her to find my number. Phones back then didn't have caller ID, the number wasn't recorded by the phone, people could make crank calls and fall back into the unknown.

"We always wondered about you. You see, Jane—she's been pretty good lately—Jane has epilepsy. She's been hospitalized I don't know how many times. She almost drowned twice—she had seizures when she was diving." Now I could hear her choking back tears.

Oh my god. My daughter has epilepsy. I understood now about the

LD, but I didn't, not really. LD and epilepsy do not go hand in glove. Wasn't Dostoevsky epileptic?

"Is there anything like that in your family?" she wants to know. "Any history of this?"

"No, no one. And not in her father's family either. Not that I've ever heard of."

"Any learning problems?"

"No."

"Did you ever hear from the agency?" I ask, "about the birth control pills I took when I was pregnant? I wrote to them a couple of times before I got a letter telling me that Jane was happy in her family. No mention of any problem."

"Yes, we got the letter, but we had tried to reach you when her seizures started—when she was five, six. The agency never even answered our doctor's letter. So, when this came, a few years later, it didn't mean much. By then her seizures had been going on—"

"What? I had started writing the agency when Jane was five or six. I asked them to find out if there was any information you needed." I remember agonizing over the words so as not to sound deranged, but there I was, trying to reach her at the same time they were trying to reach me. As if somehow, I knew there was trouble. I remembered the response because who wouldn't? That her family "have been most delighted with her." I could not get the words out of my mind for weeks. *Most delighted with her.* What did they mean, exactly? The letter implied that everything was hunky-dory.

In fact, *most delighted* can only be an ironic, if not moronic, description of what the Rhymers were going through with a child who has multiple, debilitating seizures that could strike at any moment. A child that must be protected from undue stress, a child who missed tons of school because of the seizures, a child with low self-esteem and a propensity to fudge the truth at the first sign of anything unpleasant. Most delighted? She was having seizures one after another—and her doctor was trying to reach me. His letter to the agency was not even acknowledged!

It took the agency nearly ten months to find the Rhymers and let them know about the birth control pills I'd taken. I'd written in August. No response until the following June, assuring me that the doctor has been made aware of "my prenatal history" and would take it from there. "At present, she has shown no symptoms indicating any such problems as you are concerned about," it stated. "She is doing well and is happy in her family. Of course, we are keeping all your letters in her file, and they will be available to her in the event she should return to us. I hope this sets your mind at rest."

All this whirls through my mind as I fall silent. Her other mother is silent too. Our daughter needs me. She had needed me all along. I knew, somehow, that she needed me. But the system, the awful, terrible, immoral system that is closed adoption, responded, No need to do anything. Like the doctor when he told me I was pregnant after months of taking birth control pills, the agency has its rules.

After speaking to both her mother and father—they want to be sure I am not a nutcase or a teen-snatcher—Jane is on the phone. We talk for fifteen minutes or so. She is reticent, the conversation stilted. Hello, I say. This is your . . . other mother. "I've never forgotten you. I've wanted to know you for the longest time—I always—I always thought about you every time I saw a girl who might be your age . . . "

I wait. Nothing.

"I had to find out if you knew you were adopted. That's why I made that odd phone call a half hour ago. Why I pretended to be doing a survey."

"Uh-huh."

What to say now? She is barely responding. I am getting nowhere. She's fifteen, I tell myself, an awkward age, I'm a stranger. Are her parents there, listening? Probably, and why not? Hang on. Keep trying. Tony sees me floundering and writes questions down in the margin of that day's *Times*. What color eyes? What color hair? How tall? What subjects did she like in school? I had heard that other people, when they first make this connection, blabber on for hours, but this is like pulling the proverbial teeth. Painful.

She keeps answering like a child, directly, slowly, using only a few words. Is this part of the LD? She is not embellishing anything, offering nothing that could be followed up on. Later she will tell me how stunned she was that night, that simply acknowledging she was talking to her real mother—yes, that is what she called me when she told me this—was so astonishing that she couldn't concentrate. Finally, I hit pay dirt.

"What do you want to be when you grow up?" I ask.

"A journalist."

"A journalist?" Now it is me who is stunned. "Do you know that's what your father and I are?"

"Really?" At last, there is a pitch of excitement in her voice. "You're kidding!"

"No kidding. We met on a newspaper where we both worked."

As it would turn out, she and her parents knew nothing about her background. They only knew that I was Polish, they had filled in the blanks and figured I was probably in high school. They did not even know that her father was Irish—which would have allowed her to share with her adoptive mother a common heritage and celebrate St. Patrick's Day as if this Catholic holiday belonged to her too. What about all those forms going back to our grandparents that Patrick and I had carefully filled out? Gone with the wind, apparently. Mrs. Mura had been insistent that no detail be left out—I naively thought it would be given to her parents—but none of that medical history had been passed on. Maybe it had been collected to assure that the child was not defective, that she came without faulty genes. But given the birth control pills that were surely recorded, given Jane's epilepsy, given that her doctor had tried to learn more about her health history, my shock—and Ann's frustration—were all too justified. The rules had benefited no one. The rules had done our daughter harm.

I want to keep Jane on the phone, but soon enough we run out of conversation. I couldn't very well go into my relationship with her (married!) father or babble on about my family—that felt rude. A request for more information should come from her, and she clearly is not asking. Anything. Later I learn that the anti-seizure medication dulls one's affect. Later she will tell me that her parents were listening, and she was self-conscious—she didn't want to hurt their feelings by being too enthusiastic, not after all they had done for her, a girl with seizures, a girl with problems. Yet her reticence does not dampen my soaring heart that night. She is alive. I am talking to her. No matter what, all's right with the world.

After Jane and I say our goodbyes, Ann comes back on the line. "Would you like to come and meet Jane?"

"Yes—when?" My mind is already in flight, thinking only, how soon?

"Let's make plans later."

"Sure." I contain myself. If I'm too pushy about this they will retreat.

After I hang up, I scream with the relief of a soul plucked from hell. She is not in foster care, institutionalized, the kid left at boarding school when everyone else goes home for the holidays. Her adoptive parents are not divorced, and Jane doesn't have a stepparent who doesn't want their partner's kid around. She has loving parents. A family. My daughter is alive. Yes, she has epilepsy—not good, not good at all—but that is a real fact about her, a fact to deal with, not the phantom mirage from before. She is lost no more, she is not dead, she was not left stranded by the side of the road when the adoption did not work out.

Now I'll never not know where she is again, I remember repeating like a litany, now I'll never not know where she is. With a simple phone call, the punishing wall of sealed records in the state of New York crumbles like the yellowing paper it had been written on decades earlier. No matter what happens next, the worst is over. Giving her up is an ongoing act, not simply a part of my history, a one-time event, but a dead weight on my present. For a mother like me, adoption can have no closure as long as we do not know what happened to our children.

Think of a mother who watches her child go off to war. He does not come home. No telegram arrives. No one in uniform knocks on the door with the sad news of his death. Day after day, month after month, year after year, there is no news. She eventually understands that this is how it will always be. I will never know what happened to my child, even if he lives. This is the unforgiving reality of women who relinquish their children in a closed adoption. This was my reality up until that day.

The next morning, I send her a bouquet of daisies, and ask that a single rose be included with a note that it is for her mother. Then I call my mother, my brothers, and a few close friends, including our British friend McCabe, who'd encouraged me to start down this path. He lives a few houses up the street from us, and a few hours later he rushes in, saying he and the date he brought to our wedding would like to buy my round-trip ticket to Wisconsin. Since they hadn't given us a wedding present, they would buy the ticket, and he urges—Don't you want to go meet her right away? Why wait? Call them, Dusky, and ask if you can come right away.

Well, sure, but—

Call and ask, McCabe insists. He is beaming with enthusiasm.

Ann is somewhat taken aback but agrees to let me come in three days. Oh my god oh my god I'm going to meet her. What to say? What will they think of me? Three more days, and the daughter I'd never held will be within reach. When something is this close, something that has been desired for so long, what is the point of waiting? Why indeed? Why not now?

Three more days.

What I did not know, and would not know until many years later, is that The Searcher had found my daughter long before I put my order in. From *Birthmark*, The Searcher had taken the clues and already knew who she was. He (or she) was merely waiting for me to ask and send the fee.

19   Reunion

What am I going to wear? Need to look nice, not too New York. I'm going to meet my daughter! Go casual, casual is best, the Midwest is casual, I ought to know, I'm from the Midwest, too. From Michigan—why, that's next door to Wisconsin! Some people don't like New Yorkers, think we are—I dunno, brash? Too New York? This pink sweater or that striped one? Yes, pants. Do I need to take a skirt? Will we go to church on Sunday? They are Catholic, can I wear pants to Sunday mass? In Wisconsin?

I am still trying on and rejecting sweaters—as if pink made a difference from purple—when Tony is saying we'd better leave, don't want to be late. Tony is a get-to-the-airport-early kind of guy, while I'm always cutting it close. I am a tense ball of nerves, and so I pop a muscle relaxant on the hour drive to the airport.

In a state of double consciousness—anxiety (what if this doesn't go well?) and calm (almost there!) I change planes in Pittsburgh. On the weekend after Thanksgiving, only three other people are on the plane to Madison, a middle-aged couple and a thirty-something woman with a baby who couldn't have been more than a few weeks old. We sit near each other and strike up a conversation. She's a college professor taking her newborn home to see her mother—the baby's grandmother—for the first time. She quietly breastfeeds her baby during takeoff and landing so she would be sucking to prevent her ears from popping, this new mother tells me. Oh. Good to know. She puts the baby on a blanket on the floor next to her empty seat so she will be more comfortable during the flight and sleep. Nice. The college professor is a

224

mother hen, clucking and cooing over her chick, and all of it tears my heart apart as I watch her do what I had not. She never once mentions a husband or the baby's father, and I do not ask. I think she is a single mother. She is doing this alone. She is everything I was not.

How different the world is in 1981, when having a baby outside of marriage is no big deal. I got in trouble. She made a choice. Will my daughter understand what it was like fifteen, sixteen years ago when I got pregnant? Will she forgive me? Who will be there when we meet? Both mother and father? That's going to be uncomfortable but can't be helped.

Of course they will be there.

I stare out the window and cannot concentrate enough to read. As the plane moves through a gray haze, I often turn to observe mother and child. It is cold on the plane, and I have kept my coat on. I do not tell the woman that I am going to meet my daughter. I am bland and smiling instead.

I say goodbye when we land. Have a good visit, I add, beating back thoughts of how I kept my baby secret from my mother.

I steel myself for what is coming: keep walking, do not get weepy, she doesn't want to meet a crying basket case, her parents will be there, walk off the plane, down the steps, toward the door, in a minute this is it, this is really happening.

I can see the whole scene from above, mind out of body. I am watching myself holding her, hugging her, but not so long that her father—her mother is nowhere in sight—will think it inappropriate, and besides, she is not hugging me back. Both of her arms are squarely planted in the back pockets of her jeans so that they are otherwise occupied, so that she does not have to hug me. Okay, at least she is not a limp noodle, she is standing strong and letting me hug her. Let me look at her: her hair is fine like mine and the same ash-blond color, just like mine before I met Miss Clairol. Eyes the same hazel green as mine, same skin tone. Are we the same height? Yes! Look at us, she's wearing a crew-necked sweater too: hers, lavender; mine, pink. She has on jeans; me, pin-striped pants. It would be nice if she could hug me back, but this is all right. Babies don't hug, teenagers don't hug, and her father is standing right there. It's really her. This is my daughter. All's right with the world.

The worst years of my life are over.

Later, she would tell me that she had choreographed her reaction to me so she wouldn't hurt her father's feelings, or her mother's, who would certainly get a detailed report. She had assumed I would hug her—she would keep her hands planted in her back pockets. She wanted to hug me, she says, but she felt uncomfortable doing so in front of her father. It seemed disloyal. It would seem as if she cared. Not hugging back would show him she was merely curious about the woman who gave her life.

Her father, Gary, is a slender man, on the short side, with sharp features and a warm smile. He is the soul of friendliness. Ann decided to skip the airport reunion, she's at home, he says. Thank god, I think, how much more uncomfortable with her hovering there. At Gary's urging, Jane and I sit side by side in the back seat. We stare at one another, drinking in each other's features. We need to talk, but what to say? Dad is listening. To fill the silence, I go through a laundry list of typical questions, repeating much of what I'd asked her on the phone, coming off like a school admissions officer interviewing a transfer student. What is your favorite subject? English. Oh, I said, really?

That's amazing! I'm thinking, repeating what I'd told her the other day about her father and I being writers.

Favorite color? Purple. Don't a lot of teenagers like purple? Is purple a hot color now with teenage girls? The color of royalty. Did I read that a lot of adopted people fantasize that their parents are kings and queens? What's my favorite color? Okay, not purple.

What do you like to do? Write poetry. Oh, my god, that's my daughter and Patrick's daughter—writing poetry. Wait till I tell him. Will I show her my poetry one day?

The house is a comfortable split-level—beige inside and out—in a nice suburban neighborhood with a public park across the street. All that is missing is a picket fence and dog. But wait. There is a dog, a Pekingese or near relative.

Ann. I can picture her sitting in a big chair in the living room, drinking me in—Do I pass? Do I look all right? Do I look not too New York? Gary is thin. Ann is rounded. Gary was open and welcoming; Ann eyes me warily. I sense her thinking, *So this is her.* She does not stand to greet me, and while I pick up on her coolness, her not standing also means there is no awkwardness deciding between a hug and a handshake.

Yet. Her sitting while I say hello adds exponentially to my sense of being inspected like a side of beef waiting for USDA approval.

Of course she would be dubious. Would my coming be good for Jane? What did I want? How would Jane's knowing me affect her, Ann? Would her relationship with Jane change? Where does this woman fit into our lives? All reasonable questions. In fact, what was the protocol for meeting the other mother of your child? Miss Manners has not tackled this, and we are making it up as we go along. Jane is silent, watching, waiting. I am amazed at the miracle of Jane. I am so fixated on her and my own wonderment, I do not stop to reflect on how strange and how unexpected my emergence is to Ann, nor do I pause to wonder what she might be feeling. I just know that while I am happy to be there, I feel like a stranger in a strange land. This is unmistakably their turf.

Over Ann's shoulder is a large, framed picture of the family taken outdoors, Ann, Gary, Ted, Jane, David, and Tim. Ted, who is also adopted, is darker than the rest of the family and so does not fit in so well; exaggerating his apartness, he is standing a little back, a bit off to the side. David and Tim obviously share their parents' genetic coloring—one was the spitting image of Ann, the other Gary—but Jane does not look out of place, for her coloring is like theirs, and besides, she and Ann share that Irish heritage. What is striking about the photograph is its size—not your normal eight-and-a-half-by-eleven; this had to be at least quadruple that size, an advertisement that boldly announces, This is our family, see how happy we are, do not question it.

Uh-oh, I am the gatecrasher here.

David and Tim, at twelve and nine, understand who I am, and they look at me as if I am in a glass display case, but they are simply curious kids, smiling, friendly, ready for anyone. Ted, the adopted brother, sticks his head in at some point, says hello, and disappears the rest of the weekend. If he feels as uncomfortable in my presence as I do in his—Where is his mother? Why hasn't she called?—it is just as well.

Both Ann and Gary are from Wisconsin, but Gary's company—Gary is an insurance adjuster—had transferred him to Rochester for a couple of years, seemingly just long enough for them to adopt two children. Ann is a nurse and had been working in the same hospital where I delivered Jane. One of her friends in the pediatric ward told her about this new baby. You already have a boy. Why not get a girl, too?

Had Ann's friend been one of the nurses who tended me? Was she the one who sent me off to the delivery room? Someone who took my blood pressure? Someone who saw Patrick, tall, fit, and well dressed, when he brought me roses? Was she someone who at least knew that much about the baby's bloodline? Did she know anything about me? Who was this person who had passed unnoticed in my life but was a link in the chain that brought me here to these particular people? I recall no one special.

By the time Jane was two, the family had returned to Wisconsin. After a slow start—Jane was not very responsive in the beginning, Ann says—she had been a normal little girl, smart and bright, cute as a button. A studio portrait of her before the seizures shows a slim, blond child in a flowered dress. Does she resemble me or Patrick? Him, I will eventually decide.

When Jane had her first seizure at five, right around the same time Ann gave birth for the first time, everything changed. Ann now had an infant as well as a child who suddenly needed special attention, and lots of it. Seizures landed Jane in the hospital again and again. No one could tell me exactly how often she'd fallen and cut herself, but I sensed that she wore the scars like badges of honor. Small absence seizures (previously called petit mal seizures) were so frequent that no one kept count. School? School was important, but it was more important to keep Jane quiet, removed from stress, because that could head off more seizures. Not surprisingly, Jane missed a lot of school. By the second grade, Jane began wearing a hockey helmet to school. If she fell, she wouldn't hurt her head.

This is way worse than I had anticipated. This is bad. My little girl in a hockey helmet, kids making fun of her, and her real mother nowhere to be found. Eventually, she was put on an anticonvulsant drug, valproic acid, brand name Depakene, and it controlled the worst seizures, but she still was having the variety that lasted a few seconds. At least the helmet was gone. But valproic acid, I quickly learn, has dozens of side effects, one of which is to slow down brain activity and impair concentration, and thus lower intelligence. It turns a bright person into someone not so bright. Jane could not keep up in algebra, and the school placed her in a learning-disability class. Additionally, the drug made her gums blow up, and she became even more self-conscious. Now, she covers her mouth when she laughs—and not just to hide the silver flash of her braces. I listen as my heart is being picked apart with each new revelation. I want to scream, I want Tony here, I want my mother!

She did need me. I had sensed it all along. And the adoption agency never let you know our doctor wrote to them? Ann prods. We were looking for more information about you. That would have been about the time of her first seizure, she says. I tell her again about the letters I sent to the agency around that time. I tell her that I wrote the agency and told them about the birth control pills I took.

"By the time we finally got a letter about that," Ann says, "we thought, 'Where were you when we needed you?'"

So at least they did get that information, however late it came. At the time I knew nothing about epilepsy, and that winter afternoon neither Ann nor I connected the birth control pills I took when I didn't know I was pregnant to Jane's seizures. Her doctor might have made the connection. And maybe he did, but what to do about it?

As a nurse, Ann is hyperaware of the importance of medical histories and is frustrated that the agency did not put us together years ago when their doctor wrote. I'm remembering the words *most delighted with her.* The inane cruelty of the closed system of adoption sinks in quickly, as we—two mothers—sit across from each other, with our daughter listening. I am disgusted, but not surprised. I know more about the rules governing adoption than Ann does.

They never gave you more information than that I was Polish? I ask incredulously. That's it? You don't know my father had a heart attack when he was fifty? That he almost died? And by the way, my father did die of a heart attack when he was fifty-eight. But that was after she was adopted; there is no way you would have known that, not with the current laws.

No, Ann says, we didn't know of any heart disease in your family. We didn't have any medical history on your family or her father's either.

The agency had not passed along a single piece of medical information.

And there's no history of epilepsy in your family? Ann repeats. She has to be sure I am not hiding something. She does not ask about Patrick's family regarding epilepsy, but I wouldn't have known what to say anyway except that no, no one in either family. That I know of.

We thought you might be in a mental institution, Ann continues, switching on a light as the afternoon darkness creeps up on us, as if it were normal to assume this.

A mental institution? I can't think of a thing to say. Now she quizzes me. There's no one in your family who is institutionalized? No one at all? You're sure?

No. No. And yes. Is this what she thinks of Jane? That she comes from defective stock?

The very law that I railed against when I signed the relinquishment papers prohibited the agency from disclosing my identity—but no law prevented them from contacting me or asking for information that might shed some light on the cause of Jane's seizures. Surely, I would have noted in my response that I had taken birth control pills during the pregnancy. Hadn't Mrs. Mura written that down? Had no one bothered to check the medical histories that I'd meticulously filled out? If they had, maybe her doctor would have treated her symptoms differently. Maybe Ann and Gary would have thought of Jane differently, not as someone whose mother might have been a mental patient and who-knows-what about the father. And if they had known more, almost certainly Jane would have thought of herself differently—she would have felt less like a reject. She would have been able to know that she hadn't been given up because something was wrong with her. She might not have suffered such a devastating loss of self-assurance as was evident in her diffidence and the slouch of her walk.

This is what adoption did to her, I think. This is the result of giving her up.

Years later I would learn on the internet that birth control pills back in their infancy, back when I took them, contained roughly three times the amount of estrogen they do today. I would learn that birth control pills leach vitamin B6 (pyridoxine) out of the body.[90] That popular birth control pills that contain estradiol—the primary component of oral contraceptives—increase the risk of seizures.[91] That birth control pills interact with some anti-seizure medications and may make the hormone-based contraception less effective.[92] That some epileptics respond well to high doses of B6, or pyridoxine.[93] That a lack of B6 in the diet may cause seizures.[94] And if all that was the case, surely my birth control pills, high in estradiol, leaching B6 away from the fetus, are what caused Jane's epilepsy. In today's world I would have been a candidate for a medical abortion. Or not, in some states. Maybe Jane's doctor would have tried B6 in large doses, a treatment for some epileptics—but that is usually started within weeks of birth, possibly in utero. Jane had no seizures until she was five. I could find no studies linking mothers who took birth control pills during the first months of pregnancy to seizures of the child, but given the amount of evidence today that the vitamin is related to seizures, the two are convincingly related.

Within days after the doctor told me I was not pregnant—when I was—I began taking birth control pills. This was a few weeks after conception. Now I have even more to feel guilty about. I can tell myself that I should not feel guilty, that I did what I thought I had to do, that I did what I thought best.

But still.

[90] Monica Reinagel, "How Birth Control Pills Affect Your Nutritional Needs," *Scientific American*, Sept. 23, 2015, https://web.archive.org/web/20220825211118/https://www.scientificamerican.com/article/how-birth-control-pills-affect-your-nutritional-needs/.

[91] Iyan Younus and Doodipala Samba Reddy, "Seizure Facilitating Activity of the Oral Contraceptive Ethinyl Estradiol," *Epilepsy Research* 121 (Mar. 2016): 29–32. https://web.archive.org/web/20220825211947/https://www.sciencedirect.com/science/article/pii/S0920121116300079.

[92] Doodipala Samba Reddy, "Do Oral Contraceptives Increase Epileptic Seizures?" *Expert Review of Neurotherapeutics* 17, no. 2 (2017): 129–34, doi.org/10.1080/14737175.2016.1243472.

[93] Huei-Shyong Wang and Meng-Fai Kuo, "Vitamin B6 Related Epilepsy during Childhood," *Chang Gung Medical Journal* 30, no. 5 (Sept.–Oct. 2007): 396–401, https://web.archive.org/web/20220825212401/https://pubmed.ncbi.nlm.nih.gov/18062169/.

[94] Dong-Gun Lee et. al, "Seizures Related to Vitamin B6 Deficiency in Adults," *Journal of Epilepsy Research* 5, no. 1 (Jue 30, 2015): 23–4. https://web.archive.org/web/20220825212545/https://pubmed.ncbi.nlm.nih.gov/26157671/.

I am guilty of not keeping my baby.

No matter what.

But that day I don't know any of the specifics of epilepsy, estradiol, or pyridoxine and only have a nagging fear the birth control pills might be the cause of my daughter's seizures. Ann is saying, We hope that meeting you might help, you know, Jane's self-esteem, that it will be good for her—while I'm internally nodding yes.

And then the thrilling words, words that no one and nothing will ever take back, no matter what, no matter howt I will always have these to warm me in the cold hard center of sleepless nights to come: *Jane told me that she wanted to find you one day.* I told her, Ann adds, that I would help her search when she turned eighteen.

She did? You said what? Hallelujah! I was a roaring blaze inside, but I simply nod, a poker player wearing shades at the table, wary of letting them know how thrilled I am. I don't want to freak them out. This is something I could never fully explain to anyone who hasn't been there herself, what it means to hear that my daughter wanted to find me. Now I see that my daughter needs to know me just as much as I need to know her.

Considering the freight carried by the occasion, the weekend is remarkably low-key. No big scenes, no raw emotions on display, no moments of intense bonding. I know that back in Michigan my mother is saying rosaries for me nightly as she slips off to sleep, praying that all goes well.

Time would eventually sew up the separation between mother and daughter as best it could. For the moment I will have to wait and see. Jane is fifteen, she is reticent, and we are surrounded by her family. I am nearly an alien from a faraway place, and I do not know her family, her teachers, her friends, her likes and dislikes. Her parents are watching, we are both aware of that, both holding ourselves in check for the benefit of our audience. We have dinner, watch television, take photographs, look at photographs. After she began having seizures, there are but few pictures of Jane. Photographs are for happy times.

It's hard to be alone with Jane in the house, so Ann sends us on a walk by ourselves. Jane still is not talking much. She is observing. I'm doing my

Figure 12. Lorraine at four.   *Figure 13. Jane at the same age.*

best to draw her out, succeeding little. Was it the epilepsy medication? The
strangeness of me? of the reality? her desire to seem aloof? Whatever it is, we
have no great bursts of conversation, no intense moment of bonding, and
anyway, the bitter cold has us back in twenty minutes. I am physically and
emotionally exhausted, the house is hot and dry, my sinuses revolt. I am getting sick, Ann gives me a decongestant, my nose runs uncontrollably, my eyes
are liquid. I am as much undone on the outside as I am on the inside.

Ann would later tell me how awestruck she was over the resemblance
between Jane and me, how much alike we were in gesture and speech, how
we had the same physique, the same coloring, the same eyes, all comparisons
she kept to herself that weekend. I see all that, too, but say nothing, because
none of it is remarkable to me, and I don't want to trumpet the obvious. Yet
I see her father's features in Jane, too, an unremarkable Irish nose like his.
She tells me she has a large head. Do I have a big head, too? No, I say—that
would be your father. You got that from him. Do you have unusually long
arms? I ask. Yes, she says. So do I. Is she enjoying finding these similarities as
much as I am? I think so.

Though no epiphanies occur that weekend, I do not have any thoughts of liking, or disliking, or being neutral. She is unquestionably my daughter, and it is as if she were a newborn placed in my arms. Of course I love her. She is my baby, flesh of my flesh, bone of my bone. I do not know what she is feeling, but to me the connection is immediate, deep, intense.

I give Jane a copy of *Birthmark* and sign it to "my daughter." What lovely words to write. To my daughter.

Ann offers that one of her relatives had told her about "that book," but she paid it no mind. Did the relative know it was about a Rochester adoption? Did Ann know that was in the book? That the birth was on the same day and in the same city that Jane was born? I want to ask but hold back. What goes unsaid is that she, an avid reader, had not wanted to read about a mother who gave up a child. A girl. In Rochester. In 1966. In April. So the advertisement for my daughter that I put in that book would not have yielded her up.

I nod blankly, say, Uh-huh. I am afraid of doing anything that might put her off. I need her approval. She can cut me out of our daughter's life if she wants to.

Ann tells me that her friends, save one, think my visit is a bad idea. All her coworkers at the nursing home where she works are opposed to my visit.

They think I am going to do what? Break up their family? Ruin the relationship that has been built by time and love? How might the Rhymers have reacted to my call if Jane had not had such a laundry list of needs? There is no getting around the fact that their welcome of me is to a great degree shaped by Jane's extraordinary needs. Yet by the end of the weekend, Ann and I are relaxed around each other, and she gives me a big hug when I leave. It all feels right. Given the year this occurred, in the early eighties when reunions were still rare, it is rather miraculous. No matter what will happen tomorrow, for now, we have met and accepted each other and the different roles we have in our daughter's life. All this is a good thing.

Jane and I smile and touch when pictures of us are taken, and she hugs me when I am leaving, but again it is under the eye of her parents, and we are both conscious of that. We know each other, but we are still almost strangers: mother and daughter of a special sort. Mom is Ann. I am Lorraine. Getting to know each other across the vast expanse of fifteen years will take time.

We have the rest of our lives.

Ann later tells me that when her friends wanted to know what I was like, she told them I was "a New York career woman."

In the heartland, that is not a good thing.

By the time I get back from Wisconsin, I am running a fever, my throat is raw, and I have a full-blown sinus infection, a condition with which I am all too familiar. Yes, I am one of those "seeker mothers" prone to illness.

My former roommate Barbara is getting married the next weekend in San Antonio, and I am supposed to go. Instead, I get into bed and stay three days. I am immobile. Heavy doses of antihistamines knock me out, and I sleep and sleep and sleep. My body is as exhausted as my soul. I do not know what will happen next, but whatever it is, it will be better than the last fifteen years. When I am conscious, a loop runs through my mind, like the news zipper at Times Square: I can't believe I met her and her parents did not bar the door—she is alive she is all right not totally there's this epilepsy sounds pretty bad—she cracked her skull in the swimming pool once—or was it twice—she had to be pulled out—hockey helmet in the second grade—how many years, did they say? The birth control pills oh my god the birth control pills could that be it?

My house has been constructed with solid beams of grief and worry and wonder, and now they are falling on me. To see her evoked the raw emotions of loss and surrender that had been dormant. Again, I am the mother who has just given birth, a mother who walks out of the hospital without her baby. I am the mother who has not brought her baby home.

I weep, I blow my nose and wipe my tears and drink herbal tea and orange juice, and after a few days, I ask for a splash of vodka in the OJ. It takes the edge off, but then I weep some more. Barbara calls and pleads with me to come to San Antonio. There are not enough people on her side of the aisle.

But I am incapable of going out the door.

Mothers Who Reject Reunion

Besides the debatable differences on the grief scale for those involved in open versus closed adoptions, there is a second issue: What happens later. And that requires looking at the impact of shame, humiliation, grief, and gossip—and the subsequent secrecy—that surrounded the mothers who relinquished their children decades ago.

For months, the pregnant women, some of them high school teenagers, hid their growing bellies from the outside world. They were forced to drop out of school and go into seclusion, possibly with faraway relatives or in a maternity home—some even committed to psychiatric institutions—all to shelter their families from the ignominy of the unwed and unwanted pregnancy. Every day was a reminder of how disgraceful it was to get pregnant outside marriage. Knowing that they were going to relinquish their babies to adoption, they experienced birth itself as sad, harrowing in the present and haunting in the future. A great many of these teenagers received little or no emotional support from their families and instead endured their scorn before and after the birth. For these teens and women, it was a hellish time.

Then these young mothers, still aching for their babies with the "love hormone" oxytocin running rampant in their bodies, were told to forget the whole experience! Social workers said it. So did priests, nuns, ministers, rabbis, and doctors. Some women were told their babies died, while others were told they were supposed to think of their child as dead. The mantra women in closed adoptions heard was forget, forget, forget.

They were supposed to move on with their lives and not grieve openly, the way one is allowed to grieve in any other catastrophic loss. Some dropped out of high school. Those in college often switched schools, having to integrate themselves into a world of coeds whose greatest problem was getting into the sorority of their choice. Like many others, I quit my job and moved to another town.

I was fortunate in that my social worker did not tell me I would forget. She said I would never forget but that in time, my awareness of loss would be easier to bear. There would be scar tissue, but the wound would heal somewhat. And, in truth, it did. It took a long time, but life—and acceptance of my life—did get better. Perhaps writing has been a way of expiating my own sorrow and guilt, but since writing about my life is as natural as riding a bicycle, I don't experience it that way. I do know those honest words from my social worker and adoption confidante, as I sat weeping in her office, have always been a lodestar on my life's journey. She understood as well as anyone who has not gone through this herself.

But others had the primacy of secrecy drilled into them too deep to dig themselves out. Many were left an absolute emotional mess, without a shoulder to cry on, and once they managed to squelch their pain and sorrow and get their lives back together, they had constructed a suit of emotional armor that left them unwilling ever to go there again. Opening themselves up once more to the pounding grief, embarrassment, and disgrace of that time in their lives became unthinkable.

And so, they reject reunion. Even when their grown children return, however discreetly, asking for information and hoping for connection.

These women may have told their partners. Or not. They may have told any other children they had. Or not. They may not have had other children. They may have told their best friends. Or not. Cousins and more distant family members may know of the birth and adoption. Or not. Having found no succor from their mortified families throughout the pregnancy, birth, and relinquishment, they never talk to them of it. Neighbors and work friends probably do not know. In short, dealing with reunion feels like fresh punishment for an old sin, one they thought they had atoned for. Instead of looking forward to meeting their now-grown child, they fear exposure. The overwhelming release of repressed grief on first contact—an email, a letter, or a phone call—unleashes a renewed sense of loss, guilt, shame, anger, and grief, now intensified by the loss having been shrouded in secrecy for countless years.[95]

And now, come out of the closet and tell everybody in the family? Have her or him visit and figure out how to introduce her or him to people you run into together? Tell your best friend, when for decades you kept this from her?

---

[95] Karen March, "Birth Mother Grief and the Challenge of Adoption Reunion Contact," *American Journal of Orthopsychiatry* 84, no. 4 (2014): 410.

Tell the children you've kept this from their entire lives? Everybody will look at you differently. You have been pretending to be someone you are not. You have been hiding this basic, essential truth about yourself for years! How can anyone trust you again?

These women are everywhere. They don't admit this on Facebook—or they avoid Facebook because they might be found—they don't volunteer for TV shows, and they don't end up in surveys and in academic research. Improbably, one of these women was a neighbor and friend of mine for years. She didn't approve of my work to unseal birth records and talked about it so much with her grown children that one of them suspected she had a secret child herself. Yet somehow we maintained a connection. On her deathbed, she admitted that her "oldest" child was not her firstborn. It was not hard for me or the family to figure out where and when she might have given birth—or even who the father most likely was. It had been simply too hard to come clean to her family until she lay dying, a time when they were not likely to quiz or criticize her. As noted earlier, couples who married after relinquishing a child appear less likely to welcome contact. Though I could find no data confirming this, other than anecdotal, this is commonly accepted among searchers and confidential intermediaries.

Some individuals may decide not to seek a continuing relationship—it could be the parent, it could be the child. When there are vastly different life-styles, or strongly held but conflicting religious or political beliefs, or addiction and criminal behavior, one or the other party might find reunion too daunting. Too much time has passed, and it may be impossible to build an enduring connection, no matter how much one side longs for the severed relationship to be stitched back together.

Often, adoptees initiate searches when they are about to be a parent. They may only want a medical history, not a relationship. Yet for an adoptee, reunion provides a second opportunity to claim something no one else on earth can provide: a mother's unquestioning acceptance and love. They don't speak of it in those terms because this yearning is difficult to acknowledge or articulate, yet the adoptees' posts on Facebook attest to the pain associated with rejection. They are excruciating to read. Time and more reunion stories in the media—as in-the-closet mothers read about how others handle re-union—may lessen the number of these rejections as they embolden women to open their hearts and welcome their children.

20 Jane Meets the Relatives

A month later, Jane flies to Detroit the day after Christmas to meet my mother and my husband. Jane, bubbling with excitement—her first airplane flight! an adventure of her own!—glides through the gate beaming. Since this was before 9/11, Tony, my mother and I are there at the gate, and this time, she hugs me enthusiastically and embraces her new grandmother too. All three of us are within an inch of each other's height, same coloring, similar hair—no mistaking who the three of us are that day. I notice a guy who got off the plane lingering a bit, watching. Jane flashes a big grin and waves, turns to me, and says, "I sat next to him and told him the whole story." I nod. He smiles and moves on. A chance encounter, a whole universe he's probably never thought about, acknowledged between strangers.

That night Jane sleeps on the couch in my mother's apartment, while Tony and I take a room at the Dearborn Inn. This way Jane will have the opportunity to get to know my mother a bit without anyone's intrusion, including ours, and we'll be there right after coffee in the morning. Jane is a good sport and has no qualms about this arrangement. There is no hockey helmet on this trip. No one here knows her as that girl in the LD class—and wait till she tells the kids at school! No wait, they already know! She'd done a book report on *Birthmark* and told the teacher and anybody within earshot that the book is about her, and the writer, her other mother. The teacher doubted her, but her parents cleared that up. Yes, that's true, our daughter is that girl. Jane has become a celebrity, and she relishes it.

The next day, we drive around my old neighborhood, and I show her

240

and my husband where I grew up: the red-brick bungalow on Calhoun Street my father built, St. Alphonsus, where I went to grade school, the pool where I learned to swim, and the Dearborn Tourist Motel, which was still there. While I'm immersed in an old movie reel of my life, Jane and Tony joke around. They only see ordinary structures. I see my past flying by, my future sitting next to me.

On Sunday, we go to mass at my old parish, Sacred Heart, where my mother still worships. Here is my daughter, Lord. Here is my good man, Lord. Here is my mother. The memories of Christmases past, when I didn't know where my daughter was and I forced down the tears during "Silent Night," whizz by in a flashback. Now I hear Tony singing in his deep bass, Mother singing on key, and Jane and myself decidedly off. Neither one of us can keep a tune more than four notes, and noticing that gives me a squirt of pleasure. Whether or not I believe in the God of my youth is not open for discussion that day as my heart repeats, Thank you, God. Thank you for giving me my daughter. Soon she will fly back to her other life, another mother, another family, in another state, and I will go back East.

But now I know her.

That afternoon, relatives troop into my mother's small apartment to meet not only Jane but also Tony, as most had not come east to our wedding—and now my mother wants to show them both off. Meeting Grandma was one thing, but all these other people—probably a dozen total—these strangers who are related to Jane? How is that going to play out?

Tony to the rescue. He sits side by side with her on the couch, making sly remarks about the passing parade to put her at ease, while I pass around the cheese and chat with cousins, aunts, and uncles, introducing them to Jane and Tony. I'm always careful to say, *This is Jane*, not, *This is my daughter*.

Adoptees say this kind of reunion experience is overwhelming and uncomfortable—they don't feel like a member of the new family. They already have a family, thank you very much, and they feel like they're on display. In truth, they are, just as much as if a groom had brought his new bride from

India to the gathering, just as much as a natural mother is on display when she meets the adoptive family. With Tony by Jane's side, she takes the event in stride. Fortunately, everybody is also checking out Tony, who deflects the attention from Jane, but since she carries shared genes, she is clearly the one they are more interested in—if only to see how she resembles them. My family sees her as a full member of the clan, even if she had been missing. Later, Jane tells me that the only thing that made her uncomfortable was when someone referred to me as "your mom." Mom is back in Wisconsin.

To bring us back to our little family of three—Tony, Jane, and me—we head out that evening to the revolving restaurant on the top of the Renaissance Center, the crown jewel of Detroit's riverfront and General Motor's gleaming new headquarters. Detroit might no longer be the exuberant Motor City of my youth—the automobile industry is already going down the tubes, Detroit had been through the riots of the sixties, and parts of the downtown had never recovered—but any big city viewed from high enough above provides a twinkling panorama at night. To Jane, it must be simply a big city, but to me it was familiar. Home. See the Christmas tree in Cadillac Square down there? That's where I used to go Christmas shopping with my mother. See that cool white building over there, with the structure on top that looks like a big wedding cake? That's designed by a famous architect named Yamasaki. The ladies' room has windows down to the floor, and it's kind of weird when you are washing your hands. See those lights on the other side of the river? That's Canada—yes, really it is, a town called Windsor in the province of Ontario.

Have you ever tried escargot?

What is that?

Snails?

Yuck.

Okay, steak and potatoes it is, with lots of butter. I'm from Wisconsin, the Dairy State, remember? she says. How could I forget? I joke back. I'm a sucker for revolving restaurants on top of skyscrapers, and so is she, as she discovers that night. We both love heights and revolving restaurants, no matter how corny they seem to the unknowing. Throughout the meal, I cannot stop staring at her. She is really there. My daughter. She doesn't hate me.

It is the Sunday after Christmas, but in my mind, it is the first Christmas since I found her. From now on, everything will be counted as before or after I found my daughter.

New Year's Eve is memorable that year, but not in the way that most people would think. Tony's daughter, Kate, is spending the holiday with us, and after a splendid dinner with our best china and crystal, I am more than a little out of sorts. Okay, I am a nut job, reason unknown. I'm upset, crying, creating a scene. A good tumbler—Orrefors crystal, a wedding present—breaks and I lose it, weeping as if it is not something replaceable. Finally, I take myself to bed well before midnight, and through the foggy haze of what seems to be slipping-away sanity, I wonder, What is wrong with me?

Had I turned into the harridan that my mother had been when her temper would flare up over the smallest infraction, or seemingly nothing at all? I remember one time—I must have been twelve or so—when she was yelling at me and then burst into tears, saying she was sorry she was like this, weeping profusely. I vowed never to be like that, so out of control, with such a terrible temper— "a bitch" I called her in my diary. But she wasn't always a woman on the verge of a breakdown. Just sometimes. And then it all went away in her fifties. With menopause. Was I like that? Yes. Oh my god, yes.

Lucky for me a magazine assignment soon after led to sweet, blessed release from my—ah, it pains me to write this—raging hormones. And rage mine did! While researching a revolutionary treatment for out-of-control premenstrual syndrome, or PMS, I found myself in the woman I am reading about. Two, maybe three, weeks of calm followed by the doldrums, crying jags, a hot temper. Although it seems altogether too handy—that I would suffer from the very malady I was investigating—a few months of keeping track of my down days prove that indeed my moods are cyclical—and I remember that the meltdown on New Year's Eve was a few days before my period.

I am not simply talking about a few weepy days, a few cranky comments. From my teens on, I became suicidal in my bleakest moods and, in fact, thought about killing myself off and on over the years. It began in college, even though I was managing to support myself, attend classes and work at the *Collegian*. I'd be all right, and then suddenly life would seem pointless, depressing beyond comprehension, everything black. Now these moody days and emotional jags might be due to PMS? Damn, I think, this is the eighties, not the fifties. How is this possible?

One of the doctors I interview prescribes this revolutionary treatment, a hormone called progesterone, and—*¡Ay, caramba!*—it works like a miracle. In 1982, progesterone in the US is not easy to come by—only a few pharmacies make it up because Big Pharma can't patent it—but my doctor knows where it is available. When I am in the path of PMS wrath—the week or longer before my period is due—as soon as progesterone hits my bloodstream my jangling nerves mellow, my hair-trigger temper fades, the tears retreat, and even those aggravating pimples that come on schedule dissolve overnight or nearly so. The sugar cravings, the bloating, the sore breasts—all going or gone. I might have been loath to admit to such a seemingly atavistic ailment in the flowering of feminism had not my symptoms been so severe and the relief of progesterone so complete.[96]

PMS, or premenstrual dysphoric disorder (PMDD), as the severe cases are called, is hereditary, but I do not tell my daughter, or Ann, to be on the lookout for its symptoms. Ann doesn't want to be reminded of more ways Jane is like me. Or maybe I now don't want to sound like a wacko, someone who might be a candidate for a lockup. And how serious would "severe PMS" sound to a teenager who has a whole passel of other problems that sound way more pressing? Or to her mother? Besides, Jane's a thousand miles away.

---

[96] Since progesterone cannot be patented, no one has done the comprehensive double-blind studies that might make it the preferred (and inexpensive) treatment option in the United States. Mood elevators might be the answer for some, for certainly not all psychological problems that women have are related to cyclical hormones. While acceptance of its usage for PMS has grown in this country, it is still not widely prescribed for PMS, and certainly was not when my daughter was suffering. My own positive response was to 400 mg. a day in the week or so before my period—or whenever I began to be aware of symptoms. Non-drug treatments, such as cutting caffeine and alcohol, aerobic exercise, adequate sleep, a good diet, and primrose oil may work for less severe symptoms; however, for some people these holistic treatments are akin to putting a Band-Aid on a hole in a dike.

Also, I know Jane hates the idea of having something else wrong with her. Something else that needs medication.

Yet a few years later, when Jane visits, she is on a crying jag the likes of which I recognize. *No one has ever loved me who doesn't have to* is the plaint I hear between the tears that seem to be unstoppable, the breathing in big heavy gulps, the eyes so terrifyingly sad.

When's your period due? I ask

Couple of days, she says.

Try this, I say, handing her a dose of my progesterone. I know that even if it does not help, it will not harm her. In twenty minutes, she is a different person. We go to dinner at the home of friends, she meets a young man there who calls a few days later and asks her to go out for a burger. I talk to her about seeing her own doctor and explaining progesterone and the family history, but once she gets back to Madison, who am I? Lorraine in another state. Not Mom.

Besides, she tells me later, wasn't that outburst just a momentary lapse into the blues? I'm fine now.

The magazine piece about PMS and progesterone? So strong is the sense that women could not, should not be susceptible to their hormones in this era of feminism that the assigned piece about progesterone for *Woman's Day*—available in nearly every supermarket in America then—is summarily turned down. The editor and I have a brusque phone call, there is no possibility of a rewrite, nor of any payment, even the kill fee written into their contract! Such are the slings and arrows of freelance writing. This is how the received wisdom of the masses—or current thinking—stays unchallenged.

My editor at *Cosmopolitan* has more imagination. She asks that I rewrite the piece from a first-person point of view. Apparently, the *Cosmo* Girl could have PMS.

21 Getting to Know You

Jane's hands are wrapped around my neck and she's shaking me, saying, *Why did you give me up? Why did you give me up?*

Obviously, we have to work out the kinks in our relationship.

Jane came to Sag Harbor the following spring for twelve days. Twelve whole days! We'd missed her sixteenth birthday by a couple of days, but we celebrated it on Easter, only days later. We invited a few close friends, including Arthur, my previous landlord in the house of frozen pipes. Despite my lack of house-tending skills, we had become good friends, like a cousin who lives around the corner, which he did. As he wasn't a previous boyfriend, Tony took to him, too, and the three of us formed a triumvirate of our own. Arthur was a former World War II Army Air Corps officer, navigator of twenty-three bombing missions over Germany, and a military attaché (a.k.a. spy) in Taiwan after the war. He was dashing and worldly, and he was unflaggingly chivalrous and kind to young women in need of a soft shoulder and a good dinner. His impeccable manners were stirred with a bawdy sense of humor, and he and Jane—an odd pair then, if there ever was one—hit it off right from the beginning. Arthur surprised her that Easter/birthday celebration with a small gift, but when she unwrapped a silk-and-lace lavender-scented trifle, the teenager who'd worn a hockey helmet until a few years before was puzzled and shot me an embarrassed look across the table. What was this? What to say?

Oh, what a nice sachet, I said. Your sweaters will smell so nice! Would she have known what a sachet was if I'd raised her? Who knows? Maybe not.

Yet that day, all I could think was, she might have. Do I have lavender sachets in my bureau? Of course I do. This may seem insignificant, but it signaled to me how the whole landscape of her life had changed because I had not raised her.

Though she had read my memoir, I thought I should tell her the story myself, even though it meant digging through old baggage, embarrassing to recount. One afternoon sitting on the back deck of our house, I begin, wondering how I can adequately explain the times: her father, his Catholic family and their reaction to divorce, his other children, or how our relationship began with a gallant gesture and a young woman with a freshly broken heart. I tell her how one night, after dinner at the home of the assistant city editor and his wife, I left after one a.m. and ran out of gas. The car died in the road. Some guy stopped, got me a gallon of gas, and waited until I started the car. The next day, somewhat hungover, I slept late, drove to work without stopping for gas, meant to get some during my shift but hadn't had time, and now it was late again—after eleven—and gas stations were likely to be closed. So Patrick said he would follow me home. He came up to see my place. He left. Or rather, he got partway down the steps. And turned around.

I describe how my anguish over my pregnancy turned into a mother's love, and how, against a backdrop of the all-encompassing shame of that era, I gave her up. One thing I had going in my favor was that she herself was raised in a Catholic family, for that part she would surely understand. But the rest?

How much could a sheltered sixteen-year-old really comprehend. To explain that I wasn't the only one involved with a married man, I wonder if I should go into detail about the woman who had an affair with her married high school French teacher the summer after she graduated. And that when she got pregnant everyone's concern seemed to be keeping it secret so he wouldn't lose his job or imperil his marriage. Do I talk about the woman who was raped by the father of the two kids she babysat for, and when her parents went to the police to file charges, their solution was to work out a deal instead—no charges would be filed, but the rapist would agree to pay the fees at the maternity home. Could she even imagine that kind of world? One in which I was freaked out not only that no one must know of my pregnancy but also that her father's reputation not be sullied? Could I explain how thoroughly everything conspired to convince me that somehow, she would be better off in a two-parent home, with a mother and a father, with people who could provide for her in ways that I could not? That while her father pushed the adoption, he really wasn't a bad guy?

Now it was the early eighties, and the world was a far different place. She knew kids from divorced families, she knew kids who had single mothers. She saw that Tony and I had a middle-class home on a nice street in a swell village. Could she see me as I had been when she was born? How could anyone who has not lived in those times really grasp what it was like?

All the words I could say would never erase that basic fact of her being—that her mother had not kept her. Intellectualizing the story of her life was not the same as the heart accepting. How deep was her sense of abandonment, how long her anger, how wounded her soul? These were the questions I could not answer. And she wasn't asking for the story of her conception or the details of my relinquishment.

Another afternoon, armchair psychologist that I decide to be, I suggest that we construct a little docudrama and act out our feelings. Tony and Arthur would be our audience. She would be herself, I would be myself, and we would see where our little experiment took us, right? I urge her to take the lead in directing the action, and within a minute or two, our characters are visiting the gravesite of some shared-but-unknown ancestor, and suddenly Jane has her hands around my neck. She begins shaking me violently, shouting, "Why did you give me up?" as she stares intently into my eyes, her voice rising. "Why did you give me up?"

Whoa!

At first, I am too shocked to respond, but I recover and shout, *Stop!* She may be letting out a scream from her soul, but she is also choking me. Our scene comes to an aborted ending. Over the next week, we talk some more and we move on. But I will always remember the fierce look in her eyes, her hands on my neck, and wonder if we will ever get past that feeling. Years will go by, but we will circle around and always come back to the moment of pain: Why did you give me away? Don't you know how much that hurt?

How I wish I'd simply said then, I made a mistake. A big, fat mistake. I wish I had cut out all the padding of "that's what it was like then" and "I didn't feel I had a choice" and simply said, "I'm sorry you were adopted. I'm sorry I gave you up." If a friend falls, you don't start explaining about the rug that made her trip or the crack in the pavement. Your role is simply to be solicitous. That's what I should have said that day. *I'm sorry.*

But it would be years before I could speak that plainly. I felt then, and do today, that I did not have a real choice to keep her or not. Yes, some women did summon the courage to defy convention and, with the help of family, kept their babies. Young mothers mostly had the decision taken away from them by their parents and were forced into relinquishing, and as the years go by, they are perhaps the most angry and hurt today. As for myself, could I have kept her? Found a way to support the two of us? Defied all convention and raised her while people whispered when we walked down the street? Gone back to work? Insisted Patrick face up to the reality of our child, tell his wife, and live with the result—no matter whether he married me or merely paid child support? Starting with the offspring of kings, history is rife with stories of royal bastards, of illegitimate children raised in their families of birth: She could have been with me.

She's never been to New York City, and so off we go. We camp out at a friend's apartment and are enthusiastic tourists. The reticent girl I'd met in Wisconsin is gone—this girl is chatty, fun, full of life and ready for adventure as we check off the must-see sights: the Empire State Building, United Nations, Staten Island Ferry, Chinatown and the Statue of Liberty.

We sprint off the first boat of the day from Battery Park and wordlessly acknowledge that if we hurry, we can be the first up the steps to the crown. Walking as fast as we can without breaking into a run—that would be too silly!—we manage to beat out another family with the same idea. Later we will laugh over how childish we were, but our recollection is mostly about how in sync we were at that moment, how in sync we were for three whole days. Like any mother and daughter on their good days. We do not feel strange or awkward with each other. Everything feels right. She is my daughter. My mind is doing cartwheels down the street when we stop for a hot dog from a street vendor. I am doing something as ordinary as any mother and daughter. No one seeing us would think this was unusual. But I know.

On the last day in Manhattan, we shop at Macy's cavernous Thirty-Fourth Street store for hip outfits she will take back to Wisconsin, the kind she will be asked about. Where did you get that? We discover that we have the same taste: tailored, chic, a little edgy. What's coursing through my mind is

Figure 14. Jane and Lorraine during Jane's first visit to Sag Harbor, Spring, 1982.

the memory of my mother admitting that, indeed, I looked best in the most expensive dress in the rack, the black one—even though it hadn't been her choice. Once I was the daughter, shopping with mom. Now I am the mother, and it is thrilling knowing that anyone who saw us would automatically know that we are mother and daughter. I open my wallet as far as I can that day. We have our makeup done by the makeup ladies before we meet Tony with two shopping bags of stuff. She's wearing one of her new outfits: black pants, a white cotton shirt with a tuxedo-style bib, a pin-striped vest, and a black patent-leather belt with a shiny buckle. Because Tony thought she'd get a kick out of the action, he decided we'd have dinner at a Japanese steak house where the chef slices and dices and sautés at the table. We know she likes steak. After dinner we have great tickets to *Evita* on Broadway, and then we'll drive back to Sag Harbor. It's going to be terrific—right?

Not so fast. Jane is suddenly monosyllabic, and nothing is amusing. Tony, who can pour on the charm like heavy cream, cannot break through her gloom. At the theater, same story. She is not animated, she is uninterested. Were the performances good? I have no idea, because I am so aware that she is determined not to enjoy herself. On the way home, she falls asleep. I voice my concern, Tony shrugs, says not to worry.

Much later, Jane would tell me that the days in Manhattan—in fact, the whole visit—had felt so joyful and comfortable that she ultimately became overwhelmed with guilt. Shouldn't she be aloof? She loves her other parents, doesn't she? If she's having such a good time, does that mean she is disloyal to her other family? "Mom" is who she watches *Little House on the Prairie* with. Mom, not Lorraine, has been there through the seizures, through the bad days. Where was Lorraine then?

What she was dealing with didn't occur to me. Couldn't she love us both?

The next morning, Jane is her normal, pleasant self. The rest of our time together goes swimmingly.

I am ecstatic the whole time—thrilled, excited, tense, wanting everything to be perfect. I am having such a great renaissance I do not even stop to think *what if*. What if I'd kept her?

Because, really, there is no answer for that. I had not kept her.

She calls me Lorraine. Mom is the woman who raised her; Mom is back home in Wisconsin. The first time I call her "my daughter," she bristles. We are in the little market across the street from our house. I introduce her to the woman behind the counter—This is my daughter, I say simply, not explaining further, knowing that the woman already knows the whole story. Jane smiles and says hello. But once on the street, she says she does not feel comfortable being introduced as "my daughter." She who had no control over the biggest event in her life could now control this one thing, what we call each other.

"Then what should I call you?" I ask. She has no answer. "Birth daughter" is distancing and bizarre, and furthermore "birth daughter" exudes too much information, just as it would if an adoptive mother went around introducing her "adopted daughter." Either people know or they don't need to. She suggests I call her "my friend." I make the case to Jane for some leeway in this language business because there would be some people in town who do not know our story. I need to say something other than "this is my [amazingly young] friend, Jane [who looks like she ought to be my daughter]," which then invites a follow-up question. Is she your niece? Maybe a neighbor's daughter? Jane grudgingly agrees to be introduced as my daughter when necessary. Yet when it proves expedient to her—even during that first extended visit—she refers to herself as my daughter, me as her mother.

But her point is made. She can control the language, and I'd better watch it. I do not get equal rights. In time, she would invent the name Ma-raine and use it when no one was around. In time, it was how I signed my cards and letters to her. It would take years before she addressed me as "Mother" in notes and signed her cards "Your daughter Jane." Words matter. The parameters of any relationship are outlined in the language we use.

Patrick is still at *Newsday*, whose offices are an hour away on the Long Island Expressway. Jane and her father could talk on the phone or they could meet. Jane is hopeful. I am cautiously hopeful. He hadn't been a jerk, after all—he supported me throughout the pregnancy and professed love before and after.

I recall how we once spoke of what a great kid we would have together. Now here she is in the flesh, almost grown up. Didn't he want to meet her?

But the imagined child came without the question, Why didn't you help my mother keep me? The imagined child did not make you feel like a heel. Patrick avoids emotional confrontation, this I know. This is why he never told his wife. She found out from reading *Birthmark*. This is why we didn't tell his brother we'd had a child when we met for dinner. This is why I wasn't supposed to cry when we left the hospital without our baby.

I do not know what he will do now. I am apprehensive.

I call him at *Newsday*, not wanting to interfere with his life.

There's a lot going on right now, he says. I can't deal with this now.

What's going on? I ask. This is our daughter. She's here.

Not now, he says in a tone I recognize. It was the same way he'd said, You must call the adoption agency.

When I relay this to Jane, she is unreadable, with a vacant stare that conveys nothing and everything. She does not cry, at least in my presence.

You'll be back in the summer for a longer visit, I say. We'll try then.

Sure, she says.

Occasionally I would check *Newsday* for his stories. Sometimes the paper was rife with his byline. And then they would disappear. I had no idea why.

After she leaves, I send Patrick a Xerox of a photo of Jane, along with a short note, at *Newsday*. Surely, he will see their resemblance. Our daughter wants to meet you, I say, no strings attached. Just meet her.

No response.

Summer comes, and Jane returns.

Again, I phone, and again he pleads off. His life is still in too much of an uproar—maybe some other time. Still no mention of what the uproar is. I point out I am talking about lunch, not moving in or paying bills. He says that his oldest daughter, Colleen, is still angry at him. She'd only visited him and his new family once, barely acknowledging her half sister, Kirsten.

This relates to lunch with Jane exactly how?

Silence.

Who is this man? Where is the man of integrity I thought I knew and with whom I once yearned to spend the rest of my life? All that I insisted to my ragged heart for decades—that he was a torn and troubled soul—is fading away when I ask him to do something hard and brave: Meet our daughter. I know his new wife is aware of everything—our affair, our daughter—but I don't know if that is the issue. Some women might be wary of old lovers returning with the issue of a once-torrid affair—a child in the flesh, interrupting their lives, siphoning off attention, possibly property. Who knew what a meeting could lead to? However, this is not on my mind. I only want my daughter—our daughter—to be content. Full. Complete. And she wants to meet him. She has a right to meet him, doesn't she?

I press my case. Look, Jane doesn't want anything from you. She only wants to meet you.

Lorraine . . . Exasperation leaks out of his voice.

I am no longer hopeful. I tell her of his refusal, and she turns quickly and runs out the door, and is gone for a few hours. If she were younger, I would wipe her tears and buy her an ice cream cone. There is not a single thing I can do to make her feel better. She is sixteen.

Her eyes are red when she returns.

Next visit, next spring, we are shopping again, this time at a discount clothing store where the clothes hang on long racks and the frills are nil. Jane has on a totally fab black pin-striped suit, man-tailored jacket, and pencil skirt, size four. The outfit fits her, suits her perfectly. She is smiling at herself in the mirror, my eyes meet hers there in the reflection. It's moments like this that I remember now, quiet incidents that add up to a stockpile of sweetmeats. My baby—that is what she is to me—only she is a teenager. Yes, we missed many years, now she is nearly grown up, but she is here. The suit would have been perfect for me too, so we scour the aisles looking for another one in the same size to no avail. I slap down a credit card, and the prized suit is hers.

Shopping is a frivolous pursuit, you say? But, hey—shopping is the modern equivalent of gathering, as in "hunting and gathering." Men hunt, men fish, we women gather at the mall and the market. Just like my mother

and I had once done. Jane and I weren't ever going to go deer hunting together or enjoy the spiritual communion of fly fishing that men rhapsodize
over. We would shop instead.

The first summer, Jane arrived with a pair of sandals that were the same style
as a pair I had bought only a month earlier in Manhattan. I have extremely
hard-to-fit feet—size eight, AAAA. Finding shoes that fit has always been a
trial, and I was rather pleased with these sandals, in braided saddle leather
over the instep, a strap over the heel that could be adjusted to be as narrow
as necessary, and a flat rubber sole. Nothing unusual, but well-made, and
they fit. Brand name, Famolare. Famolare, you ask? A small Italian company. Knowing the company made shoes that fit me, I had made a pilgrim-
age to the single Famolare store in Manhattan that spring. How many pairs
of that particular style of Famolare were sold in the United States in 1982? I
don't know. Their website says that their shoes are still made in "very small
quantity."

So, when Jane pulled out a pair of sandals of the exact same make and
style—purchased in Wisconsin—I was stunned. She was nonplussed—she
had no idea how great a coincidence this was—but I knew the odds. And I
remembered Florence Fisher telling me that when she first walked into her
mother's apartment, it was a similar shade of turquoise as her own.

Another year, Jane arrived with a pair of acid-washed black jeans that
were so close to mine they could have been mistaken for each other—and we
could have worn each other's. Yes, they were in style then, but to see us on
the street, you would think we had planned to dress alike, though we bought
our clothes a thousand miles apart. There was no mistaking we were mother
and daughter. In photographs we are often shown standing the same way,
one leg crossed at an angle, just so, in front of the other. I have a photo of my
mother when she was about twenty hanging on my office wall. Above it is a
picture of Jane at sixteen. A friend glanced at them quickly one day and said
she wondered why Jane had such an old-fashioned hairstyle—until my friend
took a second look.

Like me, she had fine, limp hair and couldn't carry a tune or snap her fingers on her left hand. We peppered our language with irony and words that little children are not supposed to hear, relentlessly doodled when on the phone, loved heights, and misplaced our stuff at every opportunity. She ordered BLTs with the same gusto as Patrick, reminding me how I had eaten them night after night in the early stages of pregnancy. I had my father's naturally fast stride; my daughter did, too. Both of us were immensely pleased to discover ourselves walking down the street in sync. One afternoon she and I sat on the roof of the World Trade Center for forty-five minutes, when you could still go to the open-air floor, and watched the helicopters flying lower than where we sat. For me and for her, finding these shared preferences and traits was a constant source of quiet wonder and enormous pleasure. It was almost a game. She was astonished the day she discovered that she and I used the same exact shade of makeup. One time, she surprised me and started rattling off our similarities as if she had been collecting them. In fact, she had been.

That summer, Jane walked up the stairs with her normal heavy footfall, *Stomp, stomp, stomp.* "You come up the stairs just like Lorraine," Tony said. Not critical, merely observant. Jane told me later—many years later, in fact—that this is when she knew she was "home." Yes, that is the word she used.

Home.

Oh, I said, reveling in the moment. But then she added this twist: She had grown up hearing her father say, Jane, can't you walk quieter? Can't you take the steps quieter?

Ouch.

No, she really couldn't, not without constant effort. You ought to hear your cousin, I told her. What is an accepted trait in my family—a heavy footfall, a quick gait—had been an unending annoyance to her adoptive parents. There are a lot of reasons to feel bad about inflicting adoption on your child—an inchoate sense of abandonment and dislocation, a difficulty in forming relationships, all of which have been documented by various experts and writers—but this seemingly small example singes still. The afternoon Jane told me this story, I remembered the day—I must have been no more than five—my parents took me to the zoo. Even back then, the Detroit zoo housed their animals in open-air spaces, and so my memory is of polar bears swimming and hanging out, not in an animal jail. It was a pleasant, sunny day, I was walking with Daddy, everything was right with the world. Dad and I zipped ahead from one area to another, leaving Mom behind. *You walk just like your daddy*, she said. I recall, even at five, reveling in being like my daddy. When I grew older, Mom often would ask me to "slow down" when we were walking together. And now here was my daughter, walking in step with me. I'd never noticed that I had a heavy footfall when I climbed steps because no one had ever mentioned it—it was normal in our house. What must have it been like to be told repeatedly, Slow down, can't you walk quieter? Her bedroom was upstairs, and so it must have happened repeatedly. She'd say, Sorry, and try to change. When changing felt so unnatural.

My girl had been a lead-footed kid among a family of soft-steppers. What else had there been? After I heard that, I would never lose the gnawing feeling that I should have found a way to keep her.

Family traits. We who have grown up among them cannot understand what it's like to be in a life where there are none, or maybe a few by chance. The more social scientists learn, the more various traits and unconscious acts appear to be hereditary. What characteristics are hardwired? They cluster into five basic factors in every culture that has been studied, from Britain to Korea to Ethiopia to the Czech Republic: Extraversion, the extent to which a person is outgoing—adventurous and sociable—or shy, silent, reclusive, and cautious. Neuroticism, the extent to which a person suffers from anxiety, guilt, worry and resentment. Agreeableness, the extent to which a person is good-natured—cooperative and nonjudgmental—or irritable, suspicious, and abrasive. Conscientiousness, the extent to which a person is responsible, persevering, and self-disciplined or undependable and quick to give up. Openness to experience, the extent to which a person is curious, imaginative, questioning and creative, or not open at all: conforming, unimaginative, predictable and uncomfortable with novelty.

Sounds like a lot—sounds like a whole personality. As much as the nurture-leaning culture might like us to believe it, the latest studies do not show a strong correlation between characteristics of adopted children and those of their adoptive parents. In fact, writes the social scientist Carol Tavris, "the correlation is weak to non-existent. This means that when children resemble their parents of any sort, adoptive or biological, and grandparents temperamentally, it is because they share certain genes with these relatives, not experiences."[97]

Those of us who were raised in our families of origin cannot truly comprehend what it is like to be the square peg in a round family. What's more, the square peg isn't supposed to notice or remark on the differences but instead try to fit in—when fitting in is not really possible.

Jane had grown up apart from me, in a different house in a different part of the country, but despite the enormous gap in our relationship, she fit into my family quite easily. Though I was now an agnostic (who sometimes slipped into mass on holidays), I had been raised Catholic, just as she was being raised Catholic. Both of her families were middle-class, college-educated, and politically liberal. Despite any differences in style, what we shared gave us common ground and eased the path of understanding and communication. How alike we were in temperament, style, attitude, and physical appearance—all that came from our connected genes and eased us into a comfort zone. If you grow up, as I did, surrounded by people with whom you share traits, those traits seem natural, and you are more forgiving of those traits that others might find obnoxious. It is highly likely that a lot of the adopted children who end up in therapy are there not simply because they are troubled in the sense that we think of but because they are so different from their parents that their parents have difficulty accepting the child's idiosyncrasies. Also, since social services were involved at the time of the adoption, it seems natural to adoptive parents to seek professional help sooner than a biological parent would in the same situation.

Jane did not talk a great deal about her life back in Wisconsin, but what I eventually gleaned was this: Mom took care of her when she had her worst

---

[97] Carol Tavris, "A New Start in Life," *Times Literary Supplement*, April 18, 2008, 27.

seizures but didn't have time to take her shopping, so she especially loved it when I did. Her dad was the great stabilizer who always came up with a plan. She adored her older adopted brother, Ted, who was not interested in searching for his other mother, and as for her two younger brothers, David and Tim, well, they were her younger brothers, and you know younger brothers. She was fiercely loyal to them all.

How did Jane feel about me in those early years? The photographer Jill Krementz was working on a book that would be called *How It Feels to Be Adopted*. After I'd written an essay for the *New York Times* about the sealed-records statute in New York and finding my daughter,[98] Jill asked Jane and me to be a part of her project. She'd photograph us and let Jane tell her story in her own voice. Jane was immediately enthusiastic. She was becoming someone special, someone with something to say that others wanted to hear. Jill photographed us at Rockefeller Center and taped Jane's thoughts while I wandered off to leave them alone.

In the interview, Jane reveals that though her mother was pleased that I called, she was nervous once I was on track to visit because she felt threatened. Jane says that most of her own friends were pitted against me, saying things like "I wouldn't let her just walk into your life. You should tell her to buzz off." Of our days in Manhattan, she says, "What I liked best was our just getting to know each other. . . . Now I understand the problems she had before I was born and why she put me up for adoption. . . . Being adopted had always made me feel a little insecure, and even though I loved my parents, I still had a lot of unanswered questions and strange fantasies. Actually, one of my fantasies turned out to be true. I'd always imagined my birth mother was a writer. . . ."[99]

[98] Lorraine Dusky, "Adoptees' Best Interests," *New York Times*, Feb. 6, 1982, sec. 1, 23, http://web.archive.org/web/20220825213139/https://www.nytimes.com/1982/02/06/opinion/adoptees-best-interests.html?searchResultPosition=4.
[99] Jill Krementz, *How It Feels to Be Adopted* (New York: Knopf, 1982), 78–85.

The Wily Persistence of DNA

For adoptive parents, meeting the genetic parents for the first time can be unsettling. For the natural parent, the same experience brings both a shock of recognition and comfort.

Genetic parents share a seemingly uncanny similarity in appearance, voice, personality, gait, and gesture with their offspring, and despite what adoptive parents intellectually know about the nature/nurture interplay, they are likely to be gobsmacked when coming face-to-face with the genetic stock that produced the person they share as parents. Seeing their similarities for the first time is likely to register as a loud mental *Ouch!* In contrast, the biological mother is quietly accepting or rejoicing over these same things, whether the individual resembles her side of the family or the father's, but in either case, the resemblance is evident.

The genetic influence is why yearbook photographs sometimes startle adoptees when they first see a picture of their mother or father and compare it with their own pictures at the same age. It's why my daughter's mother told me she was astonished when she first laid eyes on me. Our daughter resembled me so much she was taken aback. But it isn't just in outward appearance that time would reveal how much alike my daughter and I were. In time, she would divorce her husband and marry another, just as I had done, and my mother before me, and, yes, her mother before that. I was the third in a line of women to have two husbands, and Jane would be the fourth. Of course, she inherited many things from Patrick—starting with a head that required a large hat—but time and distance and never seeing them together prevents me from noting other similarities. Her writing poetry would have seemed as natural to him as it did to me.

Why were she and I so much alike when we had been separated at her birth, fifteen years earlier? The answer is in our genes.

The Minnesota Twin Family Study of identical twins—genetically identical, separated at birth, brought up in different families—found an uncanny number of similar traits. In 1979 America became fascinated by the Jim Twins, identical twins reared apart. After meeting at age thirty-nine, they became the founding pair of what would be a groundbreaking study at the University of Minnesota.[100] The sheer volume of shared traits of the Jim Twins was so numerous that they are still written about. They both bit their nails and were prone to tension headaches. They both did carpentry as a hobby, specializing in small objects. They preferred light beer and Salem cigarettes, drove Chevys, and vacationed on the same Florida beach. When asked to draw a picture of anything, each chose a human figure. They responded to the famous Rorschach inkblot test with similar answers. Eerily, both were named James by their adoptive parents, and both had a dog named Toy when they were children. Both married women named Linda and Betty (in reverse order) and named their sons James—with the middle name of Allan/Alan. Watch them in an old tape from *The Tonight Show* with Johnny Carson show and you'll see them sit and cross their legs (ankle above knee) in the same way.

The Minnesota research included more than a hundred pairs of identical and fraternal twins, some reared together, some apart. "On multiple measures of personality and temperament, occupational and leisure-time interests, and social attitudes, monozygotic (identical twins from a single egg) twins reared apart are about as similar as are monozygotic twins reared together,' the study concluded."[101] That is not the case with fraternal twins. Fraternal twins are found to be no more alike than any brother or sister, and data about them was excluded from the published findings discussed here.

What does that mean, exactly? It means that the identical twins are similar not only in verbal, mathematical, and general intelligence but also in a host of major personality traits that affect their outlook on life and how agreeable they would be to live with, writes Steven Pinker, a cognitive psychologist and author who popularized the twin studies:

"They have similar attitudes toward controversial subjects such as the death penalty, religion, and modern music. They resemble each other not just

---

[100] Thomas J. Bouchard et al., "Sources of Human Psychological Differences: the Minnesota Study of Twins Reared Apart," *Science* 250, no. 4978 (Oct. 12, 1990): 223–28.
[101] Bouchard et al., "Sources of Human Psychological Differences," 223.

in paper-and-pencil tests but in consequential behavior such as gambling, divorcing, committing crimes, getting into accidents, and watching television. And they boast dozens of shared idiosyncrasies such as giggling incessantly, giving interminable answers to simple questions, and dipping buttered toast in coffee."[102]

Earlier generations had the example of identical twins Eppie Lederer and her twin, Pauline Phillips, who wrote nearly indistinguishable advice columns under the pen names Ann Landers and Abigail Van Buren, respectively. Both syndicated their columns nationwide for decades. More recently, the movie *Three Identical Strangers*, about identical triplets separated at birth and united by chance in their twenties, reveals the same kind of mirroring.

But while the identical twins' similarities are fascinating, so are the synchronicities that adopted people discover when they meet their biological siblings. In 2019 *Good Morning America* had a spot about non-identical adopted twins who found two sisters through DNA testing, and the similarities between the four of them read like a textbook account of synchronicity.[103] Though the twins and their sisters were raised across the country from each other (Seattle and Virginia Beach), one of the twins moved from Seattle to Virginia Beach, where the non-adopted sisters lived, and became friends with the same group of women as her sister. Noting the similarities, a mutual friend introduced the two. A couple of weeks later, without prior knowledge of the other's plan, they attended the same country music concert in similar black dresses with bare shoulders and straps, all strikingly visible in the photo taken at the event. At different times, the Virginia Beach twin taught at the same school as one of her younger sisters. Punctuating the whole six-minute interview on *Good Morning America* was the sisters' effusive, shared laughter as well as their delight in the feeling that "we've known each other forever."

---

[102] Steven Pinker, *The Blank Slate: The Modern Denial of Human Nature* (New York: Viking, 2002), 47.
[103] "4 Women Who Learned They Were Sisters through DNA Testing Speak Out: 'It Was Pretty Mind-Blowing,'" *Good Morning America*, Feb. 26, 2019, https://web.archive.org/web/20220825213601/https://www.goodmorningamerica.com/family/story/women-learned-sisters-dna-testing-speak-pretty-mind-61320863.

They plan to get together on the kind of ceremonial events for which families universally gather.

The sisters had only met (except for the pair at the country music concert) eleven days earlier, and here they were planning family holidays, even though one sister still lived in Seattle. While one adopted twin mentioned that everyone has her other families—the adoptions were good ones, everyone agreed—that immediate planning for a traditional family ritual is not something that would be likely to occur without the pull of a shared genetic bond drawing them together.

The Minnesota Twin Family Study looked at the outcome of shared genes. It was up to others to investigate the ever-expanding study of genes themselves, a field taking a giant leap forward with the discovery of DNA and the mapping of the human genome. "When it comes to explaining human thought and behavior, the possibility that heredity plays any role at all still has the power to shock," observes Pinker.[104]

The importance of genes cannot be overstated, according to Robert Plomin, a behavioral geneticist and psychology professor at King's College in London: "Genetics is the most important factor shaping who we are. It explains more of the psychological differences between us than everything else put together. . . . I am not aware of a single psychological trait that shows no genetic influence," he writes.[105] Another behavioral scientist, David Nettle, writes, "Environmental influences on personality is a morass of unsupported or poorly tested ideas, and, ironically, it is behavior geneticists who have brought the most progress to the field."[106] This was so because they were trying to determine which traits were heritable—nature—and which could be attributed to environment—nurture. In doing so, they kept finding more to put on the nature side of the column.

Plomin's work does not totally discount environmental influence, but

---

[104] Pinker, *Blank Slate,* viii.
[105] Robert Plomin, *Blueprint: How DNA Makes Us Who We Are* (Cambridge, MA: MIT Press, 2018), viii.
[106] Daniel Nettle, *Personality: What Makes You the Way You Are* (Oxford University Press, 2007), 211.

he notes that the environmental factor includes the entire context of a child's life. It encompasses everything that happens to him or her. He also points out that inheritability can be very high for a specific trait, but the average difference between ethnic or gender groups could be entirely environmental. His critics say his views smack of old Nazi-style eugenics and could foster institutionalized racism and have profound social-engineering policy impli-cations.[107] However, given the evidence piling up, it is increasingly difficult to discount the outsized effect of DNA on personality. People will always find reasons for their prejudices. It is up to us to guard against those prejudices, whatever their basis.

Despite the possibility of race bias, advancing the liberal idea that we are blank slates has done great damage, according to Pinker: "The theory that parents can mold their children like clay has inflicted child-rearing regimes on parents that are unnatural and sometimes cruel. It has distorted the choices faced by mothers as they try to balance their lives and has multiplied the an-guish of parents whose children haven't turned out the way they hoped."[108]

Particularly compelling is his example on how environment might be shaped by genetic predisposition. Say a parent reads to a child at a young age, and that child then learns to read quite early. Plomin suggests that the reading itself is likely to occur because the child expresses delight at being read to, and thus the parent reacts to those cues, which come from his genes. So the nature of the child influences the nurturing he gets.

All this suggests that knowing as much as possible about the natural par-ents can be invaluable to the adopted person as well as the adoptive parents. One of the best accounts of how this might work is the frank account of an adoptive parent whose son battled with addiction. The mother assumed the

---

[107] Eric Joyce, "*Blueprint* by Robert Plomin: Latest Intelligence Genetics Book Could Be a Gift for Far-Right," *The Conversation*, Nov. 5, 2018; https://web.archive.org/web/20220825213759/https://theconversation.com/blueprint-by-robert-plomin-latest-intelligence-genetics-book-could-be-a-gift-for-far-right-104499; Nathaniel Comfort, "Genetic Determinism Redux, *Nature* 561 (Sept. 27, 2018): 461–63, https://web.archive.org/web/20220825214038/https://media.nature.com/original/magazine-assets/d41586-018-06784-5/d41586-018-06784-5.pdf.
[108] Pinker, *Blank Slate*, x.

"fetal environment of a stressed teenage mother, who probably drank and smoked" might have affected him. But nothing prepared her learning that both her son's natural mother and father—out of touch with each other for twenty-five years—had struggled with drug addiction their entire lives. The son spent months with both natural parents, and when his adoptive mother asked him how different he was from his biological father he answered, "Not a heck of a lot, but I have better tools."

His adoptive mother, E. Kay Trimberger, a retired professor of women's and gender studies at Sonoma State University, became enmeshed in behavioral genetics—not to disavow the influence of the home environment she had provided (nurture), but to understand how the home environment was somewhat shaped by the genetics at play in the adopted individual. She also concluded that if all the parties involved had known one another beyond, say, an initial meeting at the time of birth, this might have helped the young man:

"I wish I had had the courage to open my son's adoption sooner. If, during his teenage years, I had known about his birth parents' substance abuse, I would have been less anxious and confused and could have sought effective help and taken a stronger stand against drugs and alcohol. This may or may not have made a difference for Jamal but meeting his half brother at sixteen rather than at twenty-six could have been decisive. His brother, in all likelihood, would have told him ten years earlier what it was like growing up with addicted parents, and how it motivated him to never take a drink or use a drug."[109]

In another instance Trimberger wrote about, a family kept dismantling their son's projects because he just seemed to be tinkering away at something while ignoring his schoolbooks. Later they learned that several people in the son's natural family were web designers and engineers who had learned by tinkering. Once they became aware of this, they stopped taking down their son's projects because it "was time to clean up."

I could not help but reflect on how I might have helped my daughter.

---

[109] E. Kay Trimberger, "Adoption and Genetics: Implications for Adoptive Parents," *HuffPost Contributor*, Jan. 30, 2014, updated April 1, 2014, https://web.archive.org/web/20220825221805/https://www.huffpost.com/entry/adoption-and-genetics-imp_b_4682667.

One of the first things I learned was that she was, as her adoptive mother put it, LD, or "learning-disabled." *How could that be?* ran through my mind, and I was reminded suddenly of conversations with her father about the great kid we were likely to have. Undoubtedly, our unspoken assumption went like this—she'd be smart, witty, possibly a writer. She would be anything but LD. As Jane would later tell me, she had been only in a single special-ed class for algebra. But that she was LD was the first piece of information I learned about my daughter from her adoptive mother. If I'd been involved and the adoptive parents had known about Jane's father, the assumption that Jane had a mentally defective progenitor—possibly institutionalized—would never have existed. Whatever information I had imagined Ann's friend, the nurse in pediatrics at Strong Memorial Hospital, passing along—about Patrick and me being from good stock—was nonexistent or had been long forgotten over the years. Jane had missed a lot of school and her grades were so-so, yet she wrote poetry that found its way into her school's student magazine. Of course she would write poetry. I wrote poetry when I was her age, and later too. Patrick and I quoted poetry to each other the first time we met. Ann told me Jane was a bright, engaging toddler, learned her alphabet before kindergarten, and now she was slow? *Must be in her genes* is what I was getting from Ann. I would have been a lion protecting my daughter from false assumptions about her abilities. However, her missing so much school due to seizures, as well as the drugs she took to control them, must also figure into the equation.

Her mother was not able to completely hide her astonishment when she learned of Jane's actual lineage, that Jane was the daughter of two literate writers who met while working at a newspaper. Though I initially told Ann that there was no mental illness in my family, or in Jane's father's as far as I knew, she continued to quiz me. No one in your family has been institutionalized? I inferred that she had been convinced Jane came from feebleminded stock, for starters, and who knows what else? Thus, when Jane fell behind in algebra and was sent to the class for slow learners, Ann was not surprised, nor did she or Gary put up the opposition that I or Patrick surely would have. Many years later Jane would get her associate degree, win an award in her local Toastmasters association, and be encouraged by a professor to continue her education for a four-year degree in English. My daughter! Patrick's daughter! Of course she would gravitate to English literature!

She had her problems, to be sure, but my being involved in Jane's life from the onset would have given her adoptive parents a totally different mind-set about our daughter and affected how they reacted to her. Understanding how she struggled in a genetically strange environment full of unknowns has been the source of great guilt for me. Open adoption with the genetic mother—and, when possible, the father—directly involved from the beginning would be a great leap forward for the best possible care and nurturing of any adoptee, and most surely, my own daughter.

I did not find her a day too soon.

22   No-Show Dad

SUMMER 1983—Reunion stories tug at the heartstrings. Reunion stories get in the media. Reunion stories point out the regret of relinquishment and the relief of reunion. Reunion stories call attention to the inanity and injustice of sealed records for both mothers and their children. Reunion stories have the potential to move public opinion. So with Jane's and her parents' agreement, we talk to the media. *Today* did a segment that showed Ann and Jane at home. For *McCall's* I wrote a long first-person story.[110] Local newspapers did interviews with us, including *Newsday*, Patrick's paper.

That story fills nearly half a tabloid-sized page, with a picture of the two of us sitting on the steps of our back deck with our arms around each other. Ann is quoted, noting that while Jane had been curious about her biological mother, friends were against our meeting. "You never know how strong the ties are," she says. "But we did it for Jane's sake. . . . Here was this glamorous girl from New York. 'It had to be that, didn't it,' I thought then. I wasn't thrilled about the whole thing. I really did feel threatened." She adds that her husband was more suspicious about what I wanted, "but it was easier for him because it was a mother who came into the picture. . . . But no, it worked out nicely."[111]

The columnist notes that Jane was only uncomfortable with one question: What is Lorraine to you? "It's hard to describe to other people what

---

[110] Lorraine Dusky, "The Daughter I Gave Away," *McCall's*, July, 1983, pp. 42–46, 144.
[111] Marilyn Goldstein, "Forging a Family Bond after 17 Years," Long Island Diary, *Newsday*, July 21, 1983.

she is to me," Jane answers, neatly obfuscating, safely hurting no one's feelings. Adoptees often unconsciously learn an evasive language that masks their thoughts. They are schooled at not letting anyone know their feelings.

Left unasked is any question about Jane's father. Is the writer simply being super sensitive, or does she know who he is? After all, he works for the same paper as she does! She might see him when she goes back to the office. I calculate that she probably does know since the information mill among reporters—including reporters at different papers—works pretty well. But then, our affair was seventeen years ago. If asked, I mean to keep mum about his identity—or inquire whether she already knows. Patrick will see the story. Would it precipitate a call? One could hope.

However, my friend Judy does not leave Jane's father out of the story she writes for the *New York Times* a few weeks later.[112] Without naming him, she places him on Long Island but notes that so far he refuses to meet Jane. Judy quotes Jane as saying she had planned to start searching for her natural mother when she turned eighteen, and Jane adds, "I just feel I have two women who really care about me." Ann is quoted also, saying, "I always wondered if [our meeting] would interfere with my relationship with Jane, but finding Lorraine has freed Jane and given her much more self-confidence. And, if anything, Jane and I are as close, if not closer, than ever."

Bill Pierce, adoption reform's nemesis, states that the search movement has the "potential for human sorrow." But Elizabeth Cole from the Child Welfare League predicts that sealed birth records will be open one day, pointing out that they already are open in Britain and Israel, where her colleagues there "had not found the practice to be harmful."

Patrick does not call. Shortly before Jane arrived that summer, I made one more entreaty to him. He was now living alone. He and his second wife were not divorcing, he said, only not living together. Instead of agreeing to meet

---

[112] Judy Klemesrud, "Mothers Find the Children They Gave Up," *New York Times*, Aug. 29, 1983, https://web.archive.org/web/20220825222128/https://www.nytimes.com/1983/08/29/style/mothers-find-the-children-they-gave-up.html?searchResultPosition=1.

our daughter, again he turns the conversation to his oldest daughter Colleen's resentment of her half sister, Kirsten, meaning, if she resents her, she really would hate the idea of Jane! All I can think of is how Jane would be far from cool toward any sister she met—she would embrace Kirsten.

But. He was still not ready.

Now Jane is back, this time for the whole summer. She says she will phone him herself, at the office. He won't turn her down, right?

But still, I'm worried. Is she up to another refusal? How much more pain does she have to endure? Yet I do not interfere; this is her call. She's got grit, I tell myself. *Patrick, please come through for her, just this once.*

From the phone at the top of the stairs—the same one from which I'd taken her name down two years before—she dials his direct number at *Newsday*, which improbably has the same last four digits as our friend Arthur's in Sag Harbor. A good omen? *Please stay*, she whispers as the phone begins ringing, *I might need you.* Patrick answers. She freezes up on the spot: This is her father on the line.

His voice blows out her courage as quickly as someone snuffs out a candle. "Hello? Hello? Is anyone there?" I hear him faintly. She says nothing. She turns to me, her eyes huge and glassy. Go ahead, I nod and mouth the words *Say something.*

She cannot.

Patrick hangs up.

Jane runs down the stairs. Do you want me to come? I shout to her retreating back. No. She returns an hour later, her eyes are dry but red. She goes to her room and shuts the door.

For the first time, really, for the first time through all the years and all the hurts that had been accepted and exonerated, now I am not only disappointed with Patrick, I am angry. I had forgiven him everything—promises made and not kept, our baby gone—and mentally I always made excuses, racking everything up to a troublesome alignment of the stars, circumstances, other obligations.

But not now, not this. He is doing the inexcusable. He is hurting our child when he has the power not to. What happened to the man I thought I knew? He brought me roses when she was born, but seventeen years later he doesn't have the backbone to meet her? I understand this would be hard, but who is this man?

There is a place in the adopted person's heart that no one who has never been there can reach or understand. Even if glossed over as the years spin by, it stays on, a breathing thing that cannot quite die. I can sympathize with Jane; with Florence, who had a disappointing reunion with her natural mother; with my friend Pam, who would find a half sister but her mother deceased; with Annette, an adoptee who had given me a book of her melancholy poems; with all the adoptees I knew, but I can never completely understand what it's like to be relinquished by your mother, be rejected by your father, and grow up among genetic strangers who have taken you in, no matter how loving they might be.

That summer, Jane would get up early in the morning, around six, an hour before we stirred. She'd slip out of the house and walk downtown as the sun came up and the village was still quiet. Years later she would tell me she'd buy a *Newsday* and a coffee, go out on Long Wharf, and sit there scanning the paper, searching for her father's byline.

The kid just wanted a damn lunch.

23 The Opposite of Happiness

Mother-and-child reunions like ours are at first ecstatic, then blissful, but then you may feel as if you are swimming in a witches' brew of eye of newt and toe of frog.

From a short visit of a few days, our times together expanded to whole summers while she was in high school. I imagined a summer idyll, a fairy tale with a rainbow ending, long glorious walks on the beach, a true getting to know each other. What could go wrong?

Plenty, is the short answer. Just as mothers and daughters who are not separated have issues, we have Issues Plus. Our past clings to our present like moss on rock. We did have plenty of great moments when the world seemed clean and the sky blue and our relationship as solid as the Rock of Gibraltar. We spent afternoons at the beach, went horseback riding, rode our bikes, went to the movies, wandered through boutiques and galleries, hung out on Long Wharf downtown, and climbed the 137 steps to the top of the lighthouse at Montauk. Can I use the word "priceless" without making it sound like a credit card ad?

We hung out with Tony and his son, Evan, when he visited—he no longer lived with us during the summer—and my former landlord Arthur. He had become a constant in our lives, someone who wandered in and out like a family member. When he was in Sag Harbor, he was likely to join us for meal. If I needed a place to stay when I was in the city, I'd sleep on the day bed in his living room. Jane took to him like a favorite uncle.

But the good moments with Jane had their flip side, for they reminded me how I had failed her. Especially during the first few summers she lived with us, I regressed to that sad and confused heap of naked emotion lying alone in a hospital bed waiting for Patrick to rescue me and my baby, to say he and I would be together and we could keep our daughter. The feelings unleashed by being around Jane were as raw and messy as a fresh stab wound. Yet I was supposed to be overjoyed, right? She and her other family had accepted me, isn't that wonderful? She's in my home, everything is fantastic, right? Yet why was I such a mess? Why had I regressed to feeling like that pathetic young woman who became hysterical after her birth?

Because I was face-to-face with how I had failed her.

Our relationship would always be buffeted by the aftermath of her being adopted. Flashes of her anger came out of nowhere. She could be moody and surly. Talk of suicide would drift into her chatter over the years, nonchalantly, as if she were talking about having a ham-and-cheese sandwich for lunch. "Live fast, die young, be a good-looking corpse," she'd jokingly say. Jane! I'd say, and she'd laugh. *It was just a joke.*

Yet she was lonely and had only made a few friends of her own in town, so she needed me to be constantly on call, to be patient and solid, but I, too, was human. I could feel myself being smothered by her need. At times, I was short with her. I found it hard to carve out time to work. Sometimes I needed to be alone, in my office with the door shut. Away from all that reminded me of what I had not been. I could not be the perfect, ever-patient Madonna. The raw miasma of grief and guilt was swirling in me. The summers were long. By the end, I was as worn out as a frayed dish towel.

Her seizures. I can't write about Jane without talking about her seizures. Epilepsy was the background noise of her life, and that couldn't be turned off. Pass over the abandonment issues of adoption because they are preverbal, and anyway, you can't think of what to say about any of that except you are sorry, so very sorry, but on the road to the heart of the matter, you get to epilepsy, a mountain that overwhelms everything in sight. Jane would always be a prisoner of these two facts of her life. Adoption and epilepsy.

The Ryhmers wisely had never hidden from Jane her adoption, but they neglected to explain what the word "adopted" meant to the little girl. They began telling her "You're adopted" before she understood the meaning. Jane told me she thought they were saying "You're a doctor" and was puzzled, but she did not ask what they meant. When Jane was five—the age of simple comprehension, the age when she began to understand that babies came from mommies' bellies and that she came from someone other than the mommy she knew—Ann was pregnant with her first natural child, bringing home the meaning of "You're adopted" all too clearly. When Ann was still in the hospital after giving birth—news Jane must have learned from her joyful dad, now a father to his own blood—Jane had her first seizure. Tie them together or don't. I'm not claiming anything here, not at all—epilepsy has biochemical origins—but that is how it was. Around the time she learned she had been given away—and that certainly is how a five-year-old thinks; they are not using pretty language that obfuscates reality—Jane's seizures began.

And they came fast and furiously, and they were frequent.

No matter the biological underpinnings, how could a five-year-old not have dark thoughts? Epilepsy was the bogeyman in the closet: Was this why

Figure 15. From left to right: Tony, Jane, and our neighbor Arthur in our backyard.

her mother hadn't kept her? Was she like this, too? In learning to cope with the twin realities of adoption/epilepsy, Jane ended up in a place where disruption/commotion/turmoil became her normal. She got comfortable being the troubled child. The center of attention. In a hockey helmet. In the hospital. With doctors, nurses, teachers. She could never be "normal," she would never easily fit in anywhere that she knew, so why not revel in her otherness, why not enjoy the special treatment?

Once I overheard Evan trying to dissuade Jane from her pronouncement that being in the hospital was to be desired. I don't think she knew I was listening. Later I would understand that in a hospital she did not stand out as the girl who had something wrong with her. In a hospital she was a patient like everybody else. In a hospital, a girl with a problem was normal.

She must have gotten comfortable with making up stuff at the same time—if her place in the family was kind of fake, she had the go-ahead to be "fake" about whatever she wanted.

A psychologist who specializes in adoption issues, David Kirschner, discovered from personality tests that the adopted children he was treating had a rich fantasy life, usually spun around two sets of parents, one good, one bad. "There were also elaborate themes of loss, abandonment, and rejection; and the child's behavior problems often included lying, as they felt they had been lied to; stealing, to compensate for the theft of their identity; and truancy or running away, a symbolic effort to find their biological roots and an environment in which they felt they fit and belonged," he writes.[113] One of his young patients told him that he was going to keep some secrets: "'I'm going to leave you real curious, and hanging, like I was left. . . curious . . . with a hole in my head.'"

When I asked the late B. J. Lifton about lying, she replied in an email, "Since adoptees grow up with falsified birth certificates and secrecy about reality, in the minds of some there is no border between truth and lying. They have no true narrative, so they can make up anything they want. They are 'free spirits, not entrapped by roots,' as a cousin suggested to me."

---

[113] David Kirschner, *Adoption: Uncharted Waters: A Psychologist's Case Studies* (Woodbury, NY: Juneau Press, 2006), 7–8.

Jane became so expert at fibbing, or making up whoppers, that eventually it was difficult to accept anything she said at face value. Something she said might be true. Might not be. To make her life more fascinating than it really was or simply to shut up anyone—me, Ann, Gary, Tony, even Arthur—when we challenged her, she made up stories about herself. One afternoon I told her the fable about the boy who cried wolf one too many times, until nobody believed him. She listened in silence. Nothing changed.

So though she had her reasons, this hazy relationship with the truth about matters great and small was exasperating to everyone around her. None of us knew when we could believe her. She regaled me with tales of how she faked seizures to avoid going to school. Get out of bed, bump into a chest of drawers, fall on the floor—all enough to send signals downstairs that Jane is having a seizure upstairs. Now she would be able to avoid going to school, where the kids made fun of her. She told the story as a funny one about herself, but I didn't find it amusing. It was the story of a girl in pain. My daughter. Absence seizures were even easier to fake—you merely looked off into the distance for a few seconds and said nothing.

Yet because drugs were controlling her seizures all the time I knew her, it seemed not to play a role in her daily life. She took her anti-seizure meds—Depakote—religiously, so she went about her days now without her epilepsy being evident, and I scarcely thought about her affliction. She never had a seizure when she was with us—save maybe once. We were in the kitchen at home, arguing about her lying, and suddenly she got a vacant look in her eye and looked away for a few seconds. Because she had bragged about how practiced she was in faking seizures when it suited her, I suggested rather loudly that she was avoiding our confrontation. She snapped back to attention and did not deny it.

But while I did not live with her seizures, that is not to diminish how her well-being, sense of self, and interactions with others were shaped by her affliction. That was deep, that was visceral, that was all-encompassing. She accepted that being adopted might have made her different on some level—at that time, she didn't really want to talk about being adopted—but she was absolutely convinced that her seizures, and the drugs she had to take to control them, had a singular and abiding influence that overshadowed everything, including adoption. I didn't argue with her, but I knew that her epilepsy and her adoption were intertwined from the dawn of her comprehension.

By then, I began wondering if the birth control pills I took when I was pregnant were the probable source of her seizures. But at the time, I couldn't find any literature about that.

The anti-seizure medication Jane took? Do a search for "side effects of Depakote" and you see listed "memory loss, depression, lowering of IQ, thoughts of suicide, suicidal behavior." Drugs.com lists more than a hundred side effects for valproic acid, the generic name for Depakote and Depakene. It's a veritable catalog of her feelings: emptiness and sadness, confusion, anxiety and depression. My girl? She had more of these telltale markers than I wish to count.

While she could lace her conversation with irony, the mark of a nimble wit, it was impossible for her to keep, say, a deli order straight: ham on rye with—no, without—coleslaw, mayo instead of mustard and no pickle but lettuce, onion, and tomato. Or was that extra pickle? No pickle? Did he say Russian dressing? Lettuce? Tomato? How much is this sandwich with three extras? Oh god, I can't remember.

Over the years, she was hired and then fired from many entry-level jobs: as a nanny (twice), a deli-counter person, a cleaner at a local inn, and a worker at a garden center. I've run ahead here in the story for a bit to show how the pattern of hiring and firing that emerged in Sag Harbor was one that would dog her all her life. She so wanted to succeed at something, but emotional problems overwhelmed her. No matter how hard she tried, she would eventually screw up and be fired. Even at a gardening center, she ran into trouble. Yet I knew she wasn't stupid. She knew she wasn't stupid. That was the hardest part to accept.

Each time she was let go, her ego took another beating. Each time she went down for the count, she was slower to get back up. One summer she eventually found a job she kept: working at the busy ice cream parlor on Long Wharf where the lines in the summer for five-dollar cones can stretch to twenty people, all thinking, Dammit hurry up, we are on vacation. She might

have hated the down-market job for someone already out of high school—
many of the kids working there were younger than she was—but she did not
complain. She was succeeding at something. In Wisconsin, Burger King was
her main employer for years. Once she had a job under control, no matter
how menial, she did her best to make it work. When she was succeeding, her
spirits would lift. She wanted to become a shift manager and then manager.
She got close but never crossed the finish line. So many jobs ended in Jane in
a ruckus with the manager.

All I could do was listen. Yet every time she was let go from a job, she
would pick herself up, dust herself off, and move on. My girl might invent
fables about herself, but she had grit.

Sadly, I can't tell this story and do Jane justice by leaving out another
salient factor. Shortly before she graduated from high school, she revealed
that a member of her extended adoptive family had sexually abused her and
that it had started when she was about twelve. From what she told me, it
had been over for a while, but the man was still around, and she had to see
him occasionally. Lying is a hallmark of sexual abuse—the children who have
been abused are told they must keep it secret, so they get acclimated to lying
by omission. She had told me years earlier—probably the first summer she
visited—that one of her girlfriends was having regular sex with her doctor in
the girl's bedroom, a fabrication that made absolutely no sense. Even though
I pointed out that her story had so many holes in it that a herd of wild boars
could have torn through it, Jane stuck to it. By then I was used to her unbe-
lievable stories and gave up dissuading her. I failed to recognize that she had
been talking about herself, this absurdity was a cry for help, and the "doctor"
in the story was in fact, the man living with her adoptive grandmother.

Once she opened up about being abused—I never got any specific details—what she said never changed, as her other stories often did. Her negative
feelings about the man never wavered, and now the offhand and unfavorable
comments she'd made about him, comments that used to strike me as odd,
made a certain kind of awful sense. She had been in therapy as a youngster.
She once said that she did "not tell Connie [her therapist] the truth. Because
the truth was too dangerous." The truth was almost certainly about the sexual

Figure 16. Jane and Lorraine in Sag Harbor, Summer, 1982.

abuse. She once came upon a stray issue of *Penthouse* at our house—back then it wasn't all porn, and that issue had an art piece we'd been interested in—however, Jane was visibly shocked and perplexed. Grandma's companion had that magazine, she said, and we knew that Grandma's companion was a skunk—so how could we have the same magazine? I didn't make much of it at the time, but I'm telling it here because her reaction seemed outsized for the incident.

Adoption. Epilepsy. Sexual abuse. It's hard to see how anyone could absorb all that without deep psychological scars and aberrant behavior.

Jane did not escape. So did I feel like I failed her? How could I not?

Maybe I would have found a way to give her an education that didn't socially alienate her, a dynamic she never truly got over. I would have fought like a tiger to keep her from special-ed classes. She wouldn't have known her sexual abuser. Lying likely wouldn't have come to seem as natural as a facial tic. The daughter I raised—even with the same DNA—would have been a different person, one who would not have had to endure so many slings and arrows. Going down this road leads to an endless pit of recriminations, a road I have taken in my mind, but imagining a different life for her could not alter the reality. Despite her growing up in a stable, churchgoing family, despite wondering how I could have handled the epilepsy on my own, I could never think, Yes, I did the right thing. The justifications might repeat in my brain—it was the ethos of the times, it was the shame of it all, I was alone without anyone to turn to—but none of it reaches that damned hole in my heart.

Being Adopted

In America, where adoption today seems to be lurking in every family and around every corner, we tend to think of caregivers as interchangeable, that the ties to one's ancestral family are not important, as long as the child's basic needs are met. But the testimony of a growing number of adult adoptees blows that idea apart. So does the popularity of television shows that trace one's family roots. Heritage stories that go back generations flood the subjects' faces with emotion. Some guests are brought to tears when learning of their ancestors' hardships, courage in the face of adversity, and glorious times of triumph.

It is human to want to know where you come from. Whether the core issue is the separation from the natural mother or the severing of connection from the biological family, the result is the same: disorientation, dislocation, and the feeling of being unrooted. When natural parents are overwhelmed or ill, in other cultures family members raise the child, but that child always knows who's who, and the child maintains a connection with siblings, cousins, aunts, uncles. Often, the child has at least limited contact with the biological mother and father. The child is never in the dark.

That's not how it's done in the western world and particularly not in America. We remove a child from her connective tissue and, expecting the best outcome, graft her somewhere else where whether she fits or not is pure chance. The phrase in the letter from the adoption agency that stated Jane's other parents were "most delighted with her" never left my mind. How did the agency know? They didn't.

While Jane's seizures had a biological base, the data shows that adoptees are prone to psychological traumas that the rest of us are not. Yet the adoption industry generally ignores adoptee trauma and the public is largely unaware of it—or chooses to ignore it.

Certainly the six justices who voted to overturn *Roe v. Wade* in 2022 did. Justice Samuel Alito, who wrote the majority opinion in *Dobbs v. Jackson Women's Health Organization*, noted that "a woman who puts her newborn up for adoption today has little reason to fear that the baby will not find a suitable home." The comment is buried (footnote 46) in a long list of notes, but Alito's rationale for adoption as the answer to an unwanted pregnancy is no less noxious—the shortage of available babies: "[N]early 1 million women were seeking to adopt children in 2002 [prospective adoptive parents were creating a demand for adoptable babies], whereas the domestic supply of infants relinquished at birth or within the first month of life and available to be adopted had become virtually nonexistent."[114] Alito mentions the "safe-haven boxes" where babies can be dropped off anonymously with the obvious implication that they should make it easier and more convenient for women who want to quickly free themselves from the "burdens of parenting," as adoptive parent Justice Amy Coney Barrett stated at the hearing that led to this decision.

Nowhere is there any indication that the six justices—Chief Justice John Roberts is also an adoptive parent—are aware of any of the myriad issues that stem from being given up by one's mother to be available to fix this predicament in the supply chain of infants. The full implication is that solving this nagging problem for those wishing to adopt is a greater good than women's autonomy over their own bodies. Nowhere does the decision in *Dobbs* note that the data mentioned earlier revealing between 30 to 40 percent of the women who give up a child for adoption, whatever the reason, are *unlikely* to have another.[115] While these numbers are from women who gave up their children in the era of closed adoption, the mention of "safe-haven" boxes implies that there will be babies without birth certificates and that this will result in anonymous adoption. By including safe-haven boxes as a possible solution to an unwanted pregnancy, Alito and his cohorts encouraged—or at least did not discourage—anonymous, closed adoptions without any recourse for later discovery of familial ties other than the iffy chance of a DNA connection later on.

This kind of willful ignorance on the part of the justices who voted for the *Dobbs* decision ignores the reality of birth and adoption for both natural mother and child. The trauma of relinquishing a child and the adoption

---

[114] Dobbs v. Jackson Women's Health Organization, No. 19-1392, slip op. at 34n46 (S. Ct. 2022), https://web.archive.org/web/20220921004134/https://www.supremecourt.gov/opinions/21pdf/19-1392_6j37.pdf.

[115] Smith, *Safeguarding*, 49.

trauma experienced persist throughout their lifetimes. As I listened to Coney Barrett mention the safe-haven boxes, I felt my stomach turn. Knowing what we know about the hunger for roots, the real-life questions that adoptees have about identity, how could she encourage the use of safe-haven boxes?

She could because she can.

The *Dobbs* decision brings up the question of adoptees and abortion, for there is no way around the fact that many adoptees would not be here today if not for the difficulty of getting an abortion in the era when they were born. I'm writing soon after the *Dobbs* decision, but adoptees as a group have shown no major reaction to the overturning of *Roe v. Wade.* Adoptees are not cheering the end of constitutionally protected, legal abortion. At least two writers in the past have mentioned their own abortions in their memoirs, and without qualms or much if any internal debate. The day Sarah Saffian learned she was pregnant, after calming down upon hearing the news, she wrote in her memoir *Ithaka,* "…mechanically, I phoned the gynecologist's office and scheduled an appointment for an abortion in a few weeks, not taking the time that the doctor had offered to think over the decision."[116]

Jean Strauss, in her book *Beneath a Tall Tree,* does discuss her thinking somewhat: "I am playing God. I know this when I decide I will have an abortion. It is the right choice for me." She notes that a nurse at the hospital asks if she has considered adoption. Strauss knows the nurse is on a waiting list to adopt a child. "I've thought about it a lot, I tell her. 'I'm an adoptee.'"[117]

And what happens to far too many adoptees? "In developed countries, adopted children represent less than 1 percent of births, but may represent over 20 percent of the patients in mental health services."[118]

B. J. Lifton wrote that the number of adoptees in the adolescent and young-adult clinics and residential treatment centers is strikingly high: "Doctors from the Yale Psychiatric Institute and other hospitals that take

---

[116] Sarah Saffian, *Ithaka: A Daughter's Memoir of Being Found,* (New York: Delta), 145.

[117] Jean Strauss, *Beneath a Tall Tree* (Claremont, CA: Arete, 2001), 85–86

[118] Brigitte Prati, "Are Adopted Children at a Greater Risk of Suicide Than Their Non-adopted Peers?" *Adolescence,* abstract, <#>24, no. 1 (Jan. 2006), https://web.archive.org/web/20220825223151/https://www.cairn-int.info/journal-adolescence-2006-1-page-111.htm.

very sick adolescents have told me they are discovering that from one-quarter to one-third of their patients are adopted. A great many of these young people are in serious trouble with the law and are drug addicted."[119]

When the teenage son of close friends went through a rough patch, he ultimately ended up at a boarding school for bright but troubled kids. He stood out, he told his parents, because he was neither adopted nor from a broken home, as were most of his peers. Another friend's adopted daughter, after being kicked out of a series of boarding schools, landed at a "school for scoundrels," as her mother called it, and she said the place was rife with adoptees. Yes, anecdotal evidence, but anecdotal evidence confirms the data.

Naysayers attribute these statistics to the fact that adoptive parents tend to be wealthier and better educated than the general population and thus more likely to seek professional help. But that theory has been rebutted. What is happening is that adoptive parents throw up their hands and call in the experts sooner than biological parents.[120] And when they do, they often ignore adoption as the seat of the problem, attributing the bad behavior and acting out to bad genes. Psychologist David Kirschner writes that in dealing with young people, he interviews the parents first, "and more often than not, they were on their way out the door when they would turn to me and say, 'Oh, I don't remember whether we mentioned it, but Mark is adopted.' They would add, 'but that has nothing to do with the problem.'"[121] Of course it did, he writes.

Of course it did.

Fighting words above—to write about adoptees having special troubles, adoptees in treatment, adoptees hurting more than the rest of us—and you cannot write about this without an army of people objecting—adoptees,

---

[119] Betty Jean Lifton, *Lost and Found: The Adoption Experience*, 3rd ed. (Ann Arbor: University of Michigan Press, 2009), 45–46. Lifton adds that it is as if both sexes are experimenting with identities that seem to be related to fantasies about their biological parents. "The debate continues over the source of these maladjustments—the strain of being adopted, the adoptive parents' unresolved conflicts about infertility, or intrauterine disturbances—and doctors now admit the need for long-term studies."

[120] Sarah B. Warren, "Lower Threshold for Referral for Psychiatric Treatment for Adopted Adolescents," *Journal of the American Academy of Child & Adolescent Psychiatry* 31, no. 3 (May 1992): 512–17.

[121] Kirschner, *Adoption*, 7.

adoptive parents, friends of adoptees and adoptive parents, your dentist, your hairdresser, you name it, all of whom know adopted people who have never broken the speed limit and who got all A's in school. To them I say, Hats off!

But I write here what it was like to know my daughter, my daughter who was adopted. Delve into the growing library of books and articles about adoptee psychology, and you repeatedly come upon the word "healing." Healing? From what, if not the trauma of adoption? "Expect to be sad," Robert Anderson wrote in his excellent memoir, *Second Choice*.[122] My daughter? She was eternally sad.

There is ample evidence that my daughter is emblematic of the myriad problems of being adopted. Reunion is only the beginning of a long journey of painful discovery for many adoptees. As one blogger explained,

> at this stage of reunion, the adult me is not always in charge. Reunion can cause psychological regression. Though on one level I am still a (moderately) reasonable middle-aged woman— a wife, a mother, an employee—that's not all I am these days. There's another part of me that feels more like a toddler in the midst of a major daddy's-little-girl phase. For this inner-child-me, no amount of contact is enough. How much would it take to fill the hole left by a 46-year absence?
>
> I'm aware that this is where many reunions get into trouble, and I'm trying not to fall into the trap of expectations that can never be met. I'm trying to acknowledge the child-me and let her have her say without allowing her to be the one in charge. She can sit around wailing 'Daddy, Daddy, Daddy!' all day long, but when it's time to write an email or pick up the phone, she needs to let the grown-up handle the job.[123]

Being given up for adoption, as far as one can tell from the mountains of

---

[122] Robert Anderson, *Second Choice: Growing Up Adopted* (Chesterfield, MO: Badger Hill Press, 1993), 160.

[123] Rebecca Hawkes, "My Overtime Mind: Who's in Charge of This Reunion?," *Lost Daughters* (blog), Oct. 10, 2012, https://web.archive.org/web/20220825223359/ http://www.thelostdaughters.com/2012/10/my-overtime-mind-whos-in-charge-of-this.html.

literature about it, is one hell of a whack to many an ego, and that can carry over into the byways of a life. My daughter could read about the reasons that led up to her being adopted, I could talk about how it happened again and again, she would nod and say she understood, and, on an intellectual level, I believe she did. She once said that knowing how much medical attention she needed, it would have been incredibly difficult for me to cope alone, adding that her family's health insurance was excellent. From that standpoint alone, she said, adoption had been the better solution.

Yet. I cannot get past the *yet*. Even now.

Jane always insisted that epilepsy had a greater impact on her life than being adopted, and knowing what I did about her seizures, the drugs, how that affected her social skills and memory for detail, and thus employment, there was every reason to take her word for it. Her seizures might be under control with the medication, but that alone could not undo the years of having been the object of ridicule at school, her feelings of isolation that the hockey helmet represented, to which was added the sense of being abandoned by her mother at birth.

No matter which one held center stage, adoption or epilepsy—and let us not forget the sexual abuse—the combination was a triple whammy. She hurt. She hurt plenty. What to do about that? The summers in Sag Harbor might help—but enough? Probably not enough. Once we flew her to Michigan for a birthday party with my brothers and their kids, her cousins, all eager to bring her into the orbit of her other family. Did that help? Or did that simply highlight her otherness and alienation? We suggested therapy one summer, and she quickly agreed, never missed an appointment. But nothing could reach what felt like a bottomless pit of gloom. Eventually, I would retreat, for I was coming apart at the seams myself. I couldn't fix anything, and maybe I was to blame for everything.

One weekend, Jane stayed in Wisconsin and the Rhymers came for a visit by themselves. Over two days, the four of us talked about what we could do to give our daughter a happier, more successful life. We tried. The Rhymers tried. We were all exhausted.

No one could stop the rain.

24 Moving On

After the commotion of *Birthmark* and the reunion dies down, I step back from all public things involving adoption. I write a book called *The Best Companies for Women*. I am a book doctor for other authors, which is a step beyond merely editing another's work—it pretty much is rewriting the book. I write for magazines. I go to ALMA meetings only when Florence asks me to speak. I help a teenage neighbor locate her family in Poland—a Christmas card that arrived in her house each year was the key. Phone calls from strangers—sometimes mothers, sometimes adoptees—and letters from mothers and adoptees taper off. I still write the occasional letter to the editor or an opinion piece for this or that newspaper, but I long for a life that does not revolve around adoption. As reunions of adoptees and mothers become talk-show fodder, shows that turned me down when *Birthmark* came out now call. I turn them down. Tony and I become involved in local government and help elect a new mayor in the village. I write campaign ads for the newspaper and radio. Tony, in his low, theatrical bass, reads them over the radio, sounding like someone who must be paid attention to. He becomes the chair of the architectural review board, and I wind up as the chair of the zoning board just as Sag Harbor is undergoing the metamorphosis from largely ignored, charming whaling-fishing village to hip hamlet of the Hamptons. An active social life, jogging, yoga, and especially writing about subjects other than adoption fill my life.

My relationship with the Rhymers is mostly stable and friendly, even if I always feel I must be constantly aware of *not* doing the wrong thing. They have legal custody, and even though Jane is fully in charge of how much time she spends with Tony and me, I'm always somewhat tense talking to Ann. Going through old papers, I find a thank-you note from Ann. It's for a vase I'd sent as a Christmas gift. She writes that a friend informs her she is being roundly criticized for opening the door to me and that when Jane turns eighteen, she will leave them and "never look back." Ann says that she and Gary know they made the "right choice" to do what was best for Jane. I'm aware that my relationship with Jane raised some eyebrows in town, but until then it hasn't occurred to me that Ann and Gary are also criticized.

But as time grinds on and Jane grows up, she finds herself living in two different worlds. For the next couple of years, Jane visits or stays with us for extended periods. Part of the summer. All summer. She has her first romance with a cook at one of the many restaurants in town. Naturally, the Rhymers call, usually on a Saturday night, and as likely as not, we are having a dinner party. Tony cannot be stopped from answering the phone—no caller ID then—even though I am shaking my head no, and sure enough the call is from the Midwest. Tony answers, quickly says hello, and hands the phone to me. It is, alas, always Gary. I go to the kitchen and speak to him for an uncomfortable moment, saying I'll tell Jane to call, aware they must hear the boisterous chatter of a lively group of six or eight well into the wine. I sense their reproach, the mental tsk-tsk from a thousand miles away. Are they having a party over there every Saturday night?

After high school, Jane goes to work for Burger King in Madison, and one day after finishing the night shift, some guy follows her home, forces his way into her apartment—it had a broken lock, she says—and rapes her. She reports it to the police the next day, but the cops brush her off, adding to her despair and sense of worthlessness. We talk for hours at a time on the phone, and a few weeks later, she comes to live with us. At that point, I'm staying in one sublet or another and working in Manhattan three days a week as an editor for *Working Woman* magazine. But Tony is game. She moves in. She signs up for a semester at the local community college.

But Jane is far too tormented to make college work. Chaos soon reigns in our home. The exuberant teenager has grown up and is surly and unpleasant. She may be sleeping with one of her professors, as she tells Arthur and hints to me. Or is she instead having an affair with the married projectionist at the local movie theater, which she also implies? Or is that wishful thinking? One of her fantasies? Is she trying to make herself more interesting than she is in real life? Where is she? At the local pub? A black chador of victimhood enrobes her always, making her an easy target. I fret. I set a curfew. She is furious. What was this, jail? I do not relent. Trouble is just around the bend.

The nights I'm in the city, Tony's home alone with Jane. Tony is a patient man, up to a point. But after a few months, he takes to driving around at night instead of staying home, where her gloom and scorn have moved in. He's been a rock so far, but by the time the semester ends, he is plumb fed up. He wants tranquility back. He wants to feel at ease in his own home. Jane is always angry at both of us and wants to leave. She returns to Wisconsin.

Ann responds with a furious letter. God knows what Jane told the Rhymers, or if they are upset because she has returned, but I understand that the bedlam she created here is the same that they know all too well. Ann concludes by stating that we have "different values" from theirs. She does not mean that we have a more highly honed ethical code than the good, simple folks of the Midwest. Tony responds. All communication halts.

Jane and I do not speak for months.

25 Another Birthday

APRIL 5, 1986—It is Jane's birthday. We have not been in touch for several months, but it is her birthday. *Does she ever think of me on this day?* For adoptees, the question looms large. Jane and I had celebrated her birthday several times since reunion, if not on the actual date, near enough. I'd bake a cake and ice it with buttercream frosting made from my mother's recipe.

But this year there was no visit. After months of silence, knowing I must phone the Rhymers to reach Jane, I hesitate. Will she take the call? Hang up if she answers? Would I have to go through Ann? Even though it has been months since she sent me that angry letter, I am not all that eager to speak to her.

I phone. Her father answers.

Jane's not here, Gary says, but he is stumbling over his words, as if he is not sure what to say, even though I am not asking anything complicated. Just tell her I called to wish her a happy birthday, I say, and ask her to call back.

With that call from Jane comes news no mother, especially a reunited one, ever wants to hear: *She gave birth to a daughter two days earlier. She's planning to give her up for adoption.*

No!

Oh god, she is repeating history, why does this have to happen? Adoption passed on to the next generation, what could be sadder? My baby has had enough to deal with—now this? What awful chain of events began with me? Even my finding her could not end this. The image of the adoptee/ natural mother weeping over the sink in the ladies' room flashes by, as do the numerous faces of others who've lost children to adoption, and now, my own daughter must endure this? In recounting this, a knife in my heart spills blood from my fingertips onto the keyboard, and I know it is a cliché, but a knife in my heart it is.

How did this happen? Why?

I met him at Burger King, she says. He was a customer. No, Mom and Dad didn't know I was seeing him. He's Black.

Are you still together? I ask.

No! That's over and done.

Are you okay?

Fine.

The baby?

She's a preemie, weighs a little over two pounds.

Two pounds!

Yes. I was at the hospital feeding her when you called.

Oh, honey I am so sorry. *So* sorry.

She was so far away, I knew she was hurting. This is the real legacy of adoption, this vicious cycle: one adoption begets another.

Yet she is stoic. She is not crying and neither am I. I don't cry in front of them, she once told me, referring to her adoptive parents, and she had indeed learned how to tamp down the tears. And she is Patrick's child. *Don't cry, please don't cry*, his voice of two decades ago when we left her at the hospital echoes in my mind, reminding me that she is his child too.

Over the next couple of weeks, we talk almost every day. Whatever had been in the way before was moot. She goes to the hospital daily to feed her. She names her Sarah Nicole. Isn't that a pretty name? she says.

When I press for details, she says Marvin (the father) wants to keep her. He'll take the baby to Michigan—someplace called Inkster, he's from there, ever heard of it? He wants to raise her with his mother.

Inkster! It's right next to Dearborn, a few miles from where I grew up! Jane, this is amazing, you meet someone in Wisconsin from a town right next to the one I'm from in Michigan! He wants to keep his baby? Great! Then Sarah won't have to be adopted! I immediately like this Marvin. I also imme-

diately realize that to him, a Black man, Dearborn would be more than a simple suburb of Detroit and home of the Ford Motor Company: Dearborn is
infamous for its not-so-hidden reputation of redlining, bias, discrimination,
racism—call it what you will—that kept Blacks from moving in. Tireman, a
street that divided Detroit from Dearborn, was our own Maginot Line, and
Dearborn's longtime, headline-grabbing, racist mayor, Orville L. Hubbard,
made sure everybody knew what he stood for: a white community. He ran on
a campaign to "Keep Dearborn Clean," its meaning never in doubt. To remind those Blacks who might drive through town on the way to somewhere
else, the slogan was highly visible on the sides of all police cars. I heard that
"Bye, Bye, Blackbird" was played on a loudspeaker at his campaign rallies. A
section of town had a small Arab community, but miraculously, the Muslims
did not stoke Hubbard's ire. One might abhor Hubbard's racism, but with
generous taxes from the Ford Motor Company, he ran an efficient city hall
that provided great amenities—twice-weekly garbage collection, snow plow-
ing, city parks, neighborhood pools, free swimming instruction, artificial ice
rinks! Hubbard was elected fifteen straight times, one of the longest terms of
office for any mayor in America.

Yes, Marvin would know all about Dearborn. Jane surely would have
mentioned the improbable coincidence of my being raised next door to where
he was from. And he would unthinkingly cast me as a racist. My parents de-
spised Hubbard and all that he stood for, voted against him every time, and
because Dearborn's racist reputation was wide, I've forever been reluctant to
tell Black acquaintances the name of my hometown—but Marvin wouldn't
know any of that. I'd be just another racist white woman. But it's too late
to focus on that, and anyway, it's not important, what's important is letting
Marvin raise their baby.

No way, she says, I don't like the sound of it. She sounds definite, as if
there is no room for negotiation. But still. I cautiously forge ahead.

What? Why? She's the grandmother, Jane. Then you could know where
she is. Then she wouldn't have to be adopted. I actually say this.

Silence.

Please, other family of Sarah, I'm thinking, oppose my daughter, fight for your rights as kin—please keep this baby. Yet I say none of that. Our relationship is much too fragile to push her. But I already recognize that if she lets Marvin take the baby, she seems like a worse mother than if she gives the baby up for adoption. In society's eyes, adoption is the better choice. If Marvin takes the baby, Jane can't totally walk away. If Marvin takes the baby, Jane would have the opportunity, and responsibility, of staying involved.

Though I am persistent when I feel she leaves an opening—and those occasions are few—she is on a course to adoption, and nothing I say, no matter how many times I repeat it, will deter her. We do not discuss her keeping the baby because it has already been decided. I also recognize that she is not capable of living on her own by herself—too many jobs have been lost, too many times has Gary, her father, rescued her from an untenable living situation, and now she has a baby? Impossible. Except in passing, we do not discuss that the Rhymers see adoption as the only sane solution, for that is a foregone conclusion. That is a given.

Well, since you feel that way, I point out, you could have an open adoption—meaning you could choose the people, know who they are, even visit your daughter periodically. I'm thinking in exclamation points about this newfangled thing called an "open adoption" but keeping my eagerness in check so she won't dig in further. *You don't want to go through what I have, the nightmare of not knowing what happened to her,* I say. Open adoptions are extremely rare, but I've heard that an agency in Wisconsin is handling them, I can find out which one.

She says nothing. Her mind is slammed shut.

I do not suggest that Tony and I raise the baby. We have made a life as writers, and we have struggled financially to even hang onto our house. When we married, our pact explicitly did not include children. He had two teenagers, I had an unknown daughter. I was clear about never having another child, and if I had not been, we would not have married. Tony might have become an ersatz father to Jane, but that did not extend to taking on her baby, and I can't imagine she would have agreed. She had already turned down the baby's father and his mother. Nor will she consider open adoption.

Twenty years had passed since she was born and relinquished, attitudes were changing, but I couldn't even affect my own daughter's decision-making.

One day I ask, Why didn't you use birth control?

Because I was going to kill myself.

I do not respond. What could I say that I hadn't already? Besides, I knew she sometimes said whatever outrageous thing she thought of on the spur of the moment simply to shock me. But I had stopped playing that game.

I ask about Marvin again. What's going on with his family? And his mother—they must be good people . . .

He's around, she says, her voice turning to steel. Look, Lorraine, he got into drugs. Coke. He's an addict. I don't want to talk about it. Her voice has the finality of a done deed. I drop the subject, silently hoping that somehow this Marvin—I'm pretty sure the drug story is a crock designed to shut me up—will fight for custody. And I am also pretty sure that unless he hires a good lawyer and goes after this with full force, his chances of success are slim. They would be slim if Marvin were white. They are almost certainly nil in 1986 because he is not.

I hear more about Marvin over the next couple of weeks, how he is around, he's not giving up, but nothing deters Jane from relinquishing her baby to the unknown. When I mention open adoption, I can feel her bristle through the phone line. I don't want to alienate her—and that's always a strong possibility.

In the end, she says she went to court with her parents, that Marvin and his mother did not show up. She says she shook the hands of the adoptive parents—a Black doctor father, a white lawyer mother. End of story. I press for no more details. I don't believe what she has already told me because that is not how adoptions are done. Except in the most open of adoptions, mothers don't hand over their babies to adoptive parents. A social worker from an agency, or a lawyer, intervenes and acts as the middleman. As for what she wants me to believe, what could be more perfect than a biracial couple with multiple degrees and high-toned professions for my biracial granddaughter? How could I object? Plus, how could I check? They are about to disappear down a rabbit hole.

Of course, she assumes I will never find out.

For Mother's Day that year, Jane sends one of those elaborate greeting cards, the only one she ever sent me like that—big, expensive, covered with embossed flowers, dripping with sentiment, underlined, and signed "much love, Your daughter, Jane." While I am imagining that she never forgot Ann on Mother's Day, most years I do not hear from her at all. Yet with that card she is saying that she understands better now what giving her up had been like. It's something.

We have been through many hellos and goodbyes, and I am certain her fond feeling for me exemplified in the card is temporary, that in time she will again shut it off the relationship abruptly, without an explanation. All parent-and-child relationships go through myriad twists and turns, but perhaps none so much as that of the adoptee and natural parent brought back together. There is too much history that cannot be obliterated, too much ready anger bubbling just below the surface. One wrong word, and *bam*, that's it! She's gone again.

I am always on trial. I would always be on trial. But now is not a time to consider that, now is a time to comfort her in any way I can. She wants to visit and so, as always, we buy her a ticket.

She is shell-shocked when she arrives. All I can do is be understanding and sympathetic, try to amuse her with movies and quiet walks on the beach. She shows me pictures of Sarah. She says that Marvin came to see the baby at the hospital, but she wanted nothing to do with him. She keeps Sarah's photographs, black-and-white snapshots, on her nightstand. She gives me a color Polaroid, one of her holding Sarah in a frilly outfit, snapped on Mother's Day that year. She offers no other details about anything—the baby's father, the birth, the adoption process—and I do not press her because I do not want to hear a story I cannot believe.

Years go by, and Jane does not mention Sarah—and I am always hesitant to bring her up—but every year, as Jane's birthday approaches, I cannot help but think of her daughter, my granddaughter, born two—or was it three?—days before Jane's birthday, and imagine that Jane might be having the same feelings I had when her birthday rolled around.

One time—I'm jumping ahead here in the story—I called Jane on Sarah's birthday and left a message on her answering machine: Thinking about you, thinking about Sarah. Jane, who always called back right away when she was speaking to me, did not call back. Nor did she mention the call a few days later when I phoned on her birthday. The one time I made a reference to Sarah on her birthday, I was met by dead silence that shouted, Do not bring her up! I knew that if I persisted, I would jeopardize our relationship. Jane had constructed a wall around her heart where Sarah resided. Just like Patrick had about you, I thought. Just like Patrick. You are his daughter.

After the World Trade Center was destroyed on September 11, 2001, the *New York Times Magazine* carried a piece called "Repress Yourself." Its message was that possibly talking about trauma after it occurs makes the ordeal more embedded in the mind, and thus even more traumatic. People who repress a bad experience, rather than illuminating it in therapy, might be healthier than those who do not. "If you're stuck and scared, perhaps you should not remember but forget. Avoid. That's right. Tamp it down. Up you go. . . . Is it possible that folks who employ these techniques cope better than the rest of us ramblers?"[124]

Maybe, in fact, Jane was doing the right thing for herself. Maybe in this regard she was better off than me. Besides, Jane had enough trauma and trouble in her life for ten people. Maybe holding onto the grief of giving up her daughter was just one more sorrow she could not bear. Better to focus on life rather than what could not be fixed.

Community psychologist and trauma researcher Richard Gist is quoted in the *Times*' piece on what happens after a disaster involving many people: "Basically all these therapists run down to the scene, and there's a lot of grunting and groaning and encouraging people to review what they saw, and then the survivors get worse. I've been saying for years, 'Is it any surprise that if you keep leading people to the edge of a cliff they eventually fall over?'"

---

[124] Lauren Slater, "Repress Yourself," *The New York Times Magazine*, Feb. 23, 2003, https://web.archive.org/web/20220825223938/https://www.nytimes.com/2003/02/23/magazine/repress-yourself.html.

26 'Not Now' Becomes Never

JANUARY 1991—That the news is ominous is clear as soon as I pick up the phone. It's Judy Bender, my friend from the *Knick* in Albany who's now at *Newsday*, Patrick's paper. He died, she says, most likely of a massive heart attack; that's all she knows. He hadn't shown up for work, the paper sent someone over to his place after a day or two, and she wasn't sure how long he had been . . .

Oh. For myself, I am numb, facts are coming in as a distant telegraph message from a previous life. My mind is galloping to Jane. Now it's too late. She will never meet her father.

Judy talks about what a good writer he was, how he was generous with his knowledge with the younger reporters, but how his drinking interfered. She adds that *Newsday* had sent him to rehab. Twice. That I did not know. But now the disappearance and reemergence of his bylines makes sense. She's talking, but I'm remembering a time last summer when I was out jogging near our house. I was running in one of the narrow old streets of Sag Harbor—where we first lived—where there's only room for one-way traffic, and I sensed a car inching up on me, and, god knows why, I stopped and turned around and—Good lord, is that Patrick? In that red car? It is him! I stood there perplexed, squinting into the sun, and was about to walk up to the car and say, Hey, Patrick, let's talk, when he hastily backed up a half of a block onto busy Hampton Street. Nobody with any sense does that. Too much traffic. Then he was gone. I hadn't seen him in years—maybe fifteen—but it was him.

I know I must call Jane to tell her he died, but I hesitate. Can't I put this off until tomorrow? I certainly had not been on any list of people who had to be informed that Patrick died. If Judy hadn't been at *Newsday*, a long time might have passed before I even heard the news. Does it make any difference when Jane finds out? She is not about to go to the funeral.

Relations with Ann have stayed in the cooler. Though our contact is infrequent, her voice when I phone indicates that no matter that we had gotten along before, now I was anathema. We wouldn't have been more than nodding acquaintances if we'd lived in the same neighborhood or gone to the same school. We weren't churchgoers. I did not have other children. We assuredly gave too many raucous dinner parties. I was a New York Career Woman. The only person Ann ever said she liked in my family was my sister-in-law, and we are not talking blood, now, are we? Besides, I was *that woman*. Where Jane's problems began. With my bad genes. Certainly, I am to blame for all of Jane's problems. Off with my head!

But I must make the call. Now Jane would never meet her father. The guy with the large head like hers. The father who made her legitimately Irish. The guy who shared her affinity for barroom camaraderie. His *not now* had become *never*.

I put off the call for a day.

Jane is upset with me, stoic about Patrick. My delay of a day gives her something to focus on, and it is always handy to be angry at me. Why had I waited a day? she demands crossly. Why hadn't I called immediately? From her perspective, she is family, no matter how you slice it. Family gets called right away. Family doesn't hear about a death casually and a day late, doesn't hear, Oh, by the way, did you hear your (biological) father died? I explain that I wouldn't have known myself if not for my friend who works at *Newsday*, that he had died a few days earlier anyway, but she is still upset with me.

I'm sorry, I'm so sorry. I let her rail at me. I know this is hitting her hard.

He was sixty-two years old. Along with his obituary, *Newsday* runs a handsome photograph of Patrick in his fedora. He was still a good-looking guy with an engaging smile. The writer noted that he was the "embodiment of a bygone era . . . known for his wit, his impeccable dress and gentlemanly demeanor . . . matched by a passion for hard news and clarity in writing."[125] An editor added that "certain stories needed more than just clear writing, they begged for writing with feeling and humor . . . Pat was the master of these, he knew how to make the words dance to the tune he wanted." Someone else remarked how unselfish he was with his wealth of knowledge of newspapers, politics, and human nature.

The deputy US attorney general for civil rights then, John Dunne, said, "Pat could spot a phony a mile away. But more than political astuteness, he was a man who had a deep and sincere social conscience." His wife added that he was born with printer's ink in his blood, as his father and his brother had both been printers at the *Democrat & Chronicle*. His major awards were listed. It was an obit anybody would be proud to have.

His survivors were named. Our daughter was not on the list. Jane would want to see the obit anyway, and I sent it off.

Patrick's wife calls me a week later. We have never spoken before. Would I like to go to his apartment and see if there is anything Jane might like? In going over Patrick's papers, she came across my letter with Jane's picture, a letter we had composed together, as well as a letter from Jane that I knew nothing about. Did they ever meet? she asks.

No.

That was so like him, she says. He couldn't handle anything emotional. He just walked away.

Right.

The following Sunday, there we are—two women having coffee at the Walt Whitman Mall on Long Island. When he was living with me and Kirsten, she says, he fell asleep with a lit cigarette on the couch. The whole couch burned, the fire department came, and it was a disaster. I couldn't live

[125] Phil Mintz, "Patrick Brasley, 62, Longtime Newsday Reporter," *Newsday,* Jan. 25, 1991.

with him anymore. He could have burned down the house and killed us. I asked him to move out.

I simply nod. No point in my adding, Oh, so this is why he moved out. This is what was going on so that he couldn't meet Jane when I asked him. The image of a burning couch is pretty vivid.

If he dried out for a while, it didn't last, she continues. And he always went back to drinking.

She isn't bitter, she is just flatly stating the facts. Even then, I am finding excuses for him, thinking about how, after the high of a deadline of a late-breaking story, reporters need to let off steam and hang out with their buddies at a nearby saloon. You tell war stories, you tell what didn't get into the paper, and you have one more. The camaraderie counts. People who are not in the news business have a hard time understanding what it's like, why telling what needs to be told—what their mayors and school boards and governors are up to—is the engine that drives journalists, how the adrenaline of late-breaking stories and front-page bylines is so enticing, why we love the whole damn business. I say nothing about this, for she was fed up with it all, and, eventually, him.

I follow her in my car over to his place, turning left, turning right, knowing exactly how bizarre this is, me, his one-time love and mother of one of his children; she, his widow and mother of another child. We end up in a modest basement apartment in a neighborhood of modest middle-class homes.

Dull fluorescence from an overhead fixture supplements the grim February light that manages to sneak in through the small windows, the kind common to ordinary basements everywhere. It's chilly, and we keep our coats on. You could tell that without a steady stream of heat the place would be damp, the floor cold. There is a good-sized central room with a space off to the side for a single bed and a closet. A vest-pocket kitchen, if you could call it that, is a small unfinished space where you could make coffee and heat up a can of soup. A tiny bath with a shower is just off the "kitchen."

This is a not-quite-seedy bachelor's pad suitable for a young man starting out or an old man winding down. Patrick should have been a bigger star—would have been, if not for the bottle. At the time of his death, he was reduced to coming home to this cheerless basement in somebody else's house.

The apartment is orderly, for Patrick was ever the neat Virgo, and consequently there is a place for everything—his wardrobe of blazers, sport coats, and ties; a couple hundred LPs by all the jazz greats and then some; a good-sized pile of books that includes, most surprisingly, *Wild Spenders*, a breezy novel written by a friend of mine, stuck there like a foreigner among his jazz biographies, art books, Civil War histories, and Hemingway, Faulkner, and Steinbeck novels, the writers of his era. I'm stunned because *Wild Spenders* came out years after he and I had stopped having lunch, something that went on way longer than anybody knew except one girlfriend—the author of *Wild Spenders*. I ended the lunches somewhere in the late seventies—and this book came out in 1985—because I knew I could never fall in love with anybody else if Patrick was in my life, no matter how seemingly peripherally, no matter how infrequently we met. I hadn't left my first husband when Patrick asked me to, but Patrick was like an old song I couldn't get out of my head. Now I felt like an interloper being there with his wife—who knew nothing of the lunches—yet glad and grateful to have this opportunity to say goodbye to a man we both had loved, and maybe find a thing or two that Jane would like.

Once upon a time he'd meant everything to me, and despite all that had happened since, despite his not having the courage to meet our daughter, standing in this room where he had died, I am overwhelmed with sadness. If I shut my eyes, I can still picture him sitting there—as I do that day—a snifter with an amber inch of Hennessy VSOP in one hand, the light hazy, smoke curling from a cigarette. It's two a.m. From an old phonograph record, Lester Young on tenor sax is playing between the mournful lyrics Billie Holiday is singing. Yes, now I can even hear the song: "No Regrets." It was our anthem. It was something we once said to one another. *No regrets.* Once, we had been so very much in love.

So here's his stuff, take what you want, she says in a monotone, jolting me back to the present. Kirsten didn't want anything, and the rest? I have to clear the place out. His brother came to the funeral and took a few things, but his children from Rochester did not. A hard edge seeps into her voice. One of the boys said that he was coming to the funeral, but then he didn't, probably talked out of it by Colleen, I'm sure of it. I'm giving all this stuff away, so anything that is here now you can have. Colleen only wants to know what the records are worth. And the car.

That I am aware of the complications of Patrick's relationship with his other children I do not mention. Time has a way of muting the impact of just about anything, but Colleen had remained bitter about her parents' divorce, even now in his death. It had not mattered that the day after the divorce was final her mother got married, Patrick told me once. I suppose there was some justice in that.

I pick out a simple wooden chess set, the kind where the inlaid chess board closes to be the box holding the pieces; a few LPs of jazz greats, which ones I don't remember; some art books that Patrick had signed his name in—Jane might like to have his signature—a small collection of well-used metal toy soldiers that must have been from his childhood, two leather jackets, a couple of vests, and a gray fedora, all things I thought Jane would like. The hat? It might fit her.

She says that given Colleen's animosity, Kirsten will probably never get to know her, and since Kirsten will never have any other siblings, maybe Kirsten and Jane could be friends/sisters one day. But Kirsten's only twelve, she adds, and she doesn't know about Jane yet. I'll tell her when it feels right. Later.

Sure. Great, I think, Jane would like that. To know a sibling. To have a friend who is a sibling. To have a connection to her father. I am so pleased to hear that, happy that Jane might enjoy this redeeming possibility.

Then it is time to say goodbye. We stand outside next to Patrick's red car—a modest Chevy, a few years old—parked in the driveway. Yes, that is the same car that crept up on me in Sag Harbor. Yes, that had been Patrick, just like I thought. This I also do not mention. She says Colleen called her about the car, asking had she sold it yet and what was it worth? Not much, we agree and shrug our shoulders. If Colleen had come to the funeral, she would have seen that.

I stand there as if planted, not quite sure how to say goodbye, not hurrying the moment, not really wanting it to end. Do I lean over and kiss her on the cheek, do we shake hands, do I give her a hug? What is the protocol? I am so very grateful for all this, for my daughter, and for being able to say goodbye to Patrick. My eyes are glassy, the lump in my throat grown to painful proportions as I am trying not to weep.

"He did love you," she says, surprising me. The only other person who had ever acknowledged that was the teenager I'd shared a room with when Jane was born. He did love you. I hadn't made it up.

I had loved him. I had. For a long, long time, all through our affair and, yes, my first marriage and even after, even when all good sense and an instinct for self-preservation would have told me to stop. Maybe it was the lost child that bound us together, but when we met for lunch in Manhattan, or somewhere on Long Island, over a decade or longer ago, there was never a lull in the conversation or a break in the connection, and even years later the sexual tension had never left.

She senses the flood I am holding back and puts her hand on my arm and we stare into each other's eyes. "He did," she says again, now nodding for emphasis. I let the silence speak as I keep shut the dam inside me. A sniveling ex-lover, even the mother of one of his children, would be too much for the moment.

I drive back with the radio on loud rock, and the station plays the Stones' "Satisfaction." From that year when I was pregnant. That's how I remember the song: it was a hit when I had Jane. Darkness is descending as I get home. Tony is waiting.

Jane's legacy from her father—all she would ever know of him—fits in a single cardboard box that I get at the UPS store. It is a good size, to be sure, but it is one box. As if money could replace what would have been lost, I insure it for a couple hundred dollars and send it off to her.

Several months later, I pick up the phone, and it is Jane asking if I want to meet her for lunch. We haven't been in touch for quite a while. When she stopped returning phone calls, I stopped leaving messages. I didn't know what I had done or hadn't done, but I had yet again become unnecessary to her. Now she is asking me to lunch. She calmly says she's been in Manhattan for a few days and stayed at Arthur's apartment in the city. Now she's at his place around the corner in Sag Harbor. Lunch?

Sure.

I don't even bother saying, I didn't know you were in town! Instead, I act like I might have been waiting for her to call that very day. We meet an hour later at a Japanese restaurant in Sag Harbor. I throw in my purse a few trinkets I'd bought her when she was talking to me—Star Trek memorabilia because she collected that and a pendant made from an old Chinese coin that I knew she would like. Who knew when I will see her next, or if I ever will; our relationship is fluid—intense one day, desultory the next. Might as well give her these items now.

When I walk in she is wearing Patrick's fedora and one of his jackets, the one in gray suede. I am wearing a man's fedora myself, and anyone would have picked us out as mother and daughter. I do not point out our nearly matching hats because that might somehow annoy her. I am on probation once more. Who knows why? Maybe because she needs to show me that she can walk away whenever she feels like it.

When she takes off her hat, once his hat, and puts it down beside her, our eyes connect and linger. I do not pretend to understand how she feels, I am simply glad to see her again.

We talk about Patrick, and we talk about her visit to New York. She flew on a voucher from when her last flight to Madison from New York had been overbooked. The lunch is amiable, and my little gifts surprise her. We say goodbye in the parking lot, but I am afraid that if I hug her, she will push me away. Now I am back in her good graces.

Who knows for how long?

27 The Heart of the Matter

SEPTEMBER 1999—Jane had been married long enough to have a child, a daughter named Kimberly, whose nearly white-blond hair matched mine when I was a child, and Jane's too, as I'd seen in photographs. When Kimberly was two, the marriage crashed. Her daddy was gone, there was no child support, and Jane managed to hold everything together for a while.

Through a state welfare-to-work program, she got a job at the very place from where I mail-ordered my progesterone, the Women's International Pharmacy. It was located near the apartment complex where she lived. Damn! Working in the midst of PMS central, she's sure to be motivated to track her dark moods, if only to see whether they coincided with her hormonal cycle— and thus she would see if she was prone to the same PMS that I had, and my mother before me. So I thought. I was wrong.

By this time, I'd written a couple pieces about the salubrious effect of progesterone on severe PMS for women's magazines, and I'd sent her copies. No response. A year later, she would ask for them again. Nothing changed. No doctor of hers diagnosed it. Besides, wasn't having to take Depakote every day of her life enough? Now you want me to take something else every month? Forget about it. Besides, don't I have enough in my life to be depressed about? Talking to her about this was like throwing a pebble in the ocean. No visible impact. So I don't do anything but joke that she might one day even fill my order for progesterone.

The job was supposed to transition from being state subsidized to one that gave her full rights as a company employee, but when Jane went from counting pills to working on a computer, too many orders for Tacoma ended up in Topanga, and she was out the door.

No matter how hard she tried, Jane had too many demerits to support herself and her daughter on her own. Emotionally and physically, Jane would always need help. But talk to her about applying for state disability, and you would get that same blank stare and silence. What I finally understood was that if she applied for disability, she would once and for all fall in the category of *disabled*.

She would not do it. She was going to make it somehow. If only she could get a break. Nothing could jar her determination to hang on to this last bastion of self-respect: not to be legally disabled. You couldn't talk her out of this without further degrading her.

Then it was back to Burger King. She hung on for a while, but eventually she found juggling a minimum-wage job, working the night shift (where she was always transferred), and a child under five more than she could handle. We were talking, I'd send her checks to cover emergencies, but she did not let on how things were falling apart until one day she called and said Kimberly was living with the Rhymers and she, Jane, was moving to another city in Wisconsin where she had a friend.

Six months later, Jane herself ended up with the Rhymers, who had moved to the small town in rural Wisconsin where Ann had grown up. Jane got a job as part of the janitorial staff at a casino, a forty-minute drive away. Her mental outlook spiraled down, and then down some more.

Kimberly spent a good part of the summer with us in Sag Harbor, and she was not quite the little angel I'd heard about from the Rhymers. I was secretly delighted when she got sassy or talked back and acted up. I sensed that in the Rhymer household, her job was to be well behaved at all times.

She was a strong, resilient child, someone who appeared to be riding above her mother's difficulties with no obvious distress. Yet her impenetrable, bright blue eyes signaled that she took in everything but revealed little.

One summer she kept singing that catchy country song "I'm Doin' Alright." Underneath, I knew she was struggling to be "doing all right."

Relations between Ann and me hovered near freezing, no spring thaw in sight. When you are already in the doghouse, there are many ways to make a bad situation worse. Now I was the faraway grandmother who sent Beanie Babies and pricey Barbie dolls and outfits Ann deemed too trendy. Gary would duly send me photographs of Kimberly in her new clothes from Grandma Lorraine, and so I blithely went ahead plundering T. J. Maxx for more cute outfits, not realizing how much anything I sent only made Ann more infuriated. Yet I can see her point. To her, I was like the divorced dad who isn't there for the day-to-day tedium of raising a child but swoops in to take her to Disneyland, or in this case sends her cool stuff like the lava lamp Kimberly left on all night and day. The lamp overheated and exploded when she was at school. Blame Lorraine!

Ann's anger is palpable whenever I call. Sometimes she hands the phone to Gary as soon as she hears my voice. I'll be chattering away, trying to be friendly as all get out, when Gary interrupts and says he is on the line, embarrassing us both. I make myself stay in touch, though the calls are infrequent. Jane cannot phone herself, for if she does, the long-distance call will be on the bill, causing trouble. Why are you calling her?! Jane does not have a cell phone or easy access to email.

And then one evening when Gary puts Kimberly on the phone, she immediately reports, *Mama is sick in the head and in the hospital.*

Gary fills me in.

I reach Jane at the hospital.

She has attempted suicide. Again. One time before, she'd consumed a whole bottle of aspirin that led to her stomach being pumped—but this is more serious. She had gotten hold of some chemical used in cleaning and tried to swallow it. Once she regains her strength, she goes back to work and tells a coworker she is going to try again. The coworker calls the police. Jane is involuntarily taken back to the hospital, then assigned to a halfway house for a couple of months. Jane is racking up suicide attempts the way someone might collect Barbie dolls and keep them untouched in their boxes. Lined up in a row under their cellophane wrappings, the outfits might be different, but somehow the blond Barbies in their boxes all look the same.

Despite Ann's hostility, when the Rhymers plan their two-week vacation in September, they ask me to stay at their place and take care of Kimberly. Although Jane is also living there, after her two recent suicide attempts, the Rhymers are understandably uneasy leaving Jane in charge. Needless to say, I am mentally packing the minute Gary calls, even though this means Tony and I will spend our twentieth wedding anniversary apart.

The Rhymers' home is five miles outside town, a serene oasis on a sliver of man-made lake. In the fall, the setting is brilliant reds and golds. Early in the morning, the deer and wild turkeys parade by. Birdwatching might be ideal here, but it is isolating for Kimberly.

Before I get there, Jane has agreed to be interviewed on tape for a book about adoption that she and I are planning to coauthor. Since ALMA's lawsuit in 1979, only a few states have been added to those that do not seal the original birth certificates of adoptees. Yet nearly all the new statutes have a veto provision that allows the mother—most fathers are not named on the birth certificates of children born to single women—to block her name. Or the laws have other restrictions, such as only allowing openness from the time when the law went into effect, the same restriction Florence had walked away from in New York. As men and women who delayed starting families confront infertility, adoptable babies are in high demand, and adoption is in vogue again. Florence, B. J., and I might as well have been shouting in a wind tunnel about the dangers. All this is festering in the back of my brain when I sit down to find out what my daughter thinks about adoption.

Jane and I talk over a period of several nights, the two of us sitting on a couch in her parents' living room, lights on low, after Kimberly has gone to bed. On the tapes, I hear Jane light cigarettes, ask me to have one with her—and one night I do, to please her, though I haven't had a cigarette in a couple of decades. I hear the click of the lighter that Patrick gave me, the polished-chrome Zippo that he had engraved with a single letter, a lowercase *l* in script, the way I sign my name. I'd passed it on to Jane after he'd died. The grandfather clock on the wall announces the hours. Nine, ten, eleven.

"I thought about you way more than I let on to my parents," she begins. "When I lay in bed, I wondered why I was put up for adoption, what my history was. I'd look out my window when the moonlight is reflected on the snow, and the sky looked royal blue, and I'd see the moon. That's when I thought about you. Because that was a safe time to think about it. And the rest of the time I tried not to."

How did you imagine me? I ask.

"My mother told me you were young and poor, not married, that was it. But I had fantasies of you being older, and not being able to raise a child, that you were old and just scraping by."

"How old?"

"Probably like fifty."

We laugh.

"Or that you lied when you left your name at the agency. Or that you left the baby with neighbors and never returned. Sometimes you were a movie star. You lived in California. I saw lights and glitter."

"Did you ever imagine that I was a prostitute?"

"No! That is just too horrible."

We laugh again. "Did you ever imagine that I was just some middle-class married lady?"

"Once. You had too many kids, like fifteen, and couldn't raise them, and I was the last one. Like Agatha."

Agatha was the adoptee who lived on the next block in Sag Harbor, the one whose family we'd found in Poland, her mother still alive, and indeed, she was the late last child of a large, struggling farm family. A wealthy Polish American woman had taken Agatha to the United States, to the street where I lived, and the woman had died a few years later, leaving Agatha with the cantankerous but steadfast man the woman had married. When Jane visited, she and Agatha had become friends, and certainly adoption was a part of the equation.

Jane pauses, then goes on: "I wrote a million different endings to what would happen when I searched. I would go to Rochester, and they would have the information, and somebody would whisper something to me, or run out after me and hand me an address, and it would be old and I would have to track you down. And that had a million different endings. I would call and you would hang up. Or say, I don't know what you are talking about. Or I would knock on your door, and you would let me in and we would sit at a table and talk, like for four hours, and you would tell me why I was adopted, but that's kinda ridiculous because it doesn't take four hours to explain why someone is adopted. Or you would slam the door in my face."

The stuff of a million adoptee fantasies.

We are serious most of the time, but we find plenty to amuse us. We are ironic, reflective, bawdy. The conversation flows from the serious to the mundane. What kind of music did I listen to when I was pregnant, Mozart or the blues? she wants to know.

Billie Holiday, the Beatles, the Rolling Stones, Joan Baez, Dinah Washington, Bob Dylan. Peggy Lee. Patrick gave me one of her albums. I still have it. And the Billie Holiday albums, a set of four LPs. We'll play it next time you visit. And Herbie Hancock.

She shrugs. Who's he?

Jazz pianist. Patrick took me to hear him in New York when we were there—before . . . at a place called the Village Vanguard—and later Patrick gave me one of his albums. Your father loved jazz, you know, and the great blues singers—

Tell me about your apartment, she interrupts. When you were in Rochester.

A third-floor walk-up with burlap on the walls—I glued it up, instead of wallpaper—a western window where I hung pieces of colored glass, so the afternoon sun made colors on the floor. Not that big a place, but big enough. I guess it would qualify as a garret. You would have loved it. My mother drove with me to Rochester when I moved there, and we checked out apartments together. She wanted me to rent something less funky, more ordinary, in an ordinary building. This cost a little more, but it suited me, the way it had angles and wrapped around a corner, no one living above me. It was over a dentist's office. He owned the building. I don't think he ever knew I was pregnant. I didn't show much. I didn't let myself gain much weight and I wore a big, bulky sweatshirt when I went outside. You were born in the spring, so it didn't look funny.

She brings us back to the moment: Was Patrick nice to you? Did he open doors and take you to dinner?

Yes, yes, and yes. What she wants to hear is that we had been in love. In every way I can, I tell her that we were.

She tells me she understands how my life had been when she came into it, how I had not been able to keep her. She says she does not see how I could have coped with her epilepsy by myself and that she is thankful to have the parents she has. "I was real lucky and I know it—I wound up with pretty damn good parents," she says, now quite animated, making sure I understand.

She is silent for a half minute before adding, "My parents could have returned me. They could have sent me back." In that bald statement of fact, she has compressed every seizure, every trip to the emergency room, every accident, every anxious moment, every dollar spent—and there have been so many of all the above—that her parents have known.

Could have sent me back. If Jane were "chosen" like a pair of shoes, she could be returned, or end up like old shoes in a consignment store that nobody wants. Could have sent me back—what non-adopted person ever thinks that? There's nowhere to send one's biological child, for birth can't be undone. Could have sent me back. The concept is a particular demon of the adopted, and for my daughter this demon begins with me. I have a daughter who grew up thinking, I could be sent back.

That's some hell of an ending to something as antiseptic-sounding as an "adoption plan," the phrase adoption workers now use to blunt reality. But it actually makes giving up a child sound cold, calm, calculated. A plan is made and executed. A child is moved from one woman to another.

Where is the grieving, lamenting mother who gives up a child she cannot keep?

The warm day has cooled down considerably, and the night air is chilly. We pile on thick sweaters, go out on the deck, stand at the railing, and look up at the millions of stars in the sky visible there. A more peaceful setting there may be somewhere in the world, but I am not sure I know it. We pick out Orion and his belt, the Big and Little Dippers, the North Star. Our breath makes white fog in the chilly night. She lights up. Of course she lights up. She is Patrick's daughter; she is the Marlboro Woman. Which is, in fact, her brand.

"I had this drive to find out—it might have had a lot to do with the epilepsy and needing to belong somewhere," she continues after a few moments, without prodding. Now that she's begun, she wants to talk. "I knew that my family loved me, and I knew that I belonged there, I belonged with my family going through my stupid daily routine—that there was a reason for everything. But you get up, and you're sitting in bed thinking for a moment that you are going to go downstairs and take your pills, and then you wrap up your pills [anti-seizure medication] in tinfoil and put them in your lunch box and wait for the school bus, and then you get off the school bus and the kids start making fun of you. You try to get inside the school before anybody can get to you or make fun of you because once you are in earshot of the teacher, they are not going to make fun of you."

Pause.

She reminds me how the older boys rapped their knuckles on her helmet, how she hated recess because of the things she couldn't do: the monkey bars, the balance beam, the swings, don't play on the concrete, gym class. Instead, she sat on the grass by herself and lost any sense of belonging. "That was my stupid routine," she says of her grade-school years.

"I knew that I belonged with my family, but there was a feeling that I also belonged somewhere else. It wasn't belonging somewhere else, it was—I needed to know for a certain completeness inside of me, and if I didn't know, I wouldn't feel whole. I wouldn't have felt I belonged with you either, so it wasn't exactly belonging, it was completeness. I was this circle, and it was broken. I had this"—she holds up her hands forming an arc—"but I didn't have this"—she moves her hands to close the circle, to connect the arc, to make it whole.

"So, I felt like a part of me had been moving along, and all of a sudden *boom!* and I'm supposed to go along like this isn't happening—like one day I was this person, and the next day I was somebody else—but I still had this other person somewhere inside of me. Imagine you have an ancestor who was just yanked away, and you were supposed to keep on walking like nothing had happened. But I kept looking backward—the way an owl can turn its head all the way around, you know, and I'm saying—So where is she?" She stops now, her parents are far away, dammit, she's going to have a smoke in the house, the smell will be gone when they get back. I'm not going to stop her. A minute later she picks up the thread.

"I always felt like I was walking on a fence and could fall off at any moment."

What to say? A moment later, I point out that in the family portrait— that one on the wall I'd seen that first time I'd been to their house—she, Jane, with her light complexion and blond hair, does not look out of place—not really—in the Rhymer family. "If you don't look too closely," she scoffs, surprising me. "And look at Ted—he's got black hair and his skin is darker than everybody else's. Look at the picture. He doesn't fit in. But I'm not going to talk about him. It's his life."

Reminded of what it might be like to be her parents, she follows that thread: "Being an adoptive parent sets up a certain insecurity. While the adoptee always feels like they are going to be rejected, the adoptive parents always feel that someone is going to take their child away—that is their deepest, darkest fear, whether they admit it or not, and there are always going to be reminders of that. Take television. You see lots of adoption stories. I'd always walk out of the room, and my mother would be sitting there crying."

We have talked for a couple of hours. I'm tired and call it a night.

Right, she says, I'm going to Club 33.

Club 33 is a bare-bones juke joint on Route 33 sitting between two towns, one smaller than the other. Jane's patronage of Club 33 drove Ann wild. I wish she didn't want to go to Club 33, too—not at that hour, not now. It is ten miles away, half of that on a winding, unlit country road. She must get up early the next morning for work. I know she needs adequate sleep because of her seizures, but I also know I cannot stop her. Jane is Patrick's daughter, and he enjoyed the easy euphoria of a friendly saloon. Maybe she needs to leave adoption behind and hang out with her pals and have a beer. I don't know when she gets in. The next morning, she is up and out before Kimberly and I wake up.

Figure 17. Jane and Lorraine in the nineties in Sag Harbor.

The Beach Boys are giving a concert nearby during that visit, and while I've never been a fan—too smooth, I think, give me the Stones any day—Jane suggests we go. I'm reluctant. It's too expensive. We'll have a great time, she counters, and we'll all remember it. That seals the deal. We have too few in our stockpile of good-time memories.

It is pouring buckets as we drive the thirty miles there, but the venue is not enormous, and we have good seats in the orchestra. The group doing the show has only two or three original members, but I learn to love the Beach Boys that day. Jane and I end up in front of the stage dancing. Kimberly, old enough to be mortified at the unseemly behavior of these old people—her mother and grandmother—stays in her seat.

When we leave, the sun is out, the air full of good vibrations. Thank you, honey, for the memory.

Same visit, another night. Jane is lying on the couch. I'm sitting at the end with her feet on my lap. She has been talking about being raised in an environment where it was a given that she would search for her natural mother one day, and while that gave her no answers, her mother's appreciation of her need to know made her feel understood. What hangs in the air between us is Sarah, the daughter she chose to put in a closed adoption.

I wait, wondering if she is having the same thought. She is.

"Putting Sarah in a closed adoption, a part of that was selfish, but I was not emotionally ready to raise a child," she reflects. "I was twenty years old, I was working at Burger King, I was not going to college, I was living at home, making $4.75 an hour, and I would never see this baby.

"Was that selfish? Yes. Did I give her a better opportunity? I hope so. I think so. I wasn't going to marry him."

She adds that she was using birth control—the contraceptive sponge—but got pregnant anyway.

"You told me you were planning to kill yourself and that's why you didn't use birth control," I remind her.

"Maybe I thought that if I shocked you enough you would—pardon me—shut up about open adoption. I was a twenty-year-old kid, and if I said the most outrageous thing, I could walk out of the room and go downstairs and be moody . . . I've thought about suicide so many times, but there was no time during the pregnancy when that might have happened."

The conversation drifts off to the time she took a bottle of aspirin and had to have her stomach pumped. "I was clinically dead a couple of times."

Because of her seizures? Because of the aspirin? And was all this at least partly because she had been adopted? Sometimes I am too exhausted by the dismal cycle of the events of my daughter's life to probe deeper. This is one of those moments. There is only so much grand opera that the people around Jane can handle before the tap of empathy runs dry. Nothing helps. The tragedy of Act Two—or Three or Four—will be replaced by another soon enough.

She brings up her father. Patrick, that is. "I spent two months in mourning, trying to figure out how I felt about him, trying to create a picture of what he was like. It pissed me off that he never picked up the phone. He decided I would never know how I was like him. All I wanted was a stinking lunch." She pauses. "He was the loser," she concludes, resentment morphing into bravado.

She adds that Gary was upset that Patrick's death bothered her so much. That she cried. That she moped around the house for a while.

I could understand his dismay—what was this man to her, anyway? Gary had done all the fathering, not this guy Patrick. He only contributed sperm. Gary was the one who lived with Jane's round-the-clock drama. He is the one who rushed her to the hospital when she had seizures, he is the stable one who paid the bills, he has been her rock and has always been there for her. Who was this other guy? He wouldn't even meet her. How could she possibly mourn for him?

"One time Grandma asked my mother, when we were leaving her house, I must have been five or so, and she didn't think I heard, before my mom had

David. Don't you wish you had one of your own? My mother got all upset, angry, and my dad had to talk to her—she was his mother."

Let's have a beer, okay? she asks.

We get two cold ones out of the fridge. We go outside into the brisk night air and find another cloudless starry night. It's incredibly beautiful at this place, in the country on a lake, at this moment. Jane has her smoke, we come back in, and I turn the tape recorder back on.

Shaun was a cousin who, at sixteen, committed suicide. "Shaun's dying took away one of the few people in my family that I could relate to. Then there was the whole thing, Well, if he killed himself because his life was cruddy, then I have a better reason to do it than he did—I've got a lot better reasons than he did. Why should I have to stay here and suck up all this pain? I was eighteen when this happened. That's when I went through the whole suicide thing—Shaun gave me the idea. I couldn't perceive in my head that I would get better. I was scared shitless to go out in the workforce because I had spent my entire life in special ed with this epilepsy baggage, and you want me to go get a job? That scared the crap out of me."

"I didn't realize how much Shaun's dying affected you." I barely believed he was real.

"I didn't talk about it much to you. What would be the point? You didn't know him. He wasn't part of your family."

Jane's life was far more bifurcated than I could ever understand. There were Tony and me in Sag Harbor and the relatives in Michigan, who mostly remained strangers to her. There was Wisconsin, and the family she grew up with. Did she fit completely in either? Neither? There is so much anyone not adopted cannot fully understand.

Her mind turns to her grandmother's funeral. There had been words and wounds between them, wounds that never healed. The man her grandmother had lived with—and whom Jane accused of sexually abusing her—would be there, Grandma's grieving partner of many years. After Jane accused him, nothing had happened to him, nothing at all.

If Jane went to the funeral, she told me repeatedly, people would think she'd been lying about what he had done. She was determined to skip the event, but her parents kept insisting otherwise. They must go as a family. To show that everything was copacetic. To keep up appearances. She must have phoned me a half-dozen times about this, each time for an hour or so, in the days before the service. The family pressure was relentless. I urged her to listen to her gut, talk to her mother, her mother will eventually understand. But in the end, Jane went, and then was angry that she had caved to their pressure. And now, many years later, she is still upset when she talks about it. The only good thing that came out of it was that Ann finally believed Jane that the man had, indeed, abused her.

The conversation drifts to more mundane topics, and she brings up the rhetorical question of who we might have been in past lives. People who did some pretty awful things, we agree flippantly, because this life was not working out the way either of us would have planned. "A serial killer?" she jokes. "My life is a conglomerate of high intensity experiences—I've never had the opportunity to be normal."

There is no arguing with that. And off she goes to Club 33. Again.

During that visit, I discover that the three expensive Barbie dolls in full evening regalia that I've sent to Kimberly are lined on a shelf in her bedroom, staring out from behind their cellophane windows, unopened and untouched. Kimberly tells me that Grandma didn't want her to open them, that one day they will be worth a lot of money if they are in brand-new condition. Still in the box.

What?

Not wanting to create a problem for Kimberly, I say nothing. Her eyes say everything. The little angel hadn't wanted to make a commotion. But now I know that Ann resents me every bit as much as I'd imagined.

Another night, near the end of the trip. Soon I'll be leaving and taking the tape recorder with me. Maybe Jane is fed up with talking seriously, maybe she is testing me—would I believe her or not, could she get away with this?—but this night she talks endlessly about being "hypnotized" for life by a former friend, a friend she feels deserted her or somehow did her wrong, I'm not sure which. I can't dissuade her from saying she has been hypnotized for life by her friend, a student in a psychology class who had been instructed by the professor to hypnotize someone "for life." She goes on for more than half an hour in this vein. I turn off the tape recorder. I'm going to bed.

As we say goodnight, standing by the kitchen counter, she says, "If I told the truth, both of you [me and Ann] would be hurt."

I am too tired not to sleep that night. I drift off thinking how those words encapsulated so much: *If I told the truth, both of you would be hurt.*

In fact, I did know the truth. I knew it from the moment of her first visit when she put her hands around my neck in our little docudrama and shouted, *Why did you give me up?*

28　The Things People Say

Adoption reform, like all causes that move with the speed of the tilt of the Earth, can be grueling. To do the work means you keep revisiting the place of your greatest pain. In my everyday life, when I'm not actually working on an adoption-related project, I try to stay away from the subject that is my life's leitmotif. I write books on other subjects that have nothing to do with adoption.

Oh, I might send off a newspaper essay or write to legislators—I got so involved helping push through a good bill in New Hampshire that the bill's chief sponsor, adoptive father Lou D'Allesandro, called within the hour to tell me it had passed. I'd sent letters to all the state senators, and one of them—a woman—had taken the time to send me a handwritten note saying that my letters were largely responsible for pushing the vote over to passage. It confirmed my sense that while adoptees had to be the ones making noise and demanding their records, mothers were indispensable in seeing that reform happen. The adoptees the lawmakers met, the adoptees who lobbied, seemed strong, intelligent and smart—their lives had turned out all right. But what of those women who had been hiding their shame for years? Whose families of today might not know? Would their lives be wrecked if a stranger came knocking? Maybe they wouldn't be all right. If the law lifted their anonymity—no matter what the original intent of the law—who knew how the women would react? A great many of those legislators came from the era when an unwed pregnancy was the cause of great family shame, and that is what they remembered. One woman had told a legislator that if the law changed, she

320

would drive her car into the river. Her letter had been anonymous—or was it a phone call? I didn't know. And who could say that might not happen?

So many of the legislators were stuck trying to figure out whom the law should protect. I had taken on the job of letting them know, and although I had gotten around the law myself—possibly illegally—that wasn't reason enough to walk away from the fight. I couldn't quit.

Though my personal and professional life have become irrevocably tied together, I stay off the soapbox when I can. If a new acquaintance asks what I've written or what I'm working on, the words "I am a mother who gave up a child" rarely pass my lips. I sometimes get away with just saying I'm writing a memoir. The question—about what?—lies there. Drugs, alcohol, cancer, rape, a child's death? If I say "adoption" they assume I adopted. If I offer no further information, they get the message I don't want to 'fess up, and they leave the mystery alone. If I spill my beans, their faces will assume a look of *Oh my god, you poor woman.* Most people are willing to assume nearly any other circumstance than mine. Most people don't think about the woman who supplied their friend's or cousin's baby, and most people assume they've never met a woman who's given up a child. That's too "other." If I do come right out and say what my story is, I might be dragged into a conversation that I want no part of, and suddenly I'll be on trial.

Nevertheless, once in a while, when it feels safe, I do tell my story in a single sentence. I remember telling a woman I'd never met before at a birthday party—I don't know what made me do it, but I did—and she looked at me and whispered, Me too. When I was on my way to a CUB conference, I recall telling a woman waiting for the same late-arriving plane, and she said, *I'm an adoptive mother.* I did a mental uh-oh, but she was open and warm—she didn't want to crucify me—and we had one of those surprising and rewarding chats that can occur between strangers who will never meet again.

Revelations like this happen more than most would expect. Sometimes the person I tell is simply someone I sense is simpatico and will not pepper-spray me with questions that give me a panic attack or long discourses about Great Adoptions They Have Known.

Some people still do, though. Some bombard me with verbal pellets sharp as shrapnel.

"You are our worst nightmare," says an adoptive grandfather at a dinner party while the hostess is getting dessert. His son went to Russia to get a child, and then another, it comes out, simply to avoid those inconvenient biological mothers who might show up—what with open adoption becoming trendy.

"What part of your pie chart was not selfish when you looked for your daughter?" asks a lawyer, someone I had thought of as a friend. Not a parent himself, he has multiple friends who are adoptive parents.

I refer to my daughter's "adoptive parents"—not negatively, mind you—but find myself corrected by an adoptive mother: They are her parents, she says, no need to call them *adoptive parents*.

Really? I am speechless and feel myself go white in the face. What am I, then? The woman who merely labored with a child, as one adoptive mother wrote in an essay? A birthing person, as some are now trying to inveigle into the language? And now I'm with an adoptive mother who knows my history and who chastises me for referring to my daughter's adoptive parents as "adoptive." If this woman mentioned her daughter's "birth mother," would I be allowed to step in and correct her terminology and say, She is her *mother*, not just her *birth mother*? Is turnabout fair play?

No. If I say anything, she would think me uppity. Yes, uppity. Don't I know my place?

"Since the practice has been in place for so long, there is a legal precedent for keeping the records sealed," insists a lawyer at a family funeral. Someone has told him about me. The lawyer tells me he is adopted himself. That day I am not up to a calm legal discussion, especially with an adoptee who is arguing against opening birth records, and after a sentence or two about the why and the when of the law and how this makes adoptees second-class citizens, I shut him down. I say I don't want to talk about this at a wake. I can tell he is disappointed, but he is not pushy. I move away.

"You are nothing more than a reproductive agent!" exclaims the acquaintance who has made it clear she is against searching, reunions, and the advocacy work I do.

She read *Birthmark* overnight, wanted to hear more the next day, but did not change her mind. Yet she is a neighbor, we share other sensibilities, and we have remained friends—as long as we don't talk about adoption. However, this day she wants to press a book on me, written by someone she knows, about the difficulty he and his wife had conceiving and their eventual journey to adoption. She hopes reading this might change my mind. I tell her I don't want the book, she is insistent, her filters that afternoon have been loosened by wine when she lets go her invective. I flee out the door. She sends flowers, we talk, we make up. I've mentioned her earlier—she's the one whose son suspected that her strong reaction about this issue—which she talks about when I am not there—might be because she has a secret child of her own.

A few years later, when she is dying, when she is drugged with morphine, this woman will reveal, without being asked, that her "eldest son" is not her firstborn. Decades of denial had convinced her who she must be. Nothing more than a reproductive agent.

Then there's the conversation with a documentary filmmaker. She'd asked me what I write, I told her, and now we are in the most private of conversations. "When I adopted," she says, "I didn't want to know the mother because I'd probably have wanted to adopt her, too." The filmmaker says she assumed that one day her daughter—now in her twenties—would want to search. That she herself might make a film about it. "But I asked her if she wanted to search, and she said she wasn't interested."

These comments are the hardest to respond to. I think about all the adoptees I've met who search but say their parents do not know—it would kill them. I think about the adoptees who wait until their parents die, and then they search, only to have a reunion with a grave. I think about Tony's college friend who did just that, waited until both of his parents died. Decades earlier, his father had told him on his deathbed that if he, the son, searched, it would kill his mother.

I think about—actually, I think about wishing I didn't have to say anything to this woman, that the floor would open and—*abracadabra!*—I'd be out of there—but a response is needed. Not everybody searches, I say, but they shouldn't have to search. The information should be theirs because it is theirs.

I want to tell her that she has beat the desire to know out of her daughter by word and deed over the years. She has informed her daughter how much it would hurt her, the only mother her daughter has ever known, if such a search were initiated. Isn't this mother's love enough?

But every casual meeting where this issue of whether to search or not to search comes up can't be a point of confrontation. We've just met at a luncheon given by a mutual acquaintance. I end the conversation and move away.

At a cocktail party where I'm not present, my husband is chatting with a friend about Jane—there's been another suicide attempt. Another acquaintance—and adoptive mother—walks up and listens. The person my husband is talking to has met Jane on several occasions and simply refers to "Lorraine's daughter."

"Birth daughter," the adoptive mother quickly interjects.

Tony says the conversation stopped for a second or two. He ignored her and went on.

A few years later when I am talking with someone at a memorial luncheon for a cherished friend, this same woman is nearby—but not part of my conversation. But she overhears me say "my daughter" and she can't help herself. She jumps in and says "birth daughter!" so quickly I am stunned. I turn to her and say nothing, but she's made her point. She has reassured herself that her daughter's other mother can't possibly count for anything, that surely my connection to my daughter is tenuous. I have no right to speak of my "daughter" without modifiers! Yet if I were to correct her language to "adoptive daughter" whenever she speaks, it would be rude. This woman is also one of those who enjoys telling me how when she asked her daughter if she was interested in searching, she said no.

Then there are the seemingly endless numbers of people who want to engage. Sometimes they are merely curious and without malice, sometimes they want to argue. And since I've owned up to my own act of giving up my daughter, the subject must be open for discussion: How did "it" happen? Where's the father? How did you find her? How do the adoptive parents feel? Wouldn't it be better for adoptees never to know? Why should adoptees open Pandora's Box? What do you think about open adoption? Hasn't that changed everything? My cousin, he's adopted, never wants to search, what about that?

That woman gave him up. Shouldn't we let dead dogs lie? My son/brother/ niece is adopted, and it turned out swell—he/she has never mentioned any- thing about being adopted.

I want to say that how my daughter felt about me was more important, more germane, than how her parents reacted. I want to ask, Shouldn't adop- tion be first about the child? I want to ask if they ever had a long and deep conversation with that cousin/niece/whomever about being adopted. I want to tell them that often adoptees don't reveal to family what they do to others. I want to tell them how the scrim of adoption is peeled back when valuable family jewelry is up for grabs. The inheritance of such keepsakes often lays bare the difference between "born to" and "adopted into," as many an adop- tee learns at the time of a parent's death. Family jewels and keepsakes are meant to be inherited by family, adoptees learn. Blood family. But I digress.

Also heard is a dig wrapped up in a compliment, language straight from the garden of ideas to make giving up a child A Good Thing: "You did a brave thing. I could have never done it." A brave thing?

Telling someone they are brave in any other context would be a compli- ment. But saying that about a woman who has relinquished her child, calling that relinquishment "brave," is a massive twist of logic, a distortion of reality, and a slur at the same time. The comment plays into the idea that since you were a single, poor woman, your child certainly was better off with the wealthi- er people who took her in. At the same time, the addition of the "I never could have done it" is an admission that the better choice would have been to keep your child, as the speaker is not-so-subtly saying she would have surely done, regardless of the circumstances.

When I hear a comment about my supposed bravery, I immediately put to rest the idea that giving up a child has anything to do with courage or hero- ism. Oh, no, I say, I was broken and defeated, I was anything but brave. As for the other comment—that they "could never have done it"—I say nothing, but think, Well, good for you. I wish you would walk in my shoes for a day.

It is exhausting.

And it seems nearly everybody wants to debate this subject. So many questions! So many wonderful adoptions they know about! So many adoptive parents who are saints, or nearly so! Giving up my child was the worst thing I ever did, the worst thing that ever happened in my life, and though I have written and spoken about it for a purpose, even today—with all the emotional armor I should have by now—I cannot speak of it as if we are debating the fine points of foreign policy of a country neither of us has ever visited. I have a tough skin when I need it. Put me up against an opponent in a forum where it might make a difference, against anyone who argues that adoptees' original birth records should be sealed and locked off to them, and I am fearless. Then the issue is not about me. I am merely the entity representing women like me, women who, for one sad reason or another, gave up a child to be raised by another.

But adoption talk with strangers at a social event where I am required to defend myself over and over means exposing my wound to god-knows-what and god-knows-who. If I don't know the person well, I say, It's a social event, I don't do adoption at parties. This is such an emotional subject for me, I'd rather not talk about it now. They look at me surprised. Why, you've even written a book about giving up a child! Most writers are such egomaniacs they can't stop talking about their books! The kindhearted are merely embarrassed.

A writer who says she has no affiliation with any side or interest group, without an axe to grind, as she put it, wrote, "I began to realize that, to birth mothers, relinquishment was more than merely a life-altering turning point. For most, it was an invisible barrier separating them from the bulk of humanity."[126]

Since I came out of the closet, I stay away from high school reunions. I am too much the outlier. I never bring up my daughter unless asked. I don't say anything about adoption to acquaintances who don't know my story unless I'm pushed to do so. If I do, people will want to talk about it. Spray me with questions. And suddenly I am quite a different person to them than I was before. I am an object of curiosity, someone to criticize or pity, an alien among the rest of humanity.

When I became the woman who wrote *that book* back in 1979, I ex-

---

[126] Merry Bloch Jones, *Birthmothers: Women Who Have Relinquished Babies for Adoption Tell Their Stories* (Chicago: Chicago Review Press, 1993), xiii.

pected the slings and arrows. But if we're at a social event and we've just met, let's talk about politics, the state of publishing, the melting ice cap, the dark sky movement, going solar on your rooftop, whether leaf blowers ought to be banned, the Oscars, the existence of God, your children, our husbands—anything but adoption.

Anything else is a piece of cake.

The Injustice of Sealed Birth Records

Imagine that you are at a family gravesite. A grandmother is being laid to rest alongside her husband, perhaps a sibling or two, and other relatives connected by birth. You are standing there, head bowed, but you can't squelch the awareness that when you die you do not really belong in this family plot. You should be elsewhere. You have a whole other passel of relatives, but you don't know who they are or where they are. You are adopted.

You have no knowledge of who you really are, where you came from, or how you got here, and you have no family medical history. You don't look like anyone in this family, and you wonder where you got your flat feet or why your second toe is longer than your big toe when nobody else in the family has feet like yours. You were raised Jewish, but maybe you were supposed to be Episcopalian. You are expressive and talk with your hands, and your family finds it uncultivated and vulgar. You are dreamy and poetic, and you are in a family of deliberate and logical engineers. You are, always and forever, something else. You are an orphan in the world.

You've known since you were five or six that you came from another life, but you understand that you are not supposed to question or wonder what that life would be like or ever ask about those people who gave you life. You have a birth certificate, but the information on it doesn't tell you who gave birth to you, only who adopted you. When you were adopted, the state sealed your original birth certificate (OBC) forever, thus taking away your right to know who you were when you were born. Call it what you will, it is state-sponsored identity theft.

For the vast majority of adopted people in America, this is the way the world works. As of this writing, fourteen states grant adopted people the full sovereignty of self-knowledge: Alabama, Alaska, Colorado, Connecticut, Hawaii, Kansas, Louisiana, Maine, Massachusetts, New Hampshire, New York, Oregon, Rhode Island, and Vermont. The Hawaiian law is the broadest of all, giving access to the entire adoption file not only to the adult adoptee at age eighteen, but also giving that same access to the birth and adoptive parents. But for those born in Hawaii and adopted elsewhere, the law is murky, and those unfortunate individuals cannot get their OBCs.[127]

Elsewhere, adoptees are subject to a crazy quilt of laws with various restrictions: a natural mother (fathers are seldom listed on adoptees' OBCs) can request that her name be redacted; a state-appointed confidential intermediary will do a search for the mother or the adoptee, but either party may simply say no to being revealed; the OBC is available only to adoptees born in certain years (before the law sealed the records) but not others (those born in the years after the records were sealed).

One can appeal. The decision is up to the courts. I've heard of some cases where the judge routinely grants the request and, conversely, where the opposite happens.

Lawmakers in those states with "partial-access" laws have insisted on such vetoes because they ostensibly smack of fairness, as it requires both parties to agree to openness. Equal and fair, right?

There is nothing fair about these vetoes. The mother named on the birth certificate, unless adopted herself, has always had the right to her own original, unamended document.

Yet these vetoes give the person who wishes to remain anonymous the right to deprive adoptees of the self-knowledge that the rest of us have always taken for granted. For those of us who know who we are since the age of reason, the enormity of this blank wall in the mental makeup of another is impossible to fully grasp. Someone in your adopted family has taken up genealogy as a hobby, and now suddenly something as simple as a family tree makes you the exception, with an asterisk or a note announcing you really don't belong there. Or you are left out completely.

You were never asked if it was okay to erase your history, your ancestry, your family of original record. Yet by virtue of being adopted in the wrong state, your records are sealed, and until the law changes, you are stuck behind a wall of ancestral anonymity. Until the law changes in your state, you are

---

[127] State Adoption Laws, The American Adoption Congress, https://web.archive.org/web/20220825224732/https://www.americanadoptioncongress.org/state.php. This site is frequently updated to stay current.

always going to be a second-class citizen. Reflecting the zeitgeist of an earlier era when a birth outside of marriage was the cause of great scandal, these halfway measures are chauvinistic holdovers. Legislators who enact them insist they must protect these scandalous women from—whom?

Their own children.

But the laws that sealed birth certificates were never designed to give mothers anonymity. The goal was quite the opposite: the laws were written to shield the adoptive family from the natural mother's interference.[128] It was presumed that she would want to know what happened to her child, and these laws would prevent her from intruding. Despite how desperate a woman may have been to keep her baby's birth a secret at the time, today that assumption has been turned into the excuse to allow her to hide from that child. That is wrong.

Adopted individuals were never asked whether stripping away their identities and histories was their choice or in their best interest. These infants and children grow up into adults with all the rights and obligations of the rest of us, yet—due to a contract made by others and long ago, when that now-adult was just an infant—they are denied basic facts about themselves. Sealed birth records codify the same kind of appalling reasoning that allowed slavery to flourish in centuries past.

Slavery is the only other institution in which a contract made among individuals about another individual binds them not only as a child but into adulthood. It takes from the individual full autonomy; it makes them subject to the preferences of another, and it does so indefinitely and for all time. Anything other than full autonomy—which surely includes the right to know who one was at birth—is wrong morally, wrong legally, wrong anyway it can be interpreted. These laws make a mockery of justice for all. These laws set up a two-tier system of life: those who have free agency in the world, and those who do not.

---

[128] Elizabeth J. Samuels, "Surrender and Subordination: Birth Mothers and Adoption Law Reform," *Michigan Journal of Gender and Law* 20, no. 1 (2013): 32–81. https://web.archive.org/web/20220825224915/https://repository.law.umich.edu/mjgl/vol20/iss1/2/.

Courts in the past have held—and unquestionably courts in the future will find—that the mother has no constitutional right to remain anonymous from her child, and thus the state has no obligation to keep her identity secret from her offspring.[129]

In states where adopted individuals may obtain their unamended OBC, a mother may attach a "no contact preferred" proviso. Few women choose this option. A 2016 survey of several states revealed that only one-half of one percent did so.[130] The bottom line: one out of two thousand mothers requested no contact. It is important to note that while adoptees were given no voice when the records were sealed, neither were mothers asked if they wished to be anonymous for eternity. Women giving up their babies had no choice.

While opponents of unsealing birth records have promoted mutual-consent registries to match adoptees and natural parents, such registries have turned out to be largely ineffectual. Most people are unaware such registries exist, dead parents and dead adoptees can't register, some adoptees do not know where they were born, teenage mothers who were living in secrecy when they gave birth may be uncertain of the correct date or location of their child's birth, and both parties must file with the same registry. Even worse, some registries have inane restrictions. New York and California once required that adoptive parents give their consent before their adult child could register.

Registries, intermediaries, halfway laws—none are a solution to the central issue, which is the right of the adopted to answer a simple question. Who am I? Lacking information about their name at birth and the circumstances of that birth, adopted individuals remain a subordinate class of people, denied a right the rest of us have never questioned. This is social engineering gone awry.

Who opposes the unsealing of original birth certificates? It is not a hidden mass of natural mothers. It is legislators themselves—still largely male—who empathize with the man or woman in the closet. It is legislators listen-

---

[129] Samuels, "The Idea of Adoption."
[130] "Statistics for States Implementing Access to Original Birth Certificate Laws since 2000," American Adoption Congress, Feb. 2016, https://web.archive.org/web/20220825225048/https://www.americanadoptioncongress.org/docs/Stats_for_States_with_access_Feb_-_2016.pdf.

ing to the ghosts of the past. It is legislators themselves who may fear that a child they know about, or suspect, may come knocking at their own door. It is adoption agencies and their agents—adoption attorneys, paid lobbyists, and search companies—who perpetuate the image of the vulnerable, fearful woman at the time of her greatest anguish and place her in the present, needing protection from her own flesh and blood. But she is a straw woman created by an industry fearful of change and of being discovered to have been wrong all these years.

Inexpensive DNA testing is changing the equation in this debate. Adoptees are finding second cousins or someone even more remote, and via a friendly relative linked by DNA the identity of many an adoptee's biological mother or father is revealed. People who had gone down many alleys only to find a dead end are finding family as more individuals spit into a small tube and mail off their DNA. Mothers—and fathers—who thought they might never reveal the existence of their adopted-away child are finding their secret is not so safe. But whether DNA reveals family or not, the basic injustice of sealed birth records remains just that—an injustice.

And even if there are a great many women who have not shared the story of a child they relinquished for adoption with their families, their desire for anonymity loses all moral authority stacked against an adopted individual's right to his or her own, true identity. Difficult conversations can be withstood. Most people will be forgiving of the long silence on this major life event if they can grasp the sense of shame and scandal that unwed births generated in another era. But whether they do or not, no one should have to deal with the question that sometimes pops up at three a.m. Who was I before I was adopted?

Unsealing records and the reunions that follow do not mean that every story has a happy ending. But finding answers about one's history is an ending of its own. Years ago, someone posted this on an internet message board: "Everybody wants to know where they come from, even if it doesn't turn out like you wanted."

The right to know one's heritage should be a given, not something to be asked for as a favor. It should—in a free society, it must—belong to all individuals by the very act of being born.

29 What to Wear When You Are a Moving Target

EARLY SEPTEMBER, 2000—What to wear to her daughter's wedding has flummoxed many a mother of the bride, but perhaps few were ever as baffled as me. That woman. The other mother. Who will be an object of curiosity. And who is herself acutely aware of first impressions.

All events where adoptive families gather can be trying for natural mothers. Are we part of the family, on the receiving line, in a front pew, in family photos, or merely a guest, lost in the crowd, or even worse, an outlier whose very presence is controversial? Some mothers have felt so badly treated at such events that they recommend others skip them. Though I was apprehensive, I had been involved in Jane's life enough that when her adoptive mother gave a pass on reading a psalm at the ceremony, Jane asked me to. Of course, I was thrilled. Does the runner-up to Miss America mind taking over if the winner is somehow disqualified? Not much.

This will be a proper wedding, like my second was to Tony, when the first for both of us had been a quickie in a judge's office (mine) or city hall (hers). This second wedding of Jane's will be the whole enchilada: a diamond ring, an engagement photo, a wedding gown, bridesmaids, a nuptial mass, and a reception afterward at the local American Legion Hall.

Tony and I are flying in from New York, and my two brothers, their wives, and my younger brother's daughters—Jane's cousins, girls who are around Kimberly's age—are flying in from Michigan. Jane is surprised and thrilled, and she keeps mentioning it. That they would come. All the way from Detroit. To her wedding.

Everyone is hoping that this marriage signals a turning point in Jane's life. At last.

She and her intended, Bob, met at the nefarious Club 33. One night a tall stranger sat down next to her and said he knew where she lived.

"Are you a stalker?" she quickly replied.

No, he said, your postman.

Now it's a year later, and the wedding is weeks away. Jane is in a good place. She has a job as a home-health aide through the Lutheran Home, where she started out as an inpatient after one of her suicide attempts. Bob is a steady, salt-of-the-earth guy. Gary gives him a resounding A-plus.

But. There's always a but.

Ann is angrier at me than she has ever let it be known. There will be no perfunctory hugs as before when we met. No pretending we get along fine. Ann wants my head.

It is impossible not to see Jane's hand in unconsciously orchestrating this pre-wedding disaster. Everything has been going so smoothly, and there have been no major hiccups in a while. Where is the drama Jane craves?

Kimberly is the foil.

Ann and Gary want Jane to sign over permanent custody to them. Is this a sign something is about to change, and not for the better? Jane has tried to commit suicide on numerous occasions, yes, but now she is about to be married to someone I only hear good things about from Gary. The husband-to-be has his own cabin in the woods, he holds two jobs, he's never been married, and he treats Jane well. Jane and I chat frequently, and she sounds good. No—she sounds better than good, she sounds happy and stable.

So, what's this about a transfer of custody? Why now? While I am sorting out my reaction, Tony catapults me into the red zone. His ex-wife had done her best to alienate his two children from him, and he sees this custody change through his own lens. If the Rhymers want to, he points out, they could make it impossible for me to see Kimberly! I'd read about grandparents who lose all contact with their grandchildren after a nasty divorce. Could this be happening now?

The Rhymers asking for full custody of Kimberly affects me viscerally, as if I am losing my baby all over again. All the fears and feelings of what I lost when I relinquished Jane come gushing forth. They are taking my granddaughter away from me, and who knows if I'll ever know the other one. Jane is living with Bob, and so she is free to call me as often as she wishes. So the next time I talk to her—the same day, the next day, she is phoning several times a day—I say, "I don't think that's a good idea."

Well. The comment is repeated to Ann, and—no surprise here—Ann is livid. I have no trouble figuring out how "Lorraine doesn't think that's a good idea" resonates with Ann. Jane mentions that when my name is spoken, Ann either makes a snide comment or walks out of the room. Yes, having dinner parties on the Saturday nights when they called had irritated her, further proving what a trifling, silly person I was. Then follows another indignant letter from a furious Ann. What right had I suddenly to interfere? Where was I when they "rescued" Kimberly? That I hadn't known she needed "rescuing" is beside the point—she was living with them before I knew what was happening. They had given Kimberly a stable home. Who was I to even have an opinion? What right did I have to say anything?

Now I hear Ann is hopping mad that we are coming at all. Jane frets endlessly—will Ann even speak to me? Will she tell me off in front of everyone? Will she . . . Jane is full of what ifs, all the time assuring me we have to come. Oh, we are coming, I tell Jane. Ann's wrath is not keeping me from my daughter's wedding, unless she tells me my whole family is unwelcome.

I don't bother asking how she could not have foreseen that injecting me into the conversation over custody would cause one hell of a hullabaloo. Jane needs turmoil like an addict needs drugs, this I know, but awareness does not fix the situation. *Calm down, honey, we'll get through this. It will turn out fine, I won't create a scene, and Ann probably won't either* is the subject of hours of conversation. We send her a handsome check to pay for part of the wedding. I don't know if she even tells Ann and Gary, or if that would placate them, but it is a kind of peace offering—as in, let's get our daughter married together. Maybe this will be some kind of answer for her life.

But now, ye gods, what to wear going into this wedding? With Ann so furious? No bridal magazine to advise on outfits for the extra mother. Nor is there any suggested protocol for her—where does she sit, how close to the wedding party? With the other parents? Surely not, but where, then?

The wedding is two weeks away.

I freak out.

My good clothes are too New York–businesswoman, and my summer outfits belong in the Hamptons at some outdoor cocktail party. I shop locally, but that produces nothing remotely possible that I could remotely afford and that doesn't look like I am heading to a beach party or a fancy, big-ticket gala. I shop vintage, but the only dress I like (lime green, Norma Kamali, original label) overwhelms me—I'm only an inch or two above petite. Besides, the jersey sheath with bat-wing sleeves simply screams New York! I try the East Hampton Ladies Village Improvement Society thrift shop, beloved by all frugal fashionistas and known as the LVIS, or El-Vis, but that, too, coughs up nada. A major meltdown is on the horizon. I can feel it coming the way you feel a cold coming on.

Two weeks! And counting.

I had been delaying a trip to Manhattan to shop—it is August, it is hot, going to the city to troll the stores by myself with a limited budget sounds dreadful—but just as I am facing that prospect, Tony rides in on his white horse to rescue me. On Sunday we drive to a big mall in the center of Long Island. There is Macy's. There is Lord & Taylor. There is Bloomingdale's. There will be something.

Yet after a couple of hours of scoping out every possible department in the stores and wandering through the boutiques in the acres of the mall, I have nothing but an impatient husband to show for it. He's done the Sunday *Times'* crossword puzzle. He's spent an hour in a bookstore. He's had a cup of tea. We are driving away when we spot a humongous warehouse wrapped in black plastic and surrounded by scaffolding. A sign says, "Lord & Taylor is open! During renovations."

This is a gigantic warehouse outlet of that upscale department store, where clothes not sold in their stores end up at much reduced prices. To some, the pits; to me, Mecca! Cavernous, with a cement floor, unflattering florescent lighting high overhead, rows and rows of clothes on racks in simple categories: dresses, suits, evening wear. Hundreds, thousands of choices! And there "it" is, almost knocking us over when we walk in, on a separate rack by itself: the perfect yellow cotton-and-silk sateen suit with pearl buttons, short sleeves, and a jacket that stylishly scoops slightly lower in the back. Tony spies it first and holds it up, with that satisfied-yet-hopeful look that says *perfect.* And at seventy-nine dollars, marked down from three hundred seventy-nine, a real deal.

I slip into the suit in the communal dressing room, surrounded by two dozen or so women in various states of undress. It is the only outfit I've taken into the dressing room. It is the only outfit. The employee watching over the mayhem is nearby and notices how long I simply stand in front of the mirror. Frozen. Like a mannequin. You look great, she offers. What's it for?

Uh, my daughter's wedding, I say, adding, I mean, my daughter who is adopted.

Oh, she says, somewhat startled. Since she assumes that I am the adoptive mother, what's the big deal? But then, if I were the adoptive mother, would I have shared that? Her quizzical look demands more information.

What the hell, I might as well go all the way: "The daughter I gave up for adoption." People need to know this happens, I remember thinking. I hold my breath.

Oh, god bless her, she absorbs the news in an instant and does not act as if I have just popped up from the underworld. She nods slightly, conveying *I understand. This is going to be stressful, you poor woman.* Thank god for understanding strangers. I am ready to hug her.

The wedding is in a small town in Wisconsin, and I don't want to look too New York ... too ... but still? I shrug. My husband's outside, can I show him? She's not supposed to let me leave the dressing room, so she follows me out. I also think she wants to get a look at Tony, now that she's part of this little drama.

Great, huh? She says to Tony, flashing a smile.

Perfect. Back home, I pair the suit with gray fabric pumps already in my closet and a yellow-and-gray neck scarf plucked from T. J. Maxx tucked into the collar.

But what to wear is only part of the equation. As the days dwindle down, Ann's anger has not cooled, and Jane is still calling two, three times a day. What I want to say is, Jane, why did you pass on my comment about custody to Ann when it was bound to infuriate her? You must have known. What were you thinking?

But that's Jane. I think it was her way of saying, I'm not sure I like this idea. Does this have to happen now? It means I'm incompetent. Easier for her to put the words in my mouth.

A few days later, Tony and I fly to Madison, rent a car, check into a hotel in Reedsburg, and wait for my family to arrive.

The day before the ceremony, Tony and I invite my brother Richard and his wife, Phyllis, and the bride and groom to have lunch at our hotel. Jane is practically swooning she is in such a good mood. To Bob, we are simply the other family. Bob bonds with Richard over hunting and fishing, and after lunch, we go bowling.

At the rehearsal a few hours later, Jane is anxious. I am calm enough. The priest is the same hip guy I met when I was there taking care of Kimberly. He wears cowboy boots under his cassock and rides a Harley between his parishes. He greets me warmly. Ann does not acknowledge me and runs out as soon as the rehearsal is over. There is no pre-wedding dinner for either family. Later that evening, my brother Tom arrives with his wife, Judy, and their two daughters. My family is in place. *Que sera, sera.*

The morning of the wedding, Jane and Kimberly meet me at the local beauty salon for hair and nails, something I'd arranged with Jane weeks earlier. This is not Ann's style, but it is mine, and at that point it is meaningless not to share this mother-and-daughter moment.

The wedding? It goes off without a hitch. Bob, tall and thin as two chopsticks, is dignified in his tuxedo. Kimberly wears her frilly First Communion dress, and Jane is gorgeous: a size two in a spectacular beaded sheath falling to slightly below her knees, where it flares out in a fishtail. It's a bit much for a simple wedding in farm country, but that is undoubtedly why the six-hundred-dollar dress was knocked down to ninety-nine plus alterations. My daughter likes a bargain as much I do.

Overnight, Ann has somehow quelled her hostility. She barks a quick "hello" at the church, and, as Jane had wanted, we sit next to each other during the ceremony, our matching corsages pinned to our outfits. When we see Jane is visibly shaking as she walks up the aisle on Gary's arm, Ann nudges me and says: Uh-oh. Is a seizure coming? The shared mom bond has gone into gear. That is our daughter getting married to a good man. Who wouldn't get a tear in her eye at this wedding? We all do. Perhaps, at last, life is turning a corner.

Thank heavens for small blessings: After the ceremony and before going to the reception, Jane and Bob make a side trip to a local tavern for a beer—or two—and while it seems rude at the time, their absence removes any whisper of an official receiving line. What to do with the extra mother? And her husband, whom Jane had come to regard as a stepfather? Maybe the barroom jaunt calms Jane down, for she has no idea how to be the center of attention at a gathering at which she is not ill or having a seizure. The way to call attention to herself now is to be absent, and she succeeds as people begin to ask, whither the bride and groom? Nothing can happen until they return. The groom's mother finally retrieves them.

Lunch is a buffet, and there is no assigned seating. At the edge of the gathering, my family makes up a table of its own. If it had been only Tony and me there, it would have been a long, uncomfortable afternoon. My nieces hang out with Kimberly. One of Jane's cousins makes a point of coming over and talking to me, extending a welcome, telling me she read *Birthmark*. There's no official photographer, but plenty of snapshots are taken. I have one with Gary and Ann, Jane, Bob, and Kimberly, and Tony and me. However, in the one shot I have of my family with Jane and Bob, she is looking off into the distance while everyone else is smiling straight on. Gary took the shot. Jane looks like she doesn't want to be there. Her excuse was that she hates photographs when people looked posed, looking into the camera. But I have a clutch of photographs with her looking straight into the camera. The double-family pull was clearly troubling her, as well as the need—unconscious or not—to show Gary that my family came second, or that she really didn't belong there. Okay, you don't get whipped cream with that sundae.

When the parents of the bride dance, Tony grabs my hand and we go out on the floor with the Rhymers. No one hisses.

Several years go by before I learn the reason the Rhymers wanted permanent custody of Kimberly. Having lived with Jane's repeated suicide attempts, they could not be sure this period of tranquility, even this marriage, would last. Should something go awry again, and Jane make another attempt on her life, Ann and Gary wanted to make sure that if Kimberly's father appeared they would have a stronger legal standing if he suddenly were to demand custody. All anyone knew of his whereabouts occurred when he was picked up for vagrancy and in jail for short periods. Then a few small checks for child support would appear.

Had they told this to Jane, I wondered, and she chose not to repeat it to me because it brought up her instability, the suicide attempts? The odds are good that was the case.

30 Here Today, *Pfft* Tomorrow

2002–2003—Just when everything is going swimmingly for a couple of years, the tide shifts, and the life raft of our relationship breaks apart again on the rocky shoals of Jane's divided loyalties.

She and I speak frequently, send each other presents, and appear to have found a comfortable plateau in our relationship. I begin to relax. Our closeness reminds me of my relationship with my mother after I left home—we usually spoke once a week, and now Jane and I do the same: Here's a recipe for a canapé we call Memphis cheesies, made with Rice Krispies and cheddar. How's Bob? He's now working full-time in the post office? Great. What's Kimberly up to? You got a steamer to clean the furniture? Whoa! Tony thinks I'm a clean freak, wait till he hears about this. Arthur is going to China to visit his daughter—you do remember she lives there? With the girl she adopted from China? I'm painting the deck chairs white. You're painting outdoor furniture too? You wanted that recipe for the turkey brine? Gallon and a half each of apple juice and water, cup of brandy, one and a half cups of salt.

That Thanksgiving Day, she is a part of the event at our house, even though she is halfway across the country: she calls in the morning as my pumpkin pies are baking, she calls later when both our turkeys are roasting, she calls back later to chat with Evan, Tony's son, for a half hour before dinner, she calls again that evening to say her turkey came out great, using my brine recipe in her parents' roaster. The symbolism is not lost on either of us—my recipe, their cooker—and we joke about it. Christmas, January, early February, and all is well.

Then one day I pick up the phone to hear her weeping profusely—she has just heard that her brother David, the oldest of the Rhymers' two biological children, has died in a skiing accident. An expert skier, he died in a colossal fall at the Mammoth Mountain ski resort in California. Over the coming week, we speak a couple of times a day. She is distraught because her parents did not buy her a plane ticket to go to the memorial service out west, while they did for their biological son. Tell them you want to go, I say. She does, and the tickets for both her and Kimberly are immediately forthcoming. Jane's adopted brother, Ted, lives out west, so he will be there. Initially being left out was extremely upsetting to Jane, but once the slight was corrected, it was absorbed and smoothed over.

When she gets back, she tells me about the service, and we speak a couple of times that week. We have no fight, not even a whisper of an argument. This is great, right? This is the way it is supposed to be. But then, in early March, again our relationship hits a wall. She stops calling. She doesn't call me back. The one time I manage to speak to her, she is cold and barely responsive. Then, I only get the machine. I listen to Bob's voice on the answering machine. Please leave a message. I leave a message. She does not call back.

I wrack my brain trying to figure out what I might have said—after everything had been going so well—but come up with nothing. Her internet is dial-up and she does not have email yet. Or email that I know about.

What did I say or do?

All I can think is that for some reason she is going to show me how it feels to be abandoned, to have a relationship cut off without an explanation. Now nothing else matters—not that she found some psychic relief in my having searched for her, rather than her having to find me, not that we've been on cruise control for a couple of years. She will punish me in kind: She survived being abandoned. Now it's my turn.

God, it hurt.

Jane had done this so many times before—but this, after being close for a couple of years, really stung, for I had mistakenly assumed this kind of erratic behavior was over. If she were an ordinary friend, I would have walked away long ago, not resumed a relationship that made me crazy, that had so much power to hurt, that stopped and started seemingly without reason except the obvious one: I had given her up for adoption.

At the time, I had no idea how common this kind of behavior was, but I have discovered since that blogs and social media are littered with stories of advance, retreat, advance, retreat, usually without a word. Now, after nearly two decades of knowing Jane, after the wedding, after everything had been going so well, I was left standing in the road wondering what the hell just happened. Like a rabbit in a magic show, she had disappeared again.

I am one of the keynote speakers at the American Adoption Congress's twenty-fifth anniversary convention in Atlanta in the spring of 2003. The AAC, comprised of adoptees and both natural and adoptive parents, stands for openness in adoption, including taking down the sealed-records statutes. I talk about the early days of this movement and how far we still have to go. I do not gloss over the rabid opposition we faced then, and still do, often from legislators and academics who have close ties to adoption, as many themselves are adoptive parents. Or their sister is. Et cetera.

Throughout the conference, a part of me feels like a fraud—I am a poster mother for reform and reunion, and my own daughter isn't speaking to me. Yet my own baggage is actually immaterial: adoptees deserve to know who they were when they were born, and reform will not happen without a phalanx of mothers who gave up their children announcing that they do not want to remain anonymous from them.

There will always be those fearful few who want to stay anonymous for any number of reasons—because they have never told their husbands or their other children, because their religion has told them their children belong to another family now and forever, because their own sense of shame is emotionally incapacitating, or because they have lived the lie of omission so long they can't imagine telling their partner and other children. However, a great many of us desperately want to know our children, no matter how secretive and ashamed we were at the time we relinquished them. We and the times have changed, and in the path to unsealing the birth records, we are needed because now we are held up as the reason to keep the records sealed. This is so even though the real reason the lifelong unbreakable secrecy laws came into being was to make sure we didn't hang around after the adoption of our children. We must not stay in the closet. Our voices must be raised and heard and be more persistent than the long drumbeat coming from the opponents of open records. Still, here I am at the AAC, speaking up and speaking out and wondering why I have been relegated to my daughter's emotional trash heap.

Her birthday is two days after I get back. I had sent no gift, no card this year. This time her turning away from me felt complete. I thought about calling, but that seemed wrong. Maybe they already had caller ID (we did not) and she would not pick up anyway. Or if she did answer, I'd get a cool response. Oh, it's you. Why are you bothering me? You are nothing to me. Or I'd leave a message that went unanswered.

This would be the first time I had not acknowledged her birthday since reunion. And you know what? I am worn out by this fractious and fragile relationship, exhausted trying to figure out how to react, tired of getting beaten up by something I cannot fix. I do not call.

But I don't get off lightly. I spend a part of the day deep in the blues. When Linda, a natural-mother friend, calls, I burst into tears. We email each other pretty much every day. Unless you are one of us, you would be surprised how often adoption passes by in the culture: on television dramas, in celebrity gossip, on your street and in your office. You want to escape but can't. A never-ending supply of reminders of the biggest and saddest event of your life confronts you daily, and to each other we can make note of these reminders. With each other, Linda and I are alternately snide, satirical, infuriated, or simply sad. We can be free with our feelings without being thought obsessive or loony. Linda's daughter has cut her off too, even though her daughter is the one who searched. The reunion had been ecstatic. So why was Linda cut off? Unknown. Or maybe it was because Linda had used the guest towels hanging on the rack when she visited, as her daughter had remarked unfavorably. Linda hadn't used the right towels. You think I'm kidding? I'm not.

SUMMER 2003—I am heading for Wisconsin to pick up Kimberly. Jane and Bob are living in his small cabin in the woods, and Kimberly stays with the Rhymers during the week and attends the same elementary school as she did before Jane married. Though Kimberly had flown by herself from Wisconsin to New York before, after fanatics in airplanes brought down the World Trade Center, Gary and Ann don't want her to fly alone. They want me to come to Wisconsin to pick her up. I'll fly in on Saturday, we'll leave on Monday, and maybe I'll be able to talk to Jane and patch up whatever needed patching. Gary will try to broker this, he says.

No dice. Jane does not want to see me—not for dinner, not for anything. They say they are in the dark as much as I am. Gary shrugs—*Jane*. I do not respond.

Saturday evening the three of us—Gary, Ann, and I—have drinks outside on their deck, marvel over a scarlet tanager sighted across the narrow slice of the lake where their house sits, and make pleasant chitchat. Kimberly is still with Jane and Bob. We'll pick her up tomorrow at church, where we will see them. Despite the coolness I've felt from Ann from a distance, the intemperate letters, all goes well. After dinner, we watch television. Hey, life is complicated. These are the people who adopted my daughter, and she is rejecting me. I feel like an odd duck—we're friendly but not really friends—but there I am, enjoying their hospitality, about to fly back home with Kimberly. The weekend is remarkable simply because it occurs.

In many ways our relationship is a marvel, considering truly open adoptions like this are still rare. When Ann shares a story about Jane, she calls her "our" daughter. She says the neighbors know who I am and that when asked, she tells anyone that adoption is better this way, that adopted people ought to know their other mother early on. How can I not feel a special empathy toward this woman? Jane is difficult. She specializes in uproar. And Ann sure hadn't counted on her epilepsy, and then me. Me coming back is one thing, and I clearly am here to stay.

As we file into church on Sunday morning, Ann sees to it that I am at the end of the pew, where there will be room for Jane. When she and Bob come in, Jane stops and greets ten people before she slides in, putting off the moment before she has to acknowledge me. The time seems longer than it must have been. I am quite sure that most of the people she was stopping to greet know exactly who I am, and that they are watching this performance with avid interest. What will she do? Look, she is ignoring *her*. The other mother.

As she is about to slip in, she quite obviously turns around to say hello to one last person. If Jane could have held up a sign saying *This woman means nothing to me!* she would have. I feel humiliated, but so what? Ann is shaking her head. When Jane can put it off no longer, she steps into the pew and nods with a forced smile, as if I were a teacher she remembered none too fondly. Having caught the attention of several people, many who surely know who I am, she is playing to her audience, but what can I do? I nod back and say the first thing that comes to mind: Your hair is great.

She'd cut her long hair into a boyish bob. She looks pretty, and healthy too, as if this marriage to Bob has dissipated all the gloom of the past. She nods and is momentarily nonplussed. As I sit next to my daughter, who now is acting as if I am a post, mass is interminable. Except for these few words, we have not spoken for over a year.

Gary, always the calm patriarch, hoping for some kind of détente, gets Jane and Bob to agree to brunch with us afterward. In the car on the way, Ann, who has noticed Jane's effusive hellos, confirms what I thought, that Jane usually doesn't greet a zillion people on her way into church.

At Granny's Cafe, which is as it sounds—hot coffee, hearty omelets, and hash browns—this blended family takes over a big round table. Jane purposely does not sit next to me and acts as if being there is a trial. She will show them what she thinks of me. Not much! Ann is on one side, Kimberly on the other, both providing cover. Jane's bored and petulant demeanor tamps down everyone's mood. She does not look at me or speak to me, and she sulks when Gary asks her not to smoke. God, when is this meal going to be over, when can I get out of Dodge? Improbably enough, Kimberly and Ann are protecting me from Jane's obvious hostility.

As we leave, Jane and Bob light up outside of Granny's, and I force myself to stay behind and talk to them for ten minutes, about what, I do not know. Now that it is just the three of us, Jane has shifted into neutral—not painfully aloof or snide, simply coolly civil. I walk away thinking, at least she talked to me. The Rhymers and I do not discuss this again, for there is nothing to say. Kimberly and I leave in the morning for New York.

Kimberly—always an uncomplaining traveler who takes most things in stride—is amiable as ever when we get stuck in Milwaukee for several hours because of a storm. We have ice cream, and I buy her a Harry Potter novel. Over the entire summer, I do not speak to Jane—other than to answer the phone when she calls to speak to Kimberly. Jane's hostile tone announces she wants no conversation. I am merely the go-between for her and Kimberly, and an irritating one at that. In mid-August, I fly back to Chicago with Kimberly, meet her parents at the airport—they've driven in from Wisconsin—and return home.

A few weeks later, I am in Williamsburg, Virginia, at the annual retreat of Concerned United Birthparents. I am on a panel with two other mothers. One of them speaks rather forcefully about her therapist telling her repeatedly that "it was not your fault," words the therapist has her repeat until she believes it, she feels it, she knows it. Her relationship with the father was a one-night stand in France, and maybe she does feel that way. But I find her "not my fault" message and the insistent way she is proclaiming her therapeutic victory at odds with my own frame of mind. I did give a baby up for adoption. I don't feel exonerated the way she does. I can accept how it happened, but I cannot feel liberated by those words. When I get up to speak, I talk about taking responsibility for our actions, no matter what.

Later during the conference, I attend a healing session being led by another natural mother, Carol Schaefer,[131] longtime activist and author of *The Other Mother*. Carol's soothing voice guides our visualization: I see Jane coming toward me, walking over a bridge, carrying a small, flat package wrapped in fuchsia tissue paper—I have no idea what's in the package or why it is that color—and suddenly I am engulfed in a tsunami of tears. Cathartic tears? Not on your life. Just tears. I am way beyond catharsis; I am merely wretched. Many women in the group are in the same sorry boat—we had a reunion and then somehow it went south.

---

[131] Carol Schaefer, *The Other Mother* (New York: Soho Press, 1991), and *Searching for Healing after Reunion* (self-pub., 2014).

Those of us who have relinquished a child often feel outside of the mainstream—we are the pariahs we know we are—and so we rarely speak of our deep and abiding pain. Being among our own kind, where we are not judged or pitied, is immensely comforting. You don't have to explain or apologize or feel embarrassed by the sudden rush of tears filling your eyes. The woman sitting next to you, who is otherwise a stranger, understands. I confess to the group that my daughter has rejected me—again—and that's why I am in such pain. But in quiet moments when I walk alone that weekend, I can't help but recall the theory that the people who repress their feelings are the healthier ones.

At another session, Nancy Verrier, adoptive mother, adoption therapist, and author,[132] suggests that we tell our children, at least once, *I am sorry*. Sorry without qualifications. Just sorry that your child is adopted. That you didn't raise him or her. Sorry, plain and simple. No statement with "it was the times" or "my father/mother/priest/grandmother made me do it" or any of the other million reasons, no matter how true and valid they are. No matter if you were truly forced into signing the surrender papers. No matter if you felt you had no choice. No matter if you were raped and your parents sent you to purdah and said not to come back with that bastard. *So what?* is Verrier's argument. However it happened that you did not raise your baby, you can still be sorry, because, after all, aren't you? The adopted person might rationally understand the mitigating factors about why she was relinquished, but maybe, she explains, to hear a mother say just once, "I'm sorry you were adopted," would be healing. It would not deflect the blame to anyone or anything else; it would be an acknowledgment that no matter how the adoption turned out—good or bad or in between—you are sorry that it happened at all. She adds that a lot of after-reunion relationships improve dramatically once this is said. Do it once, she adds, not a million times. You don't have to be a whipping post.

A light bulb over my head switches on. Have I ever done this? I am pretty sure the answer is no—otherwise, why would this feel like such a revelation? On the flight home, I stare out the window of the airplane as a conversation I had with Kimberly that summer floats by like a passing cloud. She

---

[132] Nancy Verrier, *The Primal Wound: Understanding the Adopted Child* (self-pub., 1993), and *Coming Home to Self* (Baltimore: Gateway Press, 2003).

was ten or eleven—old enough to be aware that adoption meant I had given birth to her mother but then gave her up. She knew by then that there was both conflict and joy between Jane and me, and now she wanted to know, Why did you give Mama up?

She saw that Tony and I had a normal middle-class life, that we lived in a neighborhood of nice houses in a swell seaside town, so how come? We were in her bedroom at our house, it was after dinner, early evening but not yet dark. We had not yet put on a lamp. How to explain what it was like in 1966, what my situation was then, what it was like to be an unwed mother? How to explain how the rare "unwed mother" had whispers clinging to her like pollen in springtime? Kimberly knew kids who had single moms, and by the way, she herself had not seen her father since she was two, and until Jane married, her own mom had been a single mother. Kimberly had been absorbed into the family of Jane's other parents, so why hadn't that been the way with Jane and my family? She was determined to get to the bottom of this mystery.

But didn't you have an uncle or someone you could have asked for help? she wanted to know. Someone who would have helped you? Couldn't you have gone to the bank and explained to the man you needed money?

I explained the situation, the times, he was married, I was alone, I couldn't get a loan, you weren't supposed to have a baby if you weren't married, everything was so different from how it is now, the shame was great.

She wasn't buying any of it. Finally, I say, Women who had babies and weren't married were, uh, scorned. Like whores. I knew she had recently learned the word even if she didn't fully understand what it meant.

Oh.

But. The look on her face told me she was not convinced. I knew she was thinking, There must have been a way. I turned on the light. I waited.

"I made a mistake," I finally said. "A terrible mistake. I shouldn't have done it. I thought it was best for both her and me, but it turned out not to be." I raised my eyebrows and stared into her bright blue eyes, aware at that moment how much like Patrick's they were. I knew I was staring into the eyes of an old soul, one who understands much.

Ah, now she got it. A mistake.

Mistakes she understood. Grandma Lorraine made a mistake. That she can accept. It was a doozy of a mistake, but still: a mistake. She said nothing more.

By the time the plane lands, I know what I must do. I must make that call. I would simply say, "I'm sorry." No excuses, no explanations added. Said or unsaid would be this: I made a mistake.

On a gray, cold day a few weeks later, Tony is outside raking leaves, and I sit in the kitchen at the table and punch in Jane's number. Bob answers, registers neutral. He says they are working in the yard, he'll tell her I'm on the line.

Would she even come to the phone?

A minute later Jane picks up and says hello.

I breathe deeply and plunge forward. I know we talked about this before, and I've told you what it was like back then, but today I just wanted to say I'm sorry. I'm sorry I couldn't keep you. I wait.

I don't know what to say, she says.

That's all right. I wanted to say this once, I respond. Like that.

We speak for well over an hour—about how she and Bob are fixing up the yard, painting furniture, her job as a home-health aide. We speak like a mother and daughter. Maybe she'll talk to me now, I think when I hang up. Maybe. By this time, I know she has a computer, but she has not given me her email address, or asked for mine, and I have not brought it up for fear of being rebuffed.

Once again, silence.

It happens to others, why not me? One mother, whose daughter spent ten years trying to find her, says she always finds herself apologizing for something. It feels as if there are all kinds of ways adoptees punish us. Everything seemingly is going along fine, and then *pfft!* and a relationship disappears, replaced with nothing. Was it ever real, or only a phantom?

Yet there is another side to this bouncing coin that sometimes lands heads up and other times, head down: adoptees say they have endured the same kind of uncertain, off-again, on-again relationship. The years of separation, the essential act of being given up, the relationship with the adoptive parents—especially if it is a good one—all play into this new and endlessly complicated connection of reunited mother and child. And it often does not go smoothly.

Life continues. I write magazine pieces, keep up with my column in the *Sag Harbor Express*, sign a contract to rewrite a book, see friends, go to the movies. Yet Christmas is especially dreary that year. Tony and I spend a raucous Christmas Eve with his large contingent of nieces and nephews and their children in New Jersey, where he grew up, but the next morning when I go to mass—and I sometimes still do, despite my questioning whether God exists—I cannot hold back my tears when we turn to our neighbors, shake hands, and say, Peace. I have no peace in my heart. I miss my daughter.

SPRING 2004—She phones, and when I pick up I hear *Hello. How have you been?* I do not ask her why I have been in exile or why I now no longer am. I know there is no answer that she can, or will, articulate. We resume as before. Now she gives me her email address. Now we are on good terms again. But now, I am wary. Of saying the wrong thing. Of saying anything that might be misconstrued. Of relaxing too much. She could shut down at any time, for any reason.

It takes a long time to figure this one out. Over the months, she lets slip, in half-finished sentences, what had been going on. She had been determined to prove to Ann that she, Jane, deserved to be loved. There's no way to explain without telling the story that leads up to her hitting "delete" on our relationship. At the memorial service for the older of the Rhymers' two biological children, Ann let slip this comment: He was my favorite. That's a hard enough truth to hear in a family where none of the children are adopted, but in a family where there are adoptees? It confirms what they had always wondered.

The comment ate at Jane, for it was irrefutable proof that the mother she grew up with did not love her or her cherished older adopted brother in the same way Ann loved the children she bore. An unfortunate comment, yes, but we humans are always coming up short. Parents and grandparents, aunts and uncles in unbroken families don't intend to choose a favorite, but it happens, usually without the chosen one having done anything deserving. The roll of genetically coded dice has seen to it that this one will closely resemble a parent or a grandparent in face, physique, faculties, and personal quirks, and there you have it. What was regrettable was that Ann gave voice to her feelings. And all her children heard it.

In Jane's case, Ann's admission was especially hurtful because it came was on the heels of the Rhymers not automatically offering to pay Jane's airfare so that she could attend her brother's funeral. Jane lets on that her distress gave way to proving that she was a good daughter, worthy of Ann's love, and since Ann seemed to vary between deep dislike of me and toleration—well, she, Jane, would show her how little I mattered. How to do that? Ignore me, as if I, too, had skied off a cliff. Maybe Ann would love her more then. Irrational, right? Feelings by their very nature are irrational. They come out of our deepest needs, they rule when we want them to obey logic, and yet there is no logical explanation. Feelings simply are.

Jane once told me, "If I move close to you, then I have to move away from the other. I feel like a magnet torn between two poles."

It ain't easy being adopted.

Not long ago, I came across these wise words at a blog called *Fugitivus*, written by an adoptee using the pseudonym Harriet J:

> Everything About Adoption Hurts
>
> This is not to say that everything about adoption is *wrong*, but everything about adoption is *painful*. For our modern, legal concept of adoption to exist, families must be broken. Adoption is not, and can never be, a best-case scenario. It relies upon the worst-case situation having already come to fruition. From there, you're working with *what is* instead of what *should be*. That *should be* will never go away. For the entire lifetime of everybody involved in adoption, that *should be* exists, and it hurts. *What is* can still turn out to be wonderful, beautiful, incredible, but *what is* will never be what *should be*. It is that *should be* that necessitates education, sensitivity, and trigger warnings, because it never goes away.[133]

---

[133] Harriet J [pseud.], "Adoption Sometimes Gets All Fucked-Up, 101," *Fugitivus* (blog), Apr. 20, 2010, https://web.archive.org/web/20110305202911/http://www.fugitivus.net/2010/04/20/adoption-sometimes-gets-all-fucked-up-101/.

31 End Game

FEBRUARY 2007—It is Kimberly's fifteenth birthday, and she and I are having a shopping transfusion. I'm blowing through money for her birthday, Jane and Bob are wending their way up to the top of the Empire State Building, and Tony is in a coffee shop around the corner reading the *Times*. Manhattan is in the middle of an arctic freeze, but the city is particularly crowded today because this is Presidents' Day weekend, and tourists are everywhere. It's windy, yes, and hovering around two degrees Fahrenheit. The sun may be out, but we are freezing when we poke our noses outdoors.

My daughter and her family are visiting, and she is proudly showing Bob the sights. Later at Macy's, where Jane says we must go—our first shopping excursion was there, she reminds me—Kimberly gets funky tennis shoes and Jane buys a purse cool enough for her to be asked, where did you get that? so she can say, New York. Manhattan. Tony and Bob park themselves at Starbucks on the mezzanine, while Kimberly, Jane, and I have the run of the store.

Jane is in her fourth semester at a community college and doing well. When her employer, the Lutheran Home, was sold, the new owners fired everyone and offered some of them their old jobs back at lower wages. Jane either rejected the job or wasn't offered it, but whatever happened, she was able to turn misfortune into opportunity.

The State of Wisconsin was flush enough then to pay her tuition at a junior college where she could be trained for a different line of work. My daughter was off to the races! She enrolled in a business-management program at a technical college in Madison. She joined Toastmasters. She got A's and B's in her courses. A year later, she was in great spirits. Suicide was never mentioned. It mattered not that she drove seventy miles each way to school several times a week and sometimes at night. What counted was that she was a college student, not that numbskull in the hockey helmet.

We spoke often, emailed daily. She talked about her courses in economics, human resources, accounting. Because one of her teachers suggested it, she took to reading *The Economist*. She talked about current political issues along with what's for dinner. She asked me to correct her papers for grammar, as that had been taught when she was the unhappy kid faking seizures and missing school. That kid was long gone. That kid was picking up grammar rules on the fly. For Christmas she asked for a copy of *Bartlett's Familiar Quotations*, the better to bolster her Toastmaster speeches; I remembered asking my mother for a *Roget's Thesaurus* for Christmas one year.

Jane and Bob had moved to a comfortable three-bedroom house in Reedsburg, population ten thousand, and Kimberly joined them full-time before ninth grade began. Jane spoke enthusiastically about the nearly new Oldsmobile that Bob bought for her drive to Madison. It cost seven thousand, and I am going to make that money back because I'll be able to get a good job once I graduate, she said. Once I graduate. She had so much riding on that scheme, namely the good job she would get once she graduated. It would cancel all the years toiling at lowly jobs. She would show everyone. She had found her groove.

Over that long weekend, Bob, Jane, and I drive to the lighthouse at Montauk, take pictures at a scenic overlook with the ocean in the background, everybody wrapped up in copious scarves and puffy jackets. We stop for steaming bowls of chowder at the Shagwong, a joint in Montauk where a sign in the window advertises for a piano player who also "must know how to shuck clams." After dinner, three nights out of four Jane and Bob walk around the corner to her pub of choice, Murph's, for beers and darts. They are in a couples' darts league back home and brought their own set of implements with them. They're not our best set, Jane says. We'll leave them here. For next time. Next time, Bob will go ocean fishing. Next time. I will never get over liking the way that sounds. Next time. Everything seems so incredibly normal—even her mood shift one morning.

Sitting at the dining room table, she glares at me, at her cup of coffee, at anybody who walks by. What's wrong? I ask. My period is due in a couple of days, she says. No further explanation needed. I'd talked to Jane so many times about PMS and progesterone, I do not bother today. I simply nod and take Kimberly to T. J. Maxx.

Adoption, one way or another, comes up, but only briefly. One afternoon, quite determinedly, Jane tells me never to bring up Sarah.

Right, I say. Won't bring up Sarah.

Don't call me on her birthday, she adds. Patrick's daughter, I think. Patrick, who said *Don't cry, please don't cry* as we left Jane behind four decades earlier. Now his daughter says, Don't bring up Sarah. I ask that if Sarah ever contacts her, she would give her my address and let her know I'd like to meet her. But as I ask, I know that Jane will agree only to end the conversation. My request is futile. I do wonder about my missing granddaughter, but not in the same intense way that I mourned the loss of my daughter. I'd like to know her, but I do not wonder about her whenever I see someone who could be her. Mostly when I think about her birthday, I am anxious for my daughter, recalling how fraught Jane's birthdays were for me.

As for Patrick's other children, Jane tells me she has given up the idea of contacting them. The first three were undoubtedly lost, she assumed, due to their own unconcern and Colleen's unflagging resentment, which I had told her about. Though I sent Patrick's widow Christmas cards for a couple of years after he died and sent a few pictures of Jane's wedding, nothing ever came in return. A phone message I'd once left went unanswered. Clearly what had once seemed like a good idea to her no longer did. That was enough for Jane: I don't need any more rejection, she says. Yet I know how she would have flourished if any of her siblings had reached out to her.

We say goodbye at the airport with warm hugs. I snap a photograph of the three of them—Jane is looking straight into the camera, smiling broadly. She is in a good place, we are in a good place, and there is peace in my heart. Maybe it will be like this from now on.

On my computer I watch Jane graduate with honors, and I send her three stackable gold rings that had been my mother's. She loves the rings, she says, because they are something of my mother's, something with her history in them. She has them sized to fit. She is confident—hell, she is glowing with optimism—and the quest for a good job becomes her Holy Grail. Certainly, now she can get something that has some responsibility. Certainly, whatever she gets will be better than fast food service. Certainly, she will gain in status. Certainly. While she is looking for a job, she signs up for an online college course in writing by women. Now we have literary discussions about Willa Cather and Zora Neale Hurston. The teacher encourages her to go on with her studies and get a bachelor's degree. My girl, she's flying.

One day I pick up the phone and hear a sobbing Jane say *Tell me that you love me!*, a request elicited because of something Ann had said—that she never loved Jane. Surely said in a moment of anger, I thought. Surely the woman did not mean it.

Yes, she lives near Ann, yes, Ann is Mom, but she is also a mother Jane has to prove herself to over and over. I understand, up to a point, but I am tired of being the sympathetic mother whose feelings never matter. I want to shout, Jane, look at the way you treat me—I know I gave you up for adoption forty years ago, but can I ever expect to be treated better than the way you treat me now? Like you would treat anyone else? How long is this going to go on? I know being adopted sucks—even with the best parents in the world—but can we ever get past dumping on me? Ann says terrible things to you, and you call me up for sympathy, which I give you, but the minute we hit a speed bump—and sometimes they have nothing to do with me—you are gone! For months, nearly a year! Sometimes I do nothing and *poof!* you are gone. Do I always have to put up with behavior that is irrational and hurtful? Are you always going to glom onto any possible reason to treat me badly, to walk away, just to show me that you can?

I say none of that. Nor do I tell her that on more than one occasion Ann has told me that if Jane and Bob get divorced, she'll take Bob. Hearing this has always reminded me of the vast difference between *I love you as much as if you were born to me* and the opposite, which goes without saying. Does she imagine that in divorce mothers and fathers, like non-related friends, divide the couple into a "friend" and "not friend anymore" list? I stuff down my surprise and sorrow thinking how disposable Jane really is to her. If she could have gotten a refund for Jane, she would have. But what is there to say? I am silent.

I am solicitous of Jane's feelings. If I want a relationship with her, I must accept the vast difference between what is expected of me and what Ann can get away with. My job is to pick up the pieces. Oh, honey, I say as she weeps and as I try to soothe her.

They make up within the week.

Live fast, die young, be a good-looking corpse, a joke.

I admit I'd gotten somewhat numb about Jane saying it, because I'd heard it often enough—never at a time when she seemed down, but just as an offhand comment. I knew she liked to shock, and I put it down to that. I wasn't aware of any research that connected adoption with suicide, or epilepsy with suicide, and so I let it go. And I had thought about it so often myself and didn't feel that the topic was or should be verboten. I knew that one of my father's sisters had committed suicide before I was born, but I didn't know much about it, just that it involved an oven with the gas on. Aunt Jean had told me once that her younger sister used to say that she would never be an old woman, that if they passed an old woman on the street, her sister would say, I'm never going to be like that. Oh, come on, Jean would say, but her sister could not be deterred. Jean unwittingly had stored the comment in her memory bank. Jane knew this story, all of it. It was part of my background. Hers too.

Like the aunt I never knew, Jane was on the same path. A part of me knew that, even then—you had to be oblivious to not sense what was coming—but I didn't want to know it, not completely, like the wife who suspects her husband is having an affair but ignores the scent of the strange perfume on his shirt and the ten pounds he's quickly taken off. If Jane was determined to take her own life, no one could stop her. I could talk her out of a black mood one day, but I couldn't be there every second of every day or hire a bodyguard to stay with her twenty-four seven or make the sun not come up because I willed it.

Psychologists say that trauma is embedded in the body and stays with us always. She was married to a good man, she lived in a snug house at the edge of Reedsburg, she had a cute daughter on the honor roll. On a day-to-day basis, Jane appeared to be coping quite well. She accepted her seizures, the way one does arthritis. Her sense of being abandoned seemed to be in recession. She never talked of the child she gave up for adoption, and I did not bring her up.

But a good job does not materialize—not at the nearby home office of Lands' End, not at the real estate office that needed an office manager, not at the small company she briefly did the books for, not in the school district—all places that had openings. Her college experience and Toastmaster involvement gave her some confidence and polish, but she folded under pressure, and years of social ineptness caused by the seizures had left their mark. She sometimes told new acquaintances about her surprising connection to the Hamptons, the famous writers she had met, and I knew she had to be turning off her listeners in Wisconsin with the speed of sound. But pointing this out to her was too big a risk. I listened.

The failure to get what she considered a decent job, after two years of community college, would be the final blow. Her trauma was all there, lurking beneath her skin, a sleeper cell waiting for a signal, just waiting. With her self-esteem on a downward spiral and her PMS on an upward path—it does worsen with age until menopause—she was getting closer to triggering that signal.

Yet I did not, could not, acknowledge what I sensed: Jane would never suffer from the family arthritis, her mind would never grow feeble, she would be that good-looking corpse.

However, she is not yet down for the count and in the process does something quite magnificent. She plans a benefit for the Madison chapter of the Epilepsy Foundation. She gets scant guidance from the foundation; execution is totally up to her. The benefit will be a mixed-doubles darts tournament. She gets the local tavern to host the event; she gets more than a dozen merchants to donate items for a silent auction and the Budweiser distributor to pay for posters advertising the event. She asks me to write up the press releases for the local newspapers and radio stations, and she places them herself in the local media. She even gets a football signed by many of Wisconsin's beloved Green Bay Packers for the auction. Tony and I, along with the Rhymers, ante up for a fancy set of poker chips and a fifth of fine whiskey for a raffle prize. Representatives from the Epilepsy Foundation come up from Madison on the day for the event, but Jane has managed the whole kit and caboodle, down to the last detail. The tournament raises nearly $1,500. I speak to her in the middle of the event to bid on flowers from the local florist, thinking to have them sent to her. She is already planning next year's event. Not enough people showed up, she says, I would have done better if I had not made it a mixed-doubles tournament, so I'll make it an open tournament next year, no partners needed. I'll make more money next year.

Next year. Maybe everything is going to be all right.

A month later she is hired to work at a resort in Wisconsin Dells, a half hour away from Reedsburg. Hired to work the front desk, the first step in management. She is immensely pleased. Yet when she is not promoted from answering phones to checking people in, while others hired after her are, I worry. She tells me of regaling the manager with her familiarity with the Hamptons. I wince. She says she had to take her epilepsy medicine during dinner hour. To avoid an upset stomach, she has to take it with food, and the chef is not pleased: It's dinner hour, for god's sake! We're busy and you need something to eat? Someone who has epilepsy works in the pro shop, Jane adds, and her coworkers make fun of him. They say he is slow. The enthusiasm in her voice flags. I want to tell her to walk away before she is fired, to decide that the travel is too taxing, the hours too changeable, but I know nothing will deter her. Tomorrow will be a better day. She can't quit. Quitting is admitting defeat, that she can't get a job worthy of her intelligence.

She lasts five weeks. When she calls to tell me she has been let go—"It's off-season" is the reason, but another hired after her stays on—she is sobbing so hard I cannot understand her at first. What she finally chokes out is *I can't do this anymore, I can't get another job and get fired again, I can't do it anymore.*

She might get good grades in college, despite the epilepsy, despite the drugs that slowed down her brain and lowered IQ, despite everything, but to what end? She has so much riding on that degree—it would be the ticket to all she hoped for—and she so desperately needs to feel good about herself. To be able to show everyone that she is a person who is capable of doing smart things. To be able to be proud of herself. To contribute to the family income, like she had promised Bob she would. You wait and see what I can do, she had said. Now it was obvious none of that would be possible.

I suggest she write a piece about the benefit for an epilepsy website a friend of mine runs, and so she does. She watches afternoon television, specifically, *Who Wants to Be a Millionaire?*

Why, that was the ticket! She could answer a lot of the simple questions, she could get up to, say, five thousand dollars and she'd use Tony—who is full of arcane information—as her Phone-A-Friend lifeline! What could be simpler? Great!

What's the worst that can happen? she asks. I'll get to see you and maybe make a few thousand dollars! Great, I say. Her glass is half full. She tells me she can register online. I caution that there is one weekend I will be in Michigan. I hadn't visited my brothers in a couple of years, one of my nieces is graduating from high school, and the ticket is bought and paid for. It's the only time in May, June, or July when I won't be in Sag—come any other time, I said, but not those five days. Okay?

A week later, *Millionaire* confirms her application. She calls me with the news: she has a tryout scheduled, and she's already purchased a nonrefundable ticket, she says excitedly.

When? I ask.

It is precisely when I will be in Detroit, the date of my niece's graduation. The *Millionaire* website advertises tryouts several times a week, week after week. Coordinating the tryout with my schedule would have been no problem.

I cannot share her glee.

Didn't you see how often they are? I ask. You are coming to New York the one time in the entire year I am going to be away! How do you expect me to react? I'm frustrated and disappointed. Yet my words are not harsh. What would be the point? Tony and I were walking out of the house when she called, so our conversation is curtailed.

Since nothing I say convinces her to change her plans, I email her a few days later and explain why I am hurt. Now I am resigned, and anyway, I want her to do well. She'll come. I'll be in Detroit. Yes, I could have canceled my trip, but my brother and his family, and especially my niece, are expecting me. My niece's graduation, and the family celebration, cannot be moved to another weekend; the tryout for *Millionaire* could be. What I can't dislodge from my mind is how little I matter to her. She's coming to New York, and this will be the very first time in the two decades we've known each other that she would actually pay for her own ticket. One does get weary of being a doormat.

My apologetic emails—three—go unanswered. When I call, I get the answering machine. Since she is not working, I imagine she is sitting there listening as I leave a message. She does not call back.

I fly to Detroit on the very same day Jane flies into New York. She is staying with our friend Arthur at his place in Manhattan. Two days later, I call from Detroit. The answering machine answers. She does not have a cell phone. No one calls back.

Once I am back home, Arthur relays that there had been hundreds of people trying out for the show at the same time, and while she came close, she did not pass the written test. She was quite crushed, he relates, embarrassed, too. I tried to talk her into calling you, he adds, but no go.

I email her again—apologize again, and ask, Okay, can we move on? I phone, but their number is now unlisted. I email again. No response. A month later when my friend emails to say my daughter's piece for the epilepsy website is up, I cannot even share in what I know must be her joy in seeing her words published online with her photo. I can't even tell her how proud I am.

I have flown into the dead zone all over again.

June becomes July becomes August. Kimberly does not have her own email address, or one I know about, and a letter I send her—I do not men-

tion the silence from her mother—comes back with a red stamp on it:
REFUSED. Now Jane has the power not only to cut me out of her life but to
take Kimberly with her. Arthur says she emails him regularly with jokes and
news. At first Arthur keeps me informed, but hearing about her secondhand
is more upsetting than no news at all. I ask him to stop.

Tony suggests I look upon this all-too-familiar retreat as a vacation. I
know what he means, but being walled out feels far from a holiday. At the
acupuncturist, where I've gone for relief of tension in my back, I weep profusely. Summer becomes fall.

In mid-September I answer the phone one afternoon. It is her. "How are
you?" we say in unison, as if we are reading cue cards.

Once more, we pick up like we had never had a break. What we do
not mention is her trip east, the disappointing *Millionaire* cattle call, why
she stopped talking to me, or my unanswered emails. A few phone calls later, I calmly inquire why their number changed. She replies because she had
"signed up for some job on the internet, and now they are being bugged"
incessantly with phone calls. Uh-huh, I say, wondering if this has a shred of
truth to it. I couldn't help comparing the long weeks of silence with the speed
of her reconciliations with Ann. So it goes, I tell myself. So it will always be.
I will always be on trial, and my offense could be something as small as a
mental hangnail. I have no right to be irritated! With anything!

Jane tells me that during the summer she had trouble sleeping and took
Tylenol PM, but when two did not help, she took two more, and two more,
and still she couldn't sleep, and so it got up to a dozen pills a day. She says she
had not really slept for twelve days and ended up in the hospital with liver
toxicity from the Tylenol that almost killed her. She was taken off all medications, including her epilepsy drugs, to let her liver recover. She was in the
hospital for a week. Hadn't Arthur told me? she wants to know. No.

When I ask Arthur about this, he replies that this is all news to him.
Maybe she had forgotten that she had *not* told him, but this incident is no
fabrication, for the episode with Tylenol led her to a therapist. He prescribed
antidepressants. She tells me they make her feel better. I am concerned about
the combination of drugs—now she is taking some kind of stabilizers for her

mood and depressants for her seizures. But the therapist prescribed the drugs, therefore it must be okay, she says, and so antidepressants she is going to take, along with Depakote.

For the next couple of months, we enjoy an intimacy that seems clear and bright. In emails, she writes about being adopted, about feeling especially close to me and Tony and my family, saying that we are her true family. She writes that she looks forward to an email from me every morning. I feel the same about hers and always read them first. We speak a couple times a week, sometimes a couple times a day. It is as if after a long, dark winter, we have found our spring.

Then.

One Saturday morning in October, she calls and relates a story about Bob that doesn't make a lot of sense, but I listen and commiserate, even though I seriously doubt that Bob has committed an indiscretion with the tattooed lady in the leather vest on the day of their wedding. There are improbable details— Bob disappearing the afternoon of the wedding after we and everybody else had gone, and Jane supposedly sitting there with an uncle until Bob finally showed up—that seems crazy, but who am I to check? How would I? So I let her talk. And talk. I'd heard stories about Bob before that did not make a lot of sense. She says she has ripped up all the wedding pictures. She recounts how she could not get a job. She talks about suing the resort for letting her go, blaming the epilepsy. And she weeps profusely, great hulking sobs at times.

When are you having your period? I ask.

Couple of days.

Once again, I go over the PMS possibility—my mother had it until menopause, I had it, why not you—and the painless hormone remedy. Tell her how I'd felt like that. Repeat how it gets worse as women get older, tell her how progesterone saved my marriage and maybe my life. Tell her there were no known side effects to progesterone for people like us. Okay, Jane says, I'll go see a doctor and get a prescription. Promise. This time I'll do it.

She makes the appointment with her physician, but it is not until ten days hence. By the day it rolls around, she is in a good mood. She cancels the appointment. Four weeks later, she is in the same snake pit.

Try the damn progesterone! I say.

Okay, she says. This time she insists the doctor see her immediately.

Whew! I think. Maybe she will really do it.

She gets the prescription, but then she has to go to Madison to get the progesterone; the local pharmacy doesn't carry it. She gets her period and puts off the trip. She'll get it the next time she's in Madison.

Four weeks later, Jane calls on a Saturday in early December and again spews a long, complicated story about Bob. Having an affair. She is very specific about details. Even though I keep trying to poke holes in her story, she fills each improbability with yet another fantastic detail, obvious fabrications stacking up like cans in a grocery store. She is bawling the whole time. She goes on for an hour. Tony wants to know what's up. I tell him.

She calls back two hours later, only, it seems, to find out if I'd told Tony. Yes.

Oh. What did he say? she wants to know. Not much, I say. Her tone now has the mild buzz of added distress. We talk for twenty minutes or so. I know that saying Tony knows about the last conversation disturbs her.

She calls back again a couple of hours later, now crying—sobbing, actually—tells me that she loves me—loves us, loves my family—and wishes me a Merry Christmas. It's early December.

Should I call the police? I ask immediately, telegraphing my alarm. What are you planning to do? Where is Kimberly? I ask.

Outside shoveling snow.

And Bob?

Bob hasn't come home yet.

I'm all right, she says now, immediately pulling herself together. I'm not going to do anything.

Anything does not need an explanation.

It's before your period, right? I ask.

Yeah, but—

Do you have the progesterone?

Yeah.

Have you taken it?

No.

Take it! Will you get off the phone right now and take it now?

She does.

Tony walks by and says, What's going on?

Jane, I say, Jane, holding my hand over the receiver so she doesn't hear. He nods. Jane and I talk another ten minutes. She assures me that she is all right. Not to worry.

She calls an hour later, now from a bar, noise in the background, and she says, yes, she has taken the progesterone and is feeling much better. She says she is having an O'Doul's. Okay, good, I think, nonalcoholic. She sounds normal. Now we talk about her efforts to get a job for the Christmas holiday, even though it is already December 8. I suggest that maybe she could start a business that does errands for people—grocery shopping, cleaning out closets, packing for a move, taking kids to soccer games when the parents could not. I believe that she could handle such a business by herself, just as she had the epilepsy benefit. We toy with various names for the business: Lend-A-Hand. Off-Your-List. No-Job-2-Small.

I call her the next day. She sounds actually surprised to hear from me, says she's talked to Bob about the new venture, and she's planning to invest in a couple of small display ads in the local newspaper.

Sounds like a plan, I say, wondering if this is true. She says nothing about Bob's supposed affair. I assume the subject would never come up again until she needed something to have a reason to—what? Keep me on the phone? Invent a reason for her meltdown? She is so goddamned calm, you would not believe it was the same woman I spoke to the day before if you hadn't been through this emotional riptide yourself.

Sunday evening, she emails me a chatty note about having finished addressing her Christmas cards, how she and Bob are going green for Christmas and wrapping all their presents in newspaper, and how her Christmas shopping is almost done. She includes some amusing photos of squirrels.

On Monday she emails that she is upset that the Detroit Lions did not beat Dallas—as Detroit is her second-favorite team after Green Bay since she felt some allegiance to my hometown team. And she adds, "Darts tonight—we are going to get our ass kicked. Playing the number one team in the league."

On Tuesday, she emails again:

> I would of emailed you this morning but have had trouble with my computer. I and the family are fine. I am still upset Detroit did not beat Dallas. Today I cleaned the house and so forth. Baking chicken right now. Bob is outside plowing snow. Yes, we got more. I think we have had about 19 inches this month everyone is getting tired of it and the roads are bad. We lost Monday in darts all 13 games but we played a much better team. They are first or second I am not sure. Next week we will be beat again. We may take some games though. Not much else to say.
>
> Jane

Wednesday:

> Good morning up early today and plan to get a good start on my day with a nice long bath then some writing. CCD [Catholic Christian Doctrine, the catechism classes that Kimberly attends weekly] is tonight then parent teacher conference tomorrow. Friday we may go to a dart tourney. I am hoping I get a good partner. Made chicken and rice last night for dinner boy it was good. Campbells does great things for dinner. Tonight it will be something simple. I see Oprah is campaigning for Obama.
>
> Love,
> Jane

Late that night, the phone rings.

32 Peace at Last

DECEMBER 12, 2007—It's twenty to midnight. I am upstairs, Tony downstairs. We both pick up the phone. It's late, something is wrong, but I answer before my mind runs to her. It is Bob.

"Bob? Is that you? What's wrong?"

"Uh—I, I don't know how to say this, but Jane—Jane took a pistol and killed herself sometime today."

Live fast, die young, be a good-looking corpse.

"Oh my god. What are you saying, are you saying that—"

Faint stars dance in front of my eyes, and the world turns black and white. There is a moment of shock when you hear the words—you understand the words, but you don't yet want to accept their reality. But that comes in a nanosecond. She finally did it. She is at peace at last. She wanted this, and she succeeded. No more pain, no more grief, no more seizures, drugs, PMS. No more craziness, no more days of crippling sadness, no more—my baby is at last at peace.

"What happened?"

"She pried open my gun cabinet sometime today—I carry the only key with me—and took my pistol." Neither of us is crying. "When I got home from work there was a note in her printer," he continues, "and I immediately went to the police, and they went looking for her and found her about two miles from home. In her car." His voice is both edgy and eerily calm.

I am sitting at my big, cluttered desk where I usually talk to Jane, where I have heard her misery pour out in the last week. I am not thinking how much

I will miss her yet, what this means to Kimberly, or Bob, or Ann and Gary—all I am thinking is that my daughter, my complicated, troubled, sad daughter, is finally free from her demons. She has the peace she could not find living. My own sadness is suspended as if trapped in gel. I am shocked, yes, but I am not surprised. This is a day that was a long time coming, that already has the feel of inevitability. I will cry later, but now I sense only her relief.

The lighting in my office is full spectrum, replicating sunlight, and usually it makes me feel good, but that night it seems inappropriate and intrusive, highlighting the spiky leaves of an overgrown snake plant against the midnight window, the organized chaos on my desk. I am adjusting to the light, to the news, and now Tony is on the downstairs phone, saying words, any words, filling up the space. Oh god, she did it, yes, I understand everything all at once.

I picture her slumped over the front seat in the Oldsmobile she was so proud of once. Then, it was the vehicle of hope. Now it is her hearse.

Tony and I leave for Wisconsin on Thursday. We check into the same hotel we stayed in at the wedding. What had once seemed comfortable is now dark, gloomy, in need of a renovation, the strong odor of chlorine from the pool pervasive in the hallway.

I've never seen Jane's and Bob's house in Reedsburg. Bob shows us around, proud of the house Jane and he bought together. It's a compact ranch on a quiet street on the outskirts of town. Jane has turned one bedroom into her office. There's a three-car garage and a partly finished basement where they played darts in the evening. This is where we used to spend a lot of time, Bob says stoically. I'll miss her. I notice the red stoneware dishes I'd sent them the year before. Our Christmas card is taped to the wall in the living room. Bob pulls out a pair of shoes he'd ordered for Jane from Lands' End for Christmas, as Kimberly had told him that when they had visited in February Jane had borrowed a pair of brown suede loafers from me.

You did good, I say flatly, willing myself not to tear up. Who will one day wear them? I wonder. They are not Kimberly's size.

Bob has set up the new coffee table that would have been part of his Christmas surprise, and on it is the photography book with big glossy photographs of the United States that I sent them for Christmas. It has a great shot of the lighthouse at Montauk. Tucked inside is a metal bookmark with this quote on it: *Other things may change us, but we begin and end with family— Anthony Brandt.* It's a quote from a piece Tony wrote more than a decade earlier for *Esquire* magazine,[134] and the quote is all over the internet, on greeting cards, quote-of-the-day calendars, and this year on Hallmark tchotchkes. We begin and end with family. I stare at the words and the pictures in the book.

Bob carries the note Jane left in his breast pocket. It is a will of sorts, dispensing her books, her collections of coffee mugs and lighthouses. She's left me some of her autographed books. Later that night, the next night, or the night after that—the days run together like water from a faucet—we bump into Jane's cousin, the one who'd been friendly at the wedding. She's a bartender at our hotel. Another night, we meet a former pro baseball player, and he gives us an autographed photograph of himself. To distract ourselves, Tony and I go to the movies. Tony and Bob watch football on television while I take Kimberly shopping for an outfit for the funeral. We also buy a pair of high-heeled satin pumps for an upcoming dance at school. Even in the darkest moments, a healthy heart knows it must go on.

Kimberly says that before she left for school, Jane told her, No matter what happens, remember that I love you.

We are all sad, but no one asks, Why did she do it?

I know that so much about her life was leading up to this. The repeated attempts, the frequency with which she talked about suicide, the questions she asked that I could not answer about my aunt who committed suicide, the emotional spiral that folded its thick, heavy arms around her for a week or so every month. This end was foretold, and she was not going to let anyone—or anything like a locked gun cabinet—stop her.

In her small, cluttered office I sense Jane's presence the most. Kimberly and I look over the room together. It is here that Jane did her college work,

---

[134] Anthony Brandt, "Bloodlines," *Esquire*, Sept. 1, 1984, 21–22.

where she spoke on the phone, where she wrote up her résumé after college, where she applied to *Who Wants to Be a Millionaire?* The wedding photographs are intact, not ripped up. I see the fat, half-burned candles. Her desk is an old one, the kind that has a pull-out extension for a typewriter. For some reason, Kimberly pulls out the extension. Taped to it are two black-and-white snapshots of baby Sarah. Kimberly—who knew about Sarah in the abstract—is surprised. Her mother never talked about Sarah, Kimberly says.

Jane might not have wanted to talk about her first daughter or had the strength to search for her, but she had not forgotten her. The proof was in the baby pictures, right where she, Sarah's mother, could privately look at them as often as she chose.

I am not surprised.

The wake at the funeral parlor is Sunday night; the funeral, the next day. Don, my nephew from Tampa, flies in; my brother Tom drives from Detroit with his wife and daughters; my older brother Richard plans to fly in from Florida, but flu keeps him home. He sends flowers and so does his ex-wife. Among the family photographs set up at the funeral parlor, someone—either the Rhymers or Bob—has placed the studio portrait of four generations of my family taken when Kimberly was three and she and Jane came to Detroit: my mother, Jane, Kimberly, and me. Jane is smiling, her hair is shining, and she is staring straight at the camera. None of her troubles are evident. She looks like she belongs. My mother is smiling at Kimberly. My nephew Don hears a woman ask, *What is that?* when she examines the photograph. Her tone is obviously disapproving of whatever *that* is.

Don is undeterred. He points to the photograph and explains, This is my grandmother, this is my cousin, this is my cousin's daughter Kimberly, and this is my aunt Lorraine. The couple say nothing but look askance and move on. The woman, Don reports, clearly does not approve of the photograph, of Don, of me, of us. But there it is, Jane's double life on display.

Ann and I stand, for a long moment, shoulder to shoulder, in front of our daughter's open casket and agree: no more demons, no more torment, no more tears. "You really loved her," Ann whispers. "I know that you did." The time for frustration and rancor over, now we grieve together.

Both of us are thinking, I am sure, that we could have done more. Done better. Done something.

Ann says, "She is at peace at last."

I nod in agreement. *Live fast, die young, be a good-looking corpse* flickers through my brain, but I do not say the words.

Ann tells me about the first time Jane had a seizure. Ann was in the hospital having her firstborn, the son who has already died. She tells me how there had been no sign of trouble—no seizures—before that, how Jane was a bright little girl who learned her ABCs early.

Sometime during the long hours of that evening, a few of Jane's acquaintances from Toastmasters approach me. "Are you Jane's biological mother?" one woman asks. Her manner is open, friendly. She is not going to throw stones. I like that she had not used the supposedly more PC term of *birth mother*—that adoption-agency-approved wording that makes it sound like our connection begins and ends at birth. I like that she says it straight: biological mother. In a roomful of friends and family of the adoptive mother, the woman does have to distinguish me as somehow different from Jane's other mother, and *biological* says it all. For more than birth, for all time: her biological mother.

She spoke of you often, the woman says. She was so proud of you. The woman introduces me to the others with her, including the mayor, who also knew Jane from Toastmasters. Everyone is pleasant, accepting, pleased to meet me. That moment is a gift.

Later still, I sit and weep with Sue, Jane's best friend, who is bereft and whom I had met on an earlier visit, but I spend a lot of time sitting alone or with Tony, Tom, or Don. We are the other family. Jane's adopted brother is not there, but he will arrive in time for the funeral in the morning. I meet a friend of Jane's from Madison, and it turns out that between the endless stream of phone calls to me on the fateful Saturday, she was calling this friend with the same woeful tale of Bob's imaginary betrayal.

I had chosen not to tell Bob, but she does, and I chime in and say, *This is the same story I heard that day.*

Bob is stunned. He does not need to say that Jane's story is all made up.

The funeral is the next morning at Holy Family Church, and once again at a ritual of our daughter's, I sit next to Ann. The priest who married Jane officiates. In a voice as dry as dust, Gary says a few words about how Jane changed after her first seizure and the hockey helmet that would follow. Kimberly, a few months shy of sixteen, reads a psalm in a strong, clear voice. She is wise well beyond her years. Jane is to be cremated. Sometime during the reception at the church afterward, I feel someone staring at me. My eyes search the room and find Jane's older brother, the adopted brother, who flew in from the west, looking my way. I simply nod. He nods back.

There is nothing to say.

Later, from Gary, who called the Epilepsy Foundation in Madison to tell them what happened, I hear that the news was met with, *She lasted longer than most.*

Figure 18. Together in Michigan. My mother, Jane, Kimberly and Lorraine, 1995.

Epilepsy, Adoption, Pharmaceuticals, and Suicide

A few days after the first anniversary of my daughter's suicide, in December of 2008, the Food and Drug Administration announced that it would require makers of epilepsy drugs to add a warning about the increased risk of suicidal thoughts and "behaviors" to the products' prescribing information or labeling.

"Behaviors," I assume, means suicide attempts, some of them successful. Depakote, the drug Jane took, is on the list. The FDA action was based on the agency's review of 199 clinical trials of eleven epilepsy drugs—released only a month after her death—showing that patients taking those drugs had almost twice the risk of suicidal behavior or thoughts than those taking a placebo. But what was not answered was this: Had the epileptics taking the placebo had their lives upended by as many seizures, great and small, as my daughter had? I mentally add in the cocktail of drugs—an antidepressant and Depakote—that Jane was taking. What about that? And what about the adoption?

While there are no good statistics on adoptees who actually commit suicide, research on adopted populations shows that a disproportionate number are likely to. No matter how you slice the numbers, adoption increases the probability of suicide, no matter how many adoptees never have a thought of it, no matter how many adoptees are successful, smart, and may one day end up on the Supreme Court. It is unlikely there will ever be good statistics on how many adoptees commit suicide because "adopted" is not noted on death certificates.

What we do know is that more adoptees than non-adoptees think about suicide quite often. Google "suicide and adoption" and what pops up is an entry from the medical journal *Pediatrics*, "Adoption as a Risk Factor for Attempted Suicide during Adolescence." That study unequivocally states, "Attempted suicide is more common among adolescents who live with adoptive parents than among adolescents who live with biological parents." The connection between adoption and suicide persisted even after the researchers adjusted for depression, aggression, and impulsive behavior. Not surprisingly, "family connectedness," whether among the adopted or non-adopted, did decrease the likelihood of suicide attempts.[135]

Researchers at the University of Minnesota reported that adopted teens were almost four times more likely to attempt suicide than those who lived with their natural parents, even after adjustment for factors associated with suicidal behavior, such as psychiatric disorder symptoms, personality traits, family environment, and academic disengagement. Girls were more likely than boys to attempt suicide. About 75 percent of the adopted teens in the study (more than 1,200, all living in Minnesota) were adopted before the age of two and were foreign born—mostly from South Korea.[136] This deep dive into suicide and adoption followed a study by the lead researcher and others who concluded that being adopted approximately doubled the odds of having a disruptive behavior disorder and having contact with a mental health professional. Interestingly, international adoptees were less likely to exhibit behavior disorders.[137]

One of the more striking findings of this study was that the researchers found only a small discrepancy between the adoptee and non-adopted populations in actual disruptive or otherwise-troubling behavior, but that difference approximately doubled the odds of how frequently the adoptees were referred to mental health professionals. The authors granted that adoptive parents were more willing to seek professional help due to finances, education, and previous interaction with the gamut of therapists, social workers, and psychiatrists but also added this telling footnote: "The parent of an adopted child may have a lower threshold than the parent of a non-adopted

---

[135] Gail Slap, Elizabeth Goodman, and Bin Huang, "Adoption as a Risk Factor for Attempted Suicide during Adolescence," *Pediatrics* 108, no. 2 (Aug. 2001): e30, https://doi.org/10.1542/peds.108.2.e30. See also Arline Kaplan, "Adoption and Mental Illness," *Psychiatric Times,* Jan. 26, 2009. https://web.archive.org/web/20230110204141/https://www.psychiatrictimes.com/view/adoption-and-mental-illness.

[136] Margaret A. Keyes et al., "Risk of Suicide Attempt in Adopted and Nonadopted Offspring," *Pediatrics* 132, no. 4 (Oct. 2013): 639–46, https://web.archive.org/web/20220825231015/https://publications.aap.org/pediatrics/article-abstract/132/4/639/64833/Risk-of-Suicide-Attempt-in-Adopted-and-Nonadopted?redirectedFrom=fulltext.

[137] Margaret A. Keyes et al., "The Mental Health of US Adolescents Adopted in Infancy," *Archives of Pediatrics & Adolescent Medicine* 162, no. 5 (May 2008): 419–26, https://jamanetwork.com/journals/jamapediatrics/fullarticle/379446.

child for reporting a behavior as problematic."[138] In other words, while a natural parent might recognize the troubling tendency, understand and reprimand, forgive and move on, adoptive parents are twice as likely to call in outside help—an expert of some sort to deal with their unruly charge to whom they have no blood connection. And once an outsider is in the picture, the problem takes on more baggage.

A whole raft of things ran through my mind when I read these research findings. Jane in learning disability classes and her mother quizzing me about mental illness or institutionalization in my family. Jane being sexually abused and sent to therapy. Jane's severe PMS—call it premenstrual dysphoric disorder (PMDD), such as mine was—and my mother's, which went undiagnosed, and my inability to reach Jane in time about getting the kind of medical, not mental, relief that I got. I can't unwind her life and analyze every event in it because I wasn't there, but how can I not know that in this or that instance, I would have reacted quite differently? For starters, I would never have wondered whether Jane had feebleminded relatives, and thus assumed she was not capable of more than a class for the learning-disabled. That was the first thing her adoptive mother told me about Jane. It's why I can never fully forgive myself.

The suicide studies pile up as one scrolls through the list: A 2005 Swedish study focused on international adoptees and found they clearly were at greater risk for suicide than adoptees from the same country, but both groups had increased risk when compared to those who were living with their natural families.[139] Researchers at the University of Cincinnati College of Medicine, in a large-scale study of 6,500 students in grades seven through twelve, found that nearly 8 percent of the adoptees had attempted suicide in the past year, compared with only 3 percent of their non-adopted peers.[140]

B. J. Lifton wrote that at a seminar for adoptive parents when she brought

---

[138] Keyes et al., "The Mental Health of US Adolescents," 640.

[139] Annika von Borczykowski et al., "Suicidal Behavior in National and International Adoptees," *Social Psychiatry and Psychiatric Epidemiology* 41, no. 2 (Feb. 2006): 95–102.

[140] Trudy Festinger and James Jaccard, "Suicidal Thoughts in Adopted versus Non-adopted Youth: A Longitudinal Analysis in Adolescence, Early Young Adulthood, and Young Adulthood," *Journal of the Society for Social Work and Research* 3, no. 4 (Nov. 15, 2012): 280–95, www.doi.org/10.5243/jsswr.2012.17.

up the fact that the percentage of adoptee suicide was statistically high, a prominent psychiatrist asked if that nasty bit could be deleted from the tape, which
was to be later sold as a record of the talk. Lifton agreed but later wrote she was
sorry she had.[141] When I mentioned adoption and suicide at a conference a
few years ago, it was generally ignored. When I was pitted against Harvard law
professor Elizabeth Bartholet on PBS in 1993, she condescendingly referred to
all studies that showed adoptees had more problems than the non-adopted as
"garbage." A phalanx of adoption lawyers from around the country on moni-
tors were also there to put me—and any research I brought up—in their rearview mirror.[142]

Suicide, depression, addiction, and their statistical correspondence to adoption are not subjects the adoption industry wants to talk about. Increasingly,
adoption advocates find it hard to dismiss research on the link between suicide
and adoption as "junk science," as Bartholet did that day. The suicides of adopted children make news: Marie Osmond discussed her son's suicide on national
television; former Oregon senator Gordon Smith and his wife gave interviews
after their son committed suicide with sleeping pills and hanging himself; one
of Mia Farrow's adopted children died by a self-inflicted gunshot wound; the
writer Shana Alexander's daughter jumped to her death from a high floor on
Park Avenue; Carroll O'Connor's son, struggling with addiction, died of a self-
inflicted gunshot wound.

My daughter used a gun.

But suicide is kept out of the adoption discussion to such a degree that an
adoptee felt compelled to write a piece titled "We Need to Talk about Adoptee
Suicide." "It seems that adoptee suicide is still considered a taboo subject,"
wrote Angela Barra. "Alongside this, there are some adoptees who get very angry if they think they are being pathologized. I personally have experienced
this online, and it is disturbing that some adoptees (or adoptive parents) would
attack another adoptee for speaking about this issue."[143]

---

[141] Lifton, *Lost and Found*, 311.
[142] I've lost the videotape of that episode of the 1993 *MacNeil/Lehrer Report*. Elizabeth
Bartholet's book *Family Bonds* had just come out.
[143] Angela Barra, "We Need to Talk about Adoptee Suicide," *HuffPost Contributor*, May

Suicide is a subject certainly missing from adoption-agency websites, on which they advertise "confidential, nonjudgmental options" so that you, the prospective mother, can make an "informed choice." A truly informed choice would include the hard facts about adoption's long-term consequences, instead of gobbledygook about a better life with people who are almost always wealthier than the mother.

My daughter did not have a better life. She had a different life.

I don't know what kind of mother I would have made, and I make no claims about that. But no matter what, my daughter would not have been imprinted with a deep sense of abandonment. Yes, I couldn't have erased the epilepsy, which was most likely due to the strong dose of hormones I ingested while she was in utero. There is always that.

Google "suicide and epilepsy," and you get nearly 3.4 million hits. "Individuals with epilepsy have a two to four times increased mortality compared with the general population," conclude the authors of an article in *Lancet Neurology* in 2007. They found "a strong association between epilepsy and psychiatric disease, and psychiatric illness is one of the strongest risk factors for suicide."[144] A search for "adoption and suicide" gives up 363,000 sources. Google "PMDD and suicide" or "PMDD and suicidal thoughts" and another wealth of articles pops up. The number is just shy of 4,000 as I write. Add them up or take your pick.

I can't try to pinpoint what caused my daughter's despair and suicide. She was talking nonsense that weekend, but the next day she was calm and sane. And the next day. And the next day she was gone. She had not one, but two strikes against her—make that three, for I know that she committed suicide when she was suffering from PMS. I don't know if the sexual abuse fits in here anywhere, but it was woven into the complicated tapestry of her life.

I found her when she was a teenager, and after that we had an open adop-

27, 2017, https://web.archive.org/web/20220826174730/https://www.huffpost.com/entry/we-need-to-talk-about-adoptee-suicide_b_5928c632e4b07d848fdc03c9.
[144] Jakob Christensen et al., "Epilepsy and Risk of Suicide: A Population-based Case-Control Study," *Lancet Neurology* 6, no. 8 (Aug. 2007): 693, www.doi.org/10.1016/s1474-4422(07)70175-8.

tion, but decades later, nothing could stop her forward movement to a tragic end.

Resolution

33   Albany, Redux

FEBRUARY 2008—Three months after Jane's funeral, I am riding the train up to Albany, the town I fled to after Jane was born. Then, I was trying to get my life back in gear. Today I am trying to change lives. In my mind's eye is a set designed by Dickens: Somewhere in Albany in an underground cavern is a dark, musty room of many cabinets, cabinets piled one on top of another, reaching to a ceiling that goes on into the ether, with numerous recesses and alleyways filled with ever more cabinets, with locks on every drawer, tape sealing every file, all presided over by factotums of drudgery, headed by a malevolent Master of Circumlocution. Somewhere there, even today, is my daughter's file, yellowing, brittle with age.

Out the grimy window, the river is wide, brown, and choppy; the sky is the color of old pewter. It is damp and cold outside, but it's overheated and uncomfortably dry in the train. Down the track we speed, clickity-clack.

Someone at the adoption agency eventually had verified that Jane and I were mother and daughter, but the phrase the agency used to confirm our relationship was ambiguous. "She is the person you think she is." Clear enough, and one way to avoid saying "your daughter" because that would imply that a legal document does not alter reality.

That day, even Jane—born in 1966—would not have been able to obtain a copy of her original birth certificate in this new century. Neither would all those other people born before and after her in New York who were adopted, going back to the thirties. Even descendants of adoptees are unable to do a full genealogy. When they try, they hit a brick wall. Why? The keepers of those documents are told by their attorneys that maybe the law applies to birth certificates before 1936, maybe it goes back to the beginning of time, they're not sure, so to be on the safe side, they will keep them stashed and hidden away from the person they were written about and for!

Adoptees by the thousands, by the millions, need to stand up and demand what is rightfully theirs by birth, and until they do, those damn records will remain sealed shut. Far too many of the adopted are so blinded by fear of upsetting someone, by fear of hurting their adoptive parents, by fear itself that they are frozen, and the records stay sealed. They wait until their adoptive parents die—and by then, so have far too many natural mothers and fathers. Hence those reunions with a grave.

Why don't more of them speak out?

Tell someone for long enough that they can't have something, and they manage to subvert the desire for it. It's out of reach. Why go there? Mom and Dad will be mortally wounded. I can't do that. They raised me. It would kill them.

But that should never take away anyone's right to know who they are.

No one is telling the adopted they have to get their original records or go looking for kin. A lot of them say they don't want to. But people who say one year they are not interested find that the next year they are. They see something on television, they read a book, they get married, the spouse wants to know the health history before they have children, whatever, and now, suddenly, the incurious are insistently demanding, they want their information! The spouse saying "I want to know your family medical history before we have children" gives the adoptee permission, takes the onus off them. *It's not me, Mom. It's my wife/husband who wants to know.* Explaining it like that means they are not one of those ungrateful wretches who are turning their backs yadda, yadda, yadda . . . clickity-clack.

Albany, here I come.

I flip through the packet of papers the other lobbyists and I will pass out to the legislators tomorrow. Our handouts are put together by a group called

Unsealed Initiative, headed by Joyce Bahr, a mother like me. She's unearthed somewhere a copy of that letter from Sister Dominica Maria—so prescient: a sealed birth certificate "nullifies the inalienable right of a person to know the true facts of his birth." A letter from the Archdiocese of New York: "The mere fact of being unable to trace family because of the falsity of records would earmark and create distress and heartaches for the very persons it is planned to protect."[145]

Distress and heartaches. How many haunted adoptees have I met?

Far too many.

Sister Dominica peeled back the legalese—the law would take away the right to one's own true identity, history, people. A kind of emotional slavery with psychological chains instead of iron ones.

Dare I point out to anyone tomorrow that a few influential members of the legislature—in both houses—are adoptive fathers of the old school who believe in secrecy in adoption, period; who don't see what they are doing to their children? I think not. Or, god forbid, they are worried that a child they had—or maybe they had; they are not sure but suspect one was born—might come knocking at their own door and surprise the wife who never knew, the children who don't suspect. Or maybe they are protecting their brother, their uncle . . . I had found that unyielding adherence to closed records often came down to something personal.

Mostly it will be men tomorrow. How can they understand the grief of mothers? They don't have babies; they don't know that blast of hormones screaming to protect your own. Is that why I never wanted a second child? How could I give one away and keep another? I avoid infants—don't want to hold them, don't want to jiggle them on my lap, don't want to look at more than one photo of your grandchild. I can manage a courteous *Oh, how cute!* But don't show me ten more. That's one result of my—ha! adoption plan. I doubt that social workers go over this side effect to anyone considering giving up a child—that you may actually shun babies afterward; too triggering. Or that you may never have another child. That you are likely to suffer from

---

[145] Letter dated April 22, 1935. A copy is in my personal papers.

PTSD. That you may avoid high school and family reunions. That you may battle chronic depression. That low self-esteem may affect everything from job prospects to romance. That you may suffer from trust issues. That someone might say about you one day, *You don't want to end up like Lorraine.* Some words are knives you can never pull out. No one should end up like Lorraine.

Maybe this is why some women can't face reunion: memory evokes too much. Tony used to say that when Jane visited those first few years, I was an emotional wreck after she left. Just plain worn out, inside and out.

Clickity-clack.

This year Unsealed Initiative has corralled more than sixty co-sponsors and supporters. We've been at it for more than a decade, but even so, our bill is mired in the intractable morass that in Albany passes for democracy. We are aware that a couple of crucial legislators with ample clout are fiercely opposed to open records. Gotta save those mothers who haven't told a soul! One opponent is a woman, no reason given; another is an adoptive father, no explanation necessary. They rule in Albany. They chair important committees.

Today a dozen or so of us, adoptees and birth mothers, are breezing around the capitol, pressing our luck, running on the juice of the rightness of our cause. I make the rounds of legislators' offices with two adoptees: Chuck, who lives in Albany, and Cathy, who has flown up from Maryland but was born and adopted in New York. All morning our reception has been amazingly warm. We meet an aide whose adoptee husband recently had a successful reunion with his mother. One legislator says as soon as we walk in that he is going to put his name on the bill as a cosponsor and tells his assistant to follow up. We educate another legislator's aide, a man in his fifties who says he's never considered the issue before. He takes copious notes and promises to recommend that his boss support our bill. At our last stop before lunch, we meet an attorney who says that he's never met an adopted person who didn't want to know. We three are glowing with exhilaration. This is so much better than any of us expected.

Then the wind shifts as if some switch has been flicked when we weren't paying attention. We hear the refrain that has become the safe harbor of the opposition: the frightened woman in the closet. Data pours out of me—and that I'm a grandmother, I don't want to be protected, this is about the rights of the adopted—but the man on the other side of the desk looks at me as if I am speaking Urdu. What about the one woman in a hundred who doesn't want to be found, who was promised anonymity by the state? he says, daring me to respond. What about her?

Though I know the sponsor of our bill in the Senate is an adoptive father, I want to ask this guy if he has a connection to adoption—Are you an adoptive father? Do you have a daughter who wants to adopt, or already has? And if so, are you aware that a Cornell University survey of more than 1,200 adoptive parents in New York that found that close to 80 percent of them favor unsealing original birth certificates?[146]

But, for the moment, we are talking to what feels like a wall, and we're not seeing even a tiny chink. Decades later as I write, I am reminded of an essay I'd read about how rare it is that scientists identifying with either side of a contentious issue change their minds: "No wonder the historian Thomas Kuhn concluded almost fifty years ago that a scientific paradigm topples only when the last of its powerful adherents dies."[147] It seems that it will be the same with adoptees' rights. Shad Polier is dead, Bill Pierce is dead, but still we wait. Must we wait until they all die?

One of the last appointments of that long-ago day is with Danny O'Donnell, brother of Rosie, adoptive mother of several. Cathy and Chuck are speaking to one of his aides when O'Donnell rushes in and says, surprisingly, that he will see us. He motions for us to follow him into his inner office. We sit. He tells us that we are all well dressed and look like fine people.

Yeah? I am thinking. This is not starting well. Why say that? It implies that he expected us to arrive looking like bums when, in fact, we wore busi-

---

[146] Susan S. Lang, "Adoptive Parents Are Overwhelmingly in Favor of Opening Sealed Adoption Records, Cornell Study Finds," *Cornell Chronicle*, Jan. 30, 1997, https://web.archive.org/web/20220826182041/https://news.cornell.edu/stories/1997/01/adoptive-parents-are-overwhelmingly-favor-opening-sealed-adoption-records-cornell.
[147] Sharon Begley, "Why Scientists Need to Change Their Minds," *Newsweek*, Jan. 2, 2009, 17, https://www.newsweek.com/begley-why-scientists-need-change-their-minds-78309.

ness attire. After a few startled seconds, I begin talking about legislation in other states, about how even if you go to court you are denied—which Chuck was—but soon enough, O'Donnell interrupts and leans back in his chair and announces, I will never support this bill. Never. He goes on at some length. His voice leaves no wiggle room.

O'Donnell is dismissive, condescending, cold. He is a leader whose power is absolute, a man who has never had to question where he came from. I sense Chuck's mounting frustration, Cathy's escalating anxiety. Cathy is talking too fast about medical histories, unnecessary and costly medical tests, her daughter's marriage, her brother's inability to get a passport. She tears up, her voice rising in a hurried crescendo.

I will never support this legislation, O'Donnell repeats, calm as the Dead Sea. Cathy is still spilling out words.

I stand up to leave. We gotta get out of here. At that moment, I understand as well as I can what it is like to be treated like a second-class citizen, without recourse, asking for information that should be yours simply because you want it. Chuck has had it. He explodes as we leave, announcing angrily to anyone in earshot that their boss is the most obnoxious person he has ever met. Cathy's eyes are glassy. I recall hearing that O'Donnell told a previous lobbying group—maybe the one he didn't like the looks of—that he and his sister Rosie were afraid that the mothers of her numerous adopted children would come back and ask for money. At least with O'Donnell there is no pretense that he is protecting the privacy of the natural mother. He is protecting his sister Rosie, screw the kids, screw all adoptees! Even if they dress well.

A few years later, O'Donnell, who is gay, becomes one of the strong-arms pushing to legalize gay marriage in New York. One would think he would understand about being a member of a marginalized group. One would think. Later I read about his marriage in the *New York Times* to his longtime partner, a man of some culture. How unexpected. O'Donnell was so rude and cruel to people who simply wanted to know who they were when they were born.

What is so hard to understand about that?

But change would come, even to Mr. O'Donnell.

34   Dream a Little Dream

EARLY NOVEMBER, 2009—I wake up all hot and flustered in the middle of the night, having one of those dreams that cannot come to a satisfying end, something keeps preventing you from doing something—take a subway train, get on an elevator, cross the street. But this dream is a puzzlement: Tom Sawicki and I are trying to have sex—Yes! we are almost having sex—Yes! we are doing very sexy things—Yesyesyesalmost! but for unknown reasons we cannot manage to be alone without complications, someone interrupting us, the phone ringing, someone walking in, I'm getting on a train, someone is blocking his way, someone—one stupid interruption after another! What is the problem now!!?! I wake up all excited, not sure what is real and what is not.

Is Tom in bed with me?

No . . . this is a dream.

Whoa! Tom! Where did that come from? And trying to have sex . . . should have slept with him. Why didn't I? Might have changed everything. Yeah, it would have probably . . . instead, four decades later I dream about almost sleeping with him. I haven't dreamt about Tom since—god knows, ages.

Decades.

My mind wanders back to the last time my mother visited—she died before the new century began—and we were driving back from the ocean beach called Sagg Main, seven miles from our house in Sag Harbor. We are stopped at a light near a small cemetery where the highway meets Sagg Road. God knows why or how Tom comes up—I've been married to Tony fifteen years or so at this point, Tom's not on my radar—and she calmly says, You know, when Lillian, Tom's mother, was away at school, or maybe they broke up for a while, I went out with his father.

What!? Are you kidding me?

I turn to look at her, knowing the stoplight here is really a long one, it's summer and traffic is heavy, we'll be here for another minute at least.

You used to go out with Tom's father?

Yes, she says, nonchalantly, as if she had not been withholding evidence. Walter and I went out for a while, and then he and Lillian got back together.

She calls Tom's mom "Lillian." That is news to me. Lillian. Had she ever referred to Tom's parents by anything other than their pronouns? Guess not. And now Tom's mom is Lillian? I didn't even know her first name before this. And suddenly, Mr. Sawicki is Walter?

You went out with him more than once? I ask.

She's already told me yes, she did, and I am having a hard time absorbing this. If "Lillian" knew this—and now I'm assuming she did—no wonder they didn't want me in her son's life. That vixen Vicky would be her son's mother-in-law! Protocol would require that she, Lillian, at least be polite! They would have to see each other at family events—the wedding, christenings, birthdays, graduations—why, it was unthinkable! And if Tom's mother knew, then Tom's father, Mr. Sawicki—I can't think of him as "Walter"—could downplay the connection he and Mom might once have had by referring to me as "some broad." Someone not good enough for their son! And what if I tricked that son into marriage via pregnancy if he transferred to Wayne State the way he'd wanted to? Suddenly everything about their objection to me made a certain kind of sense.

Tom sure didn't know this.

How come you never told me? I ask.

Mom shrugs.

The light changes and I drive forward. On Sagg Road. In the Hamptons. In New York. Where I was apparently meant to be. Not on the road not taken, the road that would have led elsewhere, the road to a different life.

No one's life can be rewound. I am here, I have a good husband.

Good morning, Tony.

I tell him about the dream. He shrugs. Though he carries the jealous gene in his back pocket, though he knows Tom was my first love, he also knows Tom has been dead for more than thirty years.

I do not think about Tom or the dream anymore.

For a while.

35 Karmic Kickback

A week or two later, I'm cruising along, it's mid-November, late afternoon, and I'm making gołumpkies (stuffed cabbage, to the non-Slavs) for people coming to dinner the next night. The cabbage is steaming on the stove, softening the leaves before I roll them around a mix of chopped beef, brown rice and sautéed onions. The phone rings. Tony is nowhere near, there is no phone in the kitchen, and so I go into the dining/living room to answer. The sun has set, and it's nearly dark; only the light from the kitchen spills over. We still do not have caller ID—it's a landline on an old phone. I pick up and switch on the small lamp by the phone.

Is this Lorraine Dusky?

Yes.

Must be an adoptee or a mother, though she doesn't sound like one. She doesn't sound tentative like most of the strangers who call. She begins a roll call of names, speaking slowly and deliberately.

Hello, my name is Jennifer Sawicki Royal.

Wait, back up! Did you say Sawicki? As in Tom Sawicki?

Yes. I am his daughter.

Whoa! This is Tom's daughter? What could she be—

I'm calling because I found letters you wrote to my father, she says, and I looked you up and I saw that you had a daughter you gave up for adoption—and I was wondering if your daughter—could she be my sister? I never had a brother or a sister, and I do adoption searches here in Michigan and I'm familiar with all this, and I was hoping that your daughter could be my sister.

Whoa. She got this all out in one breath, it seems, in case I might hang up. First, I say, my daughter was not your sister, and second, my daughter died two years ago. Now I can say this quite calmly.

Oh, I'm so sorry, she says. She apologizes for barging in and bringing up something that is undoubtedly painful, but she is now telling me how she happened to call, saying how she does searches for adoptees and natural mothers in Michigan, her husband is adopted, she read about me and thought, well, maybe—

You are Tom Sawicki's daughter? Let's get back to that.

Yes.

And you do adoption searches? Too amazing.

I do want to talk to you, I say. Let me turn off what I've got cooking on the stove. You'll get a kick out of this. I'm actually making gołumpkies. She chuckles. How very Polish of me. In spite of my no-cooking-lessons-from-my-mother rule while I was growing up, I became a decent cook, and a couple of times a year I make the comfort food of my youth for my friends, some of whom grew up eating gołumpkies.

Now I'm back, pleased and flushed all at once, as Tom's daughter tells me that about a week ago, she found a stack of my letters to him—a four-inch stack of letters—along with a few funny cards and drawings. She tells me how they came into her possession a few years back when her grandmother—that would be the villainous Mrs. Lillian Sawicki, but I don't interrupt—lost her property and the bank got the building—that would be the store—but she, Jennifer, was able to pull a few things out before the place was locked up. She took what she could that belonged to her father—she was eleven when he died, it was a few days before her parents' divorce would have been final—but she was busy when she got the stuff—she's finally graduating from college, but that's a long story—and the letters were stashed in the basement of her house. She pulled them out a week ago and read them and one of them had my last name on the back above the return address—the rest only had a return address, no name, and, of course, you never signed your last name in a letter—and one thing led to another and she figured out who I was—Thank god for the internet!—and while she is talking I am remembering that inexplicable dream about her father about a week ago. A mere coincidence? There are no coincidences.

When Jennifer told her husband she found me and who I was, he kept interrupting. Hey, she's on Facebook, he said. We've already exchanged messages, she noticed I'm from Michigan and said she went to Sacred Heart. You know, right down the street from my office.

So he saved them. The letters.

Twenty minutes later Tony walks by. Who's that? he mouths.

Tom Sawicki's daughter, I whisper.

Ah. He looks surprised but knows immediately who she is. He doesn't believe in coincidence either. He believes in synchronicity.

Jennifer tells me the bare bones of her story. She and her mother had rough times after Tom died, and when it came to college, his insurance policy paid for the University of Michigan for two years, but when the cash dried up she dropped out and got a job as a reporter.

A reporter? Tom's daughter became a newspaper reporter? Where did you work? I ask.

Dearborn—

Dearborn! Are you kidding? I got started on the *Dearborn Guide*! You did notice that my address was Dearborn? Of course she had. She was way ahead of me.

Her newspaper turned out to be the other paper in Dearborn, but what the hell? She had no idea I existed at the time, nor of her father's connection to Dearborn. She had lived there too, about a mile from our house in east Dearborn. When she tells me where, I picture the block of English Tudor apartments near a long-gone movie theater. She had a basement apartment, and the woman who lived above her was named—*Lorraine*.

Seriously? You must be joking.

No, she says. She really was a Lorraine.

Jennifer goes on to say that she got involved in adoption when she found the son of one of her best friends who had given him up years before. She met her husband at an adoption reform meeting, and not only is he adopted, he is one of the leaders of the Michigan group working to unseal birth records for adoptees, which is why we were already Facebook friends. Michigan is a "sandwich" state, meaning some adoptees can get their original birth certificates, while most are denied.

We talk for most of an hour until the gołumpkies beckon. Adrenaline is still pumping as I'm rolling up the cabbage, telling Tony everything in a rush. Can you believe this? I keep saying, wondering if he can grasp the intense connection I feel with a woman halfway across the country, a woman I've never met. It's weird, right? She doesn't feel like a stranger at all.

His letters to me? I had saved them for decades. They went from Dearborn to Rochester, to Albany, to several apartments in Manhattan, out of the city to the suburbs where I lived for a year, back to the city, into storage once—I moved so many times during that part of my life my mother called me a gypsy. I didn't read them; I merely took them with me. Except for the first few, they were all signed, *I love you, Tom.* They finally ended up in the house Tony and I have owned since the mid-eighties.

But one afternoon while cleaning out closets, I came upon them, along with the glossy photograph of Tom and me at a dance at Wayne State the day after he asked me to marry him. The photo was taken by one of those roving photographers. Tom gave him five bucks, and the shot came in the mail to me later. I had on a borrowed black silk sheath—very Audrey Hepburn—I'd had to lose five pounds so that it fit perfectly, tight enough but not too tight. The picture seemed to glow as I held it that day, and keeping it seemed somehow unfaithful to my enduring marriage to Tony. If I died first, Tony would find all this and be surprised—maybe even hurt—that I'd kept the letters. I kept my prom picture with that German guy I had as a date—and even happy pictures of me and my first husband—but out went Tom's letters and that photograph.

They were too intense to keep.

A week later, my letters to Tom arrive by FedEx. In the evening, I pull one or more out at random, read, and dive headlong into the tide of remembrance that will engulf me for the next several nights. The letters, most handwritten in ink, a few typed, are on everything from flowery onion skin to cheap copy paper, messages from a bottle that has been drifting for decades. They are all hauntingly familiar: our plans for New Year's Eve a month after we met; his coming to Detroit the weekend we sealed the deal; my father's heart attack followed by the trouble at home; my exhaustion with my work/school schedule; even the courses I took, the papers I wrote, and what I was writing for the *Collegian*. The letters are peppered with sly sexual innuendos, and in the last batch of letters—after we got back together—I write about our plans to marry. I grumble that he doesn't write often enough, and later remark at his impudence for being upset when I don't write for an entire week! As if he did!

And there is one more letter—a letter from him to me, the letter he wrote when I didn't hear from him, the letter he said he didn't send because it was only a litany of woe. That, too, had been signed, I love you.

Reading the letters is pouring hot sauce on an old wound. This had been my fork in the road. A different life. A child not lost. A girl like Jennifer who does not carry the burden of being adopted. A daughter like Jane who did. I understand that life is too chancy to offer anything other than a qualified maybe about what might have been, but now with these tangible reminders of that different life sitting in a pile, hindsight is always whispering sweet yeses into my ear late at night. I cannot read these letters without weeping.

I read and weep, but snap myself back together every morning and go about my business.

In the first few months, Jennifer and I talk on the phone and email nonstop. Every morning, I have a fresh missive from her, and I sit there mesmerized by the story of her life, and then I write a reply as long as hers. The details of our lives emerge, every twist and turn, every joy and sadness, a Niagara of embedded experience and emotion, nothing held back. Not surprisingly, she reread all the letters after we spoke. I tell her I would have done the same. She wants to hear the particulars of my relationship with her father, for she barely remembers anyone speaking of him in glowing terms. Her mother was certainly not singing his praises, and today she and her mother rarely speak.

Recounting everything to her is like watching an old movie retrieved from obscurity. There we are kissing at my cousin's wedding the night we met, causing a minor scandal; then he is squeezing my arms not quite imperceptibly after helping me put on my coat, a telegraphed hello; then we are in my cousin's bedroom on New Year's Eve when I was getting ready and he asked if he could come up while I finish putting on my makeup. I linger on that moment when we caught each other's eyes, a fleeting intimacy that felt like an augur of our future together.

In return, I greedily lick up the details of his life—how a courageous act for the Black employees at his company ultimately got him fired, the moves to Indiana and Ohio, his crumbling marriage—just as my mother told me—and then, the worst day of Jennifer's eleven-year-old life, the day of his funeral, her mother playing the part of grieving widow, the in-laws barely speaking. Neither set of in-laws had approved of the marriage, and somehow, after his death, the child of this union got lost in the crossfire. Both sets of grandparents were missing from Jennifer's life for years, and she has had a decade-long break with her mother.

Even your mother's parents didn't stay in touch? I ask. I wouldn't put anything past Mrs. Sawicki, but your mother's parents? I ask. They weren't around either?

Them too.

Then I hear Jennifer's mother's mother was adopted. From Wisconsin. Wisconsin? Not Ohio. Or Illinois or Indiana.

Wisconsin, she says.

Aha. That's where my daughter grew up.

We learn that our ancestors have many of the same names: Blanche, Victoria, Genevieve. Yes, those were common names in that era, but one of us easily could have had ancestors called Irene, Dorothy, and Helen. Only we do not. My middle name is Blanche, the English version of Bronisława, my grandmother's name, and Blanche is the name of her grandmother from Wisconsin. There are so many coincidences I don't even bother saying, You're kidding.

She reads *Birthmark* and discovers in the first chapter that I muse about my missing daughter when I'm flying kites with a friend's daughter. I had given that imaginary girl the name Jennifer. Her name. I thought I had plucked the name out of the air, after rejecting Zoe and Chloe and trying out Jessica. Tom must have told me his daughter's name—I probably even asked—but I had no conscious memory of that.

One day I mention that the song Tom and I made ours was Harry Belafonte's "Jamaica Farewell." Do you know it?

Know it? The only time she did karaoke, "Jamaica Farewell" is what she sang.

I want to send her a small token as Christmas approaches. A poinsettia? Safe but too ordinary. I don't have a clue, I've never seen her home, checked out her closet, or even had a cup of coffee with her. Something keeps pulling me to a dragon pin I had bought a year earlier, emerald-green enamel with a ruby-red eye. I'd had it pinned to a green velvet hoodie. Will she think a dragon brooch is bizarre? One day, I stop analyzing and wrap it up, and off it goes.

The day she gets it, she emails me a photo of her cabinet—a good-sized cabinet—stuffed with her collection of—what else? Dragons. Dragons in every shape and form, dragons on cups and on boxes, in statuary and candlesticks. By now, I think, of course. Her father and I had intended to furnish our house with Asian accents, undoubtedly objects with dragons. Of course Jennifer would have dragons. And of course I would send her a brooch in the shape of a dragon—what else?

To Jennifer, I don't have to explain anything about adoption or why people search, as she knows all this. Nor does she have to explain why she and her husband are confidential intermediaries for the state of Michigan. Others might think me strangely obsessed with adoption, but not Jennifer or her husband.

Her father's Karmann Ghia was rear-ended that summer we separated, she happens to know. Oh, a careless driver plowed into my nearly new Ghia at a stop sign that fall, I instantly recall. This could happen to anyone, right? With their low-slung design, Ghias were always getting their rear ends bashed in. But still. Same summer. Same bashed-in rear end.

Things are getting curiouser and curiouser. Adoption and newspapers, Dearborn and dragons, bashed-in Ghias and "Jamaica Farewell," people named Lorraine and Blanche, her age so close to my daughter's (she was born only months earlier), my using the name Jennifer in *Birthmark*—our synchronicity feels right, warm, enveloping. We do not question it.

I take to shutting the door to my office when I open her emails. Tony's office is right next to mine, and I don't want him to hear me, I don't want to interrupt him, for I am crying now daily as the past—hers and mine—comes tumbling out in email after email. I cry for lost love, for the daughter I surrendered and who is no more, for the slings and arrows that punctuated Jennifer's life, for what might have been for both of us. I'm weeping a lot, yes, but somehow, it's all good, a vein gushing feelings that needed to be released though I did not know how many of them I'd held inside. This is all happening around the anniversary of my daughter's death, Christmas, and the death of someone in town I knew not well but liked immensely. I weep at his funeral way beyond what's appropriate, way beyond how much I can possibly miss this man. I am sure his wife thinks it peculiar. She glances at me when she leaves the church, but I can't stem the river.

As I play hopscotch with memory, landing here and there, I see that room with the fuzzy, wine-colored couch in that apartment in Saginaw, I see the moment when I tell Tom he must leave. The lights are bright, and I do not take those two steps across the floor to seal his promise with a kiss, that yes, he absolutely must come back tomorrow. I see myself sitting and waiting that day in that backyard when nothing broke the roar of silence.

Months later, Jennifer and I meet in Detroit, and our connection is further cemented. Jennifer drives me from the airport to my brother's house. He surprises us both when he tells Jennifer, *My sister talked about Tom all the time.*

This Jennifer could have been my daughter, only she wouldn't be our daughter, Tom's and mine. That woman would be a quite different person. We don't look alike, nor does she have the shared, familial qualities that I cherished in Jane. When Jennifer and I are out together, no one asks if we are mother and daughter the way people did when I was with Jane. On Jennifer's face, I see Tom. Her son, even at twelve, uncannily resembles the young man I was once loved.

Later, at her home, Jennifer begins reading a long letter Tom wrote to her mother and never sent, calling off their wedding. I stop her, I don't want to hear it to the end, too much lamentation is beginning to burble just below my surface. Tom and I zigged apart when we might have zagged together, but that was oh so long ago.

Yet in some way that is beyond logical understanding, Jennifer and I are linked, an alternate-universe mother and daughter. She is not my daughter, I am not her mother, but here we are, two women connected nonetheless, and everything feels right, warm, and comforting, a magic carpet that lifts us both up, together, as if our DNA, both psychic and physical, was meant to come together and rejoice.

Our relationship is fulfilling in a way I could never have imagined, dots connected that I did not know were still on the page, waiting for the right moment to align. Life is more than a logical series of events; life can include such mystical convergences if you let them in.

How is Tony handling this long trek down memory lane? He is a rock. He does not discount the numerous coincidences that are stacked up like pancakes at IHOP. He says Tom and I will work this out in another lifetime. I am not sure what I believe about other lifetimes, but for the moment, I do not dispute him, for his idea is far too comforting.

When Tom died, he was planning on starting his own advertising agency in New Orleans—with someone he was planning to marry, someone he met in Ohio as his marriage fizzled. If I had called when I first heard about his impending divorce—as my mother suggested—would we have reconnected?

Maybe yes. Maybe it would have been too late. I was in New York, and he was somewhere in the Midwest. One never knows how blows the wind across a changed landscape.

I will hear from you again, he said.

What did he know? I had wondered.

Now I do.

Why am I crying all the time? I ask Tony.

Don't you know? he says?

No, I don't.

You need a daughter and she needs a mother.

36 The Missing Granddaughter

There is still Sarah, the other granddaughter.

In Wisconsin where she was born and adopted, she can request that the state locate the parents named on her original birth certificate, and a confidential intermediary will find out if they are agreeable to contact. Natural mothers and fathers (if known)—and certainly grandmothers—do not have the same right. But I can put a letter in Sarah's birth and adoption file stating I would welcome her. A few months after Jane died, I write a short note and send it off to the Wisconsin Department of Children and Families. Not quite a letter in a bottle. A known destination.

There is one more thing I can do—post Sarah's birth data on the International Soundex Reunion Registry, the largest such registry for people looking for one another. It's quick and free. If she posts the same or similar data, the computer, or someone, will make the match and *voilà!*

The registry doesn't make a match, but I receive a response from someone who says she can find my granddaughter. I demur. I want my granddaughter to want to be searching too. I do not feel the same intensity I had about finding my daughter, but Sarah—if she is called that—is my granddaughter.

Life is good, right? I already have one fine—and most resilient—granddaughter, on the honor roll and college bound. Though she did not know of my Francophile tendencies—where they come from I do not know—she took four years of high school French. *Bonne!* Kimberly had to grow up fast in a situation that was not quite being adopted but nearly so, living so many years with the Rhymers when Jane was absent, unstable, or both. Kimberly's life was never easy, but she always knew who she was.

In July of 2008, I started a blog called *First Mother Forum*.[148] Some months later, when working on a post, I interviewed the person who headed the confidential intermediary program in Wisconsin. While I had more than a passing interest in what she had to say, I was not planning to press the issue of my granddaughter. Yet as we spoke my connection to Wisconsin emerged, as did my daughter's suicide. The voice on the phone asked about that, and I said that it occurred during a bad bout of PMS and that I tried to get her to use progesterone, that I also had terrible PMS.

"PMDD?" she interrupted. "Will your doctor attest to this? If that's the case, your granddaughter needs to know. If you get me a letter from your doctor about your PMDD, I will be obligated to let her know this. And I will let her know you are open to contact."

All this came to pass.

My granddaughter declined to learn who I was.

How can anyone not be interested in her own life?

I puzzled briefly over this but knew the answers. And then someone—a biracial adoptee—wrote this comment at *First Mother Forum*:

> Psychologically all of this waking up is a huge process. Huge. The mental and emotional hold that our APs [adoptive parents] have/had on us that held our adoption as a taboo and secret world cannot be put into words. Breaking free of that hold is an earth-shattering moment. It happened for me at the late age of thirty-five when I received word from my adoption agency that my bio family was searching for me. Up until then, I was living as if I was the white daughter of my adopters and desperately still trying to please them and have them love me.

---

[148] The URL is www.firstmotherforum.com (https://web.archive.org/web/20220809083922/https://www.firstmotherforum.com/). I added [Birth Mother] to the online title after a few months because that is what people search under when looking for information about related topics. Jane Edwards of Portland, Oregon, is my blogging partner.

The post made me acutely aware of the great mountain adoptees—all adoptees—have to climb before they search.

A year passed. One day, I mention my missing granddaughter on the blog. Again, I hear from the same person who contacted me earlier, a "search angel," in adoption parlance. She states this time that she can almost certainly find my granddaughter. A friend who is a mother like me points out that opportunity might not pass by twice. Even if I do nothing, I will know who she is. Fair enough, I think, and a week later I not only have my granddaughter's name but also a few basics about her family, including where she grew up and went to high school. I receive copies of photos from her school yearbook.

As I had suspected all along, she had not been adopted by a Black doctor father and a white lawyer mother. This was yet another thread in Jane's skein of fabrications. Sarah's family is white. The father has a trade and his own business. A highly skilled occupation, but he is not a doctor. The mother appears to be a homemaker. Not a lawyer. Sarah has two older sisters, almost certainly the couple's natural children. That last piece of information meant that at least Sarah did not carry the burden of compensating for anyone's infertility.

A few keystrokes on the computer revealed more: Sarah tweets. She gets *Time* magazine's tweets. She has her own blog, for god's sake. She writes poetry. She's published in an online magazine. She is our granddaughter, Patrick's and mine. Jane wrote poetry, I wrote poetry, Patrick and I quoted poetry to each other the night we met. Sarah's picture is on her university's website. She's bigger boned than I am, has a strong, defiant look in her eyes, medium-brown coloring, and a broad forehead like Patrick's. I am too thunderstruck to find any resemblance to me, but Tony sees Jane in her.

Then another photo of her surfaces, this one in a fedora, a fedora similar to the one I've worn for years. She is part of the jazz scene in a big Midwestern city and performs with them, does spoken-word. Jazz. That's Patrick's influence. It feels rich, remarkable, exhilarating.

Though she knows I am available, she is not seeking me out. I retreat. I do nothing for over a year. On Facebook, I do not ask to friend her, even though her friends number in the hundreds. Oh, I check her blog every couple of weeks, but not until one day in November—when she has a post about Kurt

Vonnegut—do I feel she is sending me a sign. I'd known Vonnegut and his wife, Jill Krementz, since the time she had interviewed Jane. Why isn't Sarah writing about *Siddhartha* and Hermann Hesse instead, or is that passé? From the post, I discover that my father and Vonnegut share a birth date, if a decade apart. Then, at the end of the year, Sarah invites anyone to tell their own stories on her blog, and she posts her email address. Surely that means something!

Or not.

But shortly after New Year's Day, I wake up one morning and spill out our connected stories in a thousand words and send the email off without second-guessing. Six months later, she is coming through the gate at MacArthur Airport on Long Island. It's the Fourth of July—of course fireworks are going off in the distance as we pull into the parking lot. I look up and remember that other Fourth of July, so many years back, when I waited for Tom. The fireworks feel momentous, poignant, electric with meaning.

Yet meeting her face-to-face is not like the first time with my daughter. Sarah was not a part of my body, in my womb, inside me. I did not give her up. I have no connection to her father. I am not having that out-of-body experience I had when I came face-to-face with my daughter. But Sarah is blood, she is my granddaughter, and I am thrilled to be with her.

We walk on the beach, talk over sandwiches outdoors, find jazz in the Hamptons at sunset, swim in a friend's pool. The truth of her first months of life comes out, and what I hear is not comforting. She spent her first eighteen months with a couple of nuns caring for her, because there had been no one to adopt her! Did Jane even know this? Given how adoption is handled, probably not. Later I will learn from Sarah's adoptive mother that during this time, her natural father visited her. By himself.

Instead of being an irresponsible drug user, he begins to sound like a prince. Sarah's adoptive mother also says that because he was Black and Jane was adamant about the adoption, he really did not have a chance to oppose it. I like her mother immensely. She is generous, honest, and hoping only for the best for Sarah. And the young woman I am getting to know is a fine, strong, and intelligent person with charisma, the kind that makes people look at her when we walk around New York City. It's easy to imagine her—Patrick's granddaughter—reciting spoken-word with a jazz backup in a nightclub. I give her one of my prized possessions, a Norma Kamali black-and-white beaded bolero. I found it at a resale shop eons ago, but its shoulder pads engulfed me and I never wore it. On Sarah, it is splendid. It will be one of my signature looks, she says. It feels as if I bought it for her, knowing that she would someday come along.

I understand that she is missing a mother, the generation between us. I don't know how much she wants to hear about her mother—she doesn't ask much—and I present Jane in the best light I can. I do not tell her about Jane's penchant for lying, or talk about her erratic behavior, or spill the fabricated story about Sarah's adoption, or reveal how Jane painted her natural father. What would be the point? Sarah already has to deal with the suicide. That is enough.

What is the one thing that Sarah must absolutely, positively do while she is in New York? Visit the Village Vanguard. She says she isn't going back to her musician friends in the Midwest and saying she'd missed their place of worship. I hear: She must go back to the very place Patrick brought me so long ago, the evening of the first time we made love. It seems incredible yet somehow singularly appropriate, a lost talisman from another era, now transformed and finding its way back.

The Vanguard is more than a bare-bones jazz club in a Greenwich Village basement. It's a national treasure, a historic institution where all the jazz greats pass through at some point. Feeling very much the mother hen, I cannot let this young woman, no matter how hip and self-possessed, roam around Greenwich Village by herself late at night. And what do you know? The featured artist is a pianist—his name escapes me—but I don't mention that the entertainment the night I was there with Patrick was a jazz pianist, Herbie Hancock, because she gives me an opaque look whenever I mention her grandfather's love of jazz. What is that to me, she seems to be saying. I was adopted. I am adopted.

Now I am in that same basement more than four decades later with our granddaughter. I don't know anything about Sarah's natural father—whatever Jane said about Marvin I no longer believe—but tonight it feels as if Sarah is channeling Patrick directly, only she doesn't know it. I am struck by how little the place has changed. A file of memories flips by—there's where Patrick and I sat at a table in the first row. Herbie Hancock and I made eye contact. I wore a lime green-linen sheath my mother made, Patrick, a blue-and-white seersucker suit. It was July. It was hot and steamy. The air was thick with smoke. We drank cognac. We would be going back to the Roosevelt Hotel.

I mumble a few words to Sarah about that summer night, naively inviting her in, but she is having none of it. To her my musing is nothing more than an oddity to be stowed somewhere, along with phone numbers she will never call. Conversation is random, a cat lazily toying with a ball of yarn. She doesn't say so, but I sense she wishes she was there alone, how much more intriguing than to be sitting there with a white woman, her grandmother. How unhip can you get?

Later, back at the friend's apartment where we are staying the night, she says she's going downstairs to call her family—she needs more privacy than the two rooms of the apartment can offer. Of course. There is a couch in the lobby. But after what seems like a long time, half an hour, forty-five minutes . . . she's still not back. It's near midnight, or it's after midnight, and until Sarah is safely back in the apartment and the door locked, this grandmother cannot drift off. Yet I am exhausted, aching for sleep. It's been a long day that began with a two-hour bus ride from Sag Harbor in the morning. We've ridden a double-decker bus all over Manhattan in sweltering heat, walked in Soho, had lunch somewhere, taken the Staten Island ferry, had a bite, gone downtown to the Vanguard. I'm weary, I'm in bed, but know I must wait until I hear her come in before I can sleep.

Finally, I throw on some clothes and go downstairs. She is not in the lobby. I find her sitting outside on the sidewalk, back against the building, talking to her father, tears streaming down her cheeks. She's come undone.

I'd like to take her in my arms and comfort her, but I know I should not. I am the wrong person to comfort her, I am the cause of her internal uproar. There is absolutely nothing I can do for her. This is the great abiding sorrow of reunion—it closes the door of the unknown, but it opens a new one with turmoil and tears on the other side. The whole world of *what if* rumples the blankets of memory. I look at her weeping and I see full force what adoption has wrought. I see my daughter's bleeding heart. I see her daughter's wound.

And it started with me.

Adoptees talk about the emotional havoc of reunion—a complex miasma of feelings of abandonment and rejection, of what might have been, of what can never be—and soon enough, they need to swim back to their comfort zone on their own familiar beach of people they know, of a lifetime of shared experience. I had my own thrashing about in those murky waters after I found Jane; what adoptees go through is the other side of that ocean. I know Sarah needs to separate, she needs space—and so do I—but together we are. I am too tired to worry about anything that night. I am not roiling about in an emotional vortex, for I did not give this girl away and tried to stop Jane from doing so. My emotions are in check, but I know tomorrow will be long and hard.

The next day, we do more sightseeing. From the discount-ticket booth in Times Square, I manage to snap up front-row seats to a matinee of David Mamet's *Race*. For a few hours we are transported to another world—this one of white bias, police shenanigans, and a curveball—and we do not need to relate to one another. The turmoil is on stage, we are enjoying a respite we both crave.

The rest of the week is tough. Our two-story home is suddenly too small. Outside the house, we trip over people who want to meet her. When we go to hear the jazz on Thursday night at a local joint, our friends are there. When we have lunch at our favorite restaurant, not introducing her to the waiters we know so well would be rude. When we go downtown for coffee, we run into more acquaintances. She wants to meet our friends who are poets and writers, and so we do. Yet now the days drip out of the week agonizingly slowly, for she has become—it happened that night at the Vanguard—blank verse impossible to read. Now I am awkward around her, like an insecure teenager, not sure of myself on my own turf, sensing that every gesture, every word is somehow foolish, inappropriate, wrong. Am I suddenly too white to be tolerated? That may be how she grew up but now, in a big city, her life is far from all white. Her poetry identifies as not white. She says she is treated differently in town because she is not white. I say maybe I am treated differently because I have been here three decades and know a lot of people. It's a small town. Who knows who is right, or quite possibly we are both right. We both yearn for space and separation, but the week has days to go. The ticket is prepaid.

Adoption is hard. Reunion is hard. Even this reunion—once removed— is hard. Yet with gentleness and decorum on both our parts, and Tony's calm strength and attention, with the diversions of the Hamptons to distract us, we get through the remaining days.

The drive to the airport is mostly in silence. It is clear she needs to bolt and run, for it feels as if she is about to explode. I do not suggest we park and wait until she boards. At the drop-off area, we give each other a perfunctory hug, and off she goes, bursting through the doors, racing away, a comet on an altered course.

I am exhausted. Meeting her has been like picking at a scab that had long hardened over and finding fresh grief, the living awareness of how one adoption begat another. When Sarah said one afternoon at the beach that she did not intend to have children, I'd been pleased. At least, I thought, it ends here.

I didn't know what to expect after that week and its hurried goodbye. Yet in the months following, through email and frequent phone conversations, Sarah and I became close for nearly a year. For Christmas I bought a rug for her apartment that we picked out together on eBay. I looked forward to her calls, near weekly, and we'd chat for almost an hour. It felt as if we had escaped the pitfalls of so many adoptee/natural parent reunions.

This was my happy ending.

I had always quietly encouraged her meeting her father. That Marvin had wanted to raise Sarah with his mother spoke volumes. I was sure he would want to meet her now. He did. He still lived in Wisconsin. Soon enough, they met. I felt he would answer the questions that bubbled up in her poetry.

I don't know what Marvin said to Sarah. I did not ask, and she did not offer. But whatever he said, Sarah's walls started going up as fast as they do on home improvement shows—why, they can redo a whole house in a week!

Jane and I had been out of touch when she was seeing Marvin, so I can only imagine that the picture Jane painted of me was not pretty. When she was living with us, friends sometimes told me what foul things she said about me. She most likely told him that I was encouraging the adoption, when I was doing the exact opposite. She most likely told him that I was from the town next to his—Dearborn, so famously racist that I surely would suffer by association. I instantly regretted that I had kept from Sarah the problematic aspects of Jane's personality, the barrage of lies, the fables she spun. Now it was too late; now saying anything would seem false.

Then she was gone.

I was upset for a while.

But I had endured this kind of push-pull relationship with Jane too many times to start another. I was not willing to go down that road again.

The people who want to be in your life will be. You don't have to chase after them.

37   How Dare She?

2011—For years, I had been writing opinion pieces on issues related to adoption—crack babies born addicted and HIV-infected, countering Republicans who railed against abortion, for syndication via *Newsday*;[149] the hidden identities of babies conceived via sperm donors for *USA Today*;[150] and, naturally, unsealing birth records of adoptees, wherever I could find a welcome home. In May of 2011, just before the legislative session ended in Albany that year when a bill trying to do just that was again in the fray, for *Newsday* I wrote a piece poking a hole in the idea that the love of adoptive parents was not enough to stem the innate curiosity about whom one came from. In the beginning. Before the adoption agency, or attorney, or stork delivered a baby to loving, willing parents.

> The thinking [when the old laws were written] was that individuals would be secure in their new families and wouldn't need to know where they came from. And with the records sealed, their mothers—their first mothers—wouldn't be able to interfere in their lives. Those mothers would grieve in silence and then "forget" their children.
>
> But that simplistic idea of how people are hasn't stood the test of time. Stories about reunited mother and child,

---

[149] Lorraine Dusky, "Who'll Adopt These Babies, Mr. Bush?" *Newsday*, Viewpoints, Oct. 20, 1988.
[150] Lorraine Dusky, "Like Adoptees, Petri-Dish Babies May Long for Past," *USA Today*, Jan. 7, 1998.

or siblings, are in the news precisely because the heart understands what the law ignores: Neither does a mother forget, nor can questions of identity be stilled. They ring deep in the breast, and neither time, nor the love of an adoptive family, can erase them.[151]

I'd met way too many adoptees not *unhappy* with their adoptive parents but nevertheless defensive and protective of them, and I understood that curiosity about one's roots was separate from whether or not one's parents were loving. What "loving" parents often did was make the adoptee feel guilty for wanting to know. But plenty of parents get past that. And I'd heard from many adoptees that their adoptive parents supported the search and supplied whatever scraps of information they had about the genetic parents.

Well, not even in 2011 was that statement going to be in print without raising the hackles of some adoptive parents. A week later, an adoptive mother came roaring back. "How dare Dusky state with such ignorant boldness that our love can't make up for the love of the person who gave our son away?"[152] The writer ignored that my point was that "love" should neither steal nor kill the desire to know one's true self and origins. True love, unencumbered by conditions, accepts the whole person, a person with a lineage that goes back to the first man and woman. True love encompasses all, acknowledges the bad and celebrates the good, but it does not erase the past. To attempt to do so is a folly; to erase the past is a crime against consciousness. Yet the failed social engineering of closed adoption unwittingly has this as its goal, as it presumes to transform individuals into new versions of themselves, refugees without a history.

All too often, loving adoptive parents, by word and deed, instill the idea that a quest for knowledge of one's origins—identity—is a blow against them and their love and all they have done for the adoptee. "Isn't my love enough?" reveals unspoken tension behind far too many adoptive relationships. It instills guilt, sets up boundaries, builds fences between the adopted and the loving

---

[151] "Help Adoptees Reach First Parents," *Newsday*, Viewpoints, May 12, 2011.
[152] "More Adoption Information May Not Be Good," Letters, *Newsday*, May 18, 2011. The letters are signed, but for the privacy of the senders, I have not included names.

parents who ignore what they have done. Such guilt, implanted early and often, tamps down many adoptees' natural and normal curiosity about their roots.

A little-known fact about individuals who search for their original heritage and families is that those individuals raised in secure, warm, and yes, loving homes—without the burden of guilt—are the most likely to eagerly search and happily reunite with their biological families. "Adoptees who come from good adoptive situations are not afraid of finding another 'family' because their experience with the idea of family is good, and so expanding their family seems like a positive thing," said a search angel (meaning she worked for free) and confidential intermediary (she took a fee—sometimes) who said she stopped counting at 1,500 searches about five years ago. Conversely, adoptees who had bad parents and a bad experience in the adoptive family are the least likely to seek out or accept more "family." They have had enough of "family." Instead, she said, they build their social network around friends and their own nuclear family. She added that this was the generally accepted knowledge among searchers.

Another letter writer wrote that for women who chose anonymity "— who may be in their seventies and older, and likely have husbands, children and grandchildren—to be 'outed' could be devastating." Since most women in the closet would be unlikely to call attention to themselves by writing such a letter, I always wondered who had taken up the cause of the poor, benighted natural mother. Was this person an adoptive parent? The sibling of someone who gave up a child but never mentioned it in the family? A sibling or parent who didn't want the family's dirty linen to be out in the open if the child, now grown, came back one day?

The letter writers who worried about mothers being outed never revealed their reasons for writing, just as the men who railed against me never revealed why they were so upset about something they seemingly had no personal stake in. That year in New York, the bill went into the circular trash can once again.

Years galloped on.

38   Justice Arrives in New York

SPRING 2019—The signs are good that the New York legislature will finally pass a law that would unseal the original birth certificates of adoptees in the state. The last decade has been a dreary waiting period, like standing outside a prison waiting for someone to be exonerated and freed, knowing it will happen—someday—but every time it's about to, the administrative machinery stops. Every time we were close, there would be another setback, another committee appointed to deliberate the sticking point: the "birth mother veto."

Oh, there might be a father on a birth certificate here or there, if the couple was married, a few fathers among the thousands of relinquishing mothers, but the veto in the legislators' muddled minds continued to center on protecting the anonymity of the mother. The disgraced sinner of yesterday now had rights that were paramount!

Then the ground shifts. After decades of houses divided by party affiliation or petty alliances, new leaders are in power. Democrats rule both the New York State Assembly and the Senate. We hear that the governor, Andrew Cuomo, a Democrat, will sign our bill once it passes. Some of our opponents have been disgraced. Republican Dean Skelos, who had been the majority leader of the state senate after Joe Bruno, is in jail. Both he and his predecessor are adoptive fathers. Sheldon Silver, the former leader of the assembly, is fighting his conviction. We have new supporters plus the old guard who have been with us for years. My assemblyman has been a sponsor of our bills for the last several years and is again this year; my senator has let me know he will

411

vote for it. Conflict among the various groups working for change in New York breaks out, but still, we all smell victory.

In March I'm back in Albany, buzzing through the hallways with activists Suzanne Bachner, adoptee and playwright, and her husband, the writer and actor Bob Brader. We number about a dozen that day—adoptees, mothers, and at least one adoptive parent, my friend, the author Adam Pertman. In separate clusters, we cajole legislators and their aides and leave literature. It is a good day, full of energy and enthusiasm. Positive responses bolster our spirits. Back home, we wait. Television spots and newspaper features about the proposed legislation appear.

In mid-May, the bill passes thirteen to zero out of the New York State Senate Health Committee. With the usual year-end flurry of bills, the legislative session inches toward dissolution. Our bill must pass before the session winds down or we will have to wait until January. At that point we will have to restart the lobbying, keep our supporters in line, and unearth new ones.

What can I do? I can write something. I bang out a thousand-word opinion piece for the *Times-Union*, the only daily left in Albany. It is the third essay I've written for the paper over the years. The editor emails me that the piece will run, but the paper does not pay for unsolicited essays, and others are ahead of it in line. I stress that it must be published as soon as possible, since the legislative session is ending.

On June 3, the Senate votes fifty-six to six in favor of passage. Everyone celebrates, together and apart. The bill has seventy-eight sponsors in the assembly, more than enough for passage in the 150-member body.

Still, something can go wrong. We've been so close before. Two years earlier, a terrible bill written by too many lawyers had to be stopped at the last minute, but this time we have a good bill. I email the *Times-Union*'s editor, expressing urgency. He responds that if I cut it down to six hundred words, he might be able get it in. Cutting that much means that it has to be almost completely rewritten. I comply. It runs on June 6, a Saturday.[153] I agonize

---

[153] See the appendix for the article that ran in the *Times-Union*.

that fewer legislators will read it, as most leave Albany for the weekend. My assemblyman, Fred Thiele, says he will send it to everyone in the assembly.

More waiting.

Sheldon Silver, who commanded the assembly like a dictator and who had opposed us for two decades, had responded to my several letters over the years with verbiage and obfuscation. Now he is awaiting word that his appeal on a corruption conviction will be overturned.

On June 20, Senate bill 3419/A5494 is up for a vote in the assembly. It's a Saturday, and they will go on late into the night to finish up everything on the agenda. Legal sausage-making at its finest. Or lowest.

Adoptees and first mothers are in the balcony in Albany. Tony and I watch the session live on television from our kitchen table. Fred and I text back and forth as we wait for the bill to come to the floor. Finally, it's up.

The chief sponsor of the bill, David Weprin, uses the words "human rights" several times when he speaks. He's been doggedly at this for nearly a

Figure 19. Bob Brader, Lorraine, and Suzanne Bachner in front of the capitol in Albany, March 2019, the day we lobby the New York State legislature to unseal the birth records of adoptees.

decade, taking over after other sponsors left the legislature, taking grief from opponents, but never backing down. He notes that if the birth certificate does not have the information the adopted person is requesting and other state documents do have it, the adopted person will get as much as the state can provide.

Getting the supplementary information is an added bonus. The bill is even better than I realized.

Assemblyman Andy Goodell isn't ready to give up the ghost and fulminates for several minutes about why the records should stay sealed, using the same old words we've heard for decades: rape victim, traumatic, interference in the parental relationship, courageous, reduce the number of children given up for adoption, consent. He points out there is a State mutual-consent registry for birth parents and adoptees. He adds that the Women's Bar Association of New York is against this bill. He quotes them, using the phrase "forced identification" when referring to birth mothers. The Women's Bar is full of family-law specialists, I point out to Tony. Their paying clients are mostly adoptive parents, not relinquishing mothers, not adoptees.

But other assembly members quickly outshine him, starting with adoptee Pamela Hunter. She efficiently shoots down the worth of the State registry—she's still waiting to hear from the State. When she's done, her impassioned speech gets a standing ovation. Andrew Raia says his mother, a town clerk for thirty-eight years, found the most difficult and disheartening task she had was to tell someone she couldn't give them their birth records. Adoptee Monica Wallace says learning her medical history became incredibly important when she became pregnant. Adoptive mother Didi Barrett says that her child from Russia sadly will never be able to find his roots, and that this bill is long overdue. Joe Lentol, who, as chair of the crucial Codes Committee, had held up our legislation for years, stands up and emotionally apologizes for doing so. A Democrat like Silver, Lentol probably had been doing Silver's bidding, and he says that he always felt guilty when he had to turn down the adoptees who lobbied him.

Back at home in Sag Harbor, tears are streaming down my face.

When it's Fred's turn, he credits my years of lobbying him for educating him about the issue, and says he is enthusiastically for passage.

The voting begins. It's done by pressing a button on one's desk. A few more members speak as the voting is underway. Richard Gottfried, who was twenty-eight when he co-chaired the public hearing at which I first testified back in 1976, is still our champion. Speaking off the cuff, he says today, thirty-eight years later, "If the government has information so profoundly important as one's birth history, no government has the right to keep that from you. Experience teaches that when people get this information, when there are reunions, they are enormously emotionally positive—on both sides."

Carmen De La Rosa, born and adopted in the Dominican Republic, says that because she found "a piece of paper" with her biological mother's name on it, she was able to reunite with siblings. She's voting in the affirmative, she says, "because sometimes you can be in a roomful of people and still feel like no one is with you because you don't know where you came from."

I'm really weeping now, blowing my nose. Tony has tears in his eyes too. Quietly and in the background, Tony's been part of this fight, standing by me, always understanding, making phone calls to legislators when I asked. Years of pent-up frustration waiting for this day are released with our tears, exhaled with each breath.

Many of the usual suspects who for years have been against legislation without a mother's veto (and some even with one) do a turnabout and vote *aye*. Danny O'Donnell, who once told me he would never vote to unseal the records, makes no speech. But he votes *aye*.

The final tally for H5494, which is the same as the Senate bill, is 140 to 6. Four abstentions.[154]

Later that day, I call Florence Fisher. We two warriors must commiserate and celebrate. We chat on the phone like the old friends we are. She lives in Brooklyn, I live more than a hundred miles away, and we haven't seen each other in years. She's past ninety now, and long ago retired from all adoption work. But you never truly leave what has defined your life for decades the

---

[154] Video of the session that passed the adoptee-rights bill (H5494) in the New York State Assembly: www.nystateassembly.granicus.com/MediaPlayer. php?view_id=7&clip_id=5185&meta_id=94776&fbclid=IwAR1aJ_4TQ8xLJAiY jj_gcSh0K4slKdlZUUoSznkDypyu6Zg5W5s3PKAR1rI.

way you might discard a pair of Capri pants that you'll never wear again. Adoption stays in your closet.

Six days later, Silver's conviction is partly overturned, which means not entirely. In July he is resentenced to prison. In August, Silver begins serving his six-and-a-half-year sentence in Otisville, New York, known as America's cushiest prison.

It is still prison.

Then it is rumored that Silver will be included in President Trump's last batch of sketchy pardons.

He is not.

Governor Cuomo signs the bill on November 14, 2019.

Fred has a signed copy of the bill framed for me. It hangs in my office.

Adoptees by the thousands begin applying for their birth certificates on the first day they can, January 15, 2020.

Connecticut did away with the doughnut hole in their laws in 2021 and thus granted all adopted people the right to their original birth records. Massachusetts did the same in 2022. Louisiana opened their records the same year. Vermont's opened in 2023. More than twenty other states allow adoptees restricted access to an original birth certificate, but more than a dozen, as well as Washington, DC, have not touched their sealed-records statutes for decades.

Justice awaits.

39 House with the Red Door

You never know how your life story will go at the beginning, when you are young and full of yourself. Since I did not slide into Tom's arms that steamy-hot summer night so long ago, I ended up with a far different life. I, who had vowed never to be ensnared by biology, ended up exactly that way. I am a woman. I had a child. I did not keep her.

Certainly, I had no idea what that young Asian woman who read my palm in Rochester meant when she said, "You will have one child, but there is a problem, like he's adopted." If I had known the meaning of that prophecy, surely, I would have tried to outwit fate, but fate undoubtedly would have found me nonetheless, keeping its own appointment in Samarra.

Relinquishing my daughter changed me, and not simply because through that act I came to a cause that shaped my life. Giving her up made me feel apart from the great forward rush that is a normal life. No one wants to end up like me. No one wants to grow up to be a woman who gives up a baby. No one would wish that for her daughter.

The celebratory way adoption is portrayed today—on television, in the movies, in magazines—largely ignores that behind every happy adoption and every happy adoptive family is another family mourning the missing link in their family tree. And there is a child who, no matter how successful and content or how open the adoption, will one day wonder, if only for a moment, Why didn't she keep me? What was wrong with me?

Life is messy, children often end up paying the price, and there will always be adoptions. Clearly having children raised in families is better than

417

having them languish in the poorhouses and orphanages of the past, with their shoddy conditions and unsparing misery. Undoubtedly a need exists for families to raise the children of addicts and felons and women who cannot manage another child for whatever reason.

Yet in America the adoption of infants by the middle and upper class is largely a cultural phenomenon, not a necessity. Babies end up being transferred from one family to another in what is ultimately a financial transaction, even though the money does not go to the mother. The lawyers, the agencies, and the social workers employed by the agencies must all be paid. If the mothers could provide, most would keep their children—as they do in some parts of the world. Far too many adoptions in America are based largely on class and money, and they are the unnecessary product of a billion-dollar industry that promotes adoption as A Good Thing. Adoption is many things, but an unencumbered Good Thing it is not.

After Jane and I reunited, we built a relationship, and, despite everything, we did reach rapprochement and had some wonderful times together. I do have good memories, even times when for a few moments, or hours, it felt as if we were hand in glove, united by blood and all the personal peculiarities we shared that bound us tight. But nothing was ever as if she had not been relinquished, as if I had kept her, as if she did not have another family, as if we had grown together rather than apart for so many years. Nothing could ever erase her sense of abandonment, nor my sense of knowing that not keeping her was wrong. No matter what closeness we came to at times, we would always have this chasm to overcome, and we would never be able to bridge it completely. That was a given once I signed the papers terminating my parental rights.

In many ways, I can never forgive myself.

Sarah? I don't know what to think about her, and so mostly I don't. Her last email said she was in a good place, don't bother her—in words harsher than that. All right. I will leave her be. As Orson Welles once said, "If you want a happy ending, that depends, of course, on where you stop your story." If this book had ended before communication halted, this ending would be different. I remind myself that the people who want to be in my life will be. I don't have to chase after them.

Do I sometimes think I made the wrong decision, that I should have moved heaven and hell and stood up against the conventional wisdom and found a way to keep my daughter? Of course. But I did what I did and have tried to make amends for it with the tools given me—writing about the injustice of closed adoption, about its pitfalls and sorrows and the long, slow burn of its aftermath.

Do I ever consider what my life might have been without giving birth to my daughter? Of course I have. Ron Martin, the assistant city editor at the *Democrat & Chronicle*—a Gannett newspaper—went on to be the first executive editor of *USA Today*, also a Gannett newspaper. Ron had been the one who brought me to Rochester. If I had stayed at the *D&C*, it's not improbable that I might have ended up at *USA Today* in Washington, DC, where the paper is based. Yes, Washington is not the Manhattan that glowed like Oz to me, but the nation's capital is a big city with a national newspaper, and that likely would have lured me in.

And I wouldn't have ended up like Lorraine.

Yet my life has been much more than a vale of tears. I have the career I always wanted—though not in the way I would have wanted it. Somewhere along the way, much to my late mother's barely contained amusement, I learned how to make her Easter prune cake with buttercream frosting, and to Tony's delight, I can bake an apple pie that turns out close enough to his mother's to pass muster. I was not a gracious pupil when my mother insisted that I learn how to sew an "invisible" seam by hand, hem a pant leg, or iron a shirt, but damn if it didn't turn out that I enjoy these simple tasks today. I've made love, made mistakes, and carried on. Like the song says, I am woman, I am strong. I too am blessed with Tony, the right companion and the long, strong love of my life; my daughter, troubled though she was—she was mine in ways that I understood and knew, until she left us; Kimberly, a strong, superb granddaughter; a wealth of compassionate family and friends; and an adoption community that, thanks to the internet and social media, spreads around the globe. It is all good.

But.

There are moments when I cannot but wonder what my life might be had I taken that step toward Tom in the middle of the night. Certainly, that would have altered the trajectory of our lives. That is a story that always includes a daughter who is kept. Movies about first loves that get second chances, or don't, take me to that place of *what if*, but only for an hour.

I remember when my mother or one of the men I dated said to me, "I don't know what's going to happen to you," as if there were some strange emanation I gave off. I wondered why they said that. What did they see or sense? Perhaps it was because my ambition seemed outsized from my station and gender.

Yet in the darkness, at those times when I feel most indelibly me, despite the heartache, despite my daughter's adoption, despite not achieving some other less convoluted career not cemented with tears, I know that I ended up exactly where I was meant to be. I would have never chosen this path if given the choice long ago, for anyone can see it is strewn with rocks that clang together to make their own ironic music. I have danced to that tune the best I know how.

When I was a forlorn teenager, I wrote a poem about someone who contentedly lived on a hill in a house with a red door. "I am lonely now but I have hopes and dreams," the poem begins. My Lochinvar did come. I have that house now. The location on a hill was ostensibly coincidence when Tony found our home on High Street. Some years later, I painted the door red, and then was taken aback when my poem came whispering through layers of ancient memory. We have moved since to another house on a small hill. Inexplicably, a red door was already in place when we found it.

I never thought that house with the red door would be mine, nor could I have imagined the zigzag path that would lead me here.

Appendix

Allow Adopted People Right to Know Their True Identity

by Lorraine Dusky

Debate over whether the original birth records of adopted people should be opened to them as adults always comes down to a "promise" made to the women who relinquished those individuals when they were infants and could not speak for themselves. The New York Senate voted Monday to do away with this outdated regulation, but the Assembly has long ignored it.[155]

Never mind if the law as written never intended to "protect" those women. Never mind the rights of those children, now adults. Never mind their need for medical histories, or an innate, unquenchable quest to know the truth of their origins and where they fit into the tree of life. Never mind that DNA matches may find one's original family. Never mind that television shows highlight the deep comfort that comes in knowing one's genealogical history, where even people who aren't adopted sometimes break out in tears when they learn about their ancestors.

Despite the overwhelming reasons to do away with an outdated 1936 law in New York, it stays on the books. There is that supposedly legal promise of "anonymity" made to mothers.

I want to scream.

When I relinquished a child in 1966, I railed against sealing my daughter's birth certificate—from her—until my exasperated social worker said that unless I agreed, "we can't help you." That "right" to anonymity was a mandate forced upon me by a state law written when Franklin Roosevelt was president, before I was born and four decades before my daughter was. I had to agree to let the state take away her right to ever know her true identity, for her

---

[155] Originally published in the Albany *Times-Union*, June 6, 2019.

birth certificate would be sealed for all time, even to future generations. Her true history would be erased.

That knowledge was the absolute cruelest part of signing those papers.

I speak not for all birth mothers, but I do speak for many. We are the women who wait and hope our children will one day find us. For myself, I paid someone a hefty sum to find my daughter decades ago and discovered that for medical reasons her parents were already trying to locate me.

But whether we mothers who want no privacy from our own flesh and blood are few or many, any such "right to privacy" loses all moral authority stacked against an adopted person's right to their own, true identity.

Yet in the arguments that keep original birth records sealed from people whom they most concern—the adopted—their well-being is conveniently swept under the dusty rug of old law and settled practice. Opponents of unsealing the birth certificates don't argue that sealed records are in the best interests of the adopted. Instead, they demand birth mothers keep a "right" that the law never included or intended and that courts have ruled is not constitutionally protected.

No other law exists that holds binding a contract between one person (the relinquishing mother) and the state over a third person (the adoptee). In doing so, the state treats adopted people as no more than chattel over which the state retains a lifelong bondage of anonymity.

No just government should exert such invasive and degrading control over any group of people, people otherwise equal under the law. Adult adoptees can marry, enlist, vote, get a driver's license, divorce, and, in short, do everything the rest of us can as fully functioning adults without anyone else's permission; but, what they cannot do is have an unamended copy of their original birth certificate. Not only is this social engineering at its worst, it is immoral and unjust.

There ought to be a law against such mindless cruelty. And there could be, if only the Assembly would act.

Additional Reading

Eldridge, Sherrie. *Twenty Things Adopted Kids Wish Their Adoptive Parents Knew*. New York: Dell, 1999.

Fessler, Ann. *The Girls Who Went Away: The Hidden History of Women Who Surrendered Children for Adoption in the Decades before Roe v. Wade*. New York: Penguin, 2006.

Glaser, Gabrielle. *American Baby: A Mother, a Child, and the Shadow History of Adoption*. New York: Viking, 2021.

Hill, Richard. *Finding Family: My Search for Roots and the Secrets in My DNA*. Sanger, CA: Familius, 2017.

————. *Guide to DNA Testing: How to Identify Ancestors, Confirm Relationships, and Measure Ethnic Ancestry through DNA Testing*. Self-published, 2014. Kindle.

Holden, Lori, with Crystal Hass. *The Open-Hearted Way to Open Adoption: Helping Your Child Grow Up Whole*. Lanham, MD: Rowman & Littlefield, 2013. Holden is an adoptive mother.

Joyce, Kathryn. *The Child Catchers: Rescue, Trafficking, and the New Gospel of Adoption*. New York: Public Affairs, 2013.

Miller, Brent C., Xitao Fan, Harold D. Grotevant, Matthew Christensen, Diana D. Coyl, Manfred H. M. van Dulmen. "Adopted Adolescents' Overrepresentation in Mental Health Counseling: Adoptees' Problems or Parents' Lower Threshold for Referral?" *Journal of the American Academy of Child and Adolescent Psychiatry*. 39, vol. 12 (Dec. 2000) : 1504–11. doi: 10.1097/00004583-200012000-00011.

Myung Ja, Janine. *Adoption: What You Should Know*. Adoption Truth & Transparency Worldwide Network, 2020. Essays by international adoptees.

Myung Ja, Janine, Michael Allen Potter, and Allen L. Vance, editors. *Adoption Land: From Orphans to Activists*. Seattle: Adoption Truth and Transparency Worldwide Network: 2014.

Pavao, Joyce Maguire. *The Family of Adoption*. Boston: Beacon Press, 1998.

Pertman, Adam. *Adoption Nation: How the Adoption Revolution is Transforming America*. New York: Basic Books, 2000.

Riben, Mirah. *The Stork Market: America's Multi-Billion Dollar Unregulated Adoption Industry*. Dayton, NJ: Advocate Publications, 2007.

Sorosky, Arthur D., Annette Baran, and Reuben Pannor. "The Reunion of Adoptees and Birth Relatives." *Journal of Youth and Adolescence* 3 (1974): 195–206. doi:10.1007/BF02214749.

Triseliotis, John. *In Search of Origins*. London: Routledge, 1973.

Wadia-Ells, Susan, editor. *The Adoption Reader: Birth Mothers, Adoptive Mothers and Adopted Daughters Tell Their Stories*. Seattle: Seal Press, 1995.

Wright, William. *Born That Way: Genes, Behavior, Personality*. New York: Knopf, 1998.

Resources

Adoptee Rights Coalition
Lobbies legislators each year at the National Conference of State Legislatures.
https://www.adopteerightscoalition.com/

Adoptee Rights Law Center
Legal practice founded by the attorney Gregory Luce.
https://adopteerightslaw.com/

Adoptees' Liberty Movement Association (ALMA)
Comprehensive registry and support for adoptees. Founded by Florence Fisher in 1971.
https://www.thealmasociety.org
https://www.facebook.com/groups/109344539097611

The Adoption History Project
Comprehensive history of adoption in the United States and elsewhere.
Created by University of Oregon historian and adoptive mother Ellen Herman.
https://pages.uoregon.edu/adoption/index.html

The Adoption Initiative
Biennial conference sponsored by St. John's University with Montclair State University in New Jersey. Promotes the study of adoption issues in training programs.
https://adoptioninitiative.dryfta.com/index.php

Adoption Knowledge Affiliates
Connection, education, and support. Includes foster-care and donor-conceived communities. For individuals and professionals.
https://www.adoptionknowledge.org/

Adoption Network Cleveland
Advocacy, education, and support. For those impacted by foster care as well.
https://www.adoptionnetwork.org

Adoption Search Resource Connection (ASRC)
Education, advocacy, community and healing. Founded in 1975.
https://asrconline.org

Alliance for the Study of Adoption & Culture (ASAC)
Publishes essays on any aspect of adoption's intersection with culture and sponsors a biennial conference with a high attendance by academics.
https://www.adoptionandculture.org/

American Adoption Congress (AAC)
Umbrella organization founded in 1978 for search-and-support adoption reform groups across the US, Canada, and around the world. Lists the laws for each state.
https://www.americanadoptioncongress.org/

Bastard Nation
Legislative advocacy for civil and human rights.
Founded in 1996. Co-founded by Marley Greiner.
https://bastards.org/

Child Welfare League of America
Coalition of hundreds of private and public agencies since 1920.
https://www.cwla.org/

Coalition for Truth and Transparency in Adoption
Lobbies for legislative change in adoption law. Founded by Richard Uhrlaub.
https://www.adoptiontruthandtransparency.org

Concerned United Birthparents (CUB)
For biological parents of adopted people in the U.S.
Founded by Lee Campbell in 1976.
https://concernedunitedbirthparents.org/

DNA Detectives
CeCe Moore, the genetic genealogist on the PBS series *Finding Your Roots*, founded DNA Detectives, which provides free assistance with a volunteer team to those searching for unknown immediate family members as well as information on how to do DNA research or connect with a search angel who does.
https://thednadetectives.com/
https://www.facebook.com/groups/DNADetectives/

National Association of Adoptees & Parents
Educational and support organization with a variety of support services, including popular weekly Zoom chats with people from the full spectrum of adoption.
https://naapunited.org/

PACER
California-based peer support and educational resources, primarily in the Bay Area and Sacramento. For all triad groups.
https://www.pacer-adoption.org/

Saving Our Sisters
Grassroots movement to provide assistance for parents in crises to prevent unnecessary adoption.
https://savingoursistersadoption.org
https://www.facebook.com/adoptionSOS

Acknowledgments

To many friends I owe thanks for their support in many ways, but for the shape and substance of this revise I especially owe Leslie Schnur a huge debt of gratitude. She said the right words at the right time, giving me the editorial suggestions that I instantly knew were right, and then read over much of the revisions with her editorial cap on. I cannot thank her enough.

Others to whom I owe a debt of gratitude are Jane Edwards, my blogging partner, who gave me both her friendship and her cogent comments; Pamela Salela, for a gimlet-eyed reading of the manuscript and her cogent comments on the history of adoption; Judith Long, for putting up with my many revisions; my brother Tom Dusky, for helping with the photographs; and Audrey Flack, Kathryn Levy, Robert Caro, Thomas Harris, and Roger Cooper for their friendship and unflagging belief in this work.

Others gave their encouragement—either financially or emotionally or both—over the many years a manuscript became this book: Jessica Anderson, Sharon Arnez, Cindy L. Aulabaugh, Susan Bernarz, Ridgley Biddle, Patty Bybee, Victoria Chadwell, Jennifer Scoggin Cowin, Cathie Creely, Eileen Drennen, Tom Flynn, Cheryl Gribskov, Leslie Griffith, Tracy Harris and Lucian Truscott, Richard Hill, Nancy Horgan, Edmund Horsey, Kathleen Horton, Louise Jaxel, Marcie Keithley, Andrea Kelley, James Lane, Lynn Langway, Faith Marshall, Kate McMullen, Eileen Mertens, Bridget Morgan, Lois B. Morris, Meagan Muladore, Marianne Novy, Glenn O'Kray, Joy Pantelis, Bonnie Parsons, Kathleen Rich, Joyce Ricker, Lisa Roberts, Diane Roberts-Hill, Katherine Ryden, Elizabeth Samuels, Virginia F. Slater, Lynn Sonberg, Martha Spector, Mary Spitzer, Michele Stickler, Barbara Thavis, and Tania Wieking.

Thanks to Suzanne Bachner and Bob Brader for their support that grew into friendship the day we spent in Albany at the legislature lobbying, and Kiana Davenport, one of the first people I shared my secret with some five decades ago.

About Marylee MacDonald, my editor, I cannot heap enough praise. She stepped in at exactly the right moment and was the kind of editor one dreams about but often does not find. She knew where to cut, knew where to expand, and the book is richer and smarter due to her fine tuning.

Lastly, I thank my husband, Anthony Brandt, who stood by me and this book through all the years of living and writing it with unflagging encouragement. He read early drafts, middle drafts, late drafts of both editions, and he never stopped believing in it. We became characters in each other's life story, and I can't imagine mine without him in it.

About the Author

Lorraine Dusky was the first to publicly declare she gave up a child for adoption in a 1975 *New York Times* Op-Ed, and she followed that with the first memoir from that perspective, *Birthmark,* in 1979. With the memoir, Dusky became a lightning rod for controversy surrounding adoption as the institution was changing and becoming more open.

Her writing on the subject has been in numerous national magazines and daily newspapers across the country, from *Newsweek* to *Town & Country* to the *New York Times.* She testified in court and at state and federal hearings on behalf of adoptee rights and made media appearances when it was shocking to hear from women who surrendered children to adoption.

But she is not simply a woman who writes about having given up a child. On other topics, she was a finalist for a National Magazine Award and won two Exceptional Merit Media Awards (EMMAs) from the National Women's Political Caucus for her writing on the political issues of the day.

Bibliography

ALMA Society, Inc. v. Mellon. 601 F.2d 1225 (2nd Cir., 1979). Cert. denied. 444, US 995, 1979.

Anderson, Robert. *Second Choice: Growing Up Adopted.* Chesterfield, MO: Badger Hill Press, 1993

Arons, Jessica. *The Adoption Option: Adoption Won't Reduce Abortion but It Will Expand Women's Choices.* Parenting with Dignity: A Series Exploring Real Supports for Pregnant Women, no. 3. Washington, DC: Center for American Progress, 2010.   www.web.archive.org/web/20220614161132/https://www.americanprogress.org/article/the-adoption-option/.

Askren, Holli Ann, and Kathaleen C. Bloom. "Postadoptive Reactions of the Relinquishing Mother: A Review." *Journal of Obstetric, Gynecologic, & Neonatal Nursing* 28, no. 4 (July 1999): 395–400. https://doi.org/10.1111/j.1552-6909.1999.tb02008.x.

Austin, Linda Tollett. *Babies for Sale: The Tennessee Children's Home Adoption Scandal.* Westport, CT: Praeger, 1993.

Baer, Janine M. *Growing in the Dark: Adoption Secrecy and Its Consequences.* Bloomington, IN: Xlibris, 2004.

Barra, Angela. "We Need to Talk About Adoptee Suicide." *HuffPost Contributor,* May 27, 2021. www.web.archive.org/web/20220614192244/https://www.huffpost.com/entry/we-need-to-talk-about-adoptee-suicide_b_5928c632e4b07d848fdc03c9.

"Birth Family's Legal Rights after Adoption." HG.org Legal Resources. Accessed Jan. 2021. www.web.archive.org/web/20220825210831/https://www.hg.org/birth-familys-legal-rights-after-adoption.html.

Borczykowski, Annika von, Anders Hjern, Frank Lindblad, and Bo Vinnerljung. "Suicidal Behavior in National and International Adult Adoptees." *Social Psychiatry and Psychiatric Epidemiology* 41, no. 2 (2006): 95–102. https://doi.org/10.1007/s00127-005-0974-2.

Bouchard, Thomas J., Jr., David T. Lykken, Matthew McGue, Nancy L. Segal, and Auke Tellegen. "Sources of Human Psychological Differences: The Minnesota Study of Twins Reared Apart." *Science,* n.s., 250, no. 4978 (Oct. 12, 1990): 223–28. https://www.science.org/doi/10.1126/science.2218526.

Brandt, Anthony. "Bloodlines." *Esquire,* Sept. 1984, 21–22.

Brodzinsky, David, Marshall Schechter, and Robin Marantz Henig. *Being Adopted: The Lifelong Search for Self.* New York: Anchor-Doubleday, 1992.

Carp, E. Wayne. *Family Matters: Secrecy and Disclosure in the History of Adoption.* Cambridge, MA: Harvard University Press, 1998.

Christensen, Jakob, Mogens Vestergaard, Preben Bo Mortensen, Per Sidenius, and Esben Agerbo. "Epilepsy and Risk of Suicide: a Population-Based Case-Control Study." *Lancet Neurology* 6, no. 8 (Aug. 2007): 693–98. https://doi.org/10.1016/s1474-4422(07)70175-8.

Comfort, Nathaniel. "Genetic Determinism Redux." *Nature* 561 (Sept. 27, 2018): 461–63. https://web.archive.org/web/20220825214038/https://media.nature.com/original/magazine-assets/d41586-018-06784-5/d41586-018-06784-5.pdf.

Deykin, Eva Y., Lee Campbell, and Patricia Patti. "The Postadoption Experience of Surrendering Parents." *American Journal of Orthopsychiatry* 54, no. 2 (Apr. 1984): 271–81. https://doi.org/10.1111/j.1939-0025.1984.tb01494.x.

Dusky, Lorraine. "The Adopted Child Has a Right to Know EVERYTHING," *Parents*, Oct. 1975, 40–43.

———. "Adoptees' Best Interests." Op-Ed. *New York Times*, Feb. 6, 1982.

———. "Allow Adopted People Right to Know Their True Identity." *Times-Union* (Albany, NY), June 6, 2019. https://web.archive.org/web/20220614214009/https://www.timesunion.com/opinion/article/Commentary-Allow-adopted-people-right-to-know-13951654.php.

———. *Birthmark.* New York: M. Evans, 1979.

———. "The Daughter I Gave Away." *McCall's*, July 1983.

———. "Help Adoptees Reach First Parents." *Newsday*, Viewpoints, May 12, 2011.

———. "I Found My Mother." *Cosmopolitan*, June 1974, 62.

———. "I Gave Away My Baby." *Family Circle*, Oct. 9, 1979, 40+.

———. "Like Adoptees, Petri-Dish Babies May Long for Past." *USA Today*, The Forum, Jan. 7, 1998.

———. "A Natural Mother Speaks Out on Adoptees' Right to Know." *Town & Country*, Oct. 1976

———. "Somewhere Out There Is a Daughter of Mine." *New Woman*, Mar.–Apr. 1977, 34–37, 52–55.

———. "Things Your Husband/Lover Never Told You about Sex." *New Woman*, June–July 1972, 62–69, 134–42.

———. [Phyllis Bernard, pseud.]. "Who Is My Daughter?" *Newsweek*, Oct. 15, 1979, 27.

———. "Who'll Adopt These Babies, Mr. Bush?" *Newsday*, Viewpoints, Oct. 20, 1988.

———. "Yearning." *New York Times*, March 1, 1975, 25. https://web.archive.org/web/20220927210527/https://www.nytimes.com/1975/03/01/archives/yearning.html.

Ellison, Marcia A. "Authoritative Knowledge and Single Women's Unintentional Pregnancies, Abortions, Adoption and Single Motherhood: Social Stigma and Structural Violence." *Medical Anthropology Quarterly* 17, no. 3 (2003): 322–47.

Federal Register 45, no. 33 (Feb. 15, 1980): 10305–748.

Festinger, Trudy, and James Jaccard. "Suicidal Thoughts in Adopted versus Non-Adopted Youth: A Longitudinal Analysis in Adolescence, Early Young Adulthood, and Young Adulthood." *Journal of the Society for Social Work and Research* 3, no. 4 (Nov. 15, 2012): 280–95. https://doi.org/10.5243/jsswr.2012.17.

Fisher, Florence. *The Search for Anna Fisher.* New York: Arthur Fields Books, 1973.

"4 Women Who Learned They Were Sisters through DNA Testing Speak Out: 'It Was Pretty Mind-Blowing.'" *Good Morning America*, Feb. 26, 2019.

Fuller, Nicole. "Dean Skelos and Son, Adam, Scheduled to Start Federal Prison Sentence Tuesday." *Newsday*, Jan. 6, 2019.

Goldman, Ari L. "State Seeks Children with Links to DES." *New York Times*, May 10, 1979, C-7.

Goldstein, Marilyn. "Forging a Family Bond after 17 Years." *Newsday*, July 21, 1983.

Graves, Kori A. "Before It Was 'A Practice of Genocide': Transracial Adoption and African Americans in the 1950s and 1960s." Presentation at the Alliance for the Study of Adoption and Culture conference, Minneapolis, MN, Oct. 28, 2016.

Hawkes, Rebecca. "My Overtime Mind: Who's in Charge of This Reunion?" *Lost Daughters* (blog), Oct. 10, 2012. https://web.archive.org/web/20220825223359/http://www.thelostdaughters.com/2012/10/my-overtime-mind-whos-in-charge-of-this.html.

Henney, Susan M., Susan Ayers-Lopez, Ruth G. McRoy, and Harold D. Grotevant. "Evolution and Resolution: Birthmothers' Experience of Grief and Loss at Different Levels of Adoption Openness." *Journal of Social and Personal Relationships* 24, no. 6 (Dec. 2007): 875–89. https://doi.org/10.1177/0265407507084188.

Herman, Ellen. *Kinship by Design: A History of Adoption in the Modern United States.* Chicago: University of Chicago Press, 2008.

Hymowitz, Kay, Jason S. Carroll, W. Bradford Wilcox, and Kelleen Kaye. *Knot Yet: Benefits and Costs of Delayed Marriage in America.* National Marriage Project, University of Virginia / National Campaign to Prevent Teen and Unplanned Pregnancy / RELATE Institute, 2013. https://web.archive.org/web/20220615171621/http://nationalmarriageproject.org/wordpress/wp-content/uploads/2013/04/KnotYet-FinalForWeb-041413.pdf.

Janson, Donald. "Adopted Children Seeking Changes in Law on Finding Natural Parents." *New York Times*, Oct. 27, 1976, 88. https://web.archive.org/web/20220614224131/https://www.nytimes.com/1976/10/27/archives/adopted-children-seeking-changes-in-law-on-finding-natural-parents.html?searchResultPosition=1.

———. "Jersey Eases Access to Adoption Records." *New York Times*, New Jersey, Feb. 5, 1977, A-1.

"Joint Public Hearing: Sealed Adoption Records and the Search for Identity." New York State Senate/Assembly, Temporary State Commission on Child Welfare, Apr. 28, 1976, Albany, NY. Bastard Nation. Accessed Feb. 2021. https://web.archive.org/web/20081109045659/http://www.bastards.org/activism/local/ny/hearings.html.

Jones, Merry Bloch. *Birthmothers: Women Who Have Relinquished Babies for Adoption Tell Their Stories*. Chicago: Chicago Review Press, 1993.

Joyce, Eric. "*Blueprint* by Robert Plomin: Latest Intelligence Genetics Book Could Be a Gift for Far-Right." *The Conversation*, Nov. 5, 2018. https://web.archive.org/web/20220825213733/https://theconversation.com/blueprint-by-robert-plomin-latest-intelligence-genetics-book-could-be-a-gift-for-far-right-104499.

Kaplan, Arline. "Adoption and Mental Illness," *Psychiatric Times*. Jan. 26, 2009. https://web.archive.org/web/20230110211807/https://www.psychiatrictimes.com/view/adoption-and-mental-illness.

Kelly, Judy A. "The Trauma of Relinquishment: The Long-Term Impact of Relinquishment on Birthmothers Who Lost Their Infants to Adoption during the Years 1965–1972." Master's thesis, Goddard College, 1999. *Birthmother Research Project*. https://web.archive.org/web/20220614224800/https://sites.google.com/site/birthmotherresearchproject/.

Keyes, Margaret A., Stephen M. Malone, Anu Sharma, William G. Iacono, and Matt McGue. "Risk of Suicide Attempt in Adopted and Nonadopted Offspring," *Pediatrics* 132, no. 4 (Oct. 2013): 639–46. https://doi.org/10.1542/peds.2012-3251.

Keyes, Margaret A., Anu Sharma, Irene J. Elkins, William G. Iacono, and Matt McGue. "The Mental Health of US Adolescents Adopted in Infancy." *Archives of Pediatrics & Adolescent Medicine* 162, no. 5 (May 2008): 419–25. https://web.archive.org/web/20220614230737/https://jamanetwork.com/journals/jamapediatrics/fullarticle/379446.

Kirschner, David. *Adoption: Uncharted Waters: A Psychologist's Case Studies*. Woodbury, NY: Juneau Press, 2006.

Klemesrud, Judy. "Mothers Find the Children They Gave Up." *New York Times*, Aug. 29, 1983. https://web.archive.org/web/20220927221853/https://www.nytimes.com/1983/08/29/style/mothers-find-the-children-they-gave-up.html?searchResultPosition=1.

Kohler, Julie K., Harold D. Grotevant, and Ruth G. McRoy. "Adopted Adolescents' Preoccupation with Adoption: The Impact on Adoptive Family Relationships." *Journal of Marriage and Family* 64, no. 1 (Feb. 2002): 93–104. https://doi.org/10.1111/j.1741-3737.2002.00093.x.

Krementz, Jill. *How It Feels to Be Adopted*. New York: Knopf, 1982.

Lang, Susan S. "Adoptive Parents Are Overwhelmingly in Favor of Opening Sealed Adoption Records, Cornell Study Finds." *Cornell Chronicle*, Jan. 30, 1997. https://web.archive.org/web/20220614233956/https://news.cornell.edu/stories/1997/01/adoptive-parents-are-overwhelmingly-favor-opening-sealed-adoption-records-cornell.

Lee, Dong-Gun, Yeonkyung Lee, Hyeeun Shin, Kyusik Kang, Jong-Moo Park, Byung-Kun Kim, Ohyun Kwon, and Jung-Ju Lee. "Seizures Related to Vitamin B6 in Adults." *Journal of Epilepsy Research* 5. 2015 , no. 1 (June 30, 2015): 23–24. https://doi.org/10.14581/jer.15006.

Lifton, Betty Jean. *Lost and Found: The Adoption Experience*. 3rd ed. Ann Arbor: University of Michigan Press, 2009.

———. *Twice Born: Memoirs of an Adopted Daughter*. New York: St. Martin's Griffin, 1998.

"Love Is Thicker Than Blood." *New Woman*, letters, July–Aug. 1977, 61–62, 64, 66.

March, Karen. "Birth Mother Grief and the Challenge of Adoption Reunion Contact." *American Journal of Orthopsychiatry* 84, no. 4 (2014): 406–19. https://doi.apa.org/doiLanding?doi=10.1037%2Fort0000013.

Martin, Joyce A., Brady E. Hamilton, Michelle J. K. Osterman, and Anne K. Driscoll. "Births: Final Data for 2019." National Vital Statistics Reports 70, no. 2 (Mar. 23, 2021). Supplemental tables. https://web.archive.org/web/20221202013221/https://www.cdc.gov/nchs/data/nvsr/nvsr70/nvsr70-02-tables-508.pdf.

Maza, Penelope L. *Adoption Trends: 1944-1975*. U.S. Children's Bureau, Aug. 1984, 1–4. Child Welfare League of America Papers, box 65, Social Welfare History Archives, University of Minnesota. https://web.archive.org/web/20220609235345/https://darkwing.uoregon.edu/~adoption/archive/MazaAT.htm.

Miller, Brent C., Xitao Fan, Harold D. Grotevant, Matthew Christensen, Diana D. Coyl, and Manfred H. M. van Dulmen. "Adopted Adolescents' Overrepresentation in Mental Health Counseling: Adoptees' Problems or Parents' Lower Threshold for Referral?" *Journal of the American Academy of Child and Adolescent Psychiatry* 39, no. 12 (Dec. 2000): https://doi.org/10.1097/00004583-200012000-00011.

Mink, Gwendolyn, and Rickie Solinger. *Welfare: A Documentary of History U.S. Policy and Politics*. New York: New York University Press, 2003.

Mintz, Phil. "Patrick Brasley, 62, Longtime Newsday Reporter." *Newsday*, Jan. 25, 1991.

Moore, Nelwyn B., and J. Kenneth Davidson. "A Profile of Adoption Placers: Perceptions of Pregnant Teens during the Decision-Making Process." *Adoption Quarterly* 6, no. 2 (2002): 29–41.

Musser, Sandy. *To Prison With Love: An Indecent Indictment and America's Adoption Travesty*. Awareness Press, 2014.

Namerow, Pearila Brickner, Debra Kalmuss, and Linda Cushman. "The Consequences of Placing versus Parenting among Unmarried Women." *Marriage & Family Review* 25, no. 3–4 (1997): 175–97. https://journals.sagepub.com/doi/10.1177/1044389418768489.

Nemy, Enid. "Adopted Children Who Wonder, 'What Was Mother Like?'" *New York Times*, July 25, 1972, 22. https://web.archive.org/web/20220927222435/https://www.nytimes.com/1972/07/25/archives/adopted-children-who-wonder-what-was-mother-like.html?searchResultPosition=1.

Nettle, Daniel. *Personality: What Makes You the Way You Are*. Oxford: Oxford University Press, 2007.

Paul, Marla. "Study Finds Oxytocin Strengthens Memories of Both Bad and Good Events." Feinberg School of Medicine, July 22, 2013. https://web.archive.org/web/20220615174601/https://news.feinberg.northwestern.edu/2013/07/oxytocin_stress/.

Pinker, Steven. *The Blank Slate: The Modern Denial of Human Nature*. New York: Viking, 2002.

Plomin, Robert. *Blueprint: How DNA Makes Us Who We Are*. Cambridge, MA: MIT Press, 2018.

Prati, Brigitte. "Are Adopted Children at a Greater Risk of Suicide Than Their Non-adopted Peers?" Abstract. *Adolescence* 24, no. 1, (2006): 111–28. https://web.archive.org/web/20220825223021/https://www.cairn-int.info/journal-adolescence-2006-1-page-111.htm.

Raymond, Barbara Bisantz. *The Baby Thief: The Untold Story of Georgia Tann, the Baby Seller Who Corrupted Adoption*. New York: Carroll & Graf, 2007.

Reddy, Doodipala Samba. "Do Oral Contraceptives Increase Epileptic Seizures?" *Expert Review of Neurotherapeutics* 17, no. 2 (2017): 129–34. https://www.tandfonline.com/doi/abs/10.1080/14737175.2016.1243472?journalCode=iern20.

Reinagel, Monica. "How Birth Control Pills Affect Your Nutritional Needs." *Scientific American*, Sept. 23, 2015. https://web.archive.org/web/20220615180558/https://www.scientificamerican.com/article/how-birth-control-pills-affect-your-nutritional-needs/.

Rothman, David J., and Sheila M. Rothman. *The Origins of Adoption*. New York, NY: Garland Publishing, 1987.

Saffian, Sarah. *Ithaka: A Daughter's Memoir of Being Found*. New York, NY: Dell Publishing, 1998.

Samuels, Elizabeth J. "The Idea of Adoption: An Inquiry into the History of Adult Adoptee Access to Birth Records." *Rutgers Law Review* 5, no. 2 (2001): 367–436.

————. "Surrender and Subordination: Birth Mothers and Adoption Law Reform." *Michigan Journal of Adoption & Law* 20, no. 1 (2013): 33–81. https://web. archive.org/web/20220927223024/https://repository.law.umich.edu/cgi/view-content.cgi?article=1030&context=mjgl.

Schaefer, Carol. *The Other Mother.* New York: Soho Press, 1991.

Seaman, Barbara. *Women and the Crisis in Sex Hormones.* New York: Rawson Associates, 1977.

Siegel, Deborah H., and Susan Livingston Smith. *Openness in Adoption: From Secrecy and Stigma to Knowledge and Connections.* New York: Evan B. Donaldson Adoption Institute, 2102. https://web.archive.org/web/20220825200140/https://www.adoptionstar.com/openness-in-adoptionfrom-secrecy-and-stigma-to-knowledge-and-connections/.

Slap, Gail, Elizabeth Goodman, and Bin Huang. "Adoption as a Risk Factor for Attempted Suicide during Adolescence." *Pediatrics* 108, no. 2 (Aug. 2001): e30. https://doi.org/10.1542/peds.108.2.e30.

Slater, Lauren. "Repress Yourself." *New York Times Magazine,* Feb. 23, 2003. https://web.archive.org/web/20220825223938/https://www.nytimes.com/2003/02/23/magazine/repress-yourself.html.

Smith, Susan Livingston. *Safeguarding the Rights and Well-Being of Birthparents in the Adoption Process.* Rev. ed. New York: Evan B. Donaldson Adoption Institute, 2007. https://www.web.archive.org/web/20220614195035/https://library.childwelfare.gov/cwig/ws/library/docs/gateway/Blob/76045.pdf?r=1&rpp=10&upp=0&w=+NATIVE%28%27recno%3D76045%27%29&m=1.

Solinger, Rickie. *Wake Up Little Susie: Single Pregnancy and Race before Roe v. Wade.* New York: Routledge, 1992.

Sorosky, Arthur D., Annette Baran, and Reuben Pannor. *The Adoption Triangle: Sealed or Opened Records: How They Affect Adoptees, Birth Parents, and Adoptive Parents.* Garden City, NY: Anchor Press, 1978.

————. "The Reunion of Adoptees and Birth Relatives." *Journal of Youth and Adolescence* 3 (1974): 195–206. https://doi.org/10.1007/BF02214749.

Spence, Virginia. "Are Open-Adoption Agreements Legally Enforceable?" Adoption.org, GLADNEY Center for Adoption, Apr. 12, 2019. https://www.web.archive.org/web/20220614195035/https://library.childwelfare.gov/cwig/ws/library/docs/gateway/Blob/76045.pdf?r=1&rpp=10&upp=0&w=+NATIVE%28%27recno%3D76045%27%29&m=1.

"State Adoption Laws." American Adoption Congress. Accessed Aug. 25, 2022. https://web.archive.org/web/20220825224732/https://www.americanadoptioncongress.org/state.php.

"Statistics for States Implementing Access to Original Birth Certificate Laws since 2000." American Adoption Congress, Feb. 2016. https://web.archive.org/web/20220825225048/https://www.americanadoptioncongress.org/docs/Stats_for_States_with_access_Feb_-_2016.pdf.

Strauss, Jean A. *Beneath a Tall Tree: A Story about Us.* Claremont, CA: Arete, 2001.

———. *Birthright: The Guide to Search and Reunion for Adoptees, Birthparents, and Adoptive Parents.* New York: Penguin, 1994.

Tavris, Carol. "A New Start in Life." *Times Literary Supplement,* Apr. 18, 2008.

Trimberger, E. Kay. "Adoption and Genetics: Implications for Adoptive Parents." *HuffPost Contributor,* Jan. 30, 2014, updated Apr. 1, 2014. https://web.archive.org/web/20220615192226/https://www.huffpost.com/entry/adoption-and-genetics-imp_b_4682667.

Triseliotis, John, Julia Feast, and Fiona Kyle. *The Adoption Triangle Revisited: A Study of Adoption, Search, and Reunion Experiences.* London: British Association for Adoption and Fostering, 2005.

Verrier, Nancy Newton. *Coming Home to Self: The Adopted Child Grows Up.* Baltimore: Gateway Press, 2003.

———. *The Primal Wound: Understanding the Adopted Child.* Self-published, 1993.

Wang, Huei-Shyong, and Meng-Fai Kuo. "Vitamin B6 Related Epilepsy during Childhood." *Chang Gung Medical Journal* 30, no. 5 (2007): 396–401. https://web.archive.org/web/20220615193311/https://pubmed.ncbi.nlm.nih.gov/18062169/.

Warren, Sarah B. "Lower Threshold for Referral for Psychiatric Treatment for Adopted Adolescents." *Journal of the American Academy of Child & Adolescent Psychiatry* 31, no. 3 (1992): 512–17. https://www.jaacap.org/article/S0890-8567(09)64031-4/pdf.

Weiser, Benjamin, and Vivian Wang. "Dean Skelos, Ex-New York Senate Leader, Gets 4 Years and 3 Months in Prison." *New York Times,* Oct. 24, 2018.

Wilson-Buterbaugh, Karen. *The Baby Scoop Era: Unwed Mothers, Infant Adoption, Forced Surrender.* Self-published, 2017.

Younus, Iyan, and Doodipala Samba Reddy. "Seizure Facilitating Activity of the Oral Contraceptive Ethinyl Estradiol." *Epilepsy Research* 121 (Mar. 2016): 29–33. https://www.sciencedirect.com/science/article/abs/pii/S0920121116300079?via%3Dihub.

Index

A

Abortion, 91–92
 birth control pills while pregnant
  and, 231
 current state of, 84, 91, 283
 effects of adoption and, 283
 in the 1970s, 62
 New York's path to legalization
  of, 91–93
 overview, xviii
 push to keep adoption and birth
  records sealed and, 140–141
 therapeutic abortions, 57
Abrazo Adoption Services, 210
Absence seizures. *See* Epilepsy
Academy of Medicine, 91
Addiction, 238, 264, 265, 284, 376
Adolescence
 benefits of open adoption and
  contact during, 210–211
 connection between adoption and
  suicide and, 373–375
 teen pregnancy, 209–210, 236
"Adopted Child Has a Right to
 Know EVERYTHING, The"
 (Dusky), 149
"Adopted Children Who Wonder,
 'What Was Mother Like?'"
 (Nemy), 119
Adoptees, 70, 108n, 128, 173–
 174, 178. *See*
 also Adoptees searching
 for information; Adoption
 curiosity; Rights of adoptees
Adoptees' Liberty Movement
 Association (ALMA)
 ALMA Society, Inc. v. Mellon
  (1979), 140–141
 growth of, 131

"I Found My Mother" (Dusky)
 article and, 129
 inception of, 119–120, 129
 Joint Public Hearing, New York
  State Senate/Assembly: Sealed
  Adoption Records and Identity
  (1976), 136–138
 overview, 308–310, 424
 support from, 129–130
Adoptees searching for
 information. *See also* Adoption
 curiosity
 mothers who reject reunion and,
  237–239
 reactions from others and,
  323–324
 stories from, 163–165
 ways birth records were obtained
  by, 200
Adoption agencies, 209–210
"Adoption as a Risk Factor for
 Attempted Suicide during
 Adolescence" (Slap, Goodman, &
 Huang), 373–374
Adoption curiosity. *See*
 also Adoptees searching for
 information; Knowledge of one's
 family; Sealed birth records
 overview, 120, 202
 reactions from others and,
  323–324
 regardless of adoptive family
  relationships and bonds,
  408–411
 stories from others regarding,
  162–166
Adoption in the 1950s, 1960s, and
 1970s, 63–64, 66, 81–84
Adoption language
 learned by adoptees, 268–269
 overview, xv–xviii, 162
 reactions from others and,
  321–327

Adoption plan, xvi, 311

Adoption records. *See also* Birth
records; Sealed birth records

ALMA Society, Inc. v. Mellon
(1979) and, 140–141

Ann Scharp trial to obtain sealed
records and, 131–134

history of, 68–71

Model State Adoption Act and,
187–189

sealed court records of, 127

searching for adoptees and,
129–130

Adoption reform movement

access to sealed birth records,
330–331

adoptee identity while also being
a natural mother and, 155

ALMA Society, Inc. v. Mellon
(1979) and, 140–141

Ann Scharp trial to obtain sealed
records and, 131–134

arguments against, 322–323

history of, 68

Model State Adoption Act and,
187–189

Orphan Voyage organization and,
128

overview, 124

progression of, 320–321, 343–344

release of *Birthmark* (Dusky) and,
177–180, 187–188

search movement and, 269

shift towards unsealing birth
records of adoptees in New
York, 411–416

Unsealed Initiative and, 383–387

Adoption Services Associates (ASA)
in San Antonio, 210

Adoption Triangle Revisited, The
(Treseliotis, Feast, & Kyle), 104n

Adoption Triangle, The (Sorosky,
Baran, & Pannor), 108

Adoptive parents. *See also* Adoption
language

adoption curiosity regardless of
adoptive family relationships
and, 409–410

adoption language and, 323–325

anger and, 128–129, 183–185

fear and, 184–186

reactions from others and,
321–327

Agreeableness personality trait, 257

Alito, Justice Samuel, 281–282

Allesandro, Lou, 320

"Allow Adopted People Right to
Know Their True Identity"
(Dusky), 421–422

ALMA Society, Inc. v. Mellon (1979),
140–141

Amended birth certificates, 126. *See
also* Birth certificates; Sealed
birth records

Joint Public Senate Hearing, New
York Senate/Assembly: Sealed
Adoption Records and Identity
(1976), 136

kinship fostering and, 211–212

searching for adoptees and,
129–130

American Adoption Congress (AAC),
343, 424

American Medical Association, 91

Anderson, Robert, 285

Anger felt by adoptees,
128, 173–174, 178

Anger felt by adoptive parents,
128–129, 183–185

Anonymous adoption. *See
also* Closed adoptions

access to birth records and,
329–330

DNA testing and, 331–332

justification for, 410

safe-haven boxes and, 282

Anti-seizure medications, 228, 277, 373
Anxiety
  effects of adoption and, 104
  post-traumatic stress disorder (PTSD) and, 104
Apologies, 348–350
Aquinas, St. Thomas, 92
Attitudes toward adoption, 103, 321–327
Avoidance, 108, 296

B

Baby Scoop Era, 81–82
Baby Scoop Era, The (Wilson-Buterbaugh), 81n
Baby Thief, The (Raymond), 69n
Bachner, Suzanne, 412
Bahr, Joyce, 383–384
Baird, Bill, 53n
Barra, Angela, 376
Barrett, Didi, 414
Bartholet, Elizabeth, 376
Beneath a Tall Tree (Strauss), 283
Biological mothers. *See also* Adoption language; Mothers; Seeker mothers
  accuracy of the term, xvii
  effects of adoption on, 103–108
  mothers' rights in open adoptions, 206–212
  mothers who are also adoptees, 155
Birth certificates. *See* Birth records; Sealed birth records; *See* Amended birth certificates
Birth control
  birth control pills while pregnant, 171–172, 174–175, 229–231
  current state of, 84
  good Catholic girls and, 83
  in the 1960s, 52–53

Birthmark (Dusky)
  adoption reform movement and, 187–189
  excerpt from, 205
  people reaching out as a result of, 201
  publishing of, 174–185
  writing of, 166–168, 175
Birthmother Research Project, 107
Birth mothers. *See* Adoption language
Birthmothers. *See* Adoption language
Birth records. *See also* Amended birth certificates; Sealed birth records
  access to, 70–71, 328–333
  adoption in the 1960s and, 63–64
  black market adoptions and, 81
  family adoptions and, 81
  injustice of sealed birth records and, 328–333
  overview, 126
  safe-haven boxes and, 282
  searching for adoptees and, 129–130
  unsealing birth records of adoptees in New York, 411–416, 421–422
Birthright (Strauss), 155
Black children, women, and families, 82
Black market, 81. *See also* Illegal "adoptions"
Blank slate concept, 264
Brader, Bob, 412
Brandt, Anthony, 369
Bravery, idea of, 325–326
Bruno, Joseph, 189
Buck, Pearl S., xv

C

Campbell, Lee, xv, 162, 187
Carp, E. Wayne, 68

Catholic Church
  abortion and, 92–93
  birth control and, 54
  release of *Birthmark* (Dusky) and, 179
  unwed mothers and, 83–84
Children's Home Society in Washington, 68
Child Welfare League of America, 179, 269, 425
Closed adoptions, 162–166. *See also* Anonymous adoption; Sealed birth records
  adoption curiosity regardless of adoptive family relationships and, 408–410
  compared to open adoptions, 103–104, 205–212
  cruelty of, 229–230
  effects of, 105–106
  reactions from others and, 321–327
  safe-haven boxes and, 282
  searching for adoptees and, 129–130
Cole, Elizabeth, 269
Communication between the natural mother and adoptive parents, 206–209, 210. *See also* Open adoptions
Concerned United Birthparents (CUB), xv, 107, 162, 425
Coney Barrett, Justice Amy, 282
Conscientiousness personality trait, 257
Contraception. *See* Birth control
Courage, idea of, 325–329
Court cases. *See* Adoption reform movement; New York legislation and court cases
Cuomo, Andrew, 411, 416
Curiosity about one's family. *See* Adoption curiosity

D

Debate regarding terminology. *See* Adoption language
De Dorlodot, Canon Henry, 92
De La Rosa, Carmen, 415
Depakene/Depakote, 228, 276, 373. *See also* Anti-seizure medications
Depression. *See* Mental health
DES. *See* Diethylstilbestrol (DES)
Didion, Joan, 160–162
Diethylstilbestrol (DES), 171–172
Discussing adoption with others, 322–326. *See also* Adoption language
DNA
  DNA testing and sealed birth records, 332
  overview, 260–264
  twins separated by adoption and, 260–264
Dobbs v. Jackson Women's Health Organization, xviii, 281–283
Donaldson Adoption Institute, 104n, 205
Drozdowska, Bronisława Maleszinska, 141–145
Drozdowski, Tomas, 141, 143f
Dunne, John Gregory, 160–162
Dusky, Harry, 23, 147f
Dusky, Jean, 143f, 144f, 145
Dusky, Lorraine, 120, 127–129, 130, 135–136, 149, 150–151, 162–163, 169, 187–189, 205, 421–422
Dusky (Wrozek), Victoria, 147f, 370

E

Edwards, Jane, 400f
Effects of adoption. *See also* Grief; Loss; Trauma

importance of including the topic of suicide in adoption discussions, 376–377

lying, 275

overview, 103–108, 281–287, 382–385

reunions between children and parents and, 285–287

Eisenstadt v. Baird (1972), 53

Emotional response to adoption

terminology that supports and honors, xvi

Environmental factors, 263–266

Epilepsy

birth control pills while pregnant and, 229–231

suicide risk and, 373, 377

Estrogen (Estradiol), 230–231

Extraversion personality trait, 257

F

Family adoptions, 81

birth records and, 81

kinship fostering, 211–212

Family histories. *See also* Knowledge of one's family, desire for; Medical histories

adoption curiosity regardless of adoptive family relationships and, 409–410

connection between adoption and suicide and, 374

cruelty of closed adoption and, 229–231

genetic and environmental factors and, 263–266

injustice of sealed birth records and, 328–333, 382

mothers who reject reunions and, 238–239

PMS and, 243–245

value of, 141–148, 281

Family Matters (Carp), 68

Family traits. *See* Genetic bonds and traits

Fantasy life. *See also* Lying behaviors

Fear, 183–184, 236–238

Feast, Julia, 104n

"First mother". *See* Adoption language

First Mother Forum blog, 400–401

Fisher, Florence, 119, 125, 131–133, 179, 188, 255, 415

Fraternal twins. *See* Twins separated by adoption

Fully open adoptions, 206. *See also* Open adoptions

G

Gender, 264

connection between adoption and suicide and, 374

genetic and environmental factors, 263

Genealogy research, 381–382

Genetic bonds and traits. *See also* DNA

genetic and environmental factors and, 263–266

importance of, 263–264

open adoption and, 211–212

overview, 184–185

personality traits, 257–258

small, shared traits, 256–257

twins separated by adoption and, 260–263

Giovanni, Nikki, 149

Gist, Richard, 296

Giving up children. *See* Adoption language

Goldman, Ari L., 171n

Goodell, Andy, 414–415

Gossip, 236

Gottfried, Richard, 415

Grezesikowski (Wrozek), Agnes Augustine, 145–146, 146f
Grief. *See also* Loss; Trauma
  failing to acknowledge, 103–104
  in closed versus open adoptions, 105–106
  mothers who reject reunion and, 236–239
  open versus closed adoptions and, 206–207, 209–210
  over time, 236–237
  research regarding, 103–104, 104–105
  role of relationships between mother and father of the relinquished child, 123
Griswold v. Connecticut (1965), 53
Gruccio, Judge Philip A., 158–159
Guilt
  adoption curiosity regardless of adoptive family relationships and, 409
  birth control pills while pregnant and, 231
  open versus closed adoptions and, 210–211
  over time, 236–237
  post-traumatic stress disorder (PTSD) and, 108
  role of relationships between mother and father of the relinquished child on, 123

H

Hawkes, Rebecca, 285
Health, Education, and Welfare, Dept. of (HEW), 187–189
Health histories, 80, 221, 382. *See also* Family histories
  cruelty of closed adoptions and, 229–231
  injustice of sealed birth records and, 385
  PMS and, 243–245

Hillside Children's Center, 185–187. *See also* Northaven Terrace
Hormone treatments. *See also* Birth control; Progesterone
  during pregnancy, 171–172, 230–231
  for PMS, 244–245
How It Feels to Be Adopted (Krementz), 259
Humiliation, 236
Hunter, Pamela, 414

I

Identical twins, 140n, 261. *See also* Twins separated by adoption
"I Found My Mother" (Dusky), 127
Illegal "adoptions"
  adoption reform movement and, 68–69
  black market and, 81
International Soundex Reunion Registry, 399
Investigators (search angels), 203n
Ithaka (Saffian), 283

J

Joint Public Hearing, New York State Senate/Assembly: Sealed Adoption Records and Identity (1976), 136–138
Jurenovich, Elizabeth, 210

K

Kinship fostering, 211–212
Kirschner, David, 275, 284–285
Klemesrud, Judy, 175, 176, 269
Knowledge of one's family, desire for. *See also* Adoption curiosity; Family histories
  "I Found My Mother" (Dusky) article and, 127–129
  importance of knowing of family histories and, 141–148

injustice of sealed birth records and, 328–333, 381–382
overview, 120, 281
Krementz, Jill, 259
Kyle, Fiona, 104

L

Lamar, Dr. Robert C., 91
Landers, Ann, 262
Language, adoption. *See* Adoption language
LDS (Church of Jesus Christ of Latter-Day Saints), 179
Legislation. *See* Adoption reform movement; New York legislation and court cases
Lehman, Gov. Herbert H., 69, 70
Lentol, Joe, 414
Lifton, Betty Jean (B. J.), 130, 136, 187, 275, 283–284, 308, 375
Lifton, Robert J., 131–134
Loss, 417–418. *See also* Grief
failing to acknowledge, 103–104
in closed versus open adoptions, 105–106
mothers who reject reunions, 236–239
research regarding, 103–104, 105–106
terminology that supports and honors, xvi
Lost and Found: The Adoption Experience (Lifton), 284n
Louise Wise Services, 137, 139–140
Love
adoption curiosity regardless of adoptive family relationships and, 409–410
adoption language and, xvi
"Love Is Thicker Than Blood" (Dusky), 162–163
Lying behaviors

effects of adoption and, 275, 276
sexual abuse and, 278

M

Mainzer, Gertrude, 131–134
Martin, Ron, 38, 43–44, 419
Medical histories. *See also* Family histories
cruelty of closed adoption and, 229–231
genetic and environmental factors and, 263–266
injustice of sealed birth records and, 328–333, 382
mothers who reject reunion and, 238–239
PMS and, 243–245
Medication during pregnancy, 171–172, 176–177
Memories
effects of adoption, 386
post-traumatic stress disorder (PTSD) and, 107
Mental health. *See also* Suicide
Ann Scharp trial to obtain sealed records and, 132
connection between adoption and suicide and, 374–375
connection between epilepsy and, 377
effects of adoption on, 104, 107, 283–285, 376
mothers who reject reunion and, 236–239
PMS and, 244
Minnesota Twin Family Study (MTFS), 260–264
Model State Adoption Act, 187–189
Mood alterations, 108
Mother-and-child reunions. *See* Reunions between children and parents
Mothers. *See also* Adoption

language; Biological mothers; Natural mothers; Rights of mothers
adoption curiosity regardless of adoptive family relationships and, 408–410
effects of adoption on, 103–108
mothers' rights in open adoptions, 206–212
who reject reunion, 236–239
Mothers seeking information about relinquished children. *See also* Seeker mothers
Musser, Sandy, 201
Mutual-consent registries, 331

N

National Council for Adoption (NCFA), 179–180, 188–189
Natural mothers. *See also* Adoption language; Mothers; Seeker mothers
accuracy of the term, xvii
Australian study of, 104
effects of adoption on, 103–108
mothers' rights in open adoptions, 206–212
mothers who are also adoptees, 155
"Natural Mother Speaks Out on Adoptees' Right to Know, A" (Dusky), 150–151
Negative adoption language, xvii. *See also* Adoption language
Neuroticism personality trait, 257
New York Council of Churches, 91
New York Foundling Home, 138–139
New York legislation and court cases
1976 bill to unseal birth certificates, 136
abortion and, 91–93
ALMA Society, Inc. v. Mellon

(1979) and, 140–141
Joint Public Hearing, New York State Senate/Assembly: Sealed Adoption Records and Identity (1976), 136–138
Unsealed Initiative and, 382–386
unsealing birth records of adoptees, 411–416, 421–422
"No contact preferred" proviso, 331
Northaven Terrace, 65, 80, 126, 158–159, 172

O

Oakes, Judge James L., 140–141
Obstetrical Society, 91
O'Donnell, Danny, 385, 415
Open adoptions, 162–166
closing, 210
compared to closed adoptions, 205–212
effects of adoption and, 105–106, 265–266
reactions from others, 321–327
stories from others regarding, 165–169
Openness to experience personality trait, 257
Original birth certificates (OBCs). *See* Birth certificates; Birth records
Orphan Voyage organization, 128
Other Mother, The (Schaefer), 347
Oxytocin, 106–107, 236

P

Partial-access laws, 329
Paton, Jean, 128n
Pauley, Jane, 150–151
Personality traits
effects of adoption and, 275
genetic and environmental factors and, 263–266
overview, 257–258

Pertman, Adam, 412
Pierce, Bill, 179–180, 269, 385
Pill, The, 52–54. *See also* Birth
  control
Pinker, Steven, 261–263
Pisani, Senator Joseph, 137
Plomin, Robert, 263
PMS, 243, 305, 363, 400. *See
  also* Premenstrual dysphoric
  disorder (PMDD)
Polier, Shad, 137–139, 385
  connection to Louise Wise
    Services and, 139
Positive adoption language, xvii. *See
  also* Adoption language
Post-traumatic stress disorder
  (PTSD), 107, 383
Premenstrual dysphoric disorder
  (PMDD), 244, 377, 400. *See
  also* PMS
Progesterone, 244–245, 305, 363
Protestant church, 179
PTSD. *See* Post-traumatic stress
  disorder (PTSD)

Q

Questions regarding one's
  family. *See* Knowledge of one's
  family, desire for; Adoption
  curiosity

R

Roe v. Wade (1973), 62, 281–283. *See
  also* Abortion
Race, 81–84, 264
Raia, Andrew, 414
Raymond, Barbara Bisantz, 69n
Reactions from others,
  103, 236–237, 320–326
"Real mother". *See* Adoption
  language
Records. *See* Adoption records; Birth
  records

Reform, adoption. *See* Adoption
  reform movement
Registries to match adoptees and
  natural parents, 331, 399
Regret
  open versus closed adoptions and,
    206
  overview, 418
  role of relationships between
    mother and father of the
    relinquished child, 123
Rejection
  fathers who reject reunion, 270
  mothers who reject reunion,
    236–239
  saying "I'm sorry" and, 348–349
Relationship between parents
  following relinquishing a child,
    123, 238
Relative adoptions
  birth records and, 82
  kinship fostering, 211–212
Relinquishment of a child. *See
  also* Adoption language
  Baby Scoop Era and, 81–82
  effects of, 103–108
  mothers who reject reunion,
    236–239
  overview, xviii
  reactions from others and,
    321–327
Reminders, 108. *See also* Memories
"Repress Yourself" (Slater), 296
Reunions between children and
  parents, 285–286
  effects of adoption and,
    287–289, 384
  emotional responses to, 404–405
  extended family and, 241–242
  fathers who reject, 270
  "I Found My Mother" (Dusky)
    article and, 127–129

mothers who reject, 236–239
Rhythm method of birth control, 54, 83n. *See also* Birth control
Rights of adoptees
  current state of, 416
  injustice of sealed birth records, 328–333, 381–382
  Unsealed Initiative and, 382–386
  unsealing birth records of adoptees in New York, 411–416, 421–422
Rights of mothers, 421–422
  injustice of sealed birth records and, 329–333, 381–382
  in open adoptions, 206–211
  shift towards unsealing birth records of adoptees in New York, 411–416
Rockefeller, Nelson, 91
Rolling Stones (the band) article, 44–45

S

Safeguarding the Rights and Well-Being of Birthparents in the Adoption Process (Smith), 104n
Saffian, Sarah, 283
Salk, Lee, 166
Samuels, Elizabeth J., 71, 127
Schaefer, Carol, 347–348
Scharp, Ann, 133–136
Sealed birth records. *See also* Birth records; Closed adoptions
  ALMA Society, Inc. v. Mellon (1979) and, 140–141
  adoption curiosity regardless of adoptive family relationships and, 408–410
  adoption reform movement and, 343–344
  illegal acquisition and adoption of children and, 68–69
  injustice of, 328–333, 381–382

Joint Public Hearing, New York State Senate/Assembly: Sealed Adoption Records and Identity (1976), 136–138
  Model State Adoption Act and, 187–189
  New Jersey court cases regarding, 158–159
  overview, 126
  searching for adoptees and, 129–130
  search movement and, 269
  unsealing birth records of adoptees in New York, 411–416, 421–422
Search angels/The Searcher, 203, 215–216n, 223
Searching adoptees. *See* Adoptees searching for information
Second Choice: Growing Up Adopted (Anderson), 285
Secrecy
  effects of adoption and, 275
  mothers who reject reunion and, 236–238
  sexual abuse and, 278
Seeker mothers, 104. *See also* Adoption curiosity; Mothers
  research regarding, 104
  stories from, 164–166
  ways birth records were obtained by, 201
Seizures. *See* Epilepsy
Selling babies, 68–69
Semi-open adoptions, 206. *See also* Open adoptions
Senate bill 3419/A5494, 411–416. *See also* New York legislation and court cases
Shame
  mothers who reject reunion and, 236

post-traumatic stress disorder (PTSD) and, 108
Side effects of treatments
anticonvulsant drugs and, 228, 277
birth control pills while pregnant and, 230–231
Silver, Sheldon, 411, 413, 416
Single/unwed mothers
in the 1960s, 63–64
white parents/families and, 82–83
Sister Maria Dominica, 70, 383
Sixteen and Pregnant reality show, 209–210
Skelos, Dean, 189, 411
Solinger, Rickie, 57n
"Somewhere Out There Is a Daughter of Mine"(Dusky), 162–163
Spence-Chapin Adoption Services, 131–134
Sperm-donor-conceived babies, 408
"State Seeks Children with Links to DES" (Goldman), 171n
Statistics, 81–83
regarding open and closed adoptions and, 205–206
Strauss, Jean, 283
Suicide. *See also* Mental health
connection between adoption and, 373–377
epilepsy medication and, 373, 377
overview, 357–358
PMDD and, 377
research regarding, 373–378
Support from others (or lack thereof), 236–237. *See also* Reactions from others
"Surrendering" children. *See* Adoption language

T

Tann, Georgia, 68–69

Tavris, Carol, 258n
Teenagers, adopted
benefits of open adoption and contact during, 211
connection between adoption and suicide and, 373–375
Teen pregnancy, 83–84. *See also* Adolescence
mothers' rights in open adoptions, 209–210
mothers who reject reunion, 236
white parents/families and, 83–84
Terminology considerations. *See* Adoption language
Thalidomide, 55
Therapeutic abortions, 57n, 91–92. *See also* Abortion
Thiele, Fred, 413, 414
"Things Your Husband/Lover Never Told You about Sex" (Bernard/Dusky), 120
Three Identical Strangers (2018) film, 140–141n, 262
Tower, Senator John, 188
Transactional nature of adoption, 68–69, 418
Trauma. *See also* Loss
as a result of adoption, 281–282
impact of, 106–107
overview, 296, 358, 383–384
Trimberger, E. Kay, 265
Triplets separated by adoption, 140n, 262
Triseliotis, John, 104n
Twins separated by adoption
Louise Wise Services and, 140–141n
Minnesota Twin Family Study (MTFS) and, 260–264

U

Union for Reform Judaism, 91

"Un-Open Adoption, An" (*First Mother Forum*), 207–208
Unsealed Initiative, 383–386
Unwed/single mothers
    current perceptions of, 84
    in the 1960s and, 63–64
    white parents/families and, 83–84

V

Valproic acid, 228
Verrier, Nancy, 348–349
Vitamin B6 (pyridoxine), 231–233

W

Wake Up Little Susie (Solinger), 57
Wallace, Monica, 414
"We Need to Talk about Adoptee Suicide" (Barra), 376
Weprin, David, 413
White children, women, and families, 81–84
"Who Is My Daughter" (Dusky), 177
Wilson-Buterbaugh, Karen
    Baby Scoop Era, The, 81n
    family records and, 81n
Wise, Louise, 139
Women's Bar Association of New York, 414
Worry, 104
    open versus closed adoptions and, 208
Wrozek (Grezesikowski), Agnes Augustine, 145–146, 146f

Y

"Yearning" (Dusky), 135–136

Made in United States
North Haven, CT
12 July 2023

38867259R00281